# BUILDING

# E 123328 DS

684.1 Blandford, Percy W.
BLA
Building better beds

13.95

| DATE | | | |
|---|---|---|---|
| AUG 21 1986 | | | |
| AUG 8 1986 | | | |
| | | | |
| | | | |
| | | | |
| | | | |
| | | | |
| | | | |
| | | | |
| | | | |
| | | | |

## Other TAB Books by the Author

# BUILDING
# BETTER BEDS

## BY PERCY W. BLANDFORD

123328

**TAB** TAB BOOKS Inc.
BLUE RIDGE SUMMIT, PA. 17214

FIRST EDITION

FIRST PRINTING

Copyright © 1984 by TAB BOOKS Inc.
Printed in the United States of America

Library of Congress Cataloging in Publication Data

Blandford, Percy W.
Building better beds.

Includes index.
1. Beds and bedsteads. 2. Woodwork. I. Title.
TT197.5.B4B53  1984    684.1′5    83-24383
ISBN 0-8306-0664-5
ISBN 0-8306-1664-0 (pbk.)

# Contents

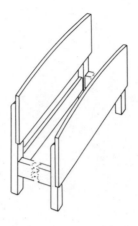

# Introduction

If you show an interest in beds in a furniture store, it will not be long before a salesman reminds you that you spend one-third of your life in a bed, so you should have a good one. He is not far off. Most of us spend about 8 hours of every 24 in bed, and that bed should provide comfort and correct support so we get the most out of each period of sleep. That is the prime function of a bed, but its appearance is important, too. It is usually the dominant feature in a bedroom, so it should be attractive and should fit in with other furniture in the room to give an overall pleasing appearance.

Perhaps surprisingly, not much information has been printed on making beds, although books and plans for all other kinds of furniture are available in great variety. Books on furniture-making and cabinetry may give plenty of designs and instructions for tables, chairs, stools, dressers, closets, and all furniture in the home, but beds may not even be mentioned. This book is an attempt to fill the gap, with coverage almost exclusively on beds of all sorts. Some beds have other items

built-in, but for instructions on making other independent furniture, the reader must look elsewhere. Many books on making furniture of many sorts have been published by TAB BOOKS Inc.

Making a bed need not be very difficult. As with other furniture, it is possible to choose a complicated and difficult design, but many satisfactory and attractive beds can be made very simply. It is easier to make a good bed with minimum skill than it is to make some other forms of furniture when your ability to work wood is not as good as you would like. This book covers all kinds of beds, from those needed by the youngest members of the family, through modern and traditional types, to beds that fold and others for special purposes. Hopefully there is something for all, from beginning woodworker to skilled craftsman. The designs at all levels embrace sound methods of cabinetry, and the finished product should be a source of pride to the maker, as well as fully functional and good-looking.

All sizes are given in inches, unless otherwise noted. All dimensional drawings are to scale. Sizes of unmarked parts can be found proportionately. If a manufactured mattress is to be used, its size may govern some dimensions in the bed parts, so it is always advisable to obtain mattress sizes before cutting wood. The materials lists are based on sizes to suit standard mattresses, but minor variations may be found and should be taken into consideration.

# Chapter 1

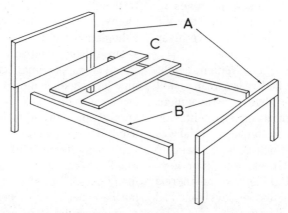

# Basic Considerations

Primitive man probably first slept on the ground in the same way that animals do. He may have searched out or made hollows to fit the shape of his body for a little more comfort, but the ground was still hard. The next step was to soften the support to conform to his body shape, even when he moved.

Comfort comes not so much from softness as from the ability of the support to spread the load over an area as large as possible. A body resting on a flat, hard surface gets its support on a few spots, mostly where bones protrude. When these contact points become painful, the body is moved, and other localized spots take the load. They begin to ache, and the body is moved again. The rest that is achieved is broken and unsatisfactory. Something more is needed to provide comfort.

A soft support pushes into the shape of the part of the body laying against it, so the area of contact may be ten times what it is on a hard, flat surface. This means that the same total weight is now spread so the load taken by each square inch is only one-tenth what it was. This condition is much more bearable. We would find the same comfort with a solid support made to the body shape, but only while we were in one position. The soft support moves with the body and conforms to the new shape exposed to it.

Primitive man may not have thought it out in that way, but he discovered that a pile of soft material was more satisfactory when he wished to sleep, particularly if he was a cave dweller, and hard stone was the alternative.

Straw, grass, leaves, and mosses were the sorts of material piled up to make a softer bed. An animal skin with the fur side upward then produced a support comparable in comfort to what most of us use. A further support might have been a network of small branches, twigs, and flexible boughs covered with straw. This network provided a springy base; so the layer of straw or similar material did not need to be as thick to get the same amount of comfort as a much thicker pile of that material only. Early man was learning about spring mattresses, although he did not realize it.

Man with his upright stance differs from most animals in preferring to sit on something near knee

1

height, rather than lowering himself to sit on the ground. A bed is more acceptable at about the same height as a seat because it is easier to get on and off a bed at that height than at floor level.

Those early ancestors may have built up their beds of boughs and coverings to this height and found the arrangement to their liking. They may have closed the sides and ends with stones or branches to keep the mass in one place. They did not know it, but they had made a primitive divan bed.

From the pile built up to a convenient height would develop the framed bed, when man's skill with tools developed. The obvious arrangement used headboards and footboards on legs, with side support pieces joining them. Softening material was supported between them. Such beds are seen in illustrations of Egyptian, Greek, and other very early civilizations. Only in the Far East was there a preference for beds at a much lower level—and an acceptance of much less padding.

By medieval days man was able to make and use a great many hand tools. He made furniture. Some of it was crude and utilitarian, but some was properly jointed and well-finished, often with turning and carving. Examples are still in existence, and drawings show us their appearance and the way they were made. By that stage beds had taken on a form not very different from what we use today, at least in their lower parts.

There was much concern about drafts. No doubt most homes were drafty. Coupled with this problem was the need for privacy in bed, since there may have been other people in the same bedroom. In a simple dwelling, the bedroom and living room may have been the same. From this situation developed beds with a roof and draperies—what is now often called a *fourposter*. Anyone in bed could then close themselves in completely, being private and draft-free at the expense of a most unhealthy atmosphere by morning. Fourposters are made and used today—some without the roof, or *tester*, and without closed draperies. Obviously, there is no longer a need for them but the design is attractive in some surroundings.

More modern beds continue the use of a head-board, which is often developed into the main feature of the piece of furniture and may be extended to take in side tables, book racks, and other supplements. There may still be a footboard, but in many beds it is no more than a support for the sides, which do not project above the bedding level.

Some padding, even into the nineteenth century and beyond, was a bag of straw, possibly supplemented with a bag of wool or feathers. It was unhygienic, and lice, bed bugs, and other vermin seem to have been accepted as a necessary evil.

The support may have been boards, or there may have been some springing provided by interlaced ropes or straps of cloth or leather. Interlaced steel strips with coil springs at their ends were also used. If these supports were too flexible, they had a hammock effect. The bodies came together in the middle, because of the sag. Since it was normal for many persons to share a bed, this situation could not have been very acceptable—except when two people wanted it to happen! With the Industrial Revolution came the development of coil springs that were coupled with iron frames to support bedding more evenly. Design was moving toward construction as we know it today.

More recently, support for sleepers featured an elaborate arrangement of coil springs permanently built into the bed frame. Over this went another arrangement of coil springs built into a cloth-covered mattress that could be lifted off. This system is still used, but the development of rubber and plastic foam has brought a simplification of support methods. An ample thickness of foam gives an even measure of padding that was difficult to achieve with coil springs alone. There may still be springs, but foam has taken the place of most of them, and may have completely replaced them in some mattresses. Water and air beds are other forms of support that out anscestors knew nothing about.

## PROPORTIONS

To be comfortable, a bed must be a size to suit the user. It is unusual today for a bed to be intended for more than two people, but there have been some very large beds in the past, and the modern king-size bed is certainly much bigger than could logically be regarded as only suitable for two.

If old beds are measured, they will mostly be found to be shorter than modern beds. Our ancestors were shorter than we are—at least an average heights comparison will show a difference of several inches. The shorter average height is also seen in the lower doorways in old houses. There are many suits of armor that were intended for men, but which would now only suit a child. Most beds from the past are less than 72 inches long, showing that their users were less than about 66 inches tall.

Today, both men and women are moving toward 6 feet, so beds are normally about 6 inches more than that. A normal length is 78 inches. The person who is well over the average height still has a problem, since mattresses, sheets, and blankets are mostly intended for people of average height, even if the bed itself is specially made at a greater length.

An adult extended straight may not have a width more than about 18 inches, but it would be unwise to expect a satisfactory bed to be little more than that. However, in the days of sailing warships packed with fighting men, a man was permitted to sling his hammock only 18 inches. Maybe the close contact produced some mutual warmth and minimized swaying. Some take-down or folding beds are made 24 inches wide, but that should be regarded as the absolute minimum for an adult. It is better to increase to 30 or 36 inches. For a double bed it is possible to manage with 48 inches, but it is better at 54 inches. Some double beds are much wider.

For a child the bed may be both narrower and shorter, maybe 24 inches by 48 inches, but children grow—often more rapidly than we expect. A child can use an adult bed, but once he has outgrown a small bed it is of no use to him and may only be worth keeping if there is a younger child in the family.

Bed sizes must be related to stock sizes of mattresses, sheets, blankets, and other things designed to go with them. Unless you intend to make all the accessories yourself, the size of any bed you build should be matched to the size of these other things, which you should get first.

A bed, particularly a double bed, is likely to be

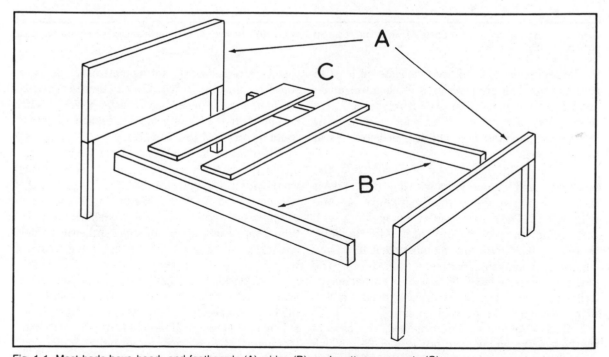

Fig. 1-1. Most beds have head- and footboards (A), sides (B), and mattress supports (C).

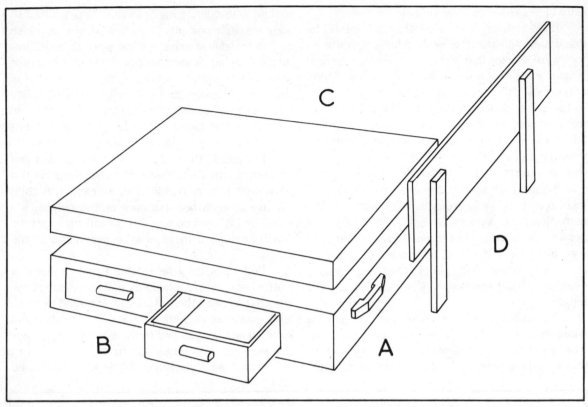

Fig. 1-2. A bed may have a box base (A), which may contain drawers (B). The mattress (C) rests on top, and there may be a headboard (D).

the largest piece of furniture in a home, at least in terms of the floor area it covers. If a bed was made as a rigid piece of furniture, it might not pass through a doorway or be suitable for carrying up or down stairs; so most beds are designed so they can be taken apart.

In the traditional method of construction, the bed's head and foot are units with legs (Fig. 1-1A); then there are two sides, which may be iron or wood (Fig. 1-1B). They may support a framework with coil springs or even be part of it. Alternatively, there may be some cross members that fit on and support a removable mattress (Fig. 1-1C). The sides attach to the head and foot in a way that makes a rigid assembly, but the joints can be disassembled if the bed has to be reduced in size.

In another construction method, the base of the bed is like an inverted box (Fig. 1-2A), which could be fitted with drawers (Fig. 1-2B). Over this

base is placed a foam or spring mattress, which is a separate unit (Fig. 1-2C). Usually there is no visible foot, but the headboard can be attached with uprights (Fig. 1-2D), or it can be a separate unit that could be attached to the wall.

Heights of the rigid parts of a bed vary according to the possible compression of the covering when sat on. Designs are usually arranged so the uncompressed mattress seems high, but when compressed, comes down to a comfortable position. This means that, in some beds, the rigid sides are only about 12 inches from the floor, but, in other beds, they are 15 inches or higher.

The backboard height is a matter of choice or fashion, but a reasonable height is one that supports the back of a person sitting up in bed. As with the side height, this should be considered in relation to the amount the mattress compresses.

It is now common practice to arrange the cov-

4

ering over the foot of the bed without a footboard projecting upward. If there is a footboard, it should be high enough to come above the level of the bed covering and be suitable for repeating the shape of the headboard, or something very similar to it.

Any other heights are decorative. Corner posts may go quite high. In some Victorian designs the footboards may be nearly as high as the headboards. That height may provide somewhere to hang your clothes and it is convenient for turning back the bedding, but this is no longer a normal arrangement. One headboard may go across two single beds, but that is done for appearance rather than necessity.

## MATERIALS

The obvious choice of construction material for a bed is wood, and the majority of beds are basically wooden. It is possible to make the exposed parts of the bed to match other furniture in the room. As that furniture is usually wooden, the bed parts could be also.

There can occasionally be considerable wracking strain on a bed. In a bed of the usual framed construction, this strain puts most of the load on the joints between the horizontal parts and the ends. The size of each corner joint may not be very large in relation to the whole assembly; so it needs to be strong. Faults at the joints can be felt if a bed is held at the head or foot and pushed backwards and forwards. Loose joints will rock.

The problem is compounded because these joints must usually be able to be disassembled to allow the bed to pass through doorways. There are suitable wood-to-wood joints, as will be seen later, but there is also substantial metal hardware that can be screwed or bolted to the wood to provide secure and rigid linkage, and still be suitable for disassembly.

An alternative is to make the bed sides of metal, either as independent pieces, usually of angle iron, or as parts of the main mattress. The metal sides have ends which link with brackets screwed to the wood ends.

In Victorian days brass bedsteads were fashionable. In nearly all cases they were made of iron, and the apparent parts were covered with thin sheet brass. Solid brass would have been too expensive and not strong enough, unless it was very massive. Most of the ironwork was cast, and some was very ornate. There is some interest in these beds today as antiques or reproductions, but making them is not within the scope of this book.

It is possible to make a bed from metal strips of various sections riveted or bolted together. They could be made of steel and painted, or made of aluminum and left untreated, if that suited the decor of the room. In any case, head and foot would need to be separate from the sides.

Many beds now have little of their construction visible. There may only be a headboard exposed. This means that there can be much more use of plywood and particleboard, which have strength, but would not usually have a pleasing appearance. In these beds, all such parts are hidden by upholstery or draped fabric. Even headboards may be upholstered, so they can be basically plywood, instead of the more expensive and difficult-to-work solid hardwood.

Changes and improvements in upholstery materials have brought about some of the changes in designs of beds in recent years. Information on upholstery materials is given in Chapter 3.

# Chapter 2

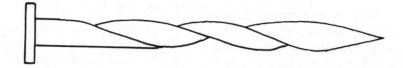

# Techniques and Materials

Most of the work in making beds from wood is the application of the common carpentry techniques. This is not a book on basic carpentry. It is assumed that you have some skill in the handling of tools and can carry out simple woodworking processes, such as cutting joints, squaring stock, and preparing surfaces. Some techniques may also be found in other branches of carpentry and cabinetmaking, but they have special emphasis in making beds. Information on them is provided in this chapter. Details of fabric working are given in Chapter 3. Information on working metal is given where examples occur in the projects.

Fortunately, a great many beds can be made with a fairly simple tool kit. A large number of designs can be made without the need to cut difficult joints. However, if you are a keen carver or turner, more elaborate designs can be selected.

If tools are being purchased, it is better to get a good selection of hand tools than to spend money on a small number of power tools. Obviously, power

tools are attractive and have their uses, but much of the work in making beds can be done just as well with hand tools, particularly if the wood is bought already planed to size. One exception may be an electric drill, which can reduce the labor of drilling and usually produces better holes. Accessories are available for many electric drills, but some of them are not always as effective as you might expect.

## SCREWS

Many parts of a bed are joined with wood screws. Driving screws is easy if you use the correct methods. If you don't, you may get increasingly frustrated and produce damaged wood and weak joints.

Screw length is given from the surface of the wood, which is the actual length of a flat head (Fig. 2-1A). On a round head, however, the head is additional to the quoted length (Fig. 2-1B). Screws are threaded about two-thirds of their length. Between

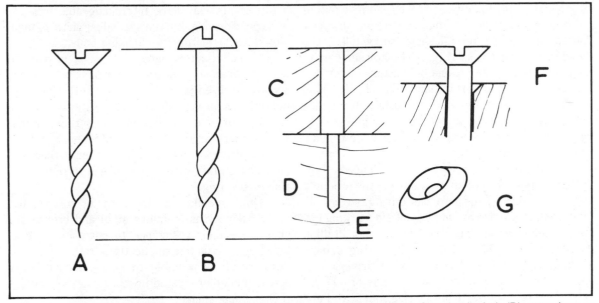

Fig. 2-1. A screw may have a flat head (A) or a round head (B). It needs a clearance hole (C) and a pilot hole (D) not so deep as the screw thread (E). The hole may be countersunk (F), or the head may go in a cup washer (G).

the head and the thread is a parallel shank. Its diameter is the size of the screw quoted by a gauge number. Some common sizes and their approximate diameters are given in Table 2-1. Screws are made in many combinations of length and gauge, but those shown suit most purposes in furniture making.

A screw holds by drawing the top piece of wood downward through the pressure of the head against the pull of the thread in the lower piece. The screw should slide through the top piece. Nothing is gained if the screw cuts into it; so there should be a clearance hole through it (Fig. 2-1C). A small screw in softwood may be started in the lower piece without a hole, but for most screws, particularly in hardwoods, there should be a pilot or tapping hole (Fig. 2-1D). Its diameter depends on the hardness of the wood; tough wood needs a larger hole than less hardwoods. A diameter one-fourth or one-third of the full screw diameter will be about right. Usually you do not need to make the tapping hole quite as deep as you expect the screw to go (Fig. 2-1E).

A flat head is intended to finish level with the surface of the wood. A countersink bit in a carpenter's brace is more effective than a similar bit in

Table 2-1. Listed Are the Sizes and Approximate Diameters of Screws Commonly Used in Furniture Making.

| WOOD SCREWS | | | |
|---|---|---|---|
| Screw Gauge | Shank Diameter (inches) | Pilot Hole Diameter (inches) | Lengths Commonly Available (inches) |
| 4 | 0.112 | 1/16 | ⅜ to ¾ |
| 5 | 0.125 | 5/64 | ½ to 1 |
| 6 | 0.138 | 5/64 | ½ to 1½ |
| 8 | 0.164 | 3/32 | ¾ to 2½ |
| 10 | 0.177 | 7/64 | 1 to 3 |
| 12 | 0.216 | 1/8 | 1½ to 4 |
| 14 | 0.242 | 9/64 | 1½ to 5 |
| 16 | 0.268 | 5/32 | 2 to 6 |
| 18 | 0.294 | 3/16 | 2½ to 6 |

an electric drill. In softwoods the head may pull in without the hole first being countersunk. In most hardwoods the countersink should not be full, or the head may pull in too far (Fig. 2-1F). For some parts of a bed, it is better to use a countersunk or cup washer under the screw head (Fig. 2-1G). This washer spreads the pressure and looks better than a head that has pulled in too far. It is particularly applicable in a place where you expect to replace the screw occasionally.

Traditionally, screws have slotted heads (Fig. 2-2A). Other types of heads are really the products of mass production to suit power driving, so there is little risk of the driver jumping off and marking the surrounding wood. The best known are Phillips heads (Fig. 2-2B) and others featuring square sockets (Fig. 2-2C). Both need screwdrivers with special ends and in sizes to suit a range of screws. They can be used for hand driving, but if you are buying screws, slotted heads are all you need.

A screwdriver should have clean slopes to the sides and a flat, true end (Fig. 2-2D). It should fit into the screw slot easily and be almost as wide as the screw head; so you need several screwdrivers, but plain ones are cheap. Pump-action and ratchet

screwdrivers may have interchangeable bits and will speed driving, but the special purchase of them would not be justified for making beds.

Common screws are made of steel and are suitable for most applications in making beds. Brass screws are used in quality cabinetwork. They are not quite as strong as steel screws, and there is a risk of thinner ones shearing off during driving. Choose a size larger than you would choose in steel. You can drive a steel screw first, then withdraw it and drive a brass screw in its place, to reduce the risk of shearing.

Other metals are also used for screws, but such examples as stainless steel and bronze are chosen for their resistance to corrosion in boat building and similar applications rather than for furniture. It is possible to get steel and brass screws plated or treated in other ways for protection and appearance.

Screw heads are not usually acceptable on a finished exposed surface. Caps and domes are made to fit over screws. Some clip on, and others are threaded into a hole in the head (Fig. 2-2E). Another way of hiding a screw head is to counterbore it. A shallow hole to take a plug comes above

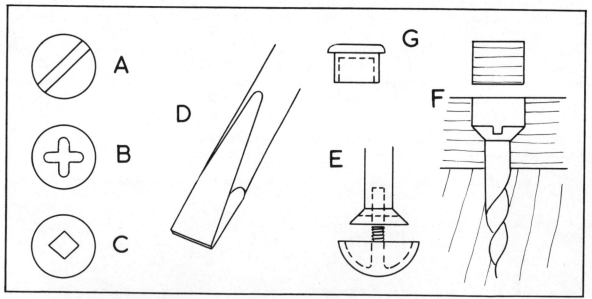

Fig. 2-2. Screw heads are slotted to take screwdrivers (A,B,C), which should not be worn away (D). A dome may cover a head (E), or the screw may be sunk and plugged (F,G).

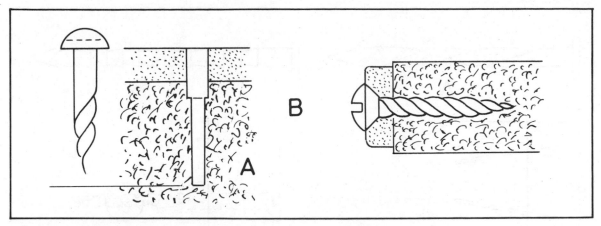

Fig. 2-3. Into particleboard there must be full drilling (A) or special screws (B).

the screw (Fig. 2-2F), but otherwise the screw is drilled for and driven in the usual way. The plug could be a piece of dowel rod, but that would show end grain on the surface. It is better to make a plug with its grain across, preferably from the same wood as that surrounding it. A plug cutter, which is a sort of hollow drill, is used to make these cross-grained plugs. Plastic plugs with shallow heads (Fig. 2-2G), originally intended for particleboard, can be used to give a neat finish, but they won't obscure the fact that there is a fastener in that position.

Driving a screw into the edge of plywood should be avoided if possible. If it must be done, choose a thin screw and make a tapping hole the full depth of the thread. There is a bursting action in the ply, and a screw tends to force the surfaces outward; so the tapping hole should be as large as can be used and still provide a grip for the threads.

Ordinary wood screws can be driven into particleboard. You cannot expect the screw to pull its way into undrilled material; so make the tapping hole too long, rather than too short. Drill a clearance hole for the parallel shank, even if part of it goes into the lower piece (Fig. 2-3A). There are special screws for particleboard that feature threads to the head and look similar to self-tapping screws for sheet metal (Fig. 2-3B). Their threads are supposed to have a better grip in particleboard. They can be used in hardboard or ordinary wood and be treated like wood screws.

## END GRAIN FASTENERS

Screws do not hold as well when driven into end grain as they do when their threads are able to grip across the grain. This is a problem particularly applicable to bed construction since wood bed sides may have to be joined to the bed head and foot, where they meet with their ends to make the joints. These are the joints where there may be severe loads when a bed is moved or strained from its ends.

### Nails

There is not much nailed construction in a bed, but where nails must be driven into end grain they should be longer than if the lower part presented side grain. Thick nails have more surface to help the wood fibers grip. Some nails give extra grip. Twisted screw nails (Fig. 2-4A) hold well, but the nails with the best resistance to pull are barbed ring (Fig. 2-4B). The rings have gradual tapers on the driven side, but the other side resists strongly any attempt at withdrawal, as may be seen if you make a mistake and try to remove a nail—it will tear back the wood fibers.

If many nails must go into a joint, it helps to drive them at alternate slight angles to produce dovetail nailing (Fig. 2-4C) and a mutual resistance to separation.

If two pieces of wood are nailed together, the grip of the nail in the lower piece provides the strength. The nail head prevents the top piece from pulling away. If the nails are to go into hardwood,

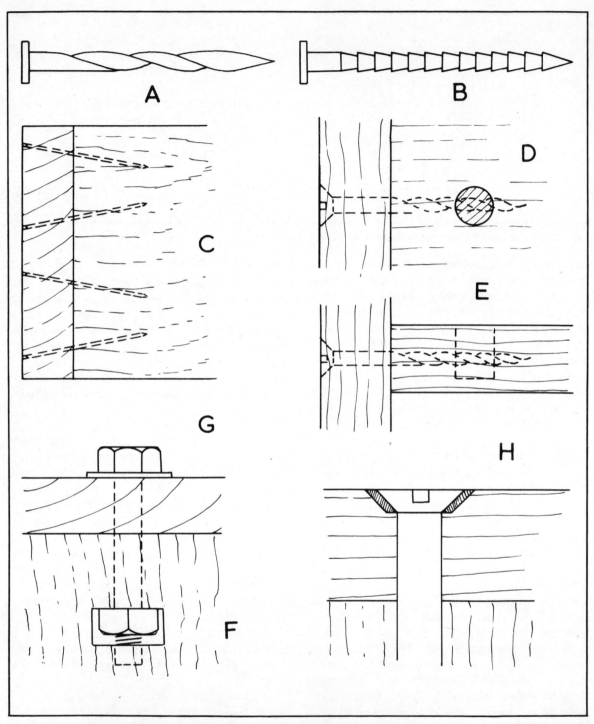

Fig. 2-4. Some nails are formed to give a better grip (A,B). Dovetail nailing (C) increases grip, as does a dowel (D,E). A nut let in (F) allows a bolt to be used (G). A cup washer sunk in the wood increases the screw head grip (H).

nothing is gained by heavy hammering to pierce the top piece, but there is the risk of buckling the nail. There is also the risk of splitting the wood, particularly near the edge of a board. A hole marginally smaller than the nail diameter can be drilled into the top piece. This hole guides the nail and keeps it straight as it goes into the important lower piece avoiding the need for a lot of effort in driving through the top wood fibers and the possibility of not drawing the nail as tight as it should be into the fibers of the lower piece.

### Screws

Screws into end grain should be longer than into side grain. It will help to use more of them, if there is enough space where the wood meets. As with nails, a thicker screw will hold better than a thin one, because the thread cuts into a greater number of fibers.

Another useful device is the provision of some cross grain in the joint, by putting a dowel through a hole, so the screw goes across it (Fig. 2-4D). The size of dowel is not very important, but it should have a diameter large enough not to split. A dowel diameter four to six times the screw diameter is about right. In many situations the appearance of the dowel on the surface will not matter, but if you do not wish the dowel to show, it can be put into a blind hole drilled from the less important side (Fig. 2-4E). Dowels may be glued in, but that is not essential. If the construction allows, dowel ends may be left to be planed off after assembly.

Although wood screws may be withdrawn and replaced, there is bound to be some lessening of the grip each time; so don't use screws as fasteners if you expect to disassemble a joint more than once or twice. Bolts, or metal-thread screws, are better for driving and withdrawing a large number of times.

### Nuts and Bolts

One way of using nuts and bolts in end grain is similar to the wood screw into a dowel. Instead, a

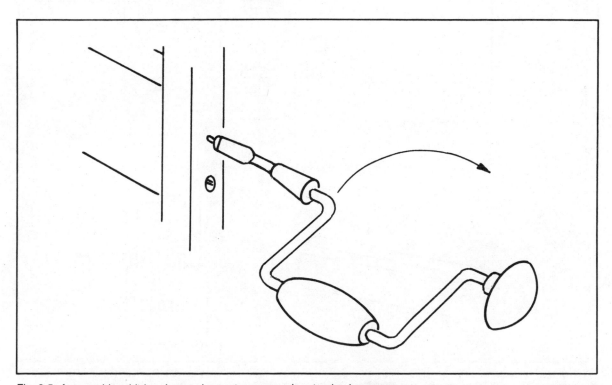

Fig. 2-5. A screwdriver bit in a brace gives extra power when turning large screws.

nut is let into the wood and the bolt engages with it (Fig. 2-4F). The nut location depends on the length of the bolt, but it should be far enough from the end of the wood so there is no risk of the wood grain breaking out under load. The nut should be further from the end in softwood than in hardwood.

A square nut is more suitable than a hexagonal one, since it presents more bearing surface to the wood. It helps to include a washer. In any case, the slot cut for the nut need not be a close fit, since it is only the bolt's pull on the nut that matters, and some slackness helps in positioning the nut on the bolt end. When you drill for the bolt, let the hole go through the slot to give clearance for the bolt end, no matter how hard you tighten the bolt. Extra

depth in the hole does not matter, but if the hole is too short it will prevent the joint from tightening.

If an exposed bolt head will not matter, the bolt will put on the greatest pressure if its head pulls against a large washer (Fig. 2-4G). If the head must finish flush with the wood surface, it may be countersunk with a screwdriver slot. In some woods it might pull in more than you wish, so it helps to line the countersunk wood with a cup washer (Fig. 2-4H).

Large wood screws and bolts with screwdriver-slotted heads are difficult to tighten fully with ordinary screwdrivers or even with many power drivers, which are intended for small fasteners. One of the best ways of tightening is with a

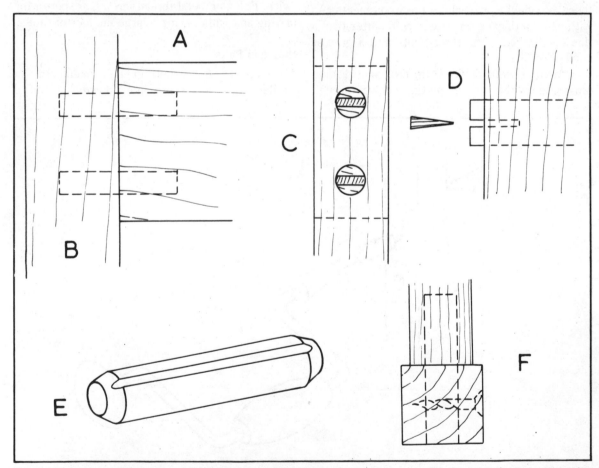

Fig. 2-6. Use at least two dowels in a joint (A,B). Wedges (C) may be driven into saw cuts (D). Grooves (E) let air and surplus glue escape. To allow later separation, a dowel may be screwed (F).

12

large screwdriver bit in a carpenter's brace (Fig. 2-5). The leverage you can apply with this tool is controllable and positive.

## Dowels

Dowels glued in make good joints in end grain parts. If the joint is to be permanent they are a good choice, but they are obviously unsuitable in a joint that must be taken apart, like the side-to-end joint in some bed constructions. Dowels should usually be between one-third and one-half the thickness of the thinnest wood in the joint. How far they go into the end grain is not very important, but between three and four times their diameter is about right. Space them to suit the wood, but distances between centers may be between three and four times the diameters (Fig. 2-6A).

If the dowels go into a substantial piece the other way, they can penetrate just as far as into the end grain (Fig. 2-6B). If the wood is thinner and the dowels go through, strength is increased by driving wedges into saw cuts across the ends (Fig. 2-6C). Leave some excess length on the dowels and cut them off after driving the wedges. Arrange the saw cuts square to the lines of grain in the wood (Fig. 2-6D), or you may split it.

If prepared dowels are used, they will probably have spiral grooves and tapered ends. If dowels are cut from long round rod, taper the ends and make a saw cut along each dowel (Fig. 2-6E). When a dowel goes into a blind hole, it is like a piston in a cylinder, compressing air and glue. Excess air and glue must escape up the saw cut, or there is a risk of bursting the wood. Always drill slightly too deep for dowels, since there is a risk of the dowel hitting the bottom of a hole and preventing the parts from coming close.

In some assemblies it is possible to arrange occasional take-down facilities by gluing the dowels into the end grain part, but fitting them dry into the other part, where a screw is driven across each dowel (Fig. 2-6F). For the closest fit, drill the wood for screws, but clamp the parts together tightly before drilling for the screws through the dowels. Choose a screw length that will pass through far enough to grip securely at the far side of the dowel.

## BRACKETED CORNERS

In joints between bed sides and ends, the inside of each joint will not normally be visible. With the usual drapes over the bed, the outside will not be visible either, except when bedding is removed.

One way of making a joint is to use a drilled iron bracket, preferably one that is stout enough not to bend and is cut as deep as the wood it is joining (Fig. 2-7A). There could be bolts through, if the appearance of exposed heads will not matter (Fig. 2-7B). If wood screws are used, stagger their positions, so they do not go through the same grain lines in nearby positions (Fig. 2-7C). If you cut and drill your own brackets, file off any sharpness that might damage fabric.

If there is sufficient width in each direction, resistance to wracking strains will be better with two or more narrower, but longer, brackets (Fig. 2-7D). Shelf brackets can be used. If screws can show on the outside, and the extra bulk in the corner would not matter, you can use triangular wood brackets (Fig. 2-7E). In some constructions it may be possible to put a wood bracket fairly low and a metal bracket higher to give clearance for a mattress.

For a take-down corner, a metal bracket may be permanently secured one way but have nuts and bolts the other way. A wood bracket can be permanently attached to a side and bolted the other way. You could put a glued dado joint, preferably dovetailed, into the side (Fig. 2-8A) instead of screws. Such a bracket could reinforce a bolted joint with one or more nuts let into the side. If the bracket is cut with its grain square to the side, it may be shaped for bolts through (Fig. 2-8B), or it could have its own inset nuts (Fig. 2-8C). This type of corner gives maximum rigidity. Make sure each bracket is exactly square to its side. Be careful that a bracket does not extend past the side it is attached to, or it will finish with a slightly open joint. Ideally the end surfaces should be level, but a bracket set back very slightly is better than one which projects.

## EDGE JOINTS

It is sometimes necessary to join boards

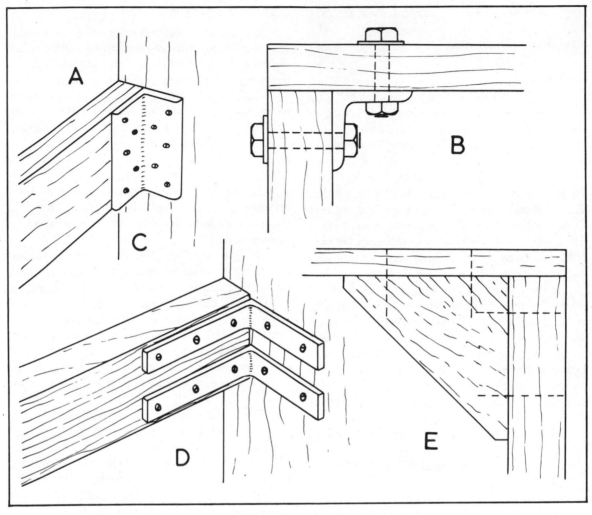

Fig. 2-7. Metal or wood brackets may be used to join bed parts.

edge-to-edge to make up a width, particularly for headboards and footboards. Most modern glues are stronger than the traditional types, and strong joints are easily made if some simple rules are followed.

Wood of a reasonable thickness can have the edges squared and glued together. Even if the edges are trued by power planing, finish with a few strokes with a hand plane. The action of a power planer tends to pound the surface of the wood and close some pores into which the glue should penetrate for the strongest joint. Hand planing removes that "case-hardened" surface.

Any tendency of a joint to open when in use may come at the ends. This tendency can be avoided by planing the edges very slightly hollow, shown exaggeratedly (Fig. 2-9A). When the joint is clamped, the ends will close tighter than the center. Before gluing, stand one board on the other to check that the finished piece will be flat (Fig. 2-9B). Pencil across the joint, so it will be put together the same way. If there are more joints, pencil each in a different way (Fig. 2-9C). If suitable tools are available, the glue area can be increased by making a tongue and groove joint (Fig. 2-9D).

A useful method of drawing glued edges

together is secret slot screwing. This method strengthens the joint and allows an edge joint to be made without clamps. Mark the meeting edges together with screw positions (Fig. 2-10A). Have one a few inches from each end and others at 9-inch to 12-inch intervals. The exact spacing is not important. Mark the centerlines of the boards, and on one piece put additional marks ½ inch from the first (Fig. 2-10B).

Choose fairly stout steel screws. For 1-inch boards they could be gauge 10 and 1 inch long. Drive a screw at each single mark (Fig. 2-10C). Leave about ¼ inch standing above the surface. At the offset positions on the other board, drill holes large enough to clear the heads (Fig. 2-10D). At the other mark on that board drill a hole to clear the neck of the screw. Draw parallel lines from that hole to mark a slot. Remove the waste from the slot with a drill and chisel (Fig. 2-10E). Make the hole and slot slightly deeper than the projection of the screw in the other board.

Insert the screw heads in the large holes and

drive one board over the other so the screw heads cut their way along the bottom of their slots (Fig. 2-10F) until the boards are in line. If this is satisfactory, drive the boards back so the screw heads can be withdrawn. Give each screw a further quarter turn, apply glue, and drive the boards back together again to complete the joint.

Wide boards, or narrower ones glued to make up a width, tend to expand and contract due to taking up or giving out moisture from the atmosphere. This has very little effect along the grain, but across the grain it can be enough to matter. If strips are put across a wide board, as they might be in fitting a headboard in place, joints should be used that allow for expansion and contraction. Do not use glue, but depend on screws.

In the case of a headboard, the bottom screw may be put through a round hole (Fig. 2-11A) to lock the lower edge in the same position. To allow for movement across the wide board, other screws should be put through slots that get longer the further they are from the bottom (Fig. 2-11B). It

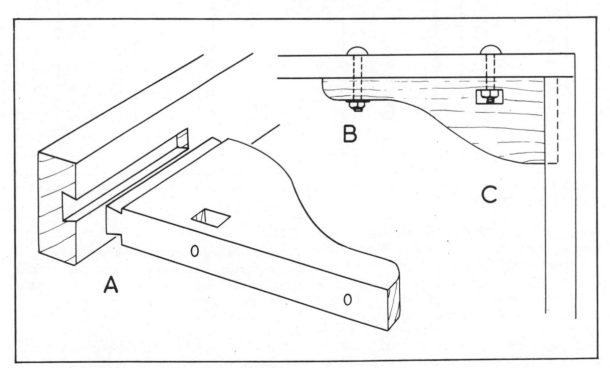

Fig. 2-8. A wood bracket may be dovetailed (A) and bolted (B,C).

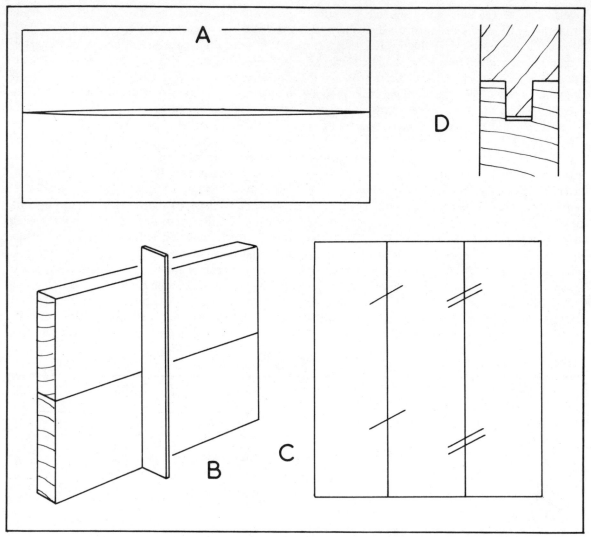

Fig. 2-9. Planing edges hollow (A) insures close ends. Check flatness (B) and put identifying marks on joints (C). Tongue and groove joints increase glue area (D).

helps to use round head screws and washers. The length of the slot depends on the wood, but ¼ inch of movement might be expected in a 12-inch width.

The risk of expansion and contraction can be reduced by storing the wood, for several weeks before it is used, in a similar atmosphere to that which the bed will be in. If wood has been stored in a damp shed and then made into a bed which is used in a centrally heated room, it will alter in width and thickness and may split or warp.

## TESTING

It is important for the sake of appearance that a bed stands true. If the legs are not upright, the head appears to tilt sideways, the footboard is not made square, or the sides are not parallel so that a mattress does not fit properly, it will be very obvious to any viewer. Checks should be made at all stages of construction, not left until final assembly only. See that individual pieces of wood are straight and have square edges.

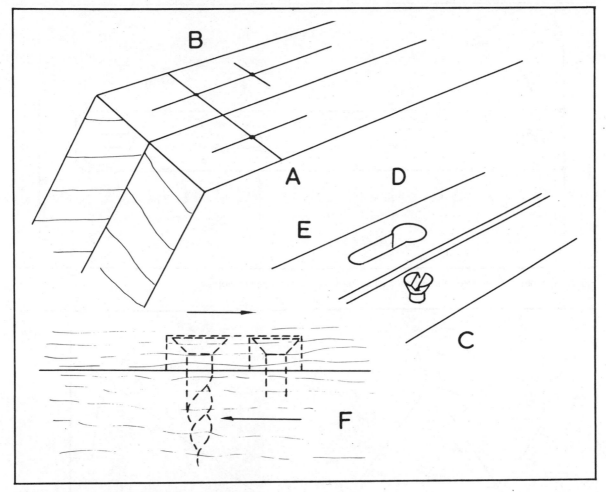

Fig. 2-10. Secret slot screwing pulls edges together.

Many parts will be longer than any available straightedge, but straightness can be seen by sighting along the edge. Squareness may also be beyond the limits of an available try square or other square. Most plywood sheets are manufactured squarely; so a corner of a sheet can be used for testing.

A triangle with its sides in the proportion 3:4:5 has a right angle between the two short sides and can be used for checking squareness. Suppose a bed head is 48 inches wide (4 units of 12 inches). Measure 3 units (36 inches) along a side. A diagonal measurement will be 5 units (60 inches) if the bed is assembled squarely (Fig. 2-12A). Any size of unit

can be used, but if you draw a line square to an edge, choose units that extend further than the line will need to be, rather than use smaller units and have to extend the line and risk of error. For instance, mark where the line is to meet the edge. Measure along the edge from its four units (Fig. 2-12B). From the mark swing a short arc of 3 units (Fig. 2-12C). From the other position measure 5 units to a point on the arc (Fig. 2-12D). A line from the edge mark through that position will be square to the edge (Fig. 2-12E).

Beds are symmetrical in all directions. Whatever their form, headboard and footboard assemblies are rarely made other than symmetrical

17

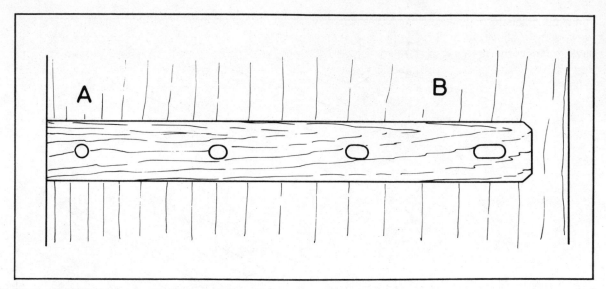

Fig. 2-11. Slot holes for screws in a batten allow for expansion and contraction.

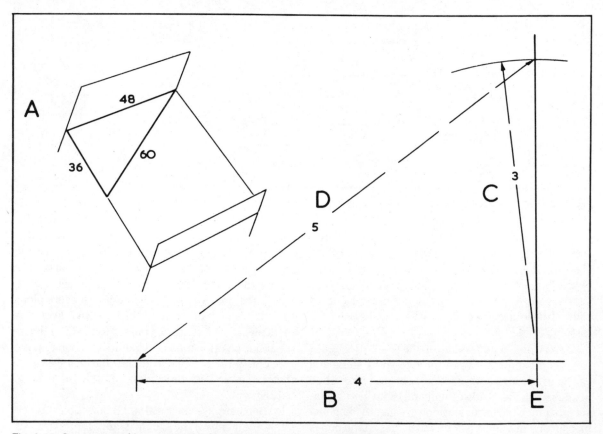

Fig. 2-12. Squareness of large parts can be checked by using a 3:4:5 triangle.

and usually square in general form. When a bed is viewed from above, it is rectangular and should have square corners. Because these shapes are too large for the usual testing tools, the way to check symmetry is by measuring diagonals. Use two pairs of matching points, preferably as far apart as the structure allows. In a rectangular headboard assembly, you can measure from the bottoms of the legs to the top corners (Fig. 2-13A). Even if the headboard has a shaped top you can find matching opposite points from which to measure (Fig. 2-13B). The shape can be tapered, providing it is supposed to be symmetrical. You can still use opposite corners (Fig. 2-13C). Squareness of a bed frame is easy to check (Fig. 2-13D), as is a bunk bed or similar assembly (Fig. 2-13E).

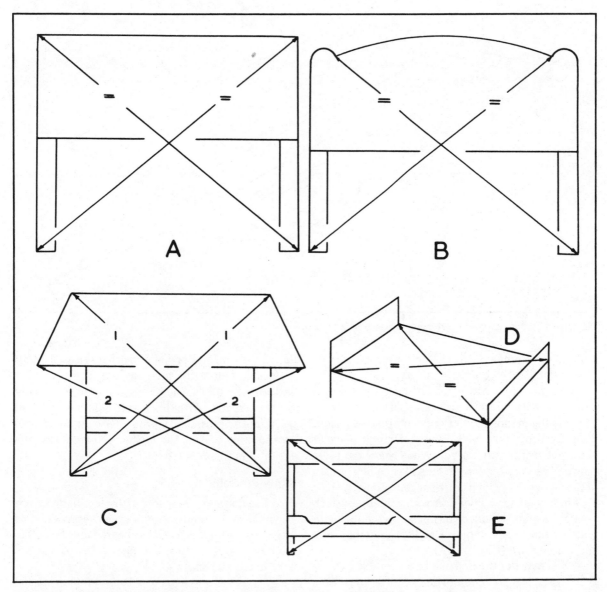

Fig. 2-13. Measure and compare diagonals to check symmetry and squareness.

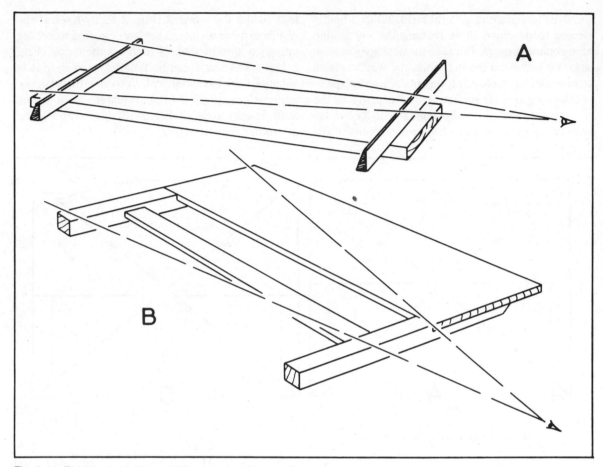

Fig. 2-14. Twist is checked by sighting across a board or frame.

A problem associated with squareness is twist, but it is not always so easy to see. It is possible to plane a board and check along its length and across its width with a straightedge to show that it is flat in those directions, yet still be twisted. This twisting may be seen by sighting along or across, but if it is not a very wide board the twist may not be very obvious. You will get a better idea of the amount of twist if you exaggerate it with a pair of winding strips. These are straightedges thick enough to stand unaided. If they are put at opposite ends of the board and you sight along, they will show any twist (Fig. 2-14A).

You may get the end of a bed assembled with a twist. Suppose you cut mortises or drill for dowels slightly out of square. The assembly may not be flat. A bed end may be sighted across (Fig. 2-14B), preferably before the glue has set. If you twist it back slightly too far the wrong way it will probably settle correctly. With this sort of sighting, you will get a more accurate assessment if you stand well back. Within reason, the further you are away, the easier it is to see a twist.

## DRAWING CURVES

The curves that most of us are familiar with are drawn with a compass. A few curves needed in laying out headboards and footboards may be within the range of a compass, but many other curves are very much bigger.

An arc of a circle up to a 10-foot radius, can be drawn with an improvised compass. Take a strip of wood, or two or more strips nailed together, slightly longer than the radius and measure the radius from one end. Push an awl through at that point (Fig. 2-15A). Put the board you want to mark on the floor. Mark a centerline across it and extend that far enough to take in the center of the circle. Make sure the board is square to the line on the floor (Fig. 2-15B). Position the end of the compass where you want it and push the awl into the floor. Put a pencil against the end and pull the compass around (Fig. 2-15C). If the strip for the compass is not very stiff, get someone to hold near the middle and pull around with you.

Decorative curves do not have to be parts of a circle, and they are often more attractive when they are not. You can get the curve for a bed head or similar piece by springing a batten to the curve and penciling along it. With help, you can get the center at the high point and the ends at the marked side positions (Fig. 2-16A). Have the batten longer than the distance between the points. You will get a

better curve if it is held and sprung to shape past the edge points. With a batten only just reaching, you will get a flattening of the curve near the ends.

A better way of getting a fair curve is to use nails to guide the batten (Fig. 2-16B) and pull it to shape outside of the end nails (Fig. 2-16C). If you are making two boards to the curve that are intended to be symmetrical, cut one to shape and use it to mark the other; then turn it over and see if the curve matches the other way. If necessary, average out the curves and plane the two until the curves match both ways.

## EQUAL DIVISIONS

Much of the marking out of beds and other assemblies can be done by measuring directly from a rule or tape, since the divisions needed may all match the calibrations. In some places, however, the spacing needed does not conform to regular rule markings, such as the spacing of the slats on bed ends (Fig. 4-4). If you divide the overall size by the

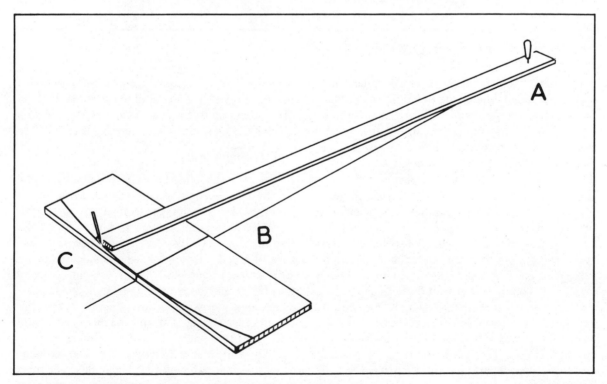

Fig. 2-15. Large curves may be drawn with an improvised compass.

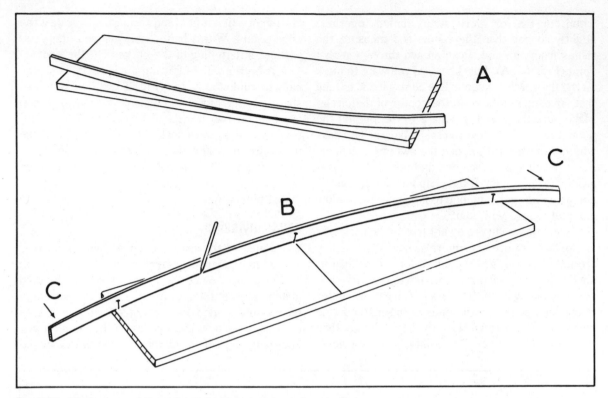

Fig. 2-16. A batten sprung through points allows a curve to be penciled.

number of divisions you get several decimal places, which are unsuitable for the practical task of marking wood.

An easier way of marking divisions is to tilt a rule until it shows a measurement that is divisible. Suppose a 19-inch width must be divided by 5. Tilt the rule so it shows 0 at one side and 20 at the other (Fig. 2-17A). Divide that by 5 at the 4-inch marks (Fig. 2-17B), and project parallel with the side line through those marks (Fig. 2-17C).

If you need to divide a line into equal divisions, you could project from the ends and divide by the same method, with lines taken up to mark the divisions. You could use a pair of dividers and step off along the line experimentally, adjusting until you get the right setting, but that could be tedious.

Another way is to draw a line at any angle from one end (Fig. 2-17D), then divide it into the required number of parts, preferably using a size that brings the final point near the length of the line to be divided (Fig. 2-17E). Join the end mark to the end of the line. Project lines parallel to it from each of the other points up to the line. One way is to slide a drawing triangle along a straightedge (Fig. 2-17F).

## SPECIAL WOOD JOINTS

Most of the joints between wooden parts of a bed are the common types used in many branches of carpentry. Dowel joints are comparatively recent. To a certain extent they are a product of the Machine Age, but they have their uses in many parts of a bed. For anyone who has doubts about their ability to cut other types of joints, a good dowel joint may be better in strength and appearance than a poorly made joint of another type. For the greatest satisfaction and maximum strength, however, other joints are usually preferred.

There are places for halved, dado, and dovetail joints in some parts of a bed, but the joint most frequently used, in several variations, is the mor-

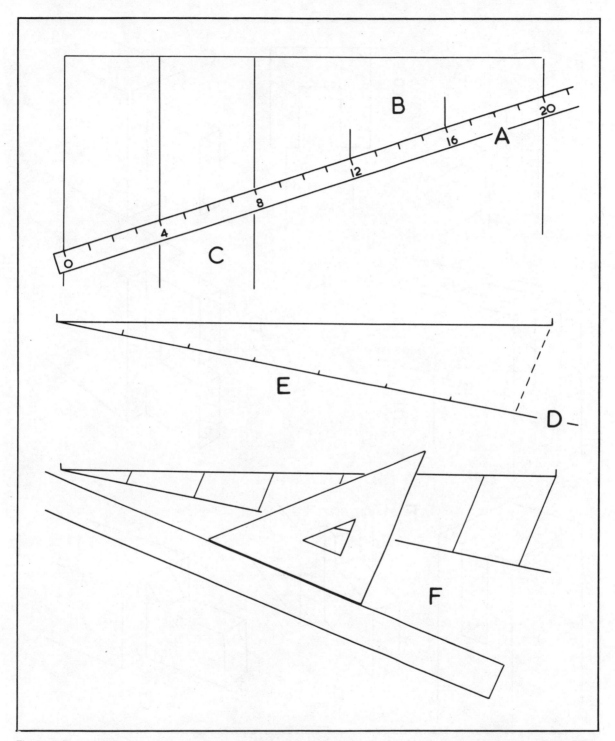

Fig. 2-17. Equal divisions in a space can be marked with a rule held diagonally (A,B,C) or by projecting another line (D, E,F).

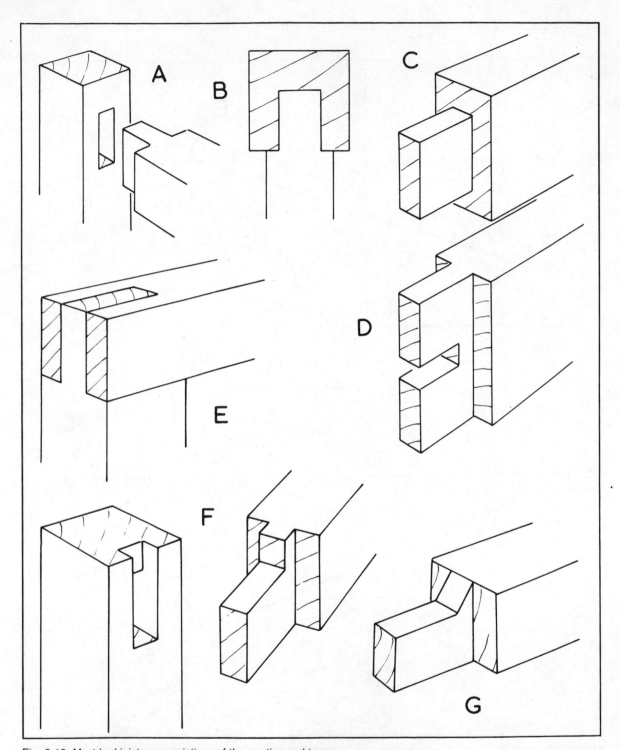

Fig. 2-18. Most bed joints are variations of the mortise and tenon.

24

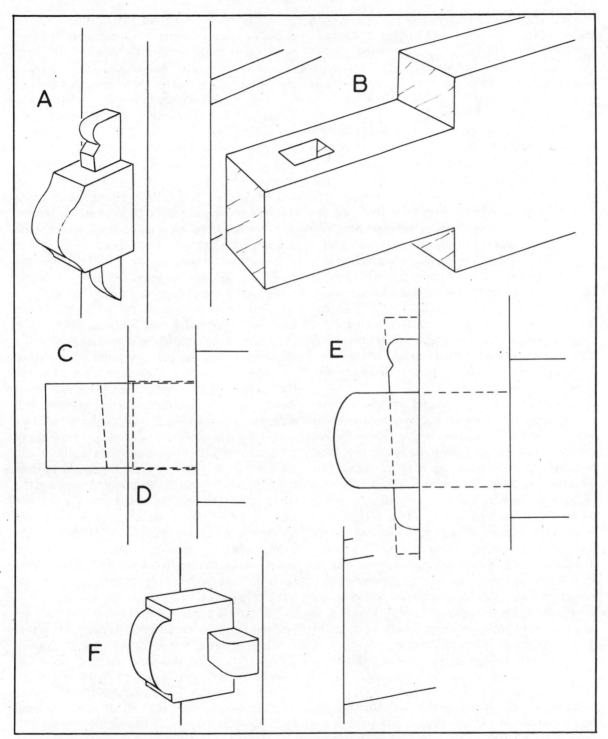

Fig. 2-19. A haunched tenon goes through (A,B,C,D) and may be wedged (E,F).

tise and tenon. In many places it is a basic joint, with the tenon made about one-third of the thickness of the wood (Fig. 2-18A). If the piece with the tenon is not as thick as the piece wth the mortise, the joint will be stronger if the tenon is thicker than that, although not necessarily one-third of the thickness of the other piece (Fig. 2-18B).

Most wracking strains on the joint of a bed try to rock the long way of the joint. Rather than cut a wide board down for a single tenon (Fig. 2-18C) it is better to keep to the full depth and divide the tenon (Fig. 2-18D).

If the mortise piece does not extend past the outside of the tenoned piece, a full width tenon would result in an open joint, sometimes called a bridle (Fig. 2-18E). A bridle might be acceptable in some positions, but it is usually better to hide the tenon. A tenon can be hidden with a haunch which will show on the surface (Fig. 2-18F), or which may be tapered to hide it (Fig. 2-18G). If both parts of the joint are grooved to take a panel, the first type of haunch must be used. When cutting a corner joint, leave some excess wood on the mortised piece until the joint has been cut.

In Colonial days people did not have a convenient supply of hardware and may not have had suitable nuts and bolts to join side rails to the bed ends. It was still necessary to be able to take most beds apart in order to transport them, even if only from room to room. A common way to join the rails to the legs was with tusk mortise and tenons, with a wedge driven through the tenon (Fig. 2-19A). This method resulted in a strong, rigid joint, but it left a few inches of wood projecting from each leg, which was fairly certain to make contact with shins occasionally. However, if you make a reproduction bed, you should use tusk tenons. At the bed head the tenons are protected against the wall. If a chest or other piece of furniture is put across the foot, the projecting tenons are unlikely to be hit.

The tusk tenon must be thick enough to take the slot for a wedge, so usually there is no reduction of the side thickness, but top and bottom are cut away to provide shoulders (Fig. 2-19B); then the tenon is made to go through and leave enough extending for the wedge slot (Fig. 2-19C). The wedge should be about one-third the thickness of the wood. Cut away the inside of the tapered slot so the wedge will come against the leg and not bear against it, even when driven tight (Fig. 2-19D). Don't shape the end of the tenon until after the slot has been cut. Do not shorten it very much, as the wedge tightens against end grain and could burst out a thin part.

Make the wedge, at a slope of about 1-in-8, too long at first. Try it in position. When you have checked how it projects when driven tightly, mark and cut the ends (Fig. 2-19E). The end of the tenon can be molded and shaped to improve its appearance, but be careful not to take away too much of the end against which the wedge thrusts.

It is less common to have a wedge across the tenon (Fig. 2-19F), however, that allows a thicker wedge and a better bearing against the leg.

You can tighten a tenoned joint with a peg, instead of a projecting tusk and wedge, if the side rail height can be arranged so that a hole through the leg is away from any part going the other way.

Make a mortise and tenon joint going through the leg, keeping the tenon as thick as the sections of wood will allow. Without the tenon in place, drill across the mortise (Fig. 2-20A), preferably slightly nearer the rail shoulder position than the center of the thickness of the wood. Mark for a similar hole in the tenon, but a little nearer the shoulder. How much nearer depends on the size of the joint and the wood used. With legs 2½ inches square and a side rail 1½ inches by 4 inches, made from oak, mahogany, or similar hardwood, the hole in the tenon could be ⅛ inches nearer the shoulder in the tenon than in the mortise. When the joint is assembled, the offset tenon hole will show through the other (Fig. 2-20B).

Choose a piece of dowel rod to suit the hole size and taper its end for perhaps one inch, so it is small enough to enter the overlapping holes (Fig. 2-20C). When you assemble the bed, drive the dowel in from outside. Leave the point projecting, but trim the outside level (Fig. 2-20D). If you ever need to disassemble the bed, drive the tapered plugs back from inside to release the tenons.

Ways have been devised to use the tusk tenon

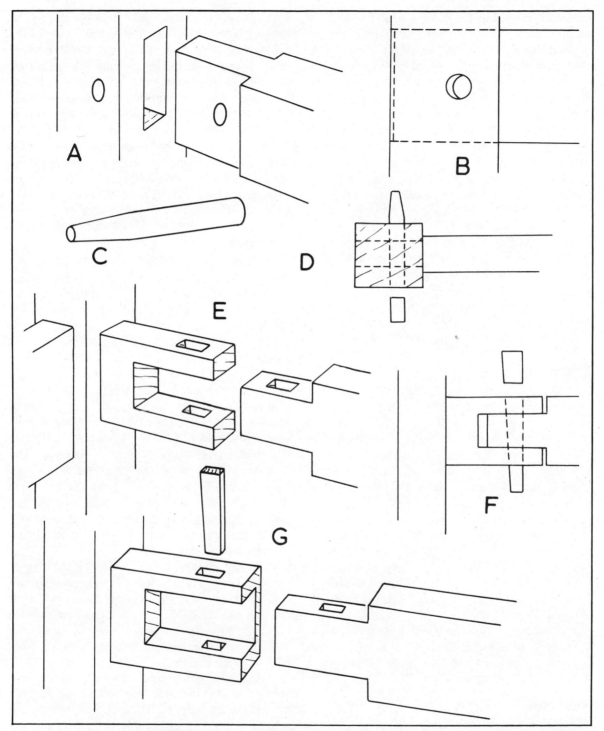

Fig. 2-20. A tenon may be doweled (A,B,C,D). Projections through an end can be avoided with a mortise piece inside (E,F,G).

principle, but keep the joint within the bed, so nothing projects past the ends. How strong they are depends on the wood and the quality of workmanship. In one method, a section of rail is permanently tenoned to the leg and allowed to project toward the main part of the rail. This projection can be cut away to allow a tenon to be inserted and a wedge driven down through (Fig. 2-20E). There must be space for the tenon to go into the stub piece without touching bottom. The action of driving a wedge tends to push open the lower part, which should be clamped until the bed has been assembled. After tightening, the top of the wedge is cut level, but the lower projection is left so it can be hit back if the bed must be taken apart (Fig. 2-20F).

The lower part can be linked to the top part of the mortised piece if the wood is thick enough to allow a web at the outside (Fig. 2-20G). The thickness of the tenon must be reduced; so there is a general weakening of the joint, unless there is ample thickness to start with.

## HARDWARE

Much hardware that is standard for other forms of woodworking may be used in beds, but there are a few special items you will also need. The place of hardware in much bed construction can be taken by wood-to-wood joints, such as mortise and tenon, where otherwise you would need a metal bracket or other device. In some situations, however, special hardware is more efficient, less bulky, and often the only feasible technique.

If a bed is to be suitable for disassembly, the joint between a bed side and a leg, or the bed end, is one that must be taken apart, yet this joint must withstand the greatest strain of any of the joints. Tenons can be taken through and wedged or pegged (Figs. 2-19 and 2-20). The less bulky and neater way of making the joint is to use bolts through into nuts set into the wood, the bolt heads are exposed on the outsides of the legs for easy disassembly, but it is difficult to disguise them.

### Cover Plates

On some antique beds, the sides were joined to the legs with bolts. A bolt head was sunk partially,

with enough clearance around it for a wrench to fit over it; then this rather large and ugly blemish on the leg was hidden by a cover plate, usually made of brass. It was domed to go over the bolt head, then decorated with a floral or geometric pattern. It may have been stamped from thin sheet brass or made by casting. One or two projecting ears took small screws to hold the cover in place until it had to be removed for the bolt to be turned. The covers are still obtainable from the makers of reproduction hardware. For a modern bed there are plain plated covers. A small glide (Fig. 2-22A) could be used and levered off later with a screwdriver.

### Metal Plates

Several types of metal fittings have been devised to make side-to-leg joints inconspicuous. Most employ some form of hooked parts, so they can be separated by lifting the bed side piece. In one type there is a plate with two slots in it to screw to the leg (Fig. 2-21A). On the end of the side goes another plate with two strong hooks projecting (Fig. 2-21B) to engage with the slots. They are tapered so they pull the parts tight as they drop into position. The metal parts are designed to have ample strength to do their job, however the screws may have considerable loads placed on their threads if the bed is given an end-to-end rocking strain. The hole size will determine the gauge of screw to use, but make them as long as the wood will allow. Drill to clear any plain neck that penetrates the wood, but make the tapping hole no bigger than is necessary for the screw to be driven, possibly using a brace and screwdriver bit.

It is the end grain of the side that is the biggest problem. In addition to using long screws, it will help to drive dowels across so that the screw thread can bite into them (Fig. 2-4D). If the metal hooked part is made to lap around the inside surface of the bed side and more screws are put there, the joint will be much stronger.

A simpler variation uses a metal plate with two screws into the bed side (Fig. 2-21C) and keyhole slots in the leg (Fig. 2-21D). The plate must be put into the leg and a recess cut behind where a screw head will drop in. The sizes of the slots determine

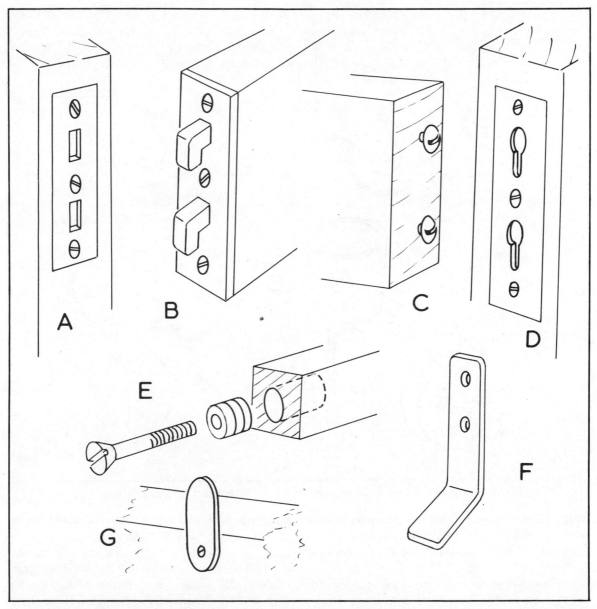

Fig. 2-21. Sides may join legs with metal fittings (A,B,C,D). A lightly loaded joint can have an insert (E). A bed iron supports a mattress (F). A turnbutton keeps it from moving (G).

the gauge of screws to use, but they should be as large as possible and preferably have raised heads. Make them fairly long and use dowels across if you do not think the grip in end grain is sufficient alone. The screws in the side must be adjusted so they drop into their slots with minimum slackness,

otherwise the bed will wobble.

This type of hardware could be made with simple metalworking equipment, to suit the sizes of wood in the bed being constructed. Use steel about ⅛ inch thick for the keyhole plate. Brass or aluminum would be too soft. The screw heads

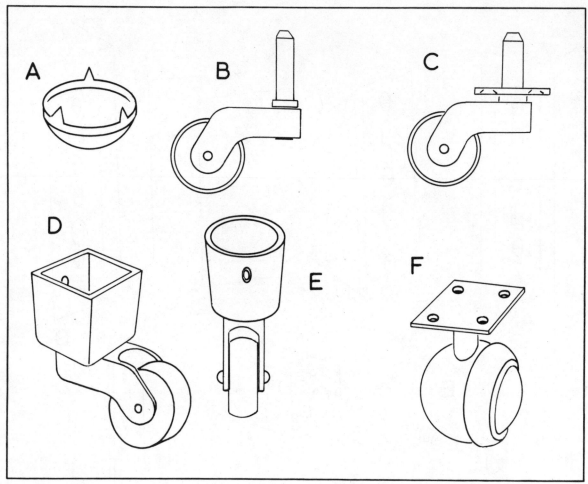

Fig. 2-22. A glide (A) may go under a leg, or a caster can be fitted (B-F), to assist in moving the bed.

would wear it away, making the joint loose and the bed wobble. Keep the keyhole slots as far apart as is reasonably possible to give maximum stiffness to the joint.

There are sheet metal angle joint plates made suitable for joining the side to something broader than the usual leg. They screw to the end, and sloping keyhole slots engage with screws in the inner surface of a side. As the side and its screws drop into the slots, the side is drawn towards the end.

### Inserts

An edge fastener that has been devised for use with particleboard has possibilities in light con-struction, such as a crib or cot, but would not be strong enough for a bed. An insert goes into the particleboard end and is threaded internally to take a bolt. The insert could go into the wood end grain of a crib side to take a bolt coming through the leg (Fig. 2-21E). The metal or plastic insert may have ridges or teeth in it to grip the wood, but it should also be glued with one of the adhesives, such as epoxy, that is suitable for metal or plastic as well as wood.

### Other Hardware

Most modern mattresses provide all the soft-ening and springiness needed by themselves and are supported on fairly rigid bases, made with plywood or slats. Another type of mattress, usually with internal springing, has a fairly rigid box form with its own solid base. This mattress can rest on strips of wood inside the bed sides, or there may be brackets, or bed irons, at intervals for the rigid edge of the mattress to rest on. These bed irons are like small shelf brackets (Fig. 2-21F). They could be made from strip steel. Make sure all exposed edges and corners are rounded before screwing into place.

On some beds the mattress is intended to rest on the tops of the sides; so it might slide out of position. To prevent this sliding position little turnbuttons (Fig. 2-21G) at wide intervals along the side. They can be bought or made from sheet brass or aluminum.

## CASTERS

A bed is quite a heavy piece of furniture. Unless there is plenty of help available, a bed is impossible to lift, so many are provided with wheels or other arrangements to ease movement without lifting. If a bed has closed-in sides, as it does when boxed in and fitted with drawers, it is usually rested close to the floor and only moved on rare occasions. If the bed is on legs, it will need to be moved more often, when the room is cleaned.

If the bottom of a leg is well-rounded, as it could be when turned on a lathe, it may be smooth enough to slide without damaging the carpet or other floor covering, but it is usual to provide another aid for sliding.

The simplest aid is a metal dome (Fig. 2-22A), usually called a *glide* or *dome of silence*. Its prongs are driven into the end grain of a leg. Put a piece of wood over the glide and hammer on the wood so you don't damage the smooth-plated surface.

It is more usual to fit *casters*. A caster is a wheel that is offset in relation to a pivot, so it will turn to trail in the right direction when the bed starts to move. There have been a very large variety of casters. Early casters had quite small wheels, both in diameter and width. These suited hard surfaces. With the more general use of carpets and other means of softening the floor surface, other casters that give a broader spread of the load

have appeared. In any case, a caster may be put in a saucer-shaped stand to spread the load further, and only lifted out when moved. To reduce marks on the floor covering, the bed position should be changed occasionally.

A basic caster has a wheel about 1 inch in diameter, offset about 1½ inches, with a pin to fit a hole in the bottom of the leg (Fig. 2-22B). The pin may be ¼ inch to ½ inch in diameter and ridged so it will grip the hole. Further strengthening may be obtained by a flange to take screws (Fig. 2-22C).

One problem in using a pin in the leg is that movement of the bed tries to bend the peg and put a bursting action on the wood around it. If the leg is fairly stout, that load will be resisted and no trouble will arise. The alternative is to enclose the wood with the metal of the caster. The traditional type has a square cup with a slight taper to fit a tapered leg end (Fig. 2-22D). For a turned leg there is a similar caster with a round cup (Fig. 2-22E). The leg should be a drive fit. It is secured with a screw through the side.

Traditional casters are still available, but there are several modern versions as well. Many of these have square base plates with holes for screws to fit up into the legs. Most are about 1½ inches square, but, if you intend to use them, make sure the leg size is suitable before making the bed. Some of these casters are deeper than the traditional types, needing perhaps 3 inches from floor to the leg end. Traditional casters only need 1½ inches, so leg lengths should be adjusted accordingly.

One modern type of caster is in the form of a ball (Fig. 2-22F), which may have a rubber tread. The hard tread suits carpets and most floor coverings, but the rubber tread is better on a hardwood or tile floor.

Casters are inconspicuous, so their appearance is not very important. Usually they are in a neutral color, but some of the modern ones have bright plastic wheels. There are casters with fairly large rubber-tired wheels, but they are more suitable for industrial use and as trolleys for moving food. They are too big for beds, except possibly for hospital beds.

For the small amount of use that bed casters

get there should be no need for lubrication, but if the wheel or pivot on a new caster does not turn easily, do not use oil, which might drip on a carpet. Rub the axle with a pencil, or smear it with wax or candle fat.

## WOOD

The most common material used for the structures of beds is wood. There are metal frames as well, but these are not as suitable for the craftsman producing individual beds. The variety of woods available is considerable, and choice can be confusing. There is insufficient space in this book for great detail. Anyone wishing to learn about woods should consult specialized books.

Wood comes from trees; so the sizes available depend on how big certain trees grow. Most woods are available in sections to suit making beds, except where wide panels are needed and boards may need to be joined. In general, small pieces are less costly than large sizes, so it is worthwhile designing a bed to use narrower pieces.

Trees that produce lumber are broadly divided into hardwoods and softwoods. In most cases, the name signifies the difference between the woods, but there are some soft hardwoods and some hard softwoods. These names indicate types and not relative hardness. Softwoods come from pines, spruces, firs, and similar needle-leafed trees. Hardwoods come from broad-leafed trees, which grow more slowly and produce wood that is denser and usually harder.

Most hardwoods are stronger than softwoods and look better when made into furniture. There has been a fashion for softwood furniture, but most tables, chairs, beds, and other furniture are hardwood. It is advisable to use hardwoods for the majority of beds. Softwoods in the same instances would need to be thicker for comparable strength.

### Drying Wood

When a tree is felled, the resulting logs contain a considerable amount of sap. Much of this moisture must be dried out before the wood is suitable for making furniture. Drying to a suitable moisture content is called *seasoning*. Usually, a log is cut across into boards, which may be stacked with spacers for air drying. Air drying could take several years, so other, quicker methods of seasoning are often employed. Some moisture must be left in the wood, but that is a controlled amount.

As wood dries, it shrinks across the lines of grain. If it absorbs moisture from the atmosphere, it expands. If possible, obtain the wood some time before you intend to use it and keep it for a few weeks in a similar atmosphere to which the finished furniture will be exposed. The wood should then stabilize, and not crack or warp from varying moisture content after being made up. Most hardwoods that have been properly seasoned should be trouble-free in use.

### Quality of Wood

As a natural product, wood can vary in quality. Cracks, called *shakes*, may occur and need to be cut around. Knots are formed where branches joined the tree trunk. Small knots that are solid with the surrounding wood will not matter and may even be decorative. Twisting and wandering grain is also decorative. Where strength is important, as in bed sides, the grain lines should be reasonably straight, and there should be no knots, other than the smallest.

### Softwoods

Softwoods can be obtained almost anywhere, since they are the woods used in general-purpose building. There are certain stock sizes, so you may have to cut them yourself to suit your needs. Sizes are as sawn. If you buy the wood planed, it will probably be about ⅛ inch less in width and thickness than the specified sizes. Quality can vary tremendously. Wood that may be good enough for a fence may be of no use for furniture.

Of the softwoods, many are unsuitable for furniture. The various pines and firs can be obtained in good qualities and may have furniture possibilities. Some exude resin around the knots, which can be a nuisance, but a coat of shellac will seal it. Pitch pine is heavy and strong, with prominent grain lines. It was used for Victorian furniture. Oregon and Columbian pines are similar to it, but lighter.

## Hardwoods

At one time, the choice of hardwoods depended on what was grown in the immediate vicinity, so if you want to make reproduction beds, this will guide you in your choice. However, with worldwide communications and transport today, hardwoods are available from all parts of the world.

A partial listing of the spread of American hardwood trees follows, but there are other woods in some regions. Some trees spread into other regions as well.

*Northern Region* — ash, aspen, basswood, yellow birch, butternut, cherry, elm, hickory, locust, hard maple, oak, walnut.

*Central Region* — white ash, basswood, beech, buckeye, chestnut, cottonwood, American elm, hackberry, shagbark hickory, locust, hard maple, white oak, yellow poplar, sycamore.

*Appalachian Region* — ash, beech, hard maple, red oak, white oak.

*Southern Region* — ash, basswood, beech, birch, cottonwood, elm, sweet and red gum, hackberry, hickory, locust, maple, red and cherry-bark oak, pecan, sycamore, black willow.

Oak has been used considerably for furniture and is very durable. Beech is one of the best woods for turning. Walnut makes attractive furniture.

Of the imported woods, mahogany is the wood most frequently used for furniture, but there are many types of this wood. Spanish and Cuban mahoganies are best for furniture, with the lighter Honduras mahogany also used. African mahogany is coarser and less suitable. Sapele looks like mahogonay and may be used with it. It is used for plywood that can be stained to match mahogany.

## Plywood

Plywood is now used in furniture in place of thin boards of solid wood which were glued to make up widths in the past. Plywood is made of three or more veneers glued together with the grains crossing. Sheets commonly available are up to 48 inches by 96 inches and in thickness from ⅛ inches. The common Douglas fir plywood is not a furniture wood, except for uses internally or under mattresses. Plywood for furniture is often made of mahogany-like hardwoods, although birch or other hardwood could be used. In some cases, the surface veneer is suitable for finishing to match surrounding solid wood. In other cases, a thin surface veneer of the surrounding wood may need to be applied.

## Particleboard

Particleboard, or *chipboard*, is a newer substitute for wide boards that has some use in making beds. It is made of chips or particles of wood in a synthetic resin. It is unsuitable for thin boards, but may be upward of ½-inch thick. In its uncovered state it is unattractive, but sheets can be obtained already covered with veneer or plastic in several finishes. It can be cut with woodworking tools, and edges can be covered with strips to match the surfaces.

## GLUE

Most of the loads in a bed are taken by screws or bolts. Glue is needed where parts of a framework are made up. They may be reinforced by screws or dowels across joints. Glue between bed parts takes similar strains to those in other pieces of furniture.

There have been many changes in glues since World War II, due mainly to the introduction of synthetic resins. Older furniture was joined with glue made from hides, fish, and other animal elements. Similar glues may still be obtained, but there are other, stronger ones that are more convenient to use. One snag with traditional glues is that they have no resistance to water; so furniture in a damp environment might open at the joints.

Modern synthetic resin glues are better known by trade names, or even by their color. Check that the glue you buy is suitable for wood only and not for a range of materials, such as paper and cardboard, as well as wood. The latter glues do not have enough strength for furniture joints. Single-part synthetic resin glues are water-resistant, but the strongest and most waterproof glues are in two parts, to be mixed before use or applied separately to meeting surfaces. They are intended primarily for boat building, but may be used for furniture, although you should avoid those that show a dark glue line.

With modern glues, follow the maker's instructions, particularly concerning temperatures. Some cannot be used in very high or very low temperatures. Once set they are hard and brittle. If excess glue squeezes out of a joint, clean it off before it sets, or it may become so hard that you chip the surface of the wood in removing a hard blob.

Joints must be reasonably close-fitting since most of these glues are not gap-filling; so their strength is reduced if they have to fill a space between parts. If you need to glue a loose-fitting joint, mix sawdust with the glue that goes into it. The bond should then be as good as if the joint parts met closely.

# Chapter 3

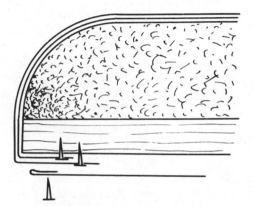

# Upholstery

From his earliest days, man has wanted to soften the things on which he sat or slept. Sitting for long on a hard surface, even if it has some shaping to the body, gets progressively more uncomfortable. The increasing discomfort becomes of more importance to the sitter than whatever should be holding his attention. There is much truth in the saying, "The brain can only absorb as much as the posterior can withstand." This also applies to beds. Most of us could not rest for a night on a hard surface.

Upholstery provides softening and padding. This term is usually applied to chairs, where seat, back, and arms may be upholstered, but the technique is expanded to take in beds and other reclining supports. All applications of upholstery are related, and the same basic considerations apply. Upholstery may be attached to a bed or chair, or it may be loose in the form of cushions, pillows, or mattresses. In many situations, there is attached upholstery that further supports removable sections. Upholstery is often arranged this way on a bed.

Another way of providing softened support is to sling the user by the method seen in a hammock. Seats and beds of this sort can be seen in ancient Greek and Egyptian drawings. A slung fabric seat can be quite comfortable. The method is used in folding stools and chairs. The traditional seaman's hammock supported by ropes to hooks is a slack version, and almost cocoons the reclining body. Use of such a hammock is unlikely to be acceptable to many people, however.

Slung fabric has possibilities for single beds, where the canvas is attached to two parallel stiff poles, held apart by end supports. If the degree of tautness is carefully arranged, such a bed may be very comfortable, either as it is, or with a light, flexible mattress over it. Application of this type of support is obviously limited to a single person. If made for two, the sag would be enough to roll them tightly together at the center. Slung fabric is suitable for take-down beds, particularly for young children, where the design limits the risk of a child falling out of bed.

## SIMPLE PADDING

The most basic requirement of upholstery is to soften a hard surface, such as a plain wood seat or some types of bed headboards. At one time this softening was done with horse hair, cotton batting, and many other materials, all of which tended to flatten and become hard themselves after much use.

It is better today to use rubber and plastic foam materials. These pads are spongelike, with large numbers of small air cells to provide cushioning. In most materials the surfaces are smooth and the air cells are contained in the thickness. In some foams the air cells are linked, which makes little difference to the padding ability, but, if the foam gets wet, it absorbs water like a sponge and is very difficult to dry out. In closed-cell foam, each cell is independent and not open to the surfaces or any other cell, so moisture cannot pass through the foam. If closed-cell foam gets wet, moisture remains on the surface and is easily removed.

Foam upholstery materials can be bought in many thicknesses, from about ⅛ inches up to 6 inches or more. The thin material may be used for lining jewelry boxes and similar applications. The thicker material gives good padding on furniture.

It is possible to get varying degrees of softness. Some fairly hard foam is not really intended for upholstery, but is used more for packing delicate things in transit. However, some foam salvaged from packing cases may have upholstery applications and is worth keeping.

Rubber or plastic foam padding several inches thick can be cut with a long, thin-bladed knife. A carving knife may be used. If the knife is sharp, a slicing action like sawing will make a clean cut. With some foam it helps to wet the blade. Always cut the pad oversize, so when the covering is drawn over it, it compresses (Fig. 3-1A). If you cut it to the exact size, compression may cause the edge of the wood to show through (Fig. 3-1B).

Since the padding must be able to expand again after compressing, air must be able to get in and out. If there is a solid base, drill a few holes so air can pass through (Fig. 3-1C). How many holes to drill is a matter of experience. Obviously it is better to have too many than too few. Four or five ½-inch

holes in a chair seat should be more than enough. Similarly, the size of the pad depends on its softness and compressibility as well as its overall size. With average foam on a chair seat, ½ inches oversize each way should be satisfactory.

If the foam is left with a square edge, the covering material will pull it slightly rounded along its top edges, but the depth will remain about upright (Fig. 3-1D). If you want to finish with a more rounded edge, as would be usual on a divan bed, bevel the foam pad. If you cut a bevel on the top edge, any slight unevenness will probably show through. Instead, bevel underneath (Fig. 3-1E) for a much better curve (Fig. 3-1F). Cut a diagonal bevel under each corner so that will curve down neatly.

## UPHOLSTERY COVERING

Almost any fabric can be, and has been, used for upholstery covering. For bed heads, the material is often similar to that used for the outer bed coverings. For general upholstery, the chosen fabric is usually stouter and thicker. For chair seats, there may be a plastic-coated fabric, with a leather look, similar to the coverings of many automobile seats. The stiffer and stouter fabrics are easier to use. The more loosely and lightly woven cloths have a tendency to pull out of shape, affecting appearance.

For traditional, loose, stuffing materials it was always customary to first cover with a light, flexible fabric. Its main purpose was to pull the padding into shape and hold it there while the outer covering was applied. This technique is still advised for upholstery finishing with a woven fabric outer covering, but with plastic-coated fabric you can go directly over the padding. It helps in some circumstances to fasten strips of fabric to the foam with adhesive and pull the foam to shape with them (Fig. 3-1G), tacking them before putting on any covering. Some plastic foams, however, do not readily accept adhesives.

Coverings can be attached to wood with tacks. Upholstery tacks are either fully tapered (Fig. 3-2A) or partly tapered (Fig. 3-2B). The alternative is to use staples, which is the usual method in mass production, where a spring or power device is also

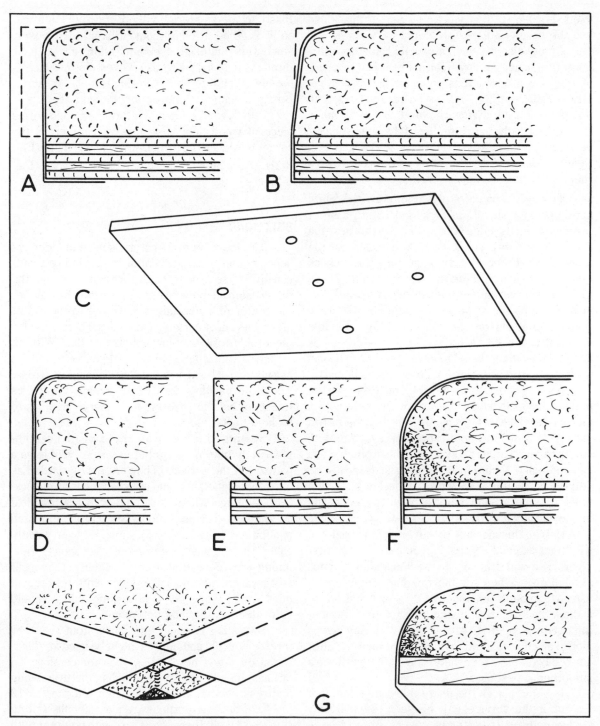

Fig. 3-1. Foam padding is compressed by its covering (A,B) and needs holes for ventilation in the base (C). A square edge does not compress much (D), but a bevel allows a greater curve (E,F). Strips stuck on will pull the foam to shape (G).

used. For small, light work you can turn back and use the base of a paper stapler.

An upholsterer uses a special hammer with a long, thin head, but any light hammer can be used. One with a narrow cross pane can be used in restricted spaces (Fig. 3-2C). To remove tacks, an upholsterer uses a *ripping chisel*, but it is not a cutting tool as the name implies. It has a thin end for getting under a tack head and may be cranked with the end notched (Fig. 3-2D). A screwdriver with a thin end will serve just as well.

To cover a piece of plywood, draw the fabric over opposite sides and tack underneath a short distance from the edge (Fig. 3-2E). Do this near the center of opposite sides, then do the same for the other sides (Fig. 3-2F). Look at the top and check that compression is about the same each way. Drive more tacks, working along the edges toward corners, keeping the same tension (Fig. 3-2G). Tack spacing depends on the material. Very flexible material will need closer spacing to avoid bumps and hollows along the edge of the padding. You can probably settle at tacks 1 inch or 1½ inch apart.

At a corner, thin, flexible material can be pulled diagonally over the corner and held with a tack underneath. The surplus can then be drawn over it to produce a smooth appearance on top. With stouter material cut away as much surplus as you can and make V cuts into the folds underneath, so you do not build up too great a thickness. Use a knife to trim around parallel with the edge and inside the lines of tacks.

If two thicknesses of covering material are used, get as good a finish as you can with the first layer. You will probably leave some slight bumps and hollows. When you put the outer covering on, use just enough tension to fit closely and try to arrange tacks in rows inside the first line, but pulling between the first tacks (Fig. 3-2H). Any bumps along the edges should level out. Fortunately, after a few days, upholstery materials tend to settle to a smoother appearance.

In some places the underside can be left as it is, but if the surface will be seen, even if only occasionally, it is better to cover with a piece of cloth. If it is a woven fabric, turn in the edges.

Plastic-coated material will not fray at a cut edge; so it could be fitted without turning in. However, since this material does not allow air to pass through, it is better to use woven cloth, which is porous, even if the top covering is a plastic fabric. Burlap is sometimes used for this purpose.

Rub down the folds of a turned-in edge with a piece of wood or a knife handle. Cut across the corner to reduce the turned-in thickness there (Fig. 3-2J). Tack outside the other lines of tacks (Fig. 3-2K).

## BUTTONING

The loose stuffing materials used in older upholstery had to be prevented from moving about, usually by sewing through. Without sewing, the filling could all move to one end, or the filling under the center of a seat might move out to the sides, leaving an uncomfortable main area. There was also the problem of keeping upholstery flat. Without some restraint the covering could curve out like a bag instead of being a flat pad, as a seat or mattress. The foam padding used today remains as flat as intended, but the covering over a large area has to be held to it.

Sewing through was traditionally accomplished by buttoning; so buttons were visible as a pattern on the surface. They are now regarded as normal on upholstery and are seen today as decoration, although stitching through still has practical advantages. It is possible to buy buttons to match upholstery materials, and suppliers can usually cover buttons with materials of your choice. Buttoning is not done until after the padding is covered, so there are no special requirements to keep in mind, except for a plywood backing, which should be drilled for stitching before covering.

Buttoning is done with fairly stout twine or thread. For thin padding, as might be used for decoration on a bed head rather than for comfort, an ordinary needle may be used, but there are long mattress needles, in lengths from 4 inches to 16 inches. For most purposes, a plain needle will do (Fig. 3-3A), but there are others with points at both ends (Fig. 3-3B). Where there would be an advan-

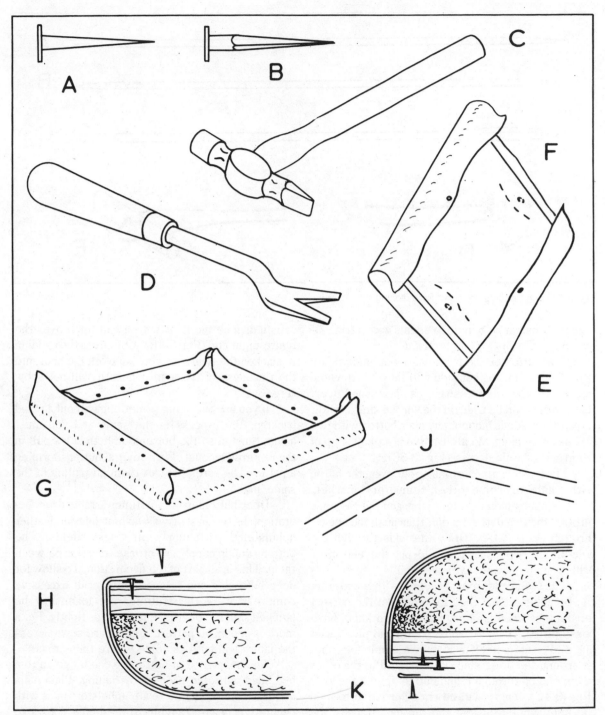

Fig. 3-2. Tacks (A,B) are driven with a light hammer (C) and removed with a ripping chisel (D). Covering tacks are spread from the center (E,F,G), and a second piece of cloth may go further than the first (H). Trim corners (J). Cloth underneath will hide tacks.

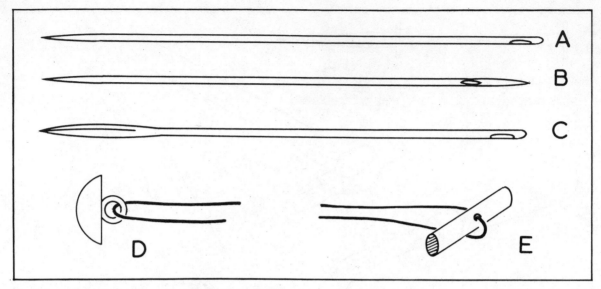

Fig. 3-3. Long needles are used for buttoning upholstery.

tage in forcing a large hole, a needle with a triangular point (Fig. 3-3C) can be used.

The button on the front has a loop underneath (Fig. 3-3D). If the other side will show, as it would in a cushion or mattress that can be turned over, that type should be used on the second side as well. If the other side is hidden, any plain button with two holes can be used. An alternative is a plain strip of wood with a hole across (Fig. 3-3E).

Mark where the buttons are to go on the fabric with chalk or some other temporary marker. Thread a button on doubled twine and put the ends through the eye of the needle, then push the needle through (Fig. 3-4A). Draw the ends through the hole in the wood backing and put the button or drilled strip of wood over one end.

The twine ends must be joined with a knot that can be adjusted and then locked when the correct tension has been applied. Several slip knots have possibilities. A figure-eight knot is simple. Twist one end back on itself as if tying a simple knot, but go around the other side (Fig. 3-4B). Put the other twine end up through it and pull to tighten the knot (Fig. 3-4C). There will be enough friction to hold the knot while you test the tension. Usually the front button is pulled back until it is a little below the covering around it (Fig. 3-4D). When you are

satisfied, lock the knot with a half hitch over the figure-eight end (Fig. 3-4E). Compress the padding to slacken the twine, so you can work the knot into the thickness of the foam where it will not show (Fig. 3-4F).

If you are buttoning something without a wood backing, the process is the same and you must adjust tension so the buttons on both sides pull in the required amount. With several buttons forming a pattern, be careful to get them all pulling in the same amount.

Deep buttoning is sometimes arranged for decoration. In the past it was fashionable for leather upholstery, particularly on Chesterfields. The buttons pull in deeply and creases develop between them. This is all part of the decoration. To allow for deep buttoning and to avoid an overall excessive compression of the stuffing, the foam may be notched and the covering not put on as tightly. For a more pronounced pattern, seams are sewn across the fabric and buttons come where they cross.

An appearance of buttoning can be given to a bed head with thin padding by nailing. Plain nails are unattractive, but there are upholstery nails with decorative heads, ranging from simple domes to patterns (Fig. 3-5A). Driven into the backing (Fig. 3-5B), they will draw in the covering in the same

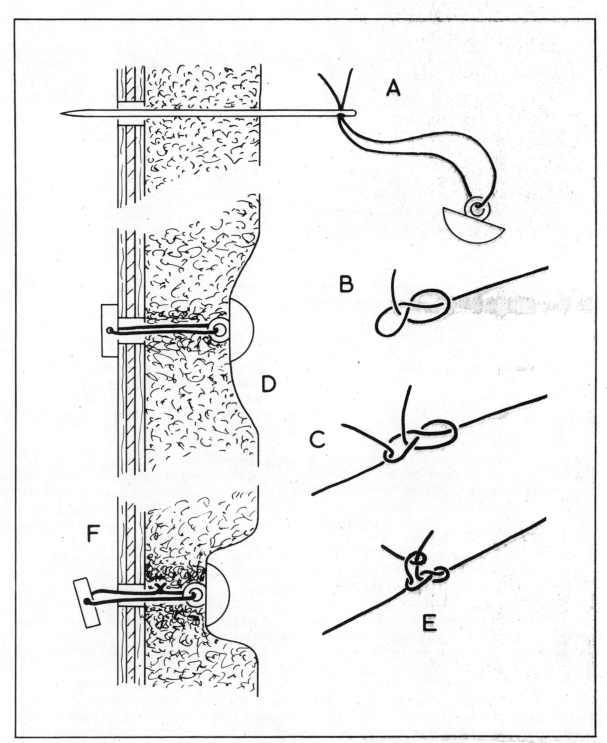

Fig. 3-4. Twine is pulled through when buttoning. Adjustment is with a slipknot.

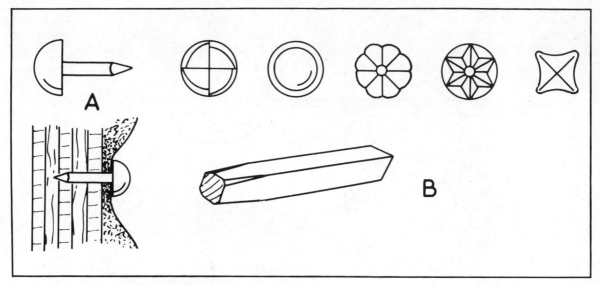

Fig. 3-5. Decorative nails give a similar appearance to buttoning.

way as buttons and twine. To avoid damaging the patterned nail head or the surrounding cloth, use a strip of square or round wood as a punch under the hammer.

## GIMP

It is not always possible to tack fabric to wood in a way that hides the tack heads. This may happen when the covering goes only partly down a wood side or one piece of cloth must be tacked over another. An upholsterer uses gimp to cover the tacks. Gimp is a woven fabric tape, usually less than ½-inch wide. It may be fairly plain or in an elaborate weave with a raised pattern on the front. Many colors are available, and combinations can be bought to either match or contrast the covering material.

With the gimp go *gimp pins*, which are fine nails, usually black, with small heads. With most gimps the head disappears in the weave and is almost invisible.

The covering may come flat on to a wood side, if it is a material that will not fray (Fig. 3-6A). Woven cloth should be turned under (Fig. 3-6B). Keep the tacks in a straight line and fairly close to the edges so the gimp will cover (Fig. 3-6C). Drive the gimp pins in a zigzag pattern and maintain a good tension on the gimp.

If the gimp is over two meeting edges, they need to be fitted carefully so the gimp hides the joint, but in some places, as when putting a flounce around the edge of a bed, the outer part may extend above the gimp (Fig. 3-6D).

## WALL EDGES

If the covering is pulled over a fairly thick block of foam from both sides, it will tend to form a bag with an indistinct edge somewhere between square and rounded, with the square-cut filling foam pad distorting unevenly. It is better to arrange a strip of fabric around the edge and separate pieces over the large surfaces. When sewn up, this arrangement provides a covering that is about the same shape as the block of foam was before covering. A mattress or a bunk cushion is an example of this treatment.

The covering is usually made inside out. When it is turned the right way, only the lines of stitches show outside. The cut edges of cloth are inside (Fig. 3-7A). Most of the seams can be machine-sewn, but a gap must be left for turning the cloth the right way and inserting the foam. The gap is then sewn by hand for a neat finish. To get a neat and tight finish, make the covering slightly smaller than the block of plastic or rubber foam.

Cut the cloth so it is ½ inch, or slightly more, oversize all around. First make the strip to go around the edges. Several pieces may need to be sewn together for a large mattress or a bunk cushion. For most purposes the mattress or cushion will be rectangular, but the technique is the same if it is to finish with a curved edge. Make the sewn strip a tight fit around the foam and put it in place inside out, with the seam widths folded outward (Fig.

3-7B). Cut the panels for top and bottom, with their seam edges folded and marked. Locate them inside out. To prevent movement while you mark the assembly, use large pins into the foam (Fig. 3-7C).

Put locating marks on the seams or cut notches to match in adjoining pieces (Fig. 3-7D), then carefully remove the covering. Pin through meeting seams, with everything still inside out. Decide where you will leave an opening for inserting the padding. Foam will compress, so the gap does not need to be very big. You can sew all around at the

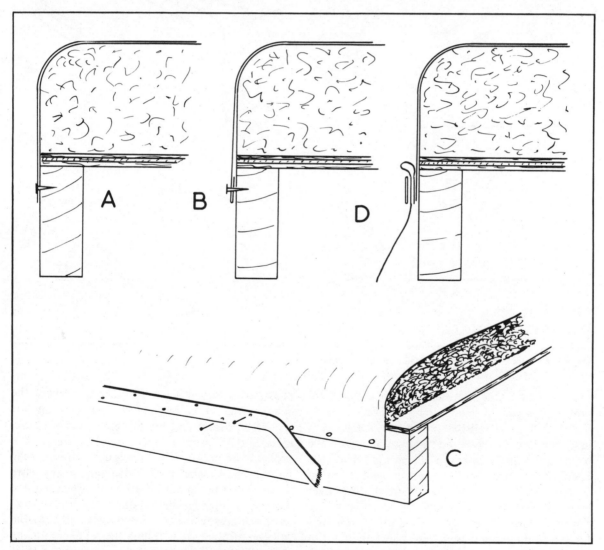

Fig. 3-6. Cloth tacked to a wood side may be covered with gimp.

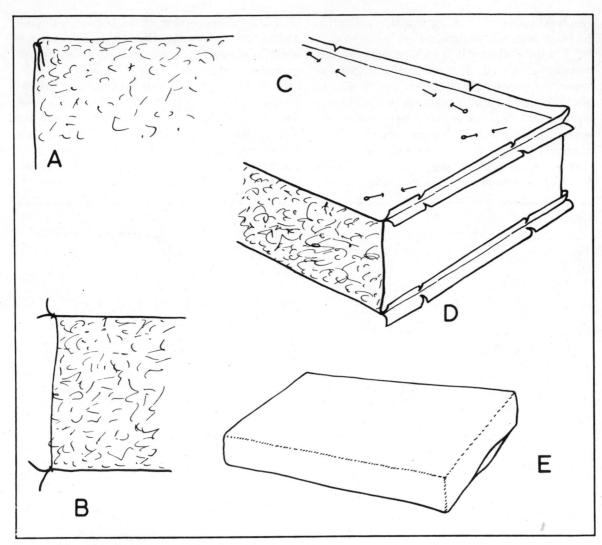

Fig. 3-7. Cloth is joined to make a wall edge and is sewn inside out.

top, but the gap must come somewhere underneath, probably as part of one end (Fig. 3-7E).

Machine-sew all the seams except the opening; then turn the cover the right way and insert the padding. In some mattresses a zipper is sewn in the opening, which avoids the need for hand stitching. It also allows the foam to be removed if the cover must be cleaned, but, since it is usual to button through a large assembly like a mattress, the buttoning stitches would need to be removed first. For hand sewing, use slip stitches, so that very little

shows outside and it is difficult to see where the seam changes from machine to hand stitching.

Use thread and needle appropriate to the material. An ordinary large sewing needle will probably be better than a thick upholstery needle for the usual mattress covering. For heavy cloth there would be an advantage in a curved needle. Turn the cloth edges in to follow along the lines of the machine-sewn seam. Sharp folds will help you to keep straight. Use double thread and knot the ends together. Take the needle into one seam (Fig.

3-8A), then up and straight across to the other seam. Go down into this and along to come up again (Fig. 3-8B). Cross straight back to the first seam and make another stitch, and so on (Fig. 3-8C). When the joint is loose, the thread is obvious, but when pulled tight, only the crossing parts of the stitches will show (Fig. 3-8D). The length of each stitch depends on the material, but they should not be more than ¼ inch. Knot the thread at the far end.

## PIPING

A wall-edged mattress showing stitches at the seams may be satisfactory where it is normally covered, but if it will double as a seat during the day and the seam will be exposed, the seam edge can be improved with piping. Piping can be seen on much upholstered furniture in the form of a small cylindrical piece projecting along a seam. Any seam that is sewn inside out can be piped. Piping can be in a color or design to match or contrast the covering material. A blue or red imitation leather might have white piping. Piping is sewn into a seam when other parts are joined and does not involve much extra work.

Piping consists of a cord enclosed in a piece of fabric, with a line of stitches close to the cord and enough cloth projecting to sew into the seam (Fig. 3-9A). It can be bought ready-made with a large range of coverings and different diameters of cord. For most upholstery, piping should not be more than ⅛ inch diameter.

You can also make piping, using offcuts of your material. Cut the strips on the *bias*—diagonal to the weave (Fig. 3-9B). Lengths can be made by joining pieces. Put two ends together with the outside surfaces meeting and sew across (Fig. 3-9C). To get a line of stitches very close to a cord, a special cording foot can be put on a sewing machine.

The piece of piping should be longer than the distance around a seam, if that is continuous. After

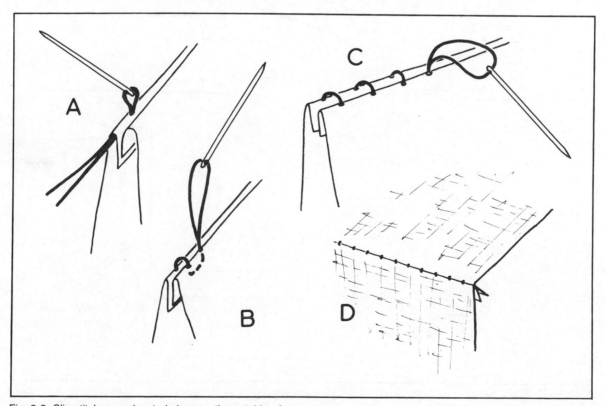

Fig. 3-8. Slip stitches are least obvious on the outside of a seam.

45

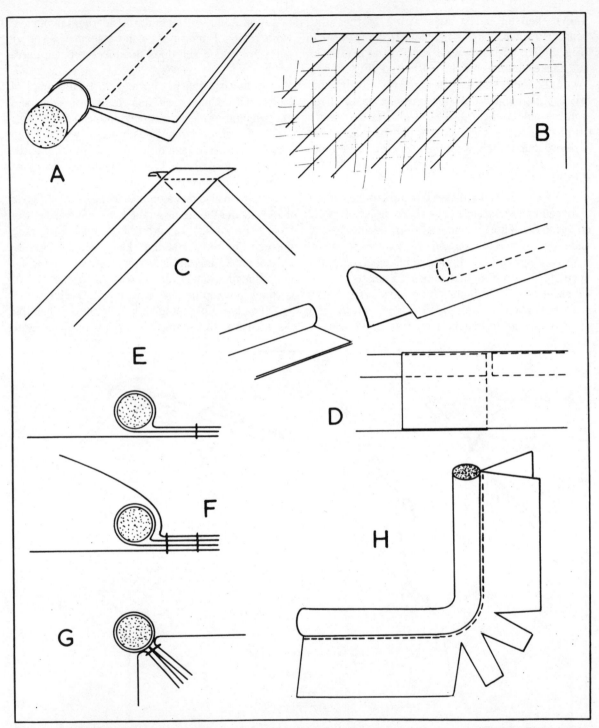

Fig. 3-9. Piping is made by enclosing cord in cloth (A), cutting on the bias (B,C), and joining ends together (D). Piping is sewn into a seam in stages (E,F,G,H).

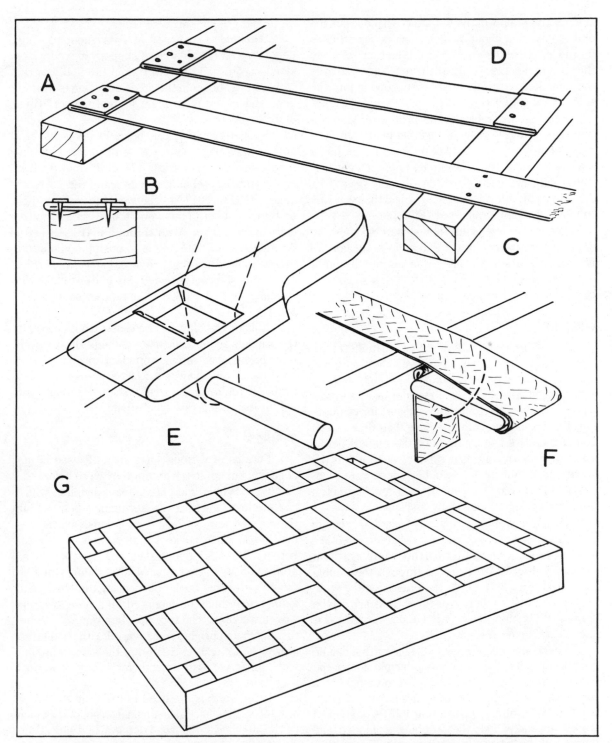

Fig. 3-10. Webbing can be tacked to a frame (A,B,C,D) and stretched (E,F). It can be woven both ways (G).

sewing the piping in, as will be described, cut the ends to overlap about ¾ inch. Unpick the stitches for the length of the overlap on one end and cut away the cord there. Bring in the other end and wrap over the unpicked cloth, then complete sewing into the seam (Fig. 3-9D).

Piping is brought into the seam where the two pieces of cloth are brought together inside out. The parts could be pinned to keep them in line, but it may be wiser to sew the piping to one piece (Fig. 3-9E), then bring the other to it and sew again (Fig. 3-9F). Finally, the assembly is turned the right way to show the piping outward (Fig. 3-9G).

When sewing inside out something must be done to permit the cloth to extend from the cord to go around a corner. Cut a few notches into the cloth, not quite up to the stitching (Fig. 3-9H), so you can bend the cord to a tight curve.

## WEBBING

Webbing is not used much in modern upholstery, but it still has a purpose. The traditional type is about 2 inches wide and strongly woven, with very little stretch. It can be interlaced across a wooden framework to provide support for cushioning, to give a more flexible base than plywood. If coil springs are used, it may be the support below them. A modern version is rubber webbing. It is the same width, but made of rubber-impregnated fabric, so it is very strongly elasticised, and there is no need for springs underneath cushions.

Ordinary webbing is usually tacked to one side of a frame, strained across, and tacked to the other side. There may be a pattern of three or five tacks at the start (Fig. 3-10A) driven through the double thickness (Fig. 3-10B). At the other side the webbing is strained while two or three tacks are driven (Fig. 3-10C), then the end is cut off, turned over, and tacked again (Fig. 3-10D).

There are many types of strainers that can be bought or made. A common principle loops the webbing through a slot in a handle, to be held by a temporary peg, while the appliance is levered (Fig. 3-10E). The simplest straining tool is a strip of wood, around which the webbing is looped and levered (Fig. 3-10F). Variations on this tool have

teeth and gripping arrangements.

Webbing is arranged at convenient spacing, depending on the amount of support needed. Gaps should not usually be more than the width of the webbing. Webbing in the other direction is worked over and under to provide mutual support (Fig. 3-10G).

Rubber webbing can be held by tacks in a similar way, but there are some metal clips intended for end fastenings. The clip is put over an end of rubber webbing and is squeezed so teeth penetrate (Fig. 3-11A). The webbing end can then go into a slot cut in the wood frame, so a screw or nail can be driven down through it (Fig. 3-11B). Another way of fastening is to push the clip into a groove plowed at a slight angle along the wood (Fig. 3-11C). In some assemblies it is better to take the webbing over the edge to a groove below (Fig. 3-11D).

Rubber webbing may be crossed both ways, in the same way as ordinary webbing. However, it often provides better and sufficient springing if it is only taken one way and placed across in close strips. If you raise the seat cushion of a chair, you will probably see this type of support.

## SPRINGS

Springs of various sorts are still used in upholstery, but not to the extent they were before the coming of rubber and plastic foam padding, which can produce much of the springing effect within themselves. Coil springs used in loose mattresses may be in cloth pockets and packed closely together, but these mattresses are best bought as professionally made units. Making them is outside the scope of this book. Coil springs in chairs and similar seats may be mounted on a base of interwoven webbing. The tops are then tied with twine to keep them upright, and covered with padding. A narrow bed might be treated in the same way, but webbing is not stiff enough for a bed of normal proportions.

If coil springs are used to make up the lower assembly, they should be on an iron support, which can be attached to the wood or metal bed sides (Fig. 3-12A). The tops of the springs must be tied to each

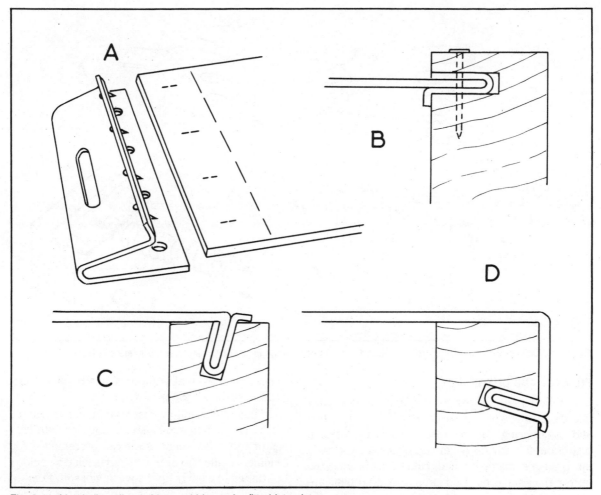

Fig. 3-11. Metal clips allow rubber webbing to be fitted into slots.

other, and to the sides, with twine, to keep them upright. It is better to obtain a complete bed assembly as a unit, in which the springs are mounted in a frame ready to mount in a bed. This assembly should be obtained first, since its size determines the measurements of the bed.

Tension springs provide support by stretching. They contrast with coil springs, which provide support by compressing. One form of tension springing can be used instead of rubber webbing. The spring goes across an opening and is attached to the wood frame. One method of attachment uses a metal plate with holes, which is screwed into a slight rabbet in the wood (Fig. 3-12B). Springs spaced only a few inches apart will support a chair cushion or bunk mattress. It is usual to put cloth over the springs to prevent chafe. Burlap is suitable. Turn the cloth under far enough to go over the spring ends to give additional chafe protection (Fig. 3-12C).

Short tension springs may be used at the ends of flexible steel laths (Fig. 3-12D). Of course, the laths do not provide springing by stretching, but they can be interleaved in the same way as webbing. With strong, short springs at the ends, they provide a sufficiently flexible support for a cushion or mattress. Burlap, with a wide turned-edge, should be put between the laths and the mattress.

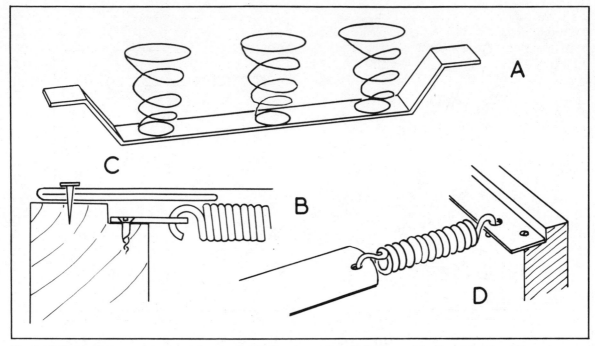

Fig. 3-12. Coil springs may be on metal supports (A). Tension springs (B,C,D) may take the place of webbing.

## PILLOWS AND CUSHIONS

Pillows are not part of the bed, but they may need to be made to suit the decor of a particular bed and its covering. Molded foam pillow interiors can be obtained ready for covering. Others can be built up. If pieces must be joined, rubber takes adhesive better than some plastic foams. Strong rubber upholstery solution will make firm joints. This solution is thicker than the solutions used for mending bicycle tire punctures.

Some molded latex rubber shapes are intended for seating and have cavities underneath to increase flexibility (Fig. 3-13A). A pair of these may be brought together and thin rubber stuck around the joint (Fig. 3-13B) to make a pillow or cushion. Another way of shaping flat foam slabs is to bevel the edges (Fig. 3-13C) and pull them together with a strip that is glued on (Fig. 3-13D). With a thick piece of foam, a similar effect can be obtained by making a V cut into its edge (Fig. 3-13E). If more curving is needed with a double thickness of foam, more pieces can be put between them (Fig. 3-13F). They need not be precisely cut or very carefully

shaped, as they will compress to give a smooth exterior shape to the pillow.

The outside pillow case will be in material to match the bedding and closed at one end with buttons or other fasteners, so it can be removed for cleaning. Inside the case it is advisable to enclose the stuffing in a fairly tight covering of soft, flexible woven cloth. Make it as a bag, either with two pieces of cloth or one folded over. If there is much shaping to the stuffing, it is better to use two pieces and give them curved edges (Fig. 3-13G) to allow for the compound curvature.

Get the sizes by fitting over the stuffing pad with the cloth inside out. Pin the parts together and sew around the seams, except for a gap to push the stuffing through when the cover is turned the right way (Fig. 3-13H). Turn the cloth the right way and sew the remaining part of a seam by hand with slip stitches, after inserting, and adjusting the stuffing.

## FLOUNCES

Many beds are given a *flounce*, or skirt, reaching almost to the floor all around. It may be just a piece of hanging cloth, but it looks better if it is pleated. In the simplest form, the pleats may be only at the corners of the foot. Pleats can be placed at fairly wide intervals along the sides and foot, or the pleats and spaces between them can be about the same, so the skirt is box-pleated and flares out for a luxurious appearance.

Unless the back of the bed will be visible, it is unnecessary to carry the skirt around the back, except for a few inches at each corner to hold the material in place. If there are pleats only at the foot corners (Fig. 3-14A), you need much less material than with full box pleating (Fig. 3-14B). A pleat that folds back 4 inches uses about 16 inches of material.

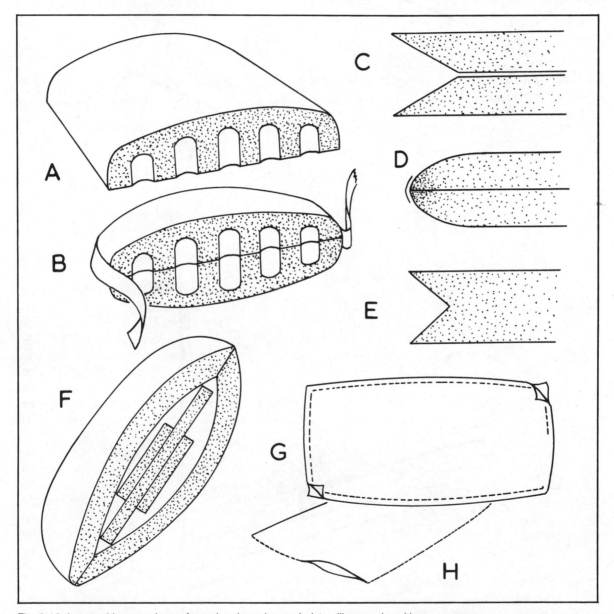

Fig. 3-13. Latex rubber may be preformed and can be made into pillows and cushions.

51

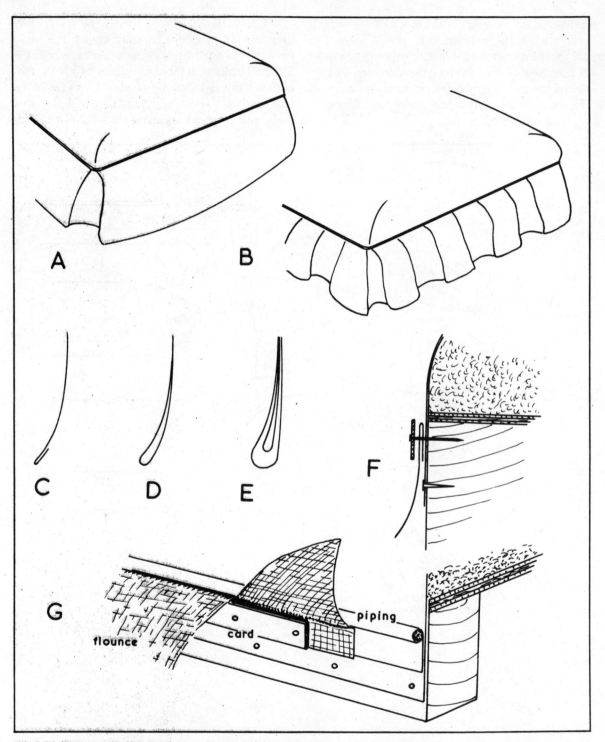

Fig. 3-14. Flounces may be lined and combined with gimp, piping, and blind tacking.

How the cloth is cut depends on the bed, but if the pleat is to follow the pattern of the top covering, you may need to cut across the material and join pieces to make up the length. A seam can be hidden in a pleat. If the flounce goes all around, the final joint can be hidden in this way. Measure around, allowing about four times as much as its width at every pleat.

You can turn back a seam along the bottom edge (Fig. 3-14C). The skirt will have a fuller appearance if the cloth is doubled (Fig. 3-14D) and look even better if it is then lined with thin cloth, such as muslin (Fig. 3-14E).

Other cloth will come down the side from the top. That cloth may be tacked first, below where the top edge of the flounce will come, then the flounce edge turned under and hidden with gimp (Fig. 3-14F). Another method of attachment helps the flounce to stand out. This is *blind tacking* combined with a length of piping (Fig. 3-14G). The tacks are driven through stiff card about ½ inch wide, which can be in several pieces. The flounce

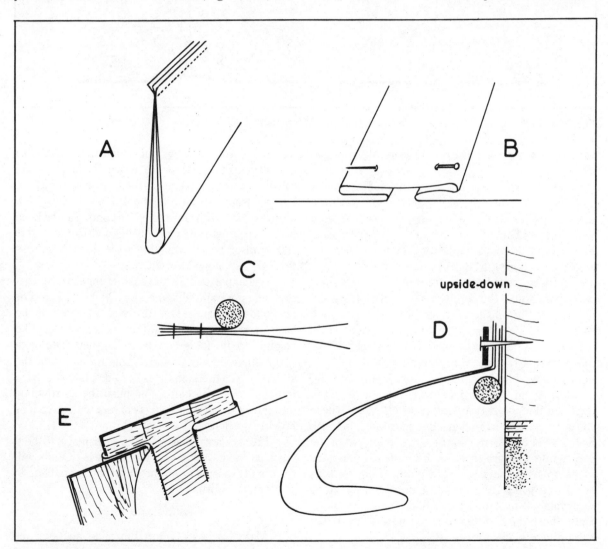

Fig. 3-15. Pleats should be carefully marked.

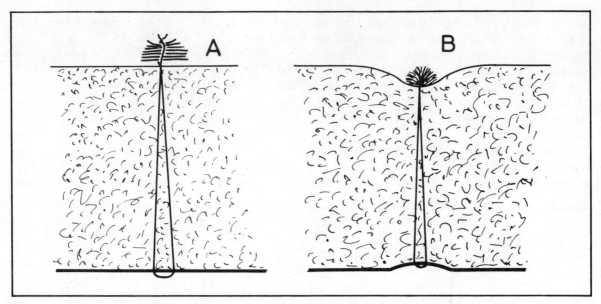

Fig. 3-16. Tufting uses pieces of wool to give a softer effect than buttoning.

fits over the card and drops with more of a rounded fold.

If the skirt is to be lined, cut the muslin about 1 inch narrower than the skirt fabric. Sew it with a line of stitches along the inside of the skirt, to keep the cloth and muslin in correct relation to each other. Fold the skirt along its center and sew the edges together (Fig. 3-15A). Press the fold.

If there are to be just corner pleats, locate their positions around the bed. Care is needed to get the pleats exactly on the corners, if they are to look right. Fold back the pleats and pin them (Fig. 3-15B). Sew across the top of each pleat and remove the pins. If the top of the flounce is to have piping above blind tacking, sew on the piping (Fig. 3-15C). At this stage make sure that you have the depth of flounce correct and parallel. Mark where the skirt comes on the bed sides and foot. It helps to have the bed inverted so the skirt hangs out of the way while you are tacking. Use a few temporary tacks to hold the flounce in place. Tack on card strips (Fig. 3-15D) with tacks at fairly close intervals—2-inch spaces will probably be about right. Turn the bed the right way up and check that the flounce hangs correctly.

If you want to use box pleating, make the pleats in the same way, but adjust their widths to give a good effect. Measure across the bed foot and calculate an even spacing, probably about 4 inches. Use the same spacing at the sides, working back from the foot, with any odd width coming at the head end. The length of material needed to make this skirt will be nearly four times the distance across the foot and along two sides.

It is important, for the sake of appearance, that the pleats are all the same size. Make two card or plywood templates. One is the total width of the back of a pleat and the other is marked for the amount to be folded in front of that. Template depths may be a little more than the depth of the skirt. To set the size of each fold, place the wide template over the cloth, and push the narrow one into the cloth until the fold is correct with the edges level (Fig. 3-15E).

Press pleats before tacking in place to help position them. Some of the sharpness of folds will eventually disappear so the cloth settles to hang in an attractive form.

## TUFTING

Mattresses are often buttoned all over the surface. With the buttons pulled below the normal surface level they are not apparent to the user. There is another way of stitching through that gives a softer effect than buttons. This is *tufting*, where a group of short pieces of wool form a tuft in a place where there would otherwise be a button. Tufting can be done on both sides, but it is more usual on a mattress that is not intended to be turned over. Use either a plywood backing or a piece of burlap. If a fairly expensive cloth is used for the visible covering, burlap can be used to provide a cheap satisfactory base.

Sew through in a similar way to buttoning, but at the back have two close holes in plywood or take the needle through and back in burlap in slightly different positions (Fig. 3-16A). At the front make a slip knot. Under the knotted twine put a group of short pieces of wool, cotton, synthetic material, or small cloth strips, all of a similar length and enough to come up into a tuft when the twine is tightened. Draw up the knot and lock it, as described for buttoning (Fig. 3-16B). Pull in all the tufts to the same depth. If the ends of twine are cut short, the knot may not show in the middle of a tuft. If it would show, compress the mattress and work the knot into the body of the foam, so only a line of twine across the tuft will show.

# Chapter 4

# Simple Traditional Beds

Beds have followed a generally similar form for several centuries, with a head, a foot, and a pair of sides. The body of the bed has some form of flexible support to provide comfort. It has usually rested on the sides, or they were incorporated in it. In some cases the sprung mattresses were built on metal sides, which took the place of wood side rails. Many sprung mattresses have been developed, but the bed that has surrounded them has followed the generally accepted form. In many cases a sprung supporting arrangement was fairly permanently mounted in the bed framework and a removable thick sprung mattress arranged on top.

Many beds are still equipped in this way, but, with the coming of rubber and plastic foam materials, the simplification of the means of providing comfort has led to adaptations. There are more beds of different designs, but there is still a preference for a bed with the traditional appearance.

The beds described in this chapter are of traditional form and can be equipped with sprung mattresses or easily adapted for foam mattresses. Headboards are provided, and most beds have foot-

boards that are intended to be exposed. It is possible, however, to arrange a footboard so its top comes about level with the bedding. Covers may then go over it. This arrangement has the advantage of preventing a mattress of bedding from slipping, while giving much of the appearance of a divan bed.

## BASIC BED

A simple bed can be embellished in many ways, but the basic design is quite functional and can be attractive in suitable surroundings. It should be made of hardwood. To get similar strength from softwood would mean increasing sections of wood that might look clumsy. In a room furnished with plain softwood pieces to give a pioneer effect, however, thicker wood for the bed might be acceptable.

Some hardwoods with attractive grain patterns do not need elaborate shaping, and they could be used for a basic bed. A clear finish would enhance their grain without the distraction of carving or other decorative shaping. The head and foot panels may need to be made up by gluing narrower pieces. An alternative is to use veneered particleboard,

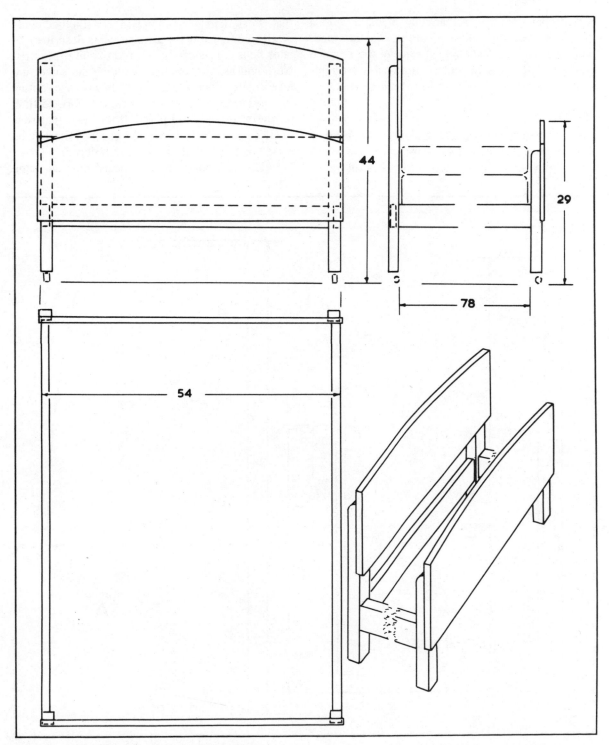

Fig. 4-1. A basic bed has ends supported on legs.

which could be kept rectangular or made with a simple curved top, as suggested for solid wood. The legs and sides should be made of wood which has been fully seasoned and is reasonably straight-grained, so the risk of warping is minimized.

## Design

The general drawing (Fig. 4-1) shows a bed to take a mattress 54 inches by 78 inches, with a boxed mattress as a base and a loose mattress on top of that. For other forms of upholstery, the bed could be altered to one of the arrangements described for later beds. Sizes can be altered to suit other mattress widths, but lengths should be the same, unless a child's bed is being built. In any case, obtain the measurements of the mattress before settling on the sizes of wood parts. If the total mattress thickness is to be less than shown, the rails may be raised or the height of the head reduced.

The headboard and footboard are the same

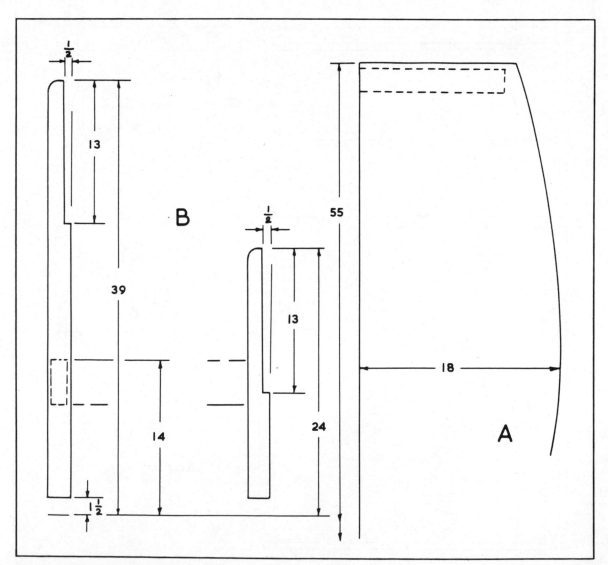

Fig. 4-2. Sizes of legs and ends for the basic bed.

58

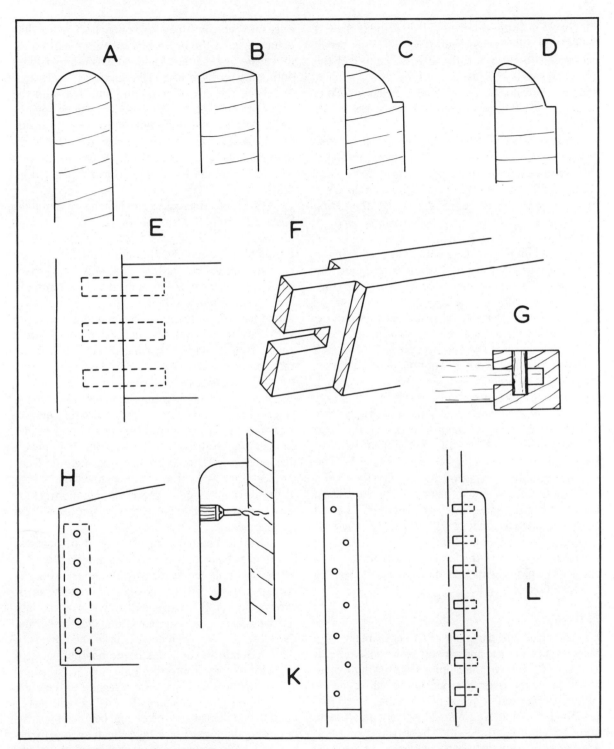

Fig. 4-3. Shaping and jointing in bed parts.

(Fig. 4-2A). At the sides they overlap the legs by ½ inch. Mark the leg positions. If the top edges are to be curved, bend a lath through the center of the edge and two points just above the legs at the side, and pencil around it. Cut and finish the curve of one piece and use it to mark around for the other piece, to get matching shapes.

Leave the bottom edges of these pieces square. The other edges could be square, with just the sharpness taken off the angular edges. They could be fully curved (Fig. 4-3A), but that does not look as good as a part curve (Fig. 4-3B). If molding facilities are available, several molding sections can be used (Fig. 4-3C). At the head it will not matter if a molding finishes with a sharp edge to the rear, but if that pattern is repeated at the foot, the sharpness should be removed by rounding (Fig. 4-3D).

Leg lengths are shown with 1½ inches allowed for casters, but that may be adjusted. In any case, raising or lowering the bed by a fraction of an inch with different hardware will not matter. Of course, if the bed is intended for someone with short or long legs, its side height could be modified.

All legs are made in the same way (Fig. 4-2B). Cut them away ½-inch deep to fit behind the head and footboards, which will then project ¼ inch. Round the tops of the legs behind the boards. The legs at the foot will get all the rigidity they need from the footboard, but at the head there should be a rail across at the same height as the sides. The rail could be joined to the legs with dowels (Fig. 4-3E), or you could use tenons (Fig. 4-3F). Either method is satisfactory, since the joints only have to supplement the rigidity gained from attaching the legs to the headboard.

### Assembly

After all the parts are cut to size, make sure they are planed true and sanded before assembly. It is easier to remove the ripples from machine planing or to level torn grain around a knot when you are dealing with a single piece of wood than when it is attached to something else. A scraper is a useful tool to remove flaws on the surface of most hardwoods. Remove sharpness from any square edges, especially where parts may be handled. For instance, a hand may be put under the bedside to move the bed, so those angles should be softened with a few strokes of a plane and some sanding.

Glue the dowel or tenon joints between the rear rail and legs, but be careful to check squareness, because the legs must stand upright. Glue should be sufficient, but, if you want to strengthen a mortise and tenon joint further, you can put a screw or dowel through each joint from the back (Fig. 4-3G).

The legs attached to the headboard and footboard gain rigidity from the joints. The joints also prevent the wide boards from warping, so they should be tight and close. A perfect contact might be sufficient for strength by glue only in a surface joint, but it is wiser to provide additional strength. Screws could be used. If driven from the front, they would have to be counterbored and plugged. Even with carefully matched wood, the plugs would show. They could be regarded as a decorative feature, and might even be made of wood of a contrasting color to draw attention to them (Fig. 4-3H).

For most beds it would be better not to have plugs showing at the front. Screws driven from the legs into the boards should be counterbored just enough for the threads to go far enough to give a maximum grip without breaking through the front surface (Fig. 4-3J). Place screws at about 2-inch intervals and stagger their arrangement (Fig. 4-3K). Plugs arranged at the rear of a leg will be inconspicuous.

Dowels could be used instead of screws. There is a choice between ½-inch dowels placed in a line centrally or ⅜-inch or ¼-inch dowels arranged in staggered lines at the same spacing as for screws (Fig. 4-3L). Drill as deeply as you can into the boards to give the maximum glue area, and therefore grip, on each dowel. Take the dowels to the full depths of the holes in the boards, but drill slightly overdepth into the legs.

How the side pieces are attached to the ends depends on circumstances. If the bed will never need to be taken apart, they could be joined permanently to the legs. For a take-down arrangement, cut the ends square and use a type of linking

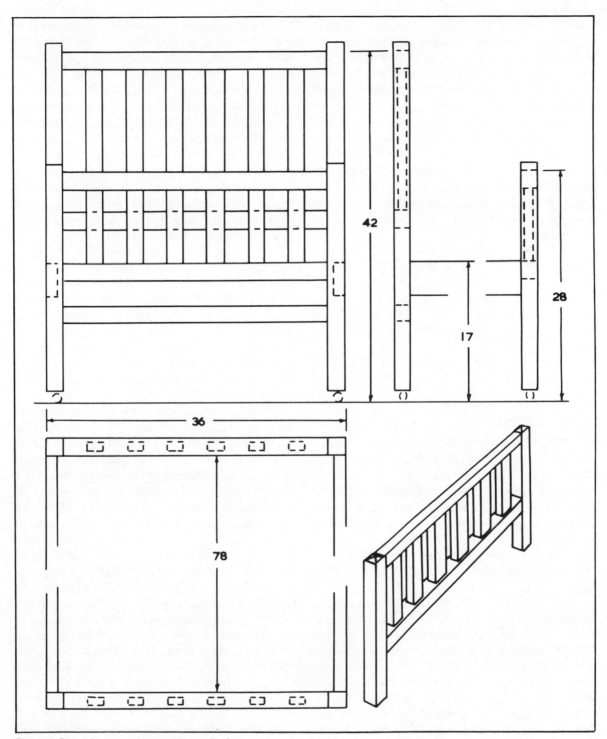

Fig. 4-4. Slats give more open ends to a bed.

hardware that has one piece screwed to the leg and its partner to the side rail. Alternatively, use bolts with nuts set into the rails (see Chapter 2). If you want to use strengthening brackets, you can carry them to the back rail under the headboard. If bolts are used, their heads may be hidden at the foot by setting them into the recesses in the legs before fitting in the footboard.

Fit casters or glides to the bottoms of the legs after checking that the bed stands level. Slight discrepancies may be adjusted by cutting a little off one leg, but this is usually unnecessary and should never be much. The bed is then completed, except for straining and polishing.

## Materials List for Basic Bed

| | | |
|---|---|---|
| 1 headboard | 18×56×¾ | |
| 1 footboard | 18×56×¾ | |
| 2 rear legs | 2×39×2 | |
| 2 front legs | 2×24×2 | |
| 1 rear rail | 4×53×1½ | |
| 2 sides | 4×79×1½ | |

## SLATTED-END BED

Wide boards are becoming difficult to find, and expensive when you can find them. The alternative of gluing up several narrower pieces to make a width still involves a large and expensive area of wood. Bed ends can be made cheaper entirely from narrow pieces, giving a more open appearance, which is very effective and may look better than solid ends in certain surroundings. Hardwood should be used. Oak would make a good-looking bed.

The general drawing (Fig. 4-4) shows a single slatted-end bed 36 inches wide, but the same method of construction could be used for a wider bed. The ends are framed with 2-inch-square pieces that give transverse stiffness and provide rigid legs. The slats are the same width, but only 1 inch thick. The sizes given allow the backboard to stand at a convenient height, while the footboard will probably not stand much higher than the usual mattress and coverings.

The legs provide the controlling sizes for several other parts, so mark them out first (Fig. 4-5A and B). Both sets of legs are shown projecting 1 inch above the top rails, allowing for strong joints. The ends can be decorated. There is an allowance of 1½ inch at the bottom for casters, but that could be modified. An extra 2-inch rail goes across the lower part of the rear legs. The tops of the side rails come level with the tops of the front lower rails.

Mark out all the legs, checking that side rail positions match at front and rear. Check the actual depths of wood being used for rails—prepared wood, as bought, is often less than the quoted size. Mark the actual depths where the joints come.

Mark out all the cross rails. The important measurements are the distances between the shoulders of the tenons, which are best marked across all of them together. Allow for the tenons outside these lines (Fig. 4-6A). Mark and cut the mortises and tenons for the joints to the legs.

You can use dowels instead of tenons. In this case, cut off the rails at shoulder length. Four ⅜-inch dowels would be better than two thicker ones in each joint.

Mark the slat lengths between shoulders from the relevant marks on the legs, then allow extra for the tenons (Fig. 4-6B). The mortises must be arranged at an even spacing along the rails. If the bed being made is a different width, choose enough slats to allow for gaps between them not much wider than the widths of the slats. The slats do not have to be all the same width. One wider slat at the center of each end would provide a variation in the design. Mark and cut the mortises so the slats will be central in the width of the wood (Fig. 4-6C).

Have all the joints cut before dealing with the tops of the legs. If there is any excess wood there, leave it until the mortises have been cut, to provide the maximum resistance to breaking out the grain. There are several ways of finishing the ends, but mark it out carefully with pencil, since these ends are very obvious in the finished bed and any errors will be seen. A simple finish has a chamfer all around (Fig. 4-5C). Keep the angles constant and make sure the top finishes level and square. For another effect there could be a shallow conical end

(Fig. 4-5D). Plane and sand the slopes flat and to a clean point. In a variation the sides curve to the point (Fig. 4-5E). Shaping can be done with a power sander or by hand with a file, followed by sanding. With any of these shapes, be careful that you don't sand too enthusiastically and round off angles excessively.

It will probably be best to glue each end entirely in one session, so you can get the assembly square and flat. If you are short of bar clamps, make

the joints to the rails with all the slats, then join to the legs after the glue has set.

When you have glued all joints in one end frame and pulled them tight with clamps, measure diagonals to see that the assembly is square. Also check that it is without twist. If you can assemble on a known flat surface and leave the end to dry there, it should finish flat. If you cannot do that, sight across one leg to the opposite one. Any twist will be apparent. If you must force the assembly out of

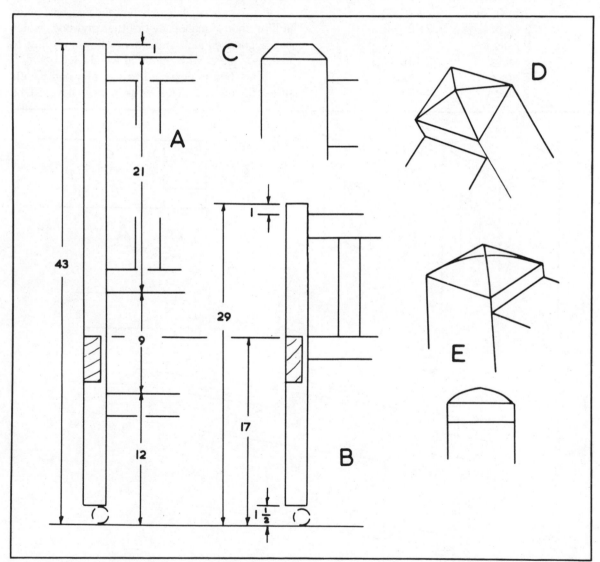

Fig. 4-5. Sizes and leg shaping of the slatted-end bed.

twist, go past flat, to allow for springing back. Before you leave it, check diagonals again to be sure you have not altered the shape.

Side rails can be made and assembled to the ends in the same way as described for the previous bed. Finish the surface and add casters to complete the bed.

## Materials List for Slatted-End Bed

| | |
|---|---|
| 2 rear legs | 2×43×2 |
| 2 front legs | 2×29×2 |
| 5 rails | 2×36×2 |
| 6 slats | 2×19×1 |
| 6 slats | 2×12×1 |
| 2 sides | 4×79×1½ |

## FLUSH-PANELED BED

It is possible to obtain plywood panels with face veneers of exotic and rare woods with attractive grain patterns. These may be single veneers with an allover pattern of grain in one direction, or the veneers may be cut and mounted to give geometric or marquetry patterns. Anyone interested in pictorial marquetry could make a picture from veneers on a plywood base. Many of the prepared panels are in suitable sizes for bed ends. You could also choose plain plywood and veneer it yourself or choose mahogany or other plywood, which has a good enough surface to allow finishing to match or blend with the solid wood used.

This bed is designed to use plywood panels fitted flush. The sizes worked may have to be

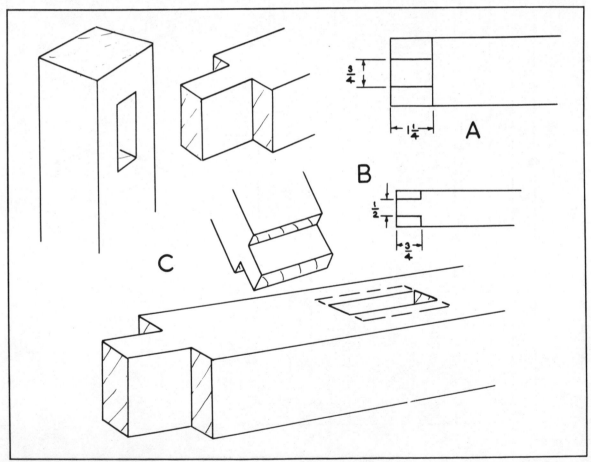

Fig. 4-6. Joints in a slatted end.

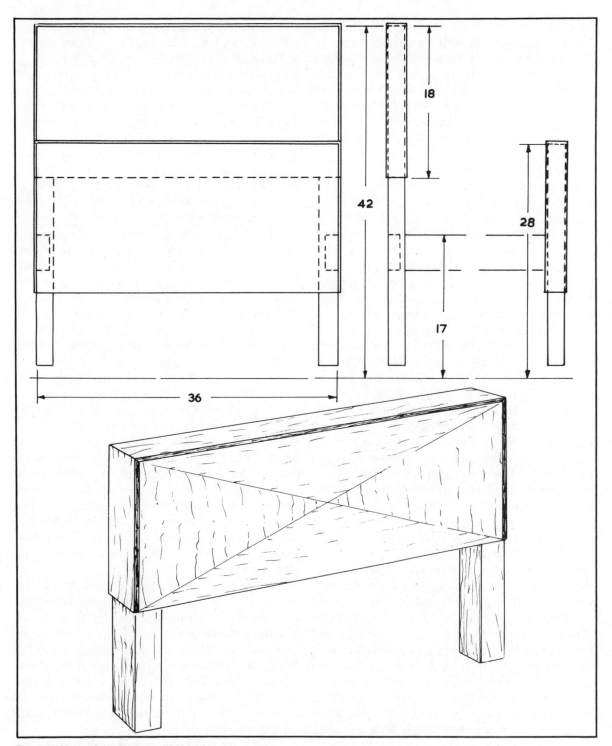

Fig. 4-7. Sizes of the flush-paneled bed.

adapted to suit available plywood panels. As drawn (Fig. 4-7), the bed is 36 inches wide and intended to use plywood pieces 18 inches by 36 inches. Head and foot panels are the same size. If the bed is located in the usual position in a room, the backs of the head and foot will not be very obvious, so you could use panels with special surfaces on the front of the bed ends and cheaper plain plywood on the backs.

The choice of plywood surface veneer will govern the choice of solid wood. You could have similar solid wood or wood of constrasting color. The plywood is framed with solid wood strips, which might be blended in, or you may prefer a dark wood border for a light-colored veneer, or the other way around. An example of a blended finish would be the choice of mahogany throughout for all parts, including the plywood faces. A contrasting design could use a near-white sycamore veneer, surrounded by oak stained dark brown, with legs and rails of oak treated in the same way. This design is not normally suitable for softwood construction, although, in some surroundings, Douglas fir plywood might be used with a matching softwood.

The paneled part of each end has the legs to the full height and framing between to take the plywood (Fig. 4-8A). The top and sides are then covered with strips to hide and frame the plywood edges (Fig. 4-8B). Make sure the wood for the legs and internal framing is all the same width, to reduce the amount of leveling to be done after assembly. The edge strips could be kept slightly too wide, for planing level with the plywood after fitting.

Mark out the four legs (Fig. 4-8C and D), leaving some surplus until the joints have been cut. There is an allowance for casters at the bottoms. It may have to be adjusted to suit available wheels.

The choice of joints in the framing that will be hidden by the panels depends on your skill and inclination. Much of the resistance to distortion of the head or foot will come from the plywood, so framing that is simply joined may be quite satisfactory. You could nail the parts together, using a strip inside each leg to take nails (Fig. 4-9A). The intermediate spacers are then simply nailed through (Fig. 4-9B).

That method may not be considered very craftsmanlike. It would be better to join the top rails to the legs with a bridle joint (Fig. 4-9C) or a dovetail joint (Fig. 4-9D). The lower rail joints may be mortise and tenon (Fig. 4-9E). Stub mortise and tenon joints will hold the spacers to the rails (Fig. 4-9F). The lower rail at the head may be tenoned or held to the legs with dowels (Fig. 4-9G).

Assemble the legs, rails, and spacers. Check for squareness and absence of twist. Try one end on top of the other to see that they match. If necessary, plane the surface level where they will come against the plywood.

It is best to fit the plywood panels in two steps. Put on the back panels for each end first and let the glue set to reduce the risk of damage to the front panel surfaces, which might come about if you turned over the end when fitting both sides during the same session. The plywood is glued on. Plane the bottom edge of a panel straight, and carefully match it to its bottom rail. If the other edges overlap slightly, they can be planed level later.

Using plenty of clamps and spreading the pressure with strips of wood, you should be able to attach the plywood with glue only. However, it is difficult to insure close contact everywhere. It is safer to also use a few very fine nails with small heads, such as brads or finishing nails. They can be punched below the surface and the hollows filled with stopping, which should be almost invisible if carefully chosen and stained to match the surrounding wood. If clamps are also used while the glue sets, nails need not be less than about 6 inches apart around the edges, with one or two more in each spacer.

With the plywood attached on both sides of both ends, plane its edges level and prepare the solid wood edge strips. Cut the side pieces level with the bottom edges of the plywood panels, but at the top corners miter and edge strips together (Fig. 4-9H). Attach the edges with glue and punched and stopped nails. Trim the edges level with the plywood; then slightly round the edges and angles. Excessive rounding would not be in keeping with the general design.

Make and fit the side rails. Finish the surfaces

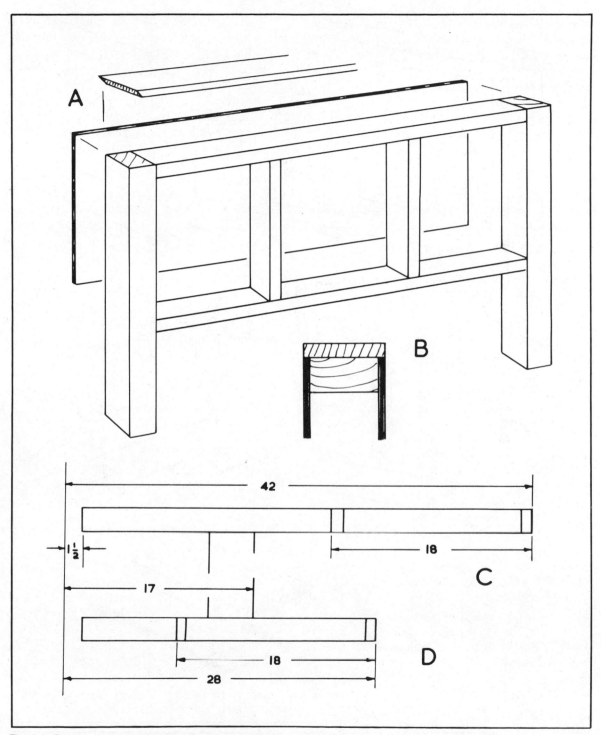

Fig. 4-8. Constructional details of the flush-paneled bed.

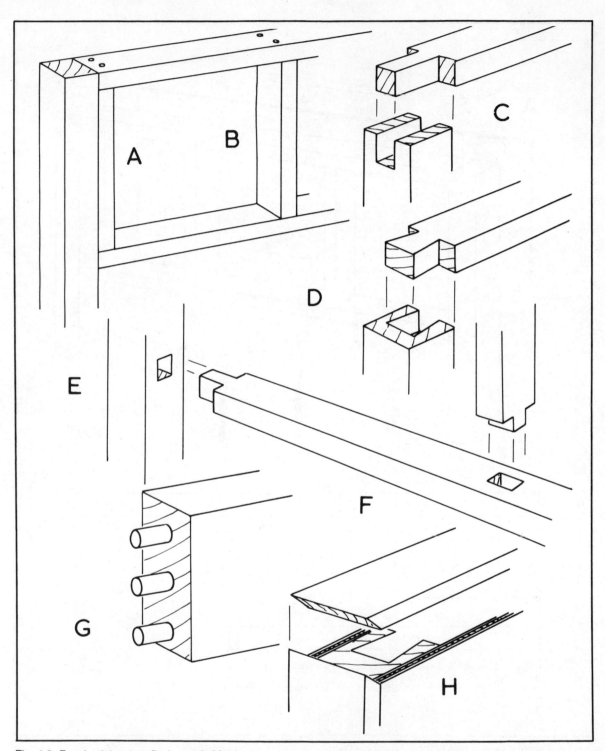

Fig. 4-9. Framing joints in a flush-paneled bed.

Fig. 4-10. Details of a bed with paneled ends and slats under the mattress.

and add casters to complete the construction of the bed.

## Materials List for Flush-Paneled Bed

| | |
|---|---|
| 2 rear legs | 2×42×2 |
| 2 front legs | 2×28×2 |
| 4 rails | 2×36×1 |
| 1 rail | 4×36×1½ |
| 4 spacers | 2×18×1 |
| 4 panels | 18×36×¼ plywood |
| 2 edge strips | 2½×38×⅜ |
| 4 edge strips | 2½×19×⅜ |
| 2 sides | 4×79×1½ |

## PANELED BED

Before the coming of plywood, the width of panels of thin wood was governed by the size of the tree trunk from which the wood was cut. Edge-gluing thin wood was unsatisfactory, and moisture taken up from a humid atmosphere and given out in dry air caused expansion and contraction across the grain, as well as the development of cracks. This problem can be seen in old doors and paneled furniture, where flaws are visible.

The restriction meant that furniture had to be designed to allow for the limited widths of possible panels; so the containing frame was arranged to divide an area into panels of a possible size, depending on the wood. This division of furniture has become accepted as a furniture form. Apart from the panel size restrictions, the arrangement of crossing rails usually looks better than a large unbroken area. Although it is now possible to have plywood furniture panels of almost any size, it is still normal to divide up areas for the sake of appearance.

The example chosen (Fig. 4-10) is a double bed with the ends paneled so each area is divided into three. Similar bed ends can be made with other arrangements. A narrow bed might be made with a single panel (Fig. 4-11A) at each end. A wider bed could have narrower panels (Fig. 4-11B) or be divided so the center panel is wider (Fig. 4-11C) or narrower than the side ones. The bed head could be made higher and the panels divided horizontally as well as vertically (Fig. 4-11D). Jacobean furniture shows many arrangements of panels. Normally, it is wiser to keep rails square to each other, but a modern arrangement might set some diagonally (Fig. 4-11E). A further step would be to set in a diamond panel (Fig. 4-11F), but that involves more complicated joints.

## Bed Head and Foot

The headboard is deeper than the footboard in the example, but construction is the same. These parts should be made first, so the sizes of other parts can be related to them. Groove all of the framing strips to suit the plywood—a depth of ⅜ inch should be enough. The intermediate strips need grooves on both sides (Fig. 4-12A).

The horizontal pieces continue through the full width of the bed, and the other parts join to them. You could use dowels, but if traditional construction is being followed, it is better to use mortises and tenons. The grooves complicate the joints slightly.

At the corners, cut back the tenon to the bottom of its groove. At the outside, cut back to the bottom of the other groove (Fig. 4-12B). The tenon should be about one-third of the wood's thickness, which is more than the width of the groove, but that does not matter. Let the tenon go about halfway through the other piece. To reduce the risk of end grain breaking out, leave some waste on the end of the mortised part until the joint has been assembled (Fig. 4-12C).

At the intermediate uprights, cut back both sides of the tenon to the bottoms of the grooves, so the end forms a standard joint (Fig. 4-12D). As with the corners, the tenons will be thicker than the width of the grooves.

Cut the plywood panels slightly undersize. If you try to make them reach the bottom of each groove, they may be so tight that they prevent the frame joints pulling together. Make sure the groove sides are not rough. Assembly is eased if the panel edges are beveled slightly (Fig. 4-12E). The mortise and tenon joints should have ample glue. There is no need for much glue around the panels, and any oozing out is difficult to remove cleanly.

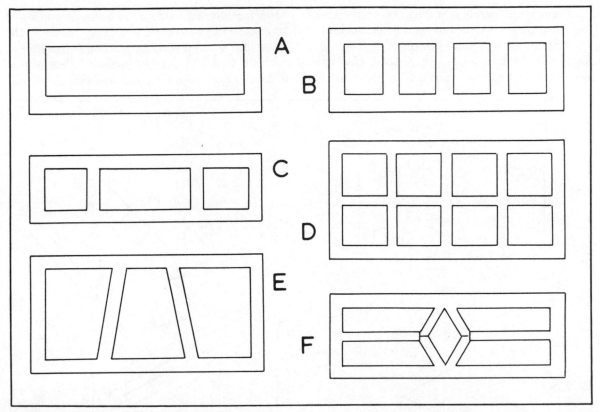

Fig. 4-11. Alternative shapes for paneled ends.

When the bed ends have been assembled, true the outsides, round the top corners, and take off sharpness from any angles. See that head and foot match.

The legs are deeper back to front to give rigidity. At the foot, notch each leg to take the framed panels (Fig. 4-13A) and bevel the tops. At the head, notch the wood similarly and mark where the lower rail goes (Fig. 4-13B). Allow for casters or glides at the bottoms of the legs. The rear lower rail may be tenoned (Fig. 4-13C) or doweled into the legs, before they are attached to the paneled headboard. The legs can be attached to headboard and footboard with dowels or plugged counterbored screws (Fig. 4-13D).

## Sides and Base

The bed sides could be single pieces held to the legs with suitable hardware or arranged with screws or bolts (see Chapter 2) to support a boxed mattress, which has enough strength in itself. A slatted form is suggested here, to support a foam or spring mattress that is not made in a stiff frame. The slats are supported on a rabbet at each side. The rabbet could cut from solid wood (Fig. 4-13E), but you may find it easier to get a clean, accurate rabbet by using two thicknesses, glued and screwed together (Fig. 4-13F). These sides may be attached to the bed ends in any suitable way for the simpler sides.

In a double bed the slats are fairly long. Although they share most loads and may be expected to spring slightly, the wood should be able to withstand occasional local loads without the risk of breaking. The slats will not show, so their appearance is not important, and they need not be the same wood as the rest of the bed. They should, however, have reasonably straight grain and be free from large knots.

You could merely rest the slats in the rabbets, but they might move and the bed sides could spring out and let a slat end drop through; so it would be better to screw the ends (Fig. 4-13G). One screw should be enough in a piece. You may find that screwing alternate slats is enough, or you could screw alternate opposite ends only. Arrange the slats with an even spacing, starting fairly close to each end. Square the bed overall by measuring diagonals before locating and screwing the slats.

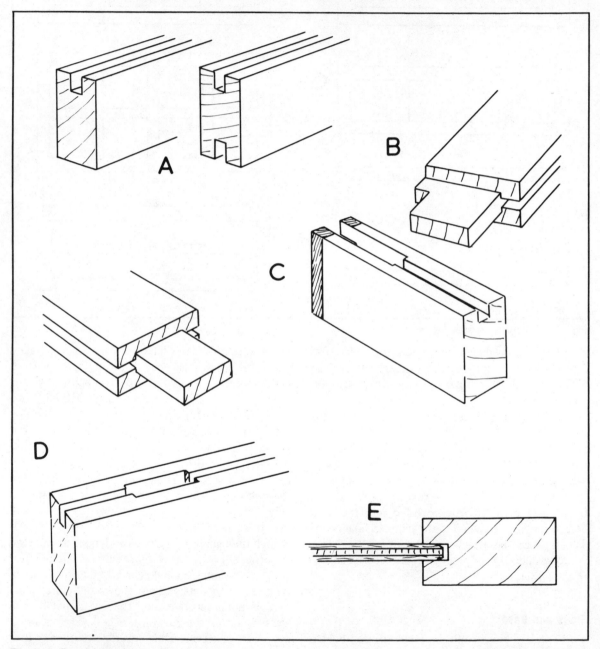

Fig. 4-12. Frame joints for paneling.

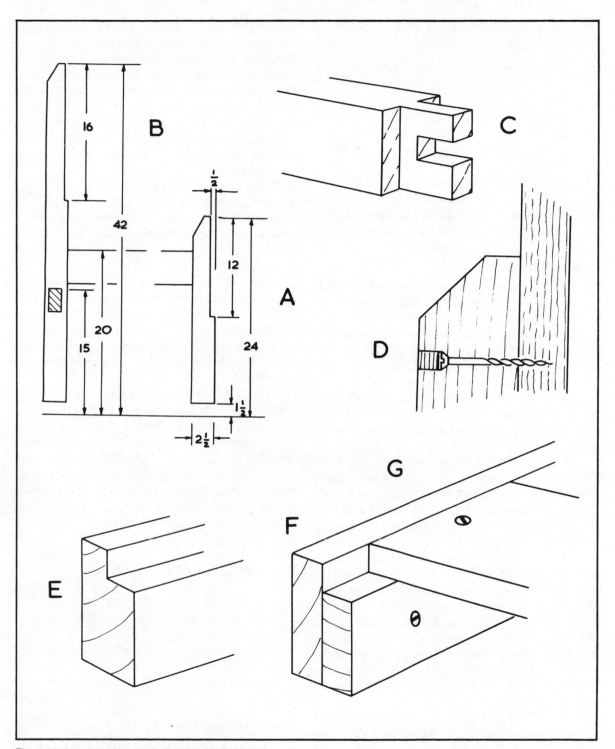

Fig. 4-13. Leg and side details for the paneled bed.

## Materials List for Paneled Bed

| | | |
|---|---|---|
| 2 rear legs | $2\frac{1}{2}\times42\times2$ | |
| 2 front legs | $2\frac{1}{2}\times24\times2$ | |
| 4 rails | $2\times22\times1$ | |
| 4 rails | $2\times56\times1$ | |
| 4 rails | $2\times19\times1$ | |
| 1 rear rail | $3\times54\times1\frac{1}{2}$ | |
| 2 sides | $4\times79\times1$ | |
| 2 sides | $3\times79\times1$ | |
| 10 slats | $5\times54\times1$ | |
| 3 panels | $18\times21\times\frac{1}{4}$ plywood | |
| 3 panels | $17\times18\times\frac{1}{4}$ plywood | |

## FENCE-END BED

The fence-end bed has its head and foot made up like a fence, with horizontal rails joining vertical posts. The design could be worked in hardwood, but it is particularly appropriate to softwood. It might form part of a room furnished in pine or other softwood, with a clear lacquer finish. The sizes given are intended for a single bed made of softwood. The visible parts could be made of knotty wood, if that is the effect you want, but the sides and slats should be straight-grained. They need not be the same wood that is used for the other parts.

As shown, the bed head has three rails above the bed level and another lower down for stiffness (Fig. 4-14). The bed foot has two rails, but it could be made deeper with three rails, if you wish.

Mark out the rear legs (Fig. 4-15A), leaving some excess length at the top until after the joints are cut. Prepare the wood for the front legs in a similar way (Fig. 4-15B). The six rails are all the same. The strongest joints are mortise and tenon (Fig. 4-15C). As the rails go into thicker uprights, the tenons may be more than the usual one-third of the rail thickness—$\frac{1}{2}$ inch or $\frac{5}{8}$ inch would be suitable for tenons $1\frac{1}{4}$ inch long. The alternative is to cut the rails with square ends and join them to the legs with dowels, preferably $\frac{5}{8}$ inch in diameter and projecting $1\frac{1}{4}$ inch (Fig. 4-15D).

After the joints have been prepared, cut the tops of the legs to length and mark them for tapering (Fig. 4-15E). Cut carefully, so the apex is central

and the slopes are even (Fig. 4-15F). Sand all parts and take the sharpness off angles and corners. This type of assembly will tend to pull out of square and may twist when gluing and clamping; so check constantly and leave the ends held square and true for the glue to set.

The sides are built up and can be attached to the legs by screwing from inside, instead of using hardware or bolts. The 2-inch strips are glued and screwed centrally on the 4-inch pieces (Fig. 4-15G), but if the sides are to be screwed to the legs, they are kept back 1 inch from each end. At the ends attach strips across, which can be drilled for screws (Fig. 4-15H). Top and bottom screws are entered squarely, but the central screw is better angled (Fig. 4-15J).

Space the slats evenly and fit them in the same way as on the previous bed (Fig. 4-10). Since this bed is narrower than the previous one, there is not as much risk of breakage or of a side springing out, but you should still use screws to prevent movement. Check and maintain squareness while screwing.

The grain of softwood will quickly absorb dirt, so do not leave the bed unfinished for long. Even if it is not yet going to be assembled in its final position, give it at least one coat of lacquer or varnish to seal the grain, while waiting. The final finish may be several coats of lacquer or varnish. A boat varnish, allowed to fully harden, may have the gloss lightly sanded off and a coat of wax applied to give an attractive clear finish. Alternatively, the bed can be painted.

## Materials List for Fence-End Bed

| | | |
|---|---|---|
| 2 rear legs | $2\frac{3}{4}\times33\times2\frac{3}{4}$ | |
| 2 front legs | $2\frac{3}{4}\times23\times2\frac{3}{4}$ | |
| 6 rails | $3\times35\times1$ | |
| 2 sides | $4\times79\times1$ | |
| 2 sides | $2\times79\times1$ | |
| 15 slats | $4\times36\times1$ | |

## MATCHED BOARD BED

One traditional way of filling a space, which

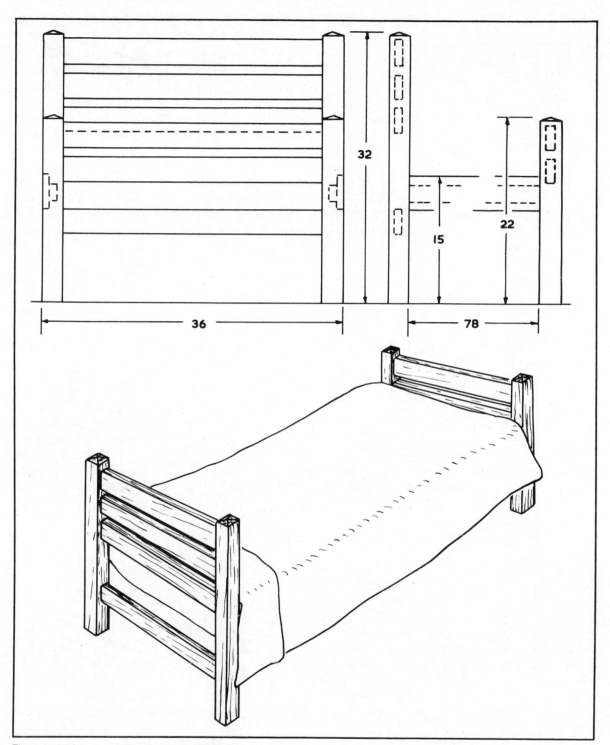

Fig. 4-14. A fence-end bed made of softwood.

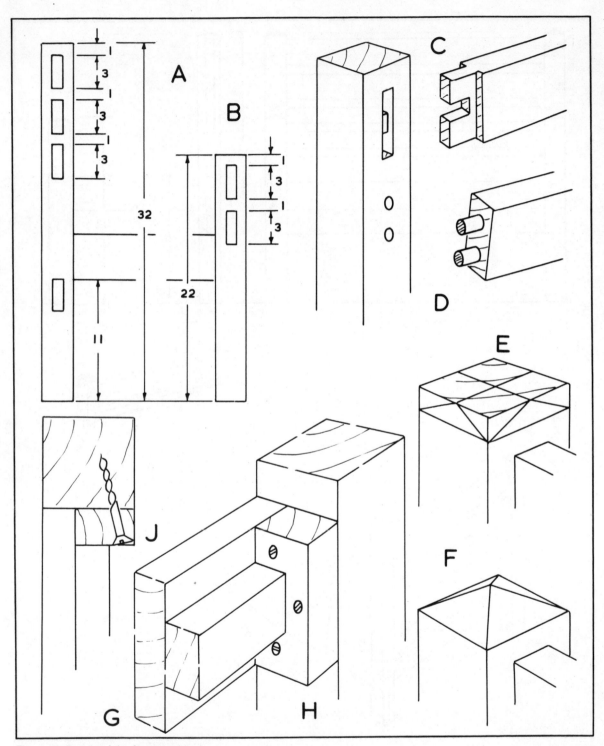

Fig. 4-15. Details of the fence-end bed.

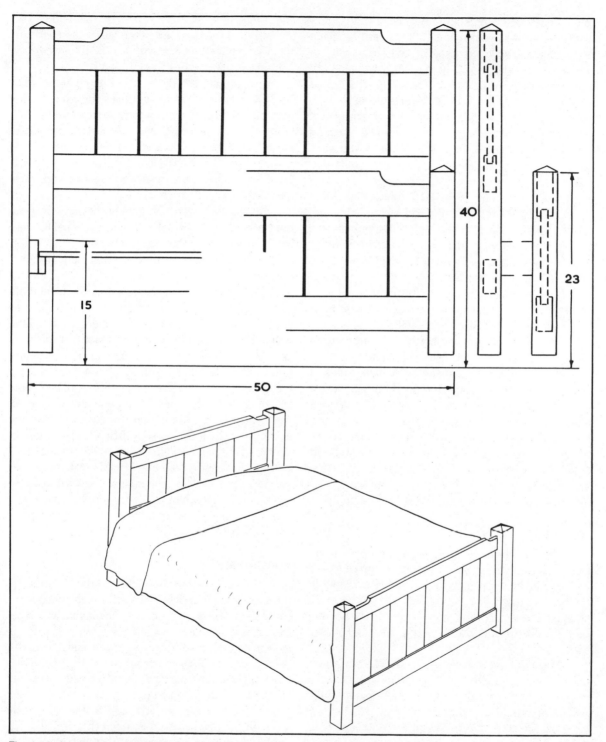

Fig. 4-16. A bed with matched board end panels.

might today be occupied by plywood or other manufactured wood, was with matched boarding. This is tongued and grooved, usually with a bead worked on the front of the joint (Fig. 4-17A). Examples can be seen in many old pieces of furniture, where door panels and the backs of closets and banks of shelves are filled by these boards, showing a pattern of vertical joints marked by beads. Matched boarding can still be obtained, or can be made if you have suitable equipment. Sizes vary so you should discover what is available before planning the layout of a bed. In the example (Fig. 4-16) it is assumed that the matched boarding is about 5 inches wide and ⅝-inch thick, which is the finished size cut from boards 6 inches wide and ¾ inch thick. Any other size could be used, but a quantity would have to be ordered to fill the spaces.

Matched boarding is normally only available in softwood, so it is appropriate to make the rest of the bed from softwood. Sizes given will suit fir, pine, or other softwood. If you use hardwood, the sections of legs and rails may be reduced slightly.

The bed could be made with plain sides to support a mattress made in a box form and stiff in itself, but it is shown with a plywood base, set below the side edges. A soft foam or spring mattress may rest on the base and be contained between the sides so it does not slide. It is advisable to get the mattress first and settle the other sizes to suit it. The materials list and drawings are for a mattress 48 inches wide and 78 inches long.

## Bed Ends

The matched boarding fits into grooves in the rails. Prepare the rails with suitable grooves—½ inch should be deep enough (Fig. 4-17B). Shape the ends of the top rails (Fig. 4-17C). Do this carefully because these parts are very obvious in the finished bed. Finish the cuts square across and sand out any saw marks.

Mark out the rear legs (Fig. 4-17D). An allowance is shown for casters. Leave some excess wood at the top for shaping after cutting the joints. The panels are the same at head and foot, so the front legs are shortened versions of the rear legs (Fig. 4-17E). The top edge of the lower rail at the head

end comes level with and supports what will be the underside of the plywood of the assembled bed. At the foot end stiffening will be on the plywood. Nothing is attached to the footboard.

Cut tenons for the rails into the legs (Fig. 4-17F). In both positions, cut back the wood to the bottoms of the grooves, but make the tenons the full width of what is left, preferably in two parts and about 1 inch thick. Two thick, or four thinner, dowels could be used. Fit the lower rail at the rear in the same way. There is no groove here to complicate the joint.

Finish the tops of the legs in the same way as the previous bed (Fig. 4-15E and F). Partially assemble the rails to the legs to check fit, but do not fully assemble any parts until the matched boarding is ready.

The outer matched boards must be planed off (Fig. 4-17G), so they can be glued to the legs. It is unlikely that the boards will make up the width without cutting. They should be arranged so there are cut boards of equal width at each side, to maintain a symmetrical appearance. When the bed ends are assembled, glue the outer pieces of matched boarding to the legs, but do not use any more glue on the boards, neither in their tongues and grooves nor in the rail slots. Leave a little clearance in the depths of the slots and do not force the tongues and grooves too tightly together. In this way there will be room for expansion and contraction, without the risk of cracks developing, as they might if the wood was restrained by glue. The beads worked along the joints disguise movement in the width.

## Sides & Base

Plain sides may be attached to the bed ends in the usual way. If the base is to be ½-inch plywood, it could be one piece, but, for ease in moving when the bed is disassembled, it is shown in two parts. Each side is made up of strips screwed and glued together (Fig. 4-18A), so the plywood can rest on the inner pieces. The projections of the pieces above hold the mattress in place.

The sides may be attached to the legs with strips inside and screwed through (Fig. 4-18B). At the bed head, the lower rear rail comes level with

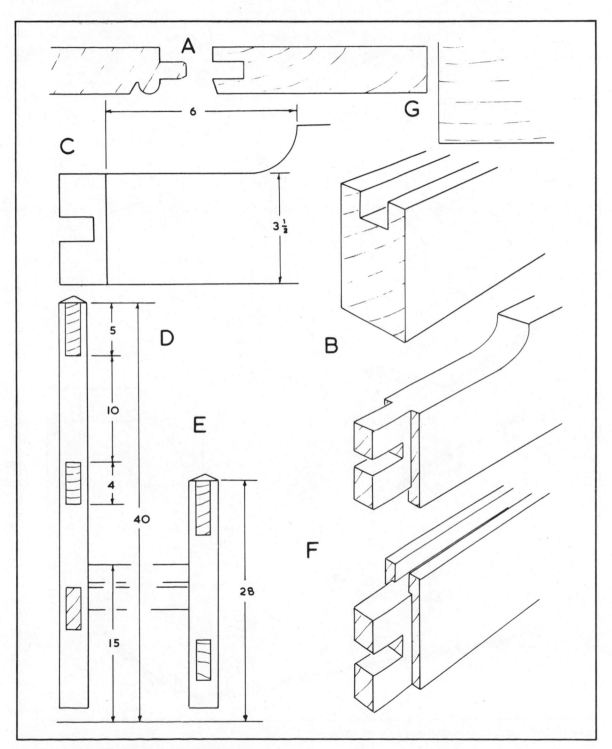

Fig. 4-17. Details of framing for the matched board bed.

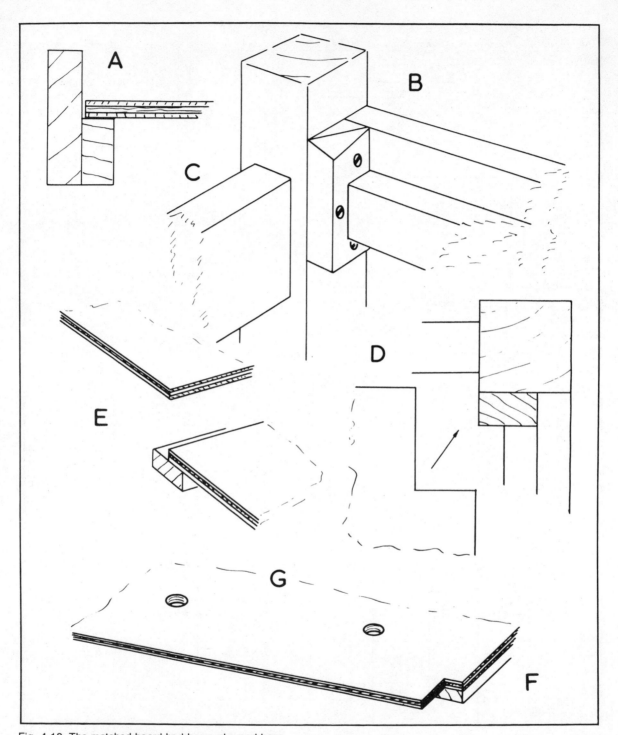

Fig. 4-18. The matched board bed has a plywood base.

the inner part of the side (Fig. 4-18C). Cut the upper piece of plywood around the legs, so it rests on the rear rail as well as the side supports (Fig. 4-18D).

Where the two base panels meet near the center of the bed, glue and screw a strip across under the lower panel (Fig. 4-18E). In normal use, it is the upper part of the bed that gets most loading, so it is best for the panel to rest on the support attached to the other panel, than the other way around. Where the lower panel comes against the footboard, put another strip below it as a stiffener (Fig. 4-18F). Cut it and the plywood to clear the block for screws into the legs.

Cut the plywood to be an easy fit in the bed framework, so the panels can be lifted out. If the plywood is cut squarely, they will keep the bed in shape. To let air through a foam mattress as it expands and contracts, drill a few holes in the plywood (Fig. 4-18G). A pattern of 1-inch holes at about 12-inch intervals should be enough. The holes also allow you to lift the plywood easily.

## Finishing

As with any other softwood construction, seal the wood fairly quickly, to prevent dirt absorption, then finish it with clear lacquer or varnish. It is unlikely that the matched boarding will shrink enough to expose bare wood in the joints, but if you want to guard against it, give the tongues a coat of the finishing material before assembling them in their grooves.

## Materials List for Matched Board Bed

| | |
|---|---|
| 2 rear legs | 2¾×40×2¾ |
| 2 front legs | 2¾×23×2¾ |
| 2 top rails | 5×48×5 |
| 3 lower rails | 4×48×1½ |
| 18 pcs. matched boarding | 5×12×⅝ |
| 2 sides | 4×79×1 |
| 2 sides | 2×79×1 |
| 2 bases | 41×48×½ plywood |
| 2 base stiffeners | 2×48×1 |

## VICTORIAN BED

The Victorians favored curves. This bed (Fig. 4-19) has a head in a simplified form of that found on some Victorian beds. Other beds with similar, but more elaborate, themes are described later. The bed shown is a single one, 36 inches wide, but the same design could be used for other widths. There could also be a foot carrying out the same design motif. This example is without a footboard and the bed covering may drape over at the foot end.

Mortises and tenons are described for all joints. You could use dowels, although the wood for the splat and uprights is not large enough for dowels greater than ¼ inch in diameter. It is more difficult to get close-fitting joints with dowels than with the type of barefaced tenons described.

Start by setting out the top rail (Fig. 4-20A). Mark the positions where the curve will come at the sides and at the center; then spring a batten through them to draw the curve. Mark where the shoulders of the tenons will come and use this marking as a gauge for marking all the other rails; so widths at all parts of the bed will be the same.

Mark out the rear legs (Fig. 4-20B). The top of the lower rail should come at the level of the notch in the sides if the bed is to be made with slats across to support a mattress. The rails will join the legs with similar mortise and tenon joints (Fig. 4-20C). The distance between the rails marked on the legs will be the same as the distance between the shoulders of the tenons on the splat and uprights; so use the leg markings as a gauge for determining the positions of markings on these parts. Leave some excess wood at the tops of the legs for shaping after the joints have been cut.

Mark across the pieces for the uprights and the splat together, to get the distances between the shoulders the same. The splat is reduced from 6 inches wide to 4 inches wide at its ends. To get a symmetrical pleasing curve, make a card template of one-fourth of it, and mark from it (Fig. 4-20D).

These pieces can be given barefaced tenons, having the single shoulder to the front (Fig. 4-20E). The mortises have to be off center in the rails if the uprights are to finish central. When the joints are

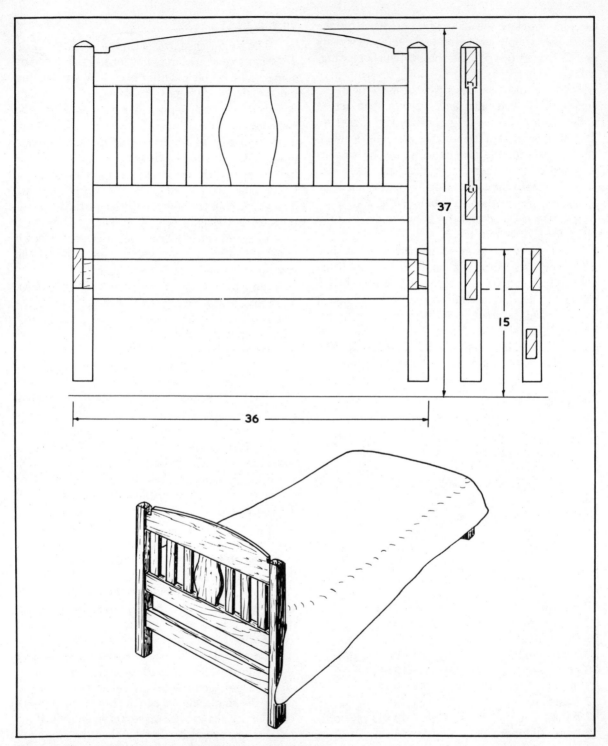

Fig. 4-19. This Victorian bed has a slatted head, but no footboard.

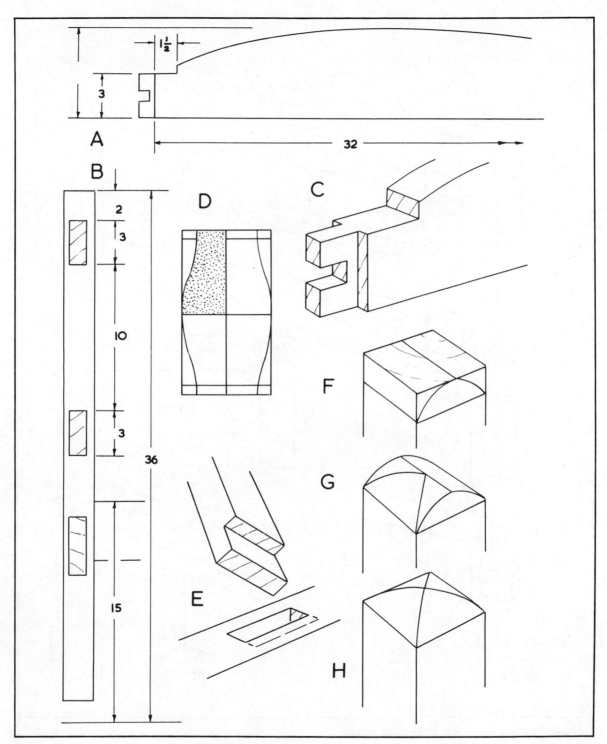

Fig. 4-20. Parts of the Victorian bed head.

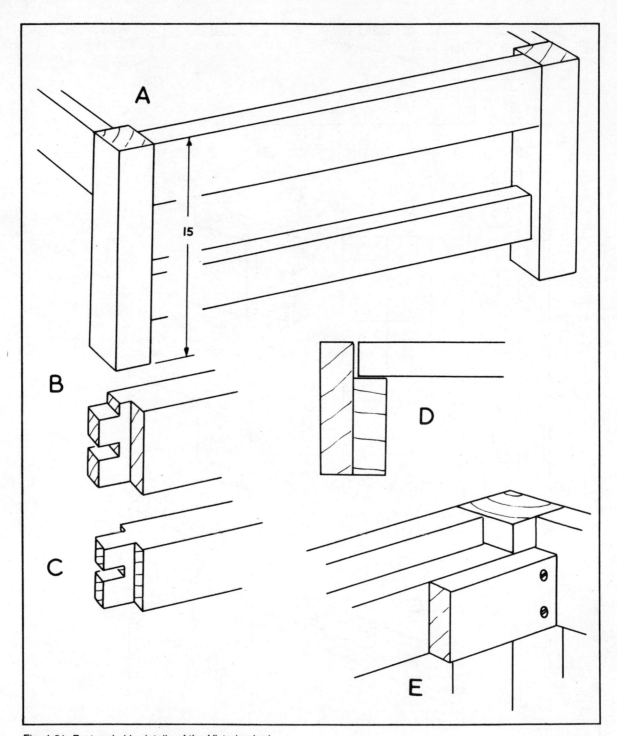

Fig. 4-21. Foot and side details of the Victorian bed.

drawn together, the single shoulders should all pull tight, and pull easier than if double shoulders were used.

The tops of the legs may be given flat-faced conical shapes, as described for some earlier beds, but to retain the curved theme, they are better rounded. Mark the shape one way (Fig. 4-20F) and cut it; then mark the other way (Fig. 4-20G) and cut to that to give uniform curved ends (Fig. 4-20H). Give the bed head parts a final planing and sanding, making sure no sharp edges are left; then glue up in two stages, putting the splat and uprights between their rails and checking for squareness. Join all three rails to the legs and check for squareness and lack of twist before allowing the glue to set.

The foot of the bed is the same height as the sides (Fig. 4-21A). Rigidity comes from the two rails, which are better tenoned than doweled. The outer surface of the top rail is level with the surfaces of the legs; so it is shouldered on one side only (Fig. 4-21B). The lower rail is central and tenoned in the usual way (Fig. 4-21C). Check the width of the foot against the head and see that it is assembled squarely.

Make up the two sides with screws and glue (Fig. 4-21D). They could be joined to the bed head and foot with bolts. Since their heads will not show at the foot under the covering and they will usually come against a wall at the head. Because the thickness of the sides is the same as the thickness of the legs, you could take a strip on the inside on to the leg for screwing (Fig. 4-21E).

Arrange the slats evenly along the sides and screw them in place in the way suggested for earlier beds. Alternatively, fit a plywood base or have plain sides to support a boxed mattress.

If you want a Victorian appearance, stain the head and any other exposed woodwork darkly and give it a gloss finish. Even if the base wood is not mahogany, a reddish mahogany stain is appropriate.

## Materials List for Victorian Bed

| | | |
|---|---|---|
| 2 rear legs | 2×36×2 | |
| 2 front legs | 2×15×2 | |
| 1 top rail | 6×36×1¼ | |
| 2 lower rails | 3×36×1¼ | |
| 2 main rails | 4×36×1¼ | |
| 1 splat | 6×12×⅝ | |
| 6 uprights | 1½×12×⅝ | |
| 2 sides | 4×79×1 | |
| 2 sides | 3×79×1 | |
| 13 slats | 4×36×1 | |

## DOWEL ROD BED ENDS

Prepared dowel rods of good quality can be used to form the main body of a bed end. Some dowel rods available may be rough and not truly circular in section. They might be satisfactory for making doweled joints, but where they are exposed as part of a bed they should be straight, smooth, and round. In any case, you should sand them by hand lengthwise to remove any marks around the rod due to the method of manufacture.

In the simplest bed head, a number of dowel rods are arranged in a frame (Fig. 4-22A). In this case, the legs and rails should be 2-inch-square hardwood and the dowels ¾ inch or 1 inch in diameter. The number of rods used in a particular width is a matter of choice. There could be very few rods spaced widely or more rods arranged closely—3-inch or 4-inch centers would be satisfactory. If the bed is to be used by a child, avoid a spacing that might allow him to get his head caught—about 5-inch centers.

If several diameters of dowel rods are available, they can be graduated from small at the sides to large at the center. This graduation may also be applied to the spacings, so the gaps are greater at the center than at the sides (Fig. 4-22B).

The dowels may supplement a flat wood splat at the center (Fig. 4-22C). This splat is shown as a simple straight piece, but it can provide some decoration. The outline could be shaped, or the wood could be pierced with a floral or other design. You could personalize the bed by fretting or carving an initial. If the bed is painted, the splat could carry a different colored decoration.

Another variation uses some horizontal dowel

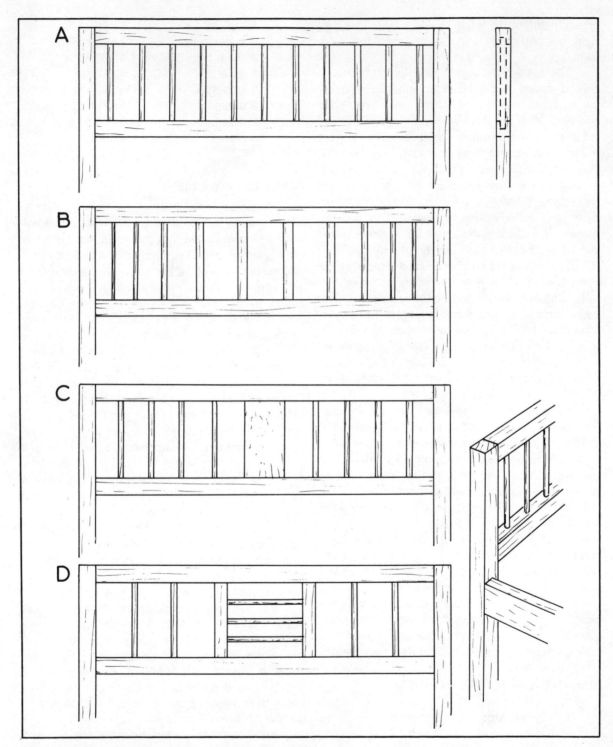

Fig. 4-22. Dowel rods can be used in many ways in bed ends.

rods (Fig. 4-22D). An exact division of the bed width into three is not as pleasing in appearance as a rather narrower central horizontal section.

The general arrangement and constructional details of the bed can be the same as described for earlier beds, but there are a few points to note. The frames shown are the same section wood all around. The rails could be a lighter section, if you wish. The legs could project above the top rail, as in some earlier beds, and be shaped similarly. As shown, the corner joints should be made to give strong connections without showing details on the surfaces.

The simplest way of dealing with the corner is to use dowels. You could arrange two large ones diagonally (Fig. 4-23A) or four smaller ones

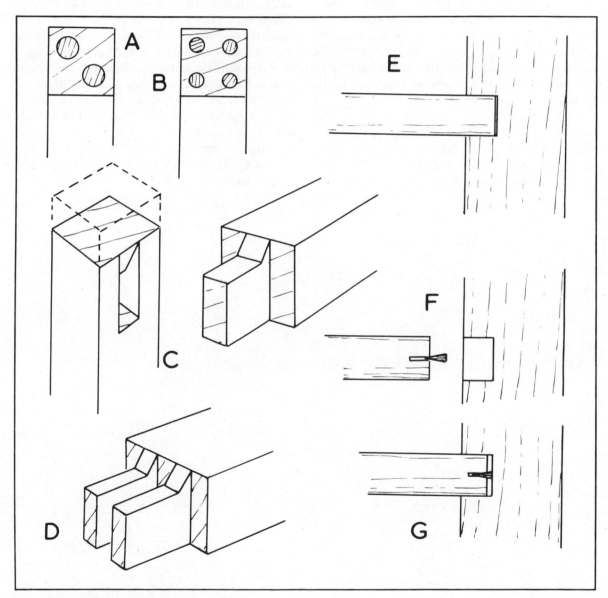

Fig. 4-23. Joints can be doweled or tenoned.

squarely (Fig. 4-23B). It will probably be easier to get the parts properly aligned with four dowels. Mortise and tenon joints should prove stronger than dowels, but the tenons must be haunched if their parts are to be hidden. Make the joints before cutting any excess wood off the tops of the legs, to reduce the risk of grain breaking out when you cut the mortises.

A haunched mortise and tenon joint must have the haunch tapered if joint details are to be hidden (Fig. 4-23C). With 2-inch wood, the tenon may be cut back to about 1½ inches wide. For square wood or rails that are wider than they are deep, cut twin tenons (Fig. 4-23D), dividing the total width by five to get a suitable proportion.

The dowels may be simply glued into suitable holes (Fig. 4-23E). There is no need to take them very deeply—½ inch should be enough. To avoid getting rails out of line when gluing, however, you may want to use some restriction on the middle rod,

and, on a wide bed, some others as well. If you clamp the bed end so one or both rails finish bowed or hollow, the appearance will be spoiled.

Foxtail wedges will help to get extra tight joints for exact adjustment at the key center dowel rod. Make saw cuts in its ends and insert some small wedges. You may have to estimate their size. Put a wedge in a saw cut as you glue the joint (Fig. 4-23F); then it will push against the bottom of the hole and spread the dowel wood (Fig. 4-23G). If you check the overall measurement as you pull the joint together, you can stop when it is right. The wedged ends should lock at that position, so the other, looser, unwedged dowel ends should settle similarly. Avoid excess glue that will squeeze out of joints, because it is difficult to remove cleanly around the ends of the dowel rods.

Any intermediate square-section wood can be joined with dowels or plain tenons, as can the ends of the lower rails.

# Chapter 5

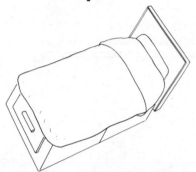

# Box-Framed Beds

Besides making a bed with sides supported by a head and foot, it is possible to make beds that are self-contained in the way the mattress and covering are supported, with or without a head and foot. This type of bed first appeared as a day bed or divan, but it is increasingly used for nighttime sleeping. It can be adapted to daytime use, so it blends with other furnishings, without being obviously a bed.

Most beds of this type are box-like. Some have the box open upward to contain or support the mattress, which fits inside or is supported by webbing or springing on the top. In another type the closed part may face upward, and be rigid or lightly padded. In this case most of the softening of the sleeping surface is in a thick foam mattress. Either type may be on legs, or the structure may reach the floor; so separate legs are not needed. A deep box assembly can be made with drawers under the bed, operating from either or both sides or from the foot, increasing the usefulness of the bed, particularly in a room with little space for other furniture. Drawers are particularly appropriate in a child's room, as one way of encouraging tidiness.

## FRAMED BOX MATTRESS

A spring or foam box mattress is almost a bed in itself. It could be put on the floor for a comfortable night, but it would be too low. This bed is a support for it at a convenient height (Fig. 5-1). The mattress may be supported on strips inside the frame (Fig. 5-2A). If the base of the mattress does not appear to have enough rigidity in itself there could be a few widely spaced slats (Fig. 5-2B), or there could be angle bracket bed irons at intervals around the frame (Fig. 5-2C). The chosen method of support will determine the size of the frame. In any case, do not make the frame a very close fit on the mattress. It should be easy to lift out.

The frame should be solid wood, although thick plywood could be used. The best joints at the corners are dovetails (Fig. 5-2D). Screwing would be satisfactory, either with screw heads counterbored and plugged or with caps on the screw heads (Fig. 5-2E). If it is a large bed that would have to be taken apart for transport, the latter arrangement would be preferable.

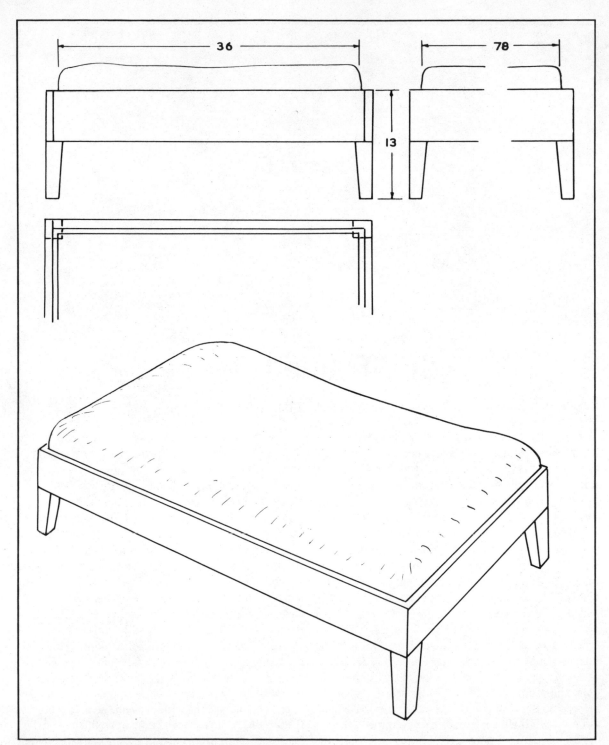

Fig. 5-1. A framed box mattress can make a bed without raised ends.

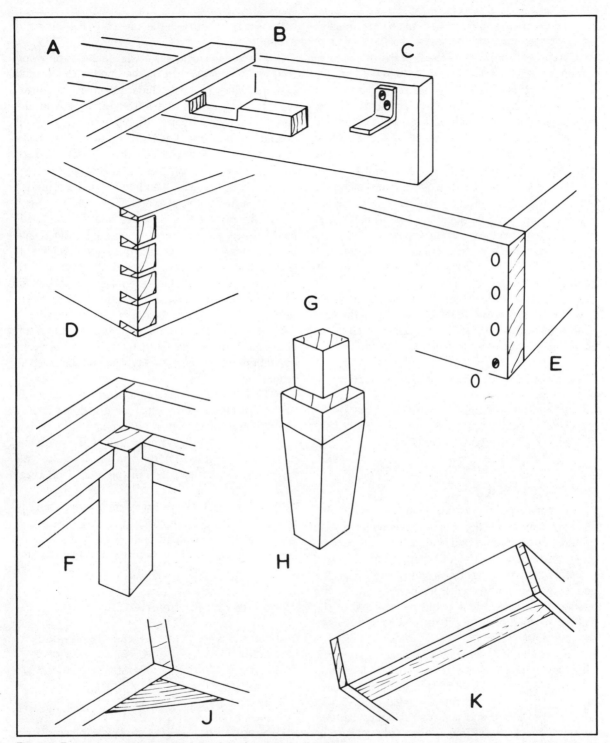

Fig. 5-2. Frame, leg, and support details of the framed box mattress.

The mattress supports should be arranged so most of the mattress projects above the frame. Attach the legs below this level. If the bed is to be arranged to take down, screw through the legs one way only; otherwise screw both ways for greater strength. With the usual mattress the legs need only project about 7 inches to give a comfortable height to the top. In the simplest form they are left square and fitted inside (Fig. 5-2F). They could be brought flush by notching (Fig. 5-2G), or they might be tapered (Fig. 5-2H). However, do not make the bottoms too small, or they will damage carpets.

The bed could be supported by prepared legs of the type with a flange at the top for screwing on. A triangular block in each corner might allow for screws from the legs (Fig. 5-2J) or a strip could go across (Fig. 5-2K).

If a headboard is required, it could be attached to the wall only, without any connection to the bed. If an attached headboard is required, it could be added in one of the ways described for later beds.

## Materials List for Framed Box Mattress

| | |
|---|---|
| 2 sides | 6×82×1 |
| 2 ends | 6×39×1 |
| 4 legs | 2×12×1 |

## INVERTED BOX BED

The inverted box bed is a narrow bed suitable for a growing child. It could be made wider, but, if brought up to double bed width, it would become bulky for transport. It would then be better in sections, as described later. As shown (Fig. 5-3), the bed is made as a box with its base upwards. If a headboard is desired, it could be attached to the wall. A method of fitting it to the bed so it can be adjusted is described.

Make the ends and sides with strips along the top edges, cut back at the corners for the legs (Fig. 5-4A). The legs could have their full squares inside or be notched to come flush outside (Fig. 5-4B). Glue all the joints and also use finishing nails or screws. Check the stiffness of the plywood to be used for the top. If it seems too flexible, put a few

battens across between the sides before gluing and nailing the top.

The headboard is shown as a piece of plywood (Fig. 5-4C), wider than the bed and with rounded corners. Many other headboard designs are possible, and ideas can be drawn from other beds in this book. The two supports (Fig. 5-4D) are screwed behind the headboard and slotted to fit over bolts through the back of the bed (Fig. 5-4E)—3/8-inch bolts are suitable. Choose bolts that will project enough to take washers and nuts. To aid stiffness put strips inside the plywood (Fig. 5-4F).

If the plywood used for the bed and the headboard has a good surface, it may be stained and lacquered or varnished with the legs matching. If the surface is not good, it could be covered with cloth, preferably matching the mattress or the bed covering. In the simplest form, the cloth goes directly on the wood, but the effect is more pleasing if the wood is first covered with thin plastic foam between 1/8-inch and 1/2-inch thick. To prevent movement use adhesive at a few key points, such as around edges.

Tack or staple the cloth for the sides and ends to the top. There is no need to turn the edges under. Pull evenly down to tack underneath (Fig. 5-4G) and turn in for the best finish, unless the cloth has no tendency to fray. On top, turn in the edges all around to cover the edges of the side cloth (Fig. 5-4H).

Cover the headboard in a similar way. There is no need for cloth on the back (Fig. 5-4J) if the bed will be against a wall. If cloth is to be put on the back, it is easier done before the supports are screwed on.

## Materials List for Inverted Box Bed

| | |
|---|---|
| 1 top | 31×79×1/2 plywood |
| 2 sides | 6×79×1/2 plywood |
| 2 ends | 6×30×1/2 plywood |
| 2 joint strips | 1×79×1 |
| 2 joint strips | 1×30×1 |
| 4 legs | 2×10×2 |
| 1 headboard | 15×36×1/2 plywood |
| 2 supports | 2×21×1 |

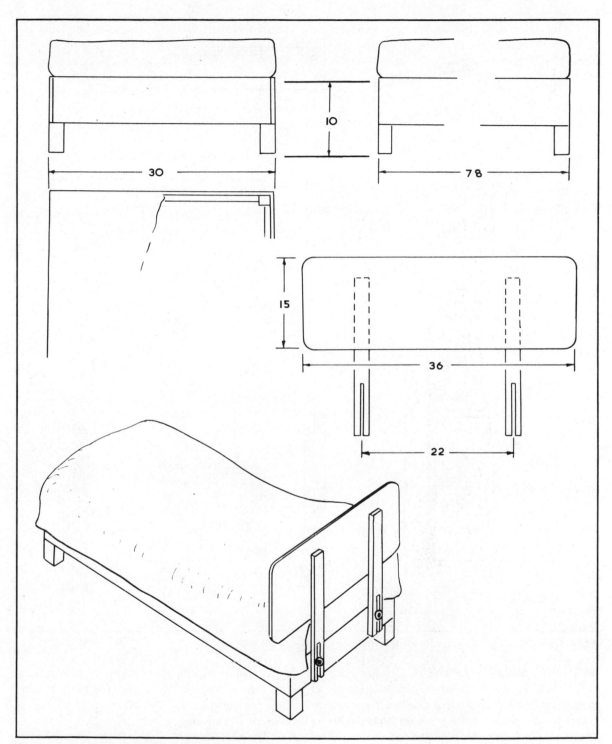

Fig. 5-3. An inverted box bed with adjustable head.

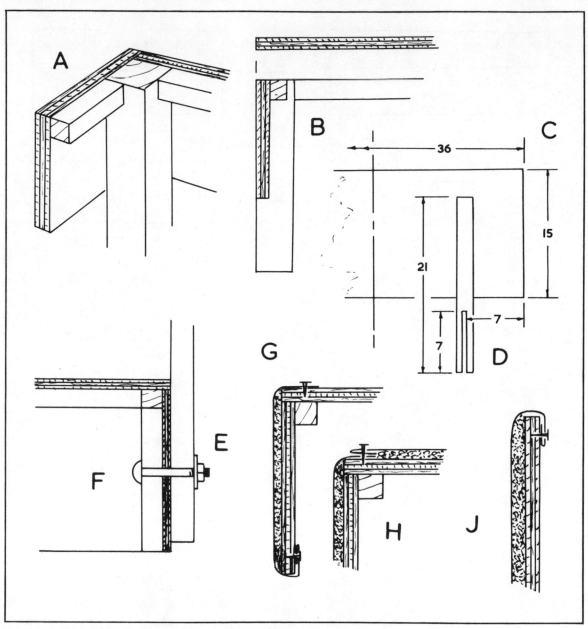

Fig. 5-4. Details of the box structure of the inverted box bed.

## SECTIONAL BED WITH DRAWERS

A bed large enough for two adults is too big to conveniently be transported or moved from room to room in one piece in the average home. This is particularly so with the inverted box construction. The size of plywood needed for its top may be bigger than is usually available in one piece. If the bed is divided across its center, the two parts are more manageable, and the plywood is within the limits of stock sizes.

The sectional bed with drawers (Fig. 5-5) will support a mattress 54 inches wide and 78 inches long. The two similar sections are each 39 inches by 54 inches and 15 inches deep. Two drawers are shown in each section, but if one side of the bed comes against a wall, it would be better to have drawers at one side only. They could be longer to give extra capacity. The general drawing (Fig. 5-6) shows the main dimensions and a suggested shape for a head.

## Boxes

The boxes are made of ½-inch plywood framed around inside with 1-inch strips. The two sections are the same, except for the attachments for the headboard supports. The key parts are the sides with the drawer openings (Fig. 5-7A). Besides the

edge framing there will be stiffening around the openings (Fig. 5-7B). You can probably use punched finishing nails to supplement glue when the plywood parts are framed.

At each side of a drawer opening is a strip 1 inch by 2 inches on edge, with a 1-inch-square strip across the bottom of the opening. Glue and nails should be sufficient, but a dowel or stub tenon between the parts will keep them in line (Fig. 5-7C). Make up the four sides with their framing. Note that the sides overlap the plywood going across the bed.

Make the plywood pieces to go across the bed. They are plain except for their edge stiffening. The drawer guides are made of 1-inch-by-2-inch strips

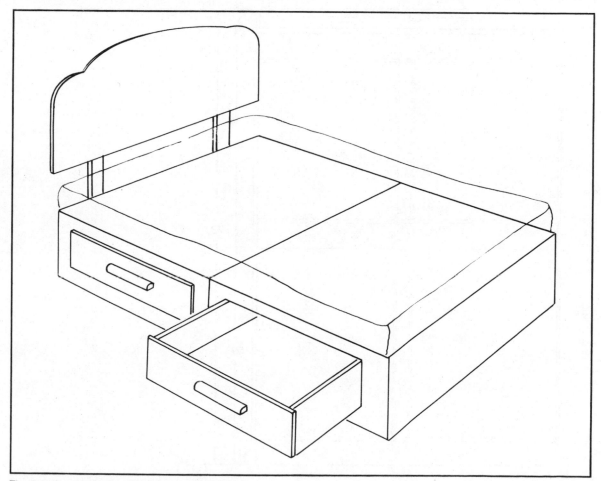

Fig. 5-5. The box base with drawers is in two parts.

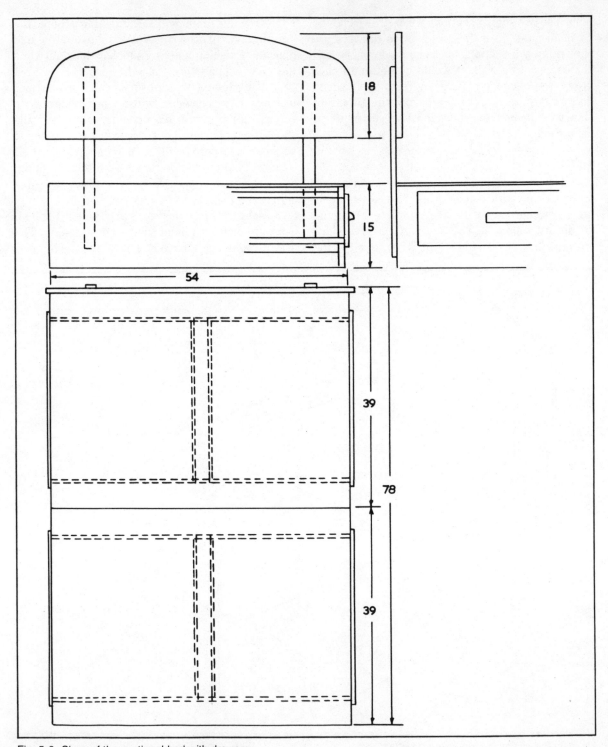

Fig. 5-6. Sizes of the sectional bed with drawers.

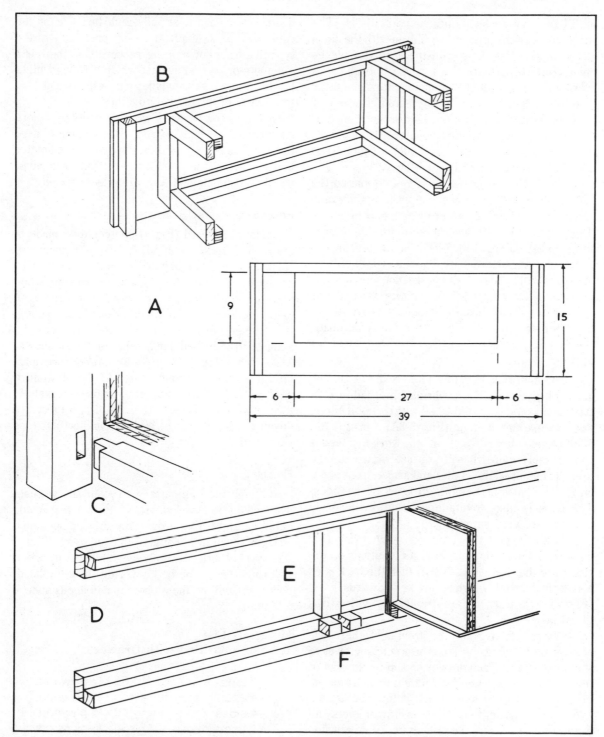

Fig. 5-7. Framing of the box bases and drawers.

with 1-inch-square strips attached (Fig. 5-7D). The wide pieces of the strips must line up with the sides of the drawer openings, and the narrower pieces must come level with the top and bottom, so a drawer passing through the opening runs smoothly on to the guides. Choose straight-grained wood for these parts, as later warping could be a nuisance. It will be best to use stub tenons where these guides meet the uprights, but they could be glued and nailed if they are carefully lined up.

To guard against the weight of people on the bed bending the top guides and pinching the drawers, put a strut at the center of each pair of guides (Fig. 5-7E). You will also need to provide drawer stops on the guides (Fig. 5-7F), but final fitting can be left until the drawers are made. It is unlikely that the stops will be identical, but that does not matter. You can position each stop to suit its drawer. The overlapping drawer front will also act as a stop, but the other stop on the guide will prevent strain on it.

## Drawers

The materials list allows for the drawers to be made of plywood. The traditional method of construction would use solid wood with dovetail joints. You can use this method (Fig. 5-8A), but it is difficult to get suitable wood, and the work involved is considerably more than if you use plywood. The front has stopped dovetails, and a false front is put on it. The bottom goes into grooves in the sides. The back is also dovetailed. Traditionally made drawers are very satisfying.

For plywood construction, each drawer is made as a box. The bottom rests on strips on the sides and the front (Fig. 5-8B); then the back goes above the bottom, which is screwed upwards into it (Fig. 5-8C). Corners are reinforced with strips glued inside.

The sides overlap the front and there are screws into it (Fig. 5-8D). The front is subject to the most strain. Each drawer should be an easy fit into its opening and guides. There is no need for the precision fit that is more usual in fine cabinetry.

Cut each front to overlap its drawer evenly all around and make sure the drawer fronts at each side match. Secure each false front with screws from inside. Wooden drawer pulls could be made, or you could use metal or plastic ones, preferably of the type that hang down or are recessed, so there is a minimum projection against which bare legs might hit. Bolts holding the handles will help to secure the front parts of the drawer together.

Get all the drawers working properly before adding the tops of the sections. Drill for bolts where the sections come together. Two ⅜-inch diameter bolts, with washers under the heads and nuts, should be sufficient if they are widely spaced.

## Headboard

The headboard (Fig. 5-9A) could be made of plywood or thicker solid wood. To get it symmetrical make a template of half the curves, to turn over on the wood (Fig. 5-9B). The edges of solid wood may be molded. Plywood may be covered with cloth, as described for the previous bed.

The supports could be slotted to fit over bolts at the head of the bed, but another method is shown. Make cleats (Fig. 5-9C) to fit a short distance apart on the plywood. Reinforce inside the plywood if necessary. Drill the supports at close intervals-½ inch should do. Taper the ends of two pieces of dowel rod to push into the holes and act as stops (Fig. 5-9D).

## Finishing

Finish the box parts with stain and varnish. They could be covered with cloth, but that would entail careful fitting around the drawer openings, and extra clearance would be needed there. Even if the plywood surface is not very good, very little of it will show under the bed covering. It is the headboard that will be most obvious and needs special attention.

## Materials List
## for Sectional Bed with Drawers

| | |
|---|---|
| 2 tops | 40×55×½ plywood |
| 4 ends | 15×55×½ plywood |
| 4 sides | 15×40×½ plywood |
| 1 headboard | 18×56×½ plywood |
| 2 supports | 2×33×1 |

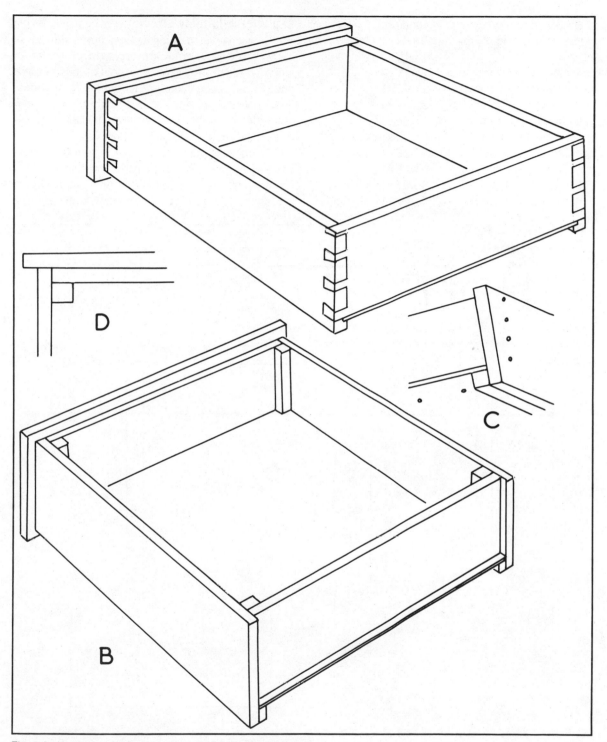

Fig. 5-8. Alternative drawer constructions for the sectional bed.

| | |
|---|---|
| 8 side framing | 1×40×1 |
| 4 end framing | 1×54×1 |
| 8 corners | 1×16×1 |
| 4 drawer hole framing | 1×28×1 |
| 8 drawer hole framing | 2×15×1 |
| 8 drawer guides | 2×54×1 |
| 8 drawer guides | 1×54×1 |
| 4 drawer fronts | 10×29×½ plywood |
| 4 drawer fronts | 9×28×½ plywood |
| 4 drawer backs | 9×28×½ plywood |
| 8 drawer sides | 9×27×½ plywood |
| 4 drawer bottoms | 27×27×¼ plywood |

## BED WITH END DRAWER

For ease in moving in and out a drawer is better if it is deeper back to front than it is side to side. A wide drawer of shallow depth tends to move out of square and catch on the guides. In a double bed, as in the previous example, drawers at opposite sides of the sections have reasonable proportions for ease of movement. However, if the same arrangement is planned for a single bed, the drawers will be much wider than they are deep. They could be single and one-sided and taken almost across the bed, or there could be one drawer at the

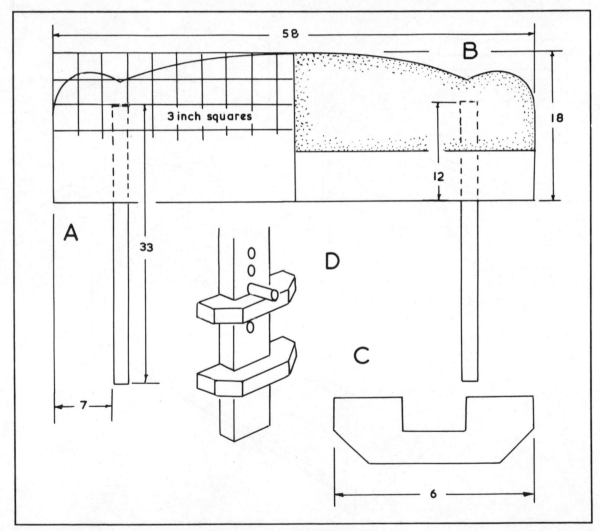

Fig. 5-9. Bed head shaping and fitting for the sectional bed with drawers.

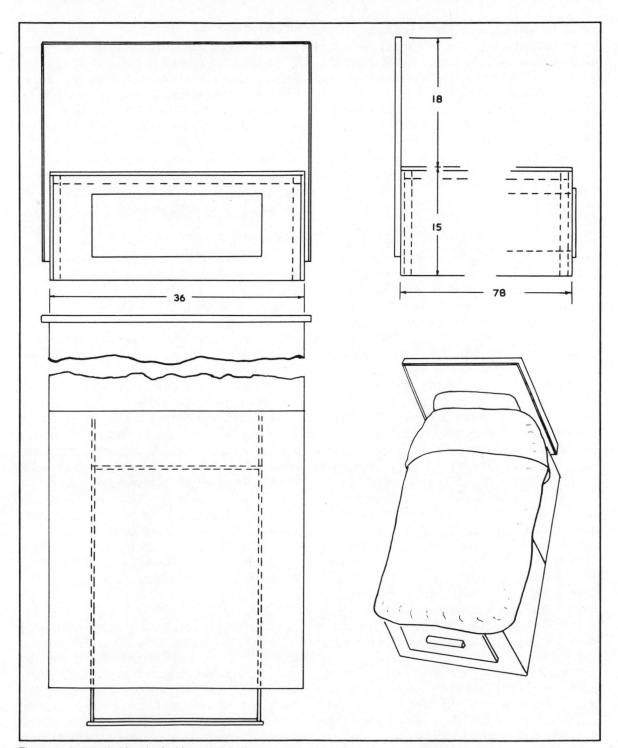

Fig. 5-10. An inverted box bed with an end drawer.

foot of the bed. There could still be a drawer across the top section. The feasibility of either, or both, of these arrangements depends on the amount of space around the bed for the drawers to slide out.

The bed with end drawer (Fig. 5-10) is intended for one person and is shown with a drawer at the foot only. Another drawer could be fitted across the other section, with details similar to the previous bed. The head is a simple one attached directly to the bed, but it could be made adjustable, as already described.

## Boxes

The bed is divided across its center, so the two boxes must be made up to overall sizes of 36 inches across the bed, 39 inches along it, and 15 inches high. The sides overlap the ends, and the tops overlap the sides and ends. Make up the boxes with 1-inch strips inside the joints, using glue and finishing nails. The two boxes should be identical in overall sizes and details, but the one at the foot must be made to take the drawer.

Prepare the plywood parts for both boxes. All will remain plain, except for the end at the foot, which must be pierced for the drawer (Fig. 5-11A). The top edge and the corners of the box are stiffened with strips in the same way as the other box parts. In this case, the drawer guides are shown as pieces of plywood (Fig. 5-11B). If you prefer, they could be made of strips, as described for the previous bed. Make the plywood guides to go the full length of the box and notch around the framing at the top. Stiffen the top and bottom edges (Fig. 5-11C) and arrange guide strips in line with the opening in the plywood (Fig. 5-11D). Vertical strips on the plywood provide attachment to the end beside the opening. Use the same method of attachment at the other end, even though there is no opening. Stiffen above and below the opening between the guides (Fig. 5-11E).

When you assemble that box, be sure that the guides are parallel and square to the end, so the drawer will slide correctly. Complete both boxes by adding the tops. Drill their meeting ends for two ⅜-inch bolts that will hold them together in use.

## Drawer

The drawer is of generally similar construction to those in the previous bed (Fig. 5-8). Make the drawer sides first, to slide easily in the guides; then make the front and back to allow an easy fit in the available space. Fit the bottom to strips at the lower edges of the sides and arrange the back above it. Add the false front to overlap all around. Make a handle or use a metal or plastic drawer pull. The false front will keep the drawer from going back too far, but you can put small blocks as stops on the guides to reduce strain on the front.

## Bed Head

The bed head shown (Fig. 5-12) is intended to be made of plywood and stiffened by framing. It could be plywood faced with a special veneer, or plain plywood painted. It might be covered with cloth. In any case, it is framed with some border strips, which could be given a contrasting finish. If cloth is put over the plywood, attach it before the border pieces are added.

Square the plywood and add the framing strips. Since the edges will be hidden, there is no need to miter the framing corners nor to cut any special joints there. There is no need for a framing piece across the bottom edge. Arrange two upright stiffeners, which will take screws driven from inside the box. The greatest strain will come near the top of the box; so arrange long, stout screws there—1¾-inch-by-12-gauge would be ideal. Two more screws in each stiffener should be enough.

Miter the corners of the border pieces. When the glue has set, round these joints and take off the sharpness of exposed edges.

## Finishing

The border could be finished in a contrasting color to the panel. The exposed parts of the box may be stained and varnished or covered with cloth. If a thick mattress is being used, the rigid, untreated tops of the boxes will provide a good support, but they could be covered with cloth over foam padding. This covering might be thick enough to provide some additional cushioning, or just thick enough to

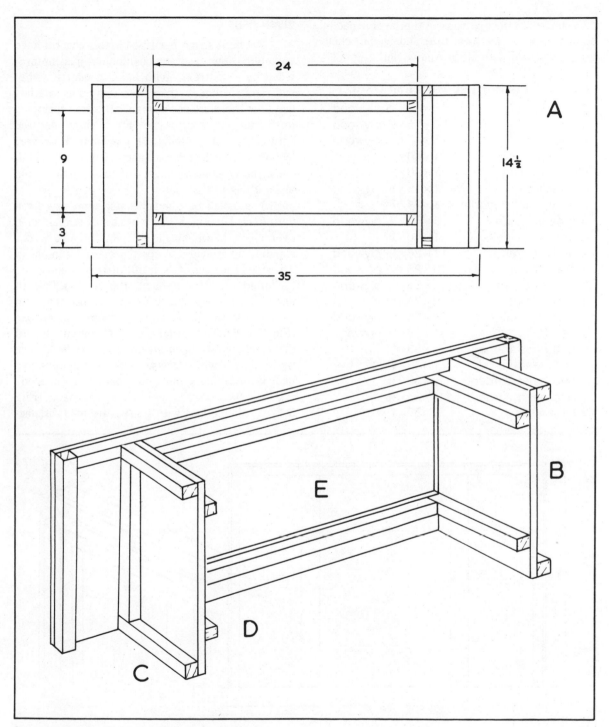

Fig. 5-11. Framing of the box base and end drawer.

form a base for the mattress. A thin layer of padding helps to stop the mattress from sliding, particularly if it is covered with fairly coarse cloth.

## Materials List for Bed with End Drawer

| | |
|---|---|
| 2 tops | 36×40×½ plywood |
| 4 ends | 36×15×½ plywood |
| 4 sides | 15×40×½ plywood |
| 4 side framing | 1×40×1 |
| 4 end framing | 1×36×1 |
| 10 uprights | 1×15×1 |
| 2 drawer hole frames | 1×24×1 |
| 2 drawer guides | 15×40×½ plywood |
| 8 drawer guides | 1×40×1 |
| 1 drawer front | 11×26×½ plywood |
| 1 drawer front | 10×25×½ plywood |
| 2 drawer sides | 9×36×½ plywood |
| 1 drawer back | 9×24×½ plywood |
| 1 drawer bottom | 24×36×¼ plywood |
| 1 bed head | 34×38×½ plywood |
| 2 bed head frames | 1×33×1 |
| 1 bed head frame | 1×39×1 |
| 1 bed head border | 1½×39×⅜ |
| 2 bed head borders | 1½×34×⅜ |
| 2 stiffeners | 2×33×1 |

## DIVAN BEDS

The beds so far described in this chapter have unyielding tops, and any cushioning must be provided by a mattress. With modern mattresses of sufficient thickness, these tops are quite satisfactory, but there are occasions when some springing in the support is desirable. For a single bed the springing can be provided with webbing. However, webbing would be less satisfactory on a wider bed, since the combined weights of two people would make it sag to the center.

A suitable single bed may also serve as a divan during the day (Fig. 5-13). It has a substantial frame over which the webbing is stretched; then a border standing up around it keeps the mattress in place. The sides and ends of the frame are thickened at the top for attaching the webbing (Fig. 5-14A). Legs fit inside the corners and stiffeners are put across to prevent the sides from bowing inwards under load (Fig. 5-14B). The border strips are not put on until the webbing has been strained and tacked; then they are fixed with screws, so they can be removed later if the webbing must be repaired or replaced.

The best corner joints are dovetails (Fig. 5-14C). Simple laps with screws are also satisfac-

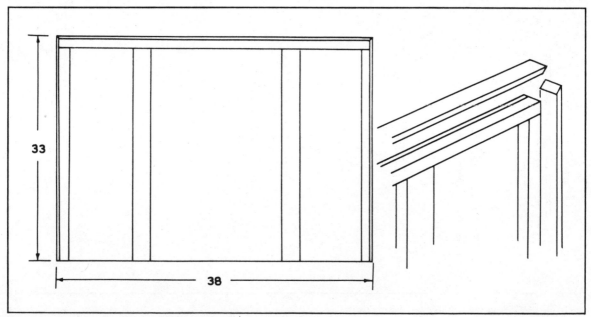

Fig. 5-12. Construction of the head of the bed with end drawer.

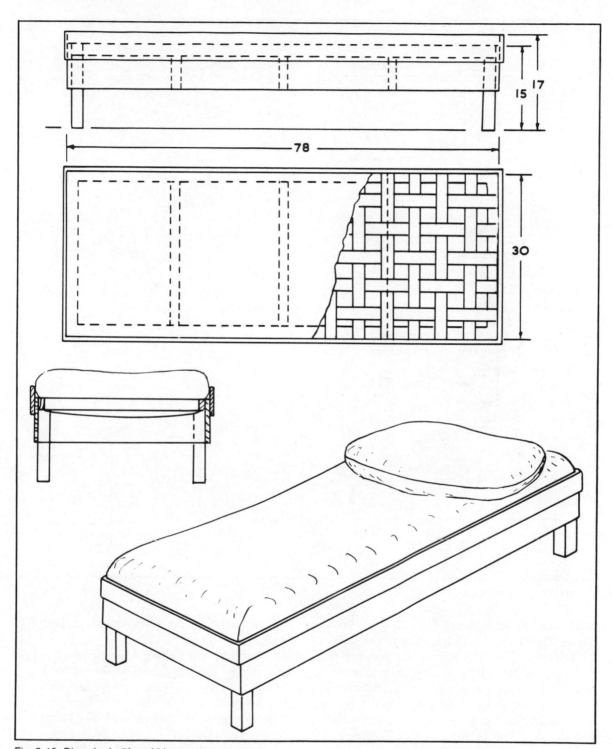

Fig. 5-13. Divan bed with webbing mattress support.

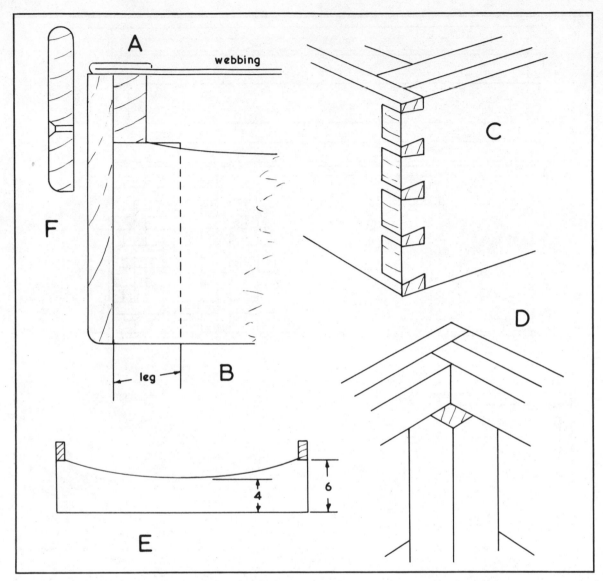

Fig. 5-14. Divan bed framing.

tory since the corners are reinforced by the legs inside (Fig. 5-14D). Attach the thickening strips to the top edge. They can be nailed or screwed from outside, as well as glued, since heads will be hidden under the border strips. The three stiffeners are equally spaced between the sides. Their top edges come under the top stiffening strips, and so are 2 inches below the webbing. It is unlikely that the webbing will sag that far under load, but, in case it does, hollow the top edges about two inches (Fig. 5-14E).

Make up the main frame completely. See that it is square. Measure diagonals. Round the lower edges of the sides and ends. Remove any sharpness from the inner edges of the top stiffening pieces, where webbing could chafe under load. Leave other edges square.

Make the border strips (Fig. 5-14F). They

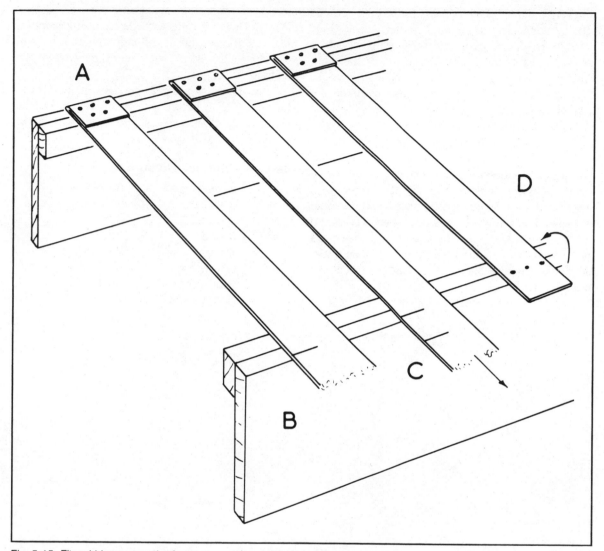

Fig. 5-15. Fit webbing across the frame.

stand 2 inches above the tops of the sides and ends, then overlap enough for screws at about 6-inch intervals into the framing. Miter the corners. Drill these pieces and round their edges, but do not fit them until after all the webbing is in place.

The webbing could be the plain fabric type, with little stretch, or it could be rubber-reinforced. In either case, arrange the stretching and attaching uniformly, so the support and amount of flexing is the same all over the bed. Webbing 2 inches wide can be arranged with spaces between 2 and 3 inch-

es. Pencil along the sides and ends where the webbing is to go, to get an even and square spacing.

It is the bands of webbing across the narrow way which mainly determine the amount of support that is given; so deal with that direction first. Tack a piece of turned-over webbing to one side, using five tacks (Fig. 5-15A). Pull it across just hand tight and pencil on it where the edge of the wood comes (Fig. 5-15B). Strain the webbing (see Chapter 3) until you judge there is enough tension. Mark where the edge of the wood is now (Fig. 5-15C) and note the

107

difference. Drive three tacks near the edge and cut off the webbing with enough to turn back (Fig. 5-15D). Fold that over and tack again with two tacks. Deal with the other strips across in the same way, but try to get the same amount of stretch, indicated between pencil marks, as you did on the first piece.

The lengthwise webbing supplements the support provided from the crosswise pieces, but do not expect to get such a relatively tight tension. Thread each piece over and under the crosswise pieces. It will be easiest to judge the correct tension if you start with a central strip. Tack one end and stretch at the other end, using pencil marks to check tension. Deal with the other lengthwise parts in the same way. You should finish with an interlaced pattern that only yields slightly when you press on it.

Ordinary upholstery tacks should hold well in most hardwoods, but make sure they are driven closely. Direct hitting with the face of a hammer may be sufficient, but it will help to then use a nail set over each head to bed it into the weave of the webbing.

It will be easier to get a good, even finish if you stain and polish before you finally screw on the border pieces. Since the screw heads will show, they look well if they are brass.

## Materials List for Divan Bed

| 2 sides | $8 \times 79 \times \frac{3}{4}$ |
| 2 sides | $2 \times 79 \times 1$ |
| 2 ends | $8 \times 30 \times \frac{3}{4}$ |
| 2 ends | $2 \times 30 \times 1$ |
| 4 legs | $2 \times 14 \times 2$ |
| 2 borders | $5 \times 80 \times \frac{3}{4}$ |
| 2 borders | $5 \times 31 \times \frac{3}{4}$ |
| 3 stiffeners | $6 \times 30 \times 1$ |

# Chapter 6

# Beds with Turned Parts

A lathe can be used to make parts of beds. Posts and rails look lighter and more graceful than when left square in section, and still retain enough strength. Many traditional beds have turned parts. The use of turning had practical advantages for furniture makers in the days when most cutting and shaping of wood had to be done laboriously by hand. Instead of hand sawing and hand planing wood straight and true, a more roughly shaped piece could be mounted in a lathe and turned. The lathe had to be treadled, or an assistant had to drive it with a wheel, A symmetrical straight piece of the bed structure resulted from a total expenditure of labor less than might have been expended to make a similar, but less attractive, piece of square section by hand.

There may not be a labor-saving reason now for having round instead of square parts. With modern methods of working wood it would be less trouble to leave the wood square, but turned parts are attractive, both on traditional designs and modern pieces. Even if the main part of the bed has square-sectioned wood, some turned parts improve

appearance, even when they are quite small in relation to the whole thing.

Most woods can be turned. The close-grained hardwoods are needed for finer detail. Coarse-grained hardwoods, such as most oaks, are used for bigger, flowing curves, avoiding cross-grained projections that might break off. Softwoods have similar problems, but they take easy curves well if you avoid deep beads, and acutely angled projections and very fine detail. Much depends on the particular piece of wood, but every piece should be fully seasoned if you expect it to keep its shape after turning. If you have doubts about the dryness of a piece of wood, turn it roughly to shape, leaving at least ⅛ inch yet to be removed. Put it aside for one or two weeks, before mounting it in the lathe again for finishing.

Some practical limitations may need to be considered. You can turn knobs, feet, and finials as separate items in any lathe, but the distance between centers will limit how long a part you can make. Many lathes have a capacity only a little over 30 inches. That capacity is arranged so table legs can be made, but for some bed parts it is not enough. You could not deal with a fourposter, and even a rail across a single bed might not fit the lathe. There are ways of getting over these problems. If an antique bed was broken up, you would probably find that some apparently long turned parts were actually formed of several pieces, showing that our ancestors did not always have large lathes.

One of the first uses of turned parts may be as knobs for the tops of square legs, instead of tapering or otherwise shaping the leg itself, as suggested for some beds. Knobs may be turned with their own dowels to fit into holes drilled in the legs. If the leg is shorter than the capacity of the lathe, the knob may be turned in the same piece of wood. This method may be possible with some legs at the foot of a bed, but, if the legs at the head are too long, it will look better if you add separate knobs to all the legs.

A knob at the top of the leg will finish with minimum trouble if the diameter at the base of the knob is almost the same as the thickness of the leg (Fig. 6-1A). You can make a bead, then a quirk and a smaller bead before the knob. Turning a true sphere is difficult (Fig. 6-1B); so it is better avoided. In any case a shorter (Fig. 6-1C) or higher (Fig. 6-1D) knob looks better.

A knob may be developed into a finial to continue up just a short distance, (Fig. 6-1E) or quite high, as on some traditional beds. There is, however, the problem of strength. If someone swings on it, will it break? A normal knob should stand up to any abuse. In most cases the turned dowel should be ¾ inch or 1 inch in diameter and project about twice that length.

Obviously, the hole in the leg for the dowel must be carefully centered, since a slightly offset knob will be very obvious. Take the corners off the leg before fitting the knob (Fig. 6-1F).

Feet may be turned in a similar way to the knobs (Fig. 6-1G). You can arrange a similar pattern so the top and bottom of a leg will match, but a fairly squat ball will usually be adequate. The bottom of a leg does not get the attention its top does. If there is a caster, the foot must be a suitable size for it. If there is a glide, a ball foot is a good backing for it (Fig. 6-1H). You could dispense with a glide by turning the foot to a slightly domed curve of sufficiently broadbase to spread the load on the carpet (Fig. 6-1J).

## Joining Turned Parts

Where rails or other parts have to be made up to a greater length than can be turned, they can be joined with dowels in holes. This arrangement is best done where beads or other turned shapes leave cuts around the wood (Fig. 6-2A). The joints should meet closely outside, so if you turn the meeting surfaces slightly hollow (Fig. 6-2B), the joint will not show on the assembled work.

If you want to make a long rail you could use one joint near the center (Fig. 6-2C), but it may be more convenient and stronger to have two joints nearer the sides (Fig. 6-2D).

Sometimes a turned part must appear to pass through a flat or square piece. If this piece is thick enough, doweled ends can go through a hole in it (Fig. 6-2E). If the wood is thinner, the dowel on one piece may go right through into the other one (Fig. 6-2F), or it may be better to have a thick dowel on one piece and take the other into a hole in it (Fig. 6-2G).

## Matching Pieces

For most beds you must make two or four turned parts that match each other. They may be far apart, and minor variations may not be obvious, but overall sizes and general appearance must be the same. It will help to make a full-size drawing of the design and try to work closely to it each time, or you may turn the first piece and use that as an example.

A strip of wood with the key distances on it may form a rod (Fig. 6-3A). When the wood has been turned around, use a pencil and the rod to mark cutting positions (Fig. 6-3B). It may help to draw the intended shapes and the diameters behind the marks on the rod (Fig. 6-3C). Use calipers to check diameters before shaping the detail; then you will get matching sizes, even if curves are slightly different.

It is usually sufficient to work from a rod, but if

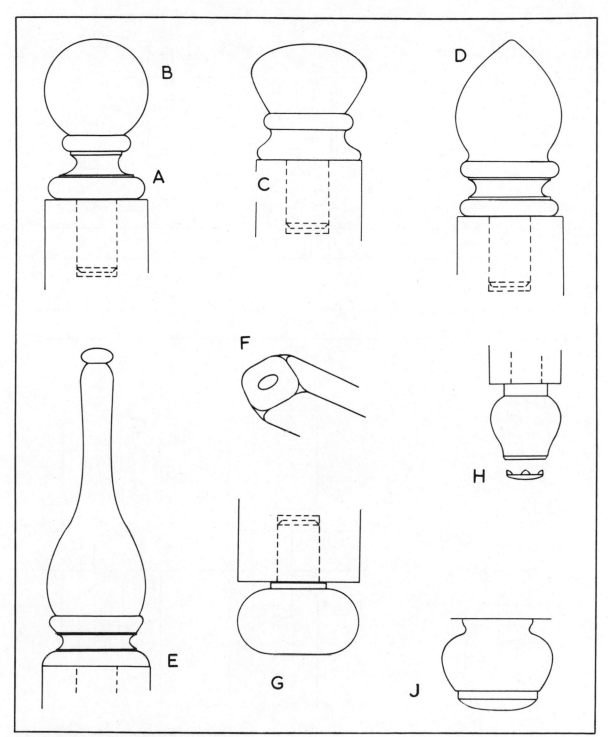

Fig. 6-1. Knobs, finials, and feet may be turned.

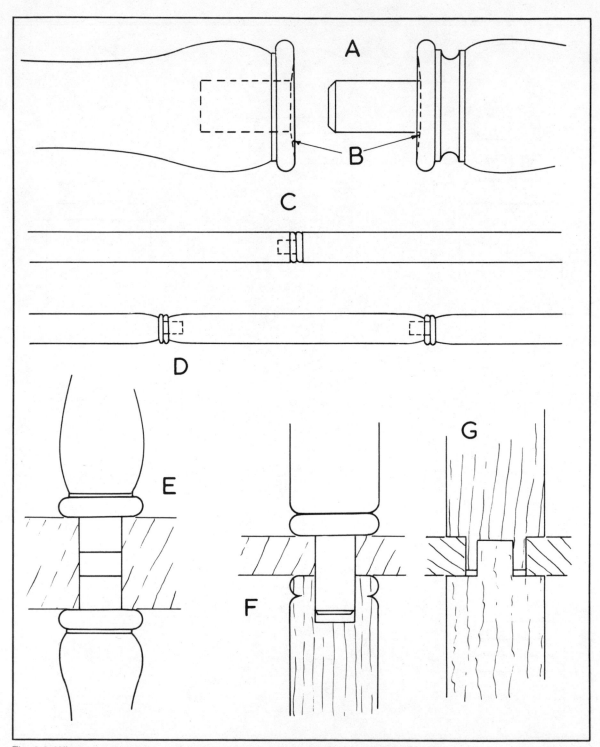

Fig. 6-2. When turned parts must be joined, a dowel on one may fit into a hole in the other.

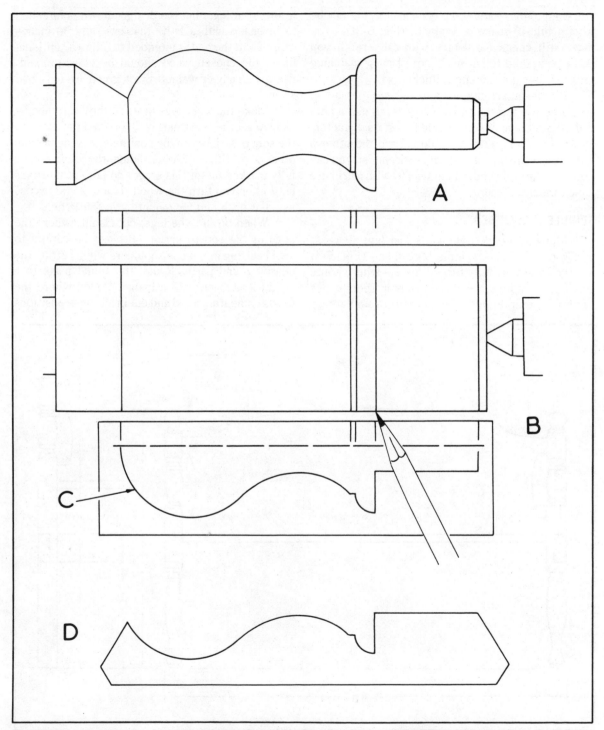

Fig. 6-3. A rod may be used to mark key distances (A), and the shape may be drawn on it (B,C), or you can make a template (D) of a turned part.

you want to make several pieces identical it may be worthwhile to make a template (Fig. 6-3D). You must still check diameters with calipers. If you don't you could finish with parts having matching profiles, but not matching thicknesses.

If you can arrange for a dowel end to come in the lathe toward the tailstock, you can use a hole drilled in a piece of scrap wood to test its diameter. However, if one end has a dowel and the other a hole, make the hole at the tailstock end, so you can bore it accurately and concentrically with a drill in a chuck mounted there.

## SPINDLE-LEGGED BED

Many Colonial-style beds had legs at least partly turned. This spindle-legged bed (Fig. 6-4) has the front legs fully turned, except where joints go. The rear legs are turned only in their upper parts. The rear legs could be turned in a similar way

to the front legs, but the design shown is intended to be made with a lathe that has only 30 inches capacity. If the bed is intended to follow traditional lines, the chosen wood should be close-grained, like mahogany or walnut. Sizes given are for a bed 48 inches wide.

Make the front legs first, so they can then be used to set the sizes and layout of other parts. Mark the square strips with the positions of the joints and other parts (Fig. 6-5A). Although the joints can be fully marked out at this stage, do not cut mortises until after you turn the wood. Leave some excess wood at each end for mounting in the lathe.

When turning the legs, cut cleanly where the ends of the square parts come and be careful to avoid cutting into these shoulders when cutting the nearby round parts. Rough the round parts to a cylindrical shape with a gouge. Pencil where the beads come from a rod and cut in all these positions

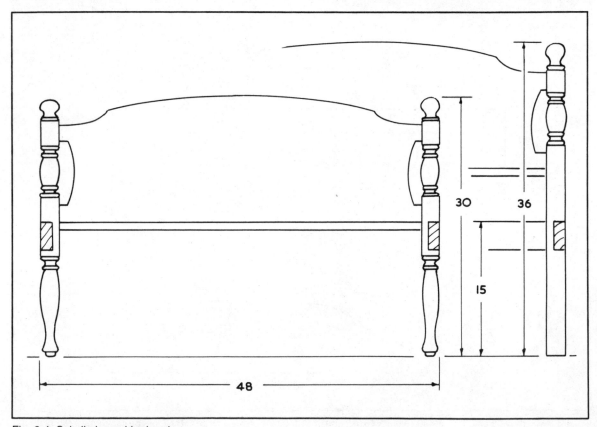

Fig. 6-4. Spindle-legged bed ends.

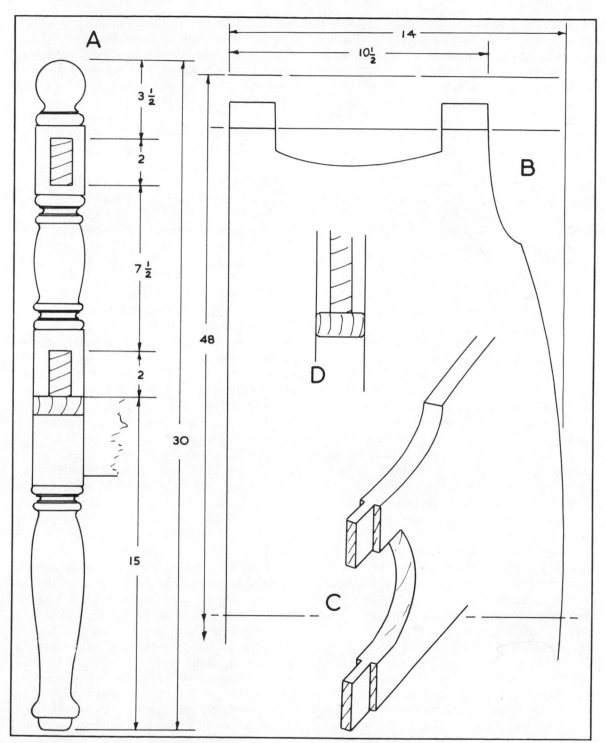

Fig. 6-5. Sizes of a spindle-legged bed.

with the long point of a chisel. Round the beads first and they will set the limits for the other shaping. The leg bottom is shown rounded to form its own glide, but if casters are to be used, shorten the leg and leave an end large enough to take the caster.

If you have a lathe large enough to take the length of the rear legs, they can be turned full length. The lower part could be turned in the same way as the front legs, if you wish. If your lathe will not take the whole leg between centers, it can be made in two parts. Make one square piece up to the turned part and drill centrally to take a dowel from the upper turned part. You can make the turned section, with the top square part included, as a unit down to the meeting with the lower square part, where it may have a 1-inch dowel about 1½ inches long projecting to make the joint.

It is the grain pattern of the panels (Fig. 6-5B) that provides the main decorative feature of the bed ends, to supplement the turned legs. If the wood is rather plain, you could add carving or piercing at the center, but otherwise it is better to stain and give a clear finish to emphasize the grain. The ends are reduced for tenoning and cut back between the tenons (Fig. 6-5C). Be careful to get the shaping symmetrical. A half template will help, or you can mark and cut half of one panel, and use it to mark half of the other panel. Reverse each on the other and use them to mark the second halves. Finally, turning one panel over on the other will show any discrepancies that need corrections.

The top profiles of the panels should first be finished smoothly square across, so all tool marks are removed, then sharpness should be taken off the angles. To remove the plainness of the bottom edges there are strips across (Fig. 6-5D), as wide as the legs, but rounded where they project. A strip might be made only wide enough to project forward, then come level with the rear of the panel, but it is shown extending on both sides of it.

The strip may have tenons or dowels into the legs. It could be only glued to the panel edge, but a few dowels would be advisable, or screws could be driven from below, where they would not show.

At the back there is a rail to provide stiffness at the level of the sides. Tenon or dowel it to the legs.

The side strips may be attached in any of the ways previously described. In the original Colonial furniture they would probably have been given tusk tenons taken through the legs and wedged, but, if those projections are to be avoided, you may use bolts or special hardware.

## Materials List for Spindle-Legged Bed

| | |
|---|---|
| 2 rear legs | 2¼×38×2¼ |
| or 2 | 2¼×25×2¼ |
| and 2 | 2¼×15×2¼ |
| 2 front legs | 2¼×31×2¼ |
| 2 panels | 14×48×1 |
| 2 panel edges | 2¼×48×1 |
| 1 rear rail | 4×48×1½ |
| 2 sides | 4×79×1½ |

## SPINDLE-PANELED SINGLE BED

Even with a lathe of small capacity, it is possible to embellish a bed with turned work, if the main structure is left in square sections. In this spindle-paneled single bed, (Fig. 6-6) the legs and rails forming the ends are of 2-inch-square sections. Instead of plywood or slat panels, there are turned spindles, while the tops of the legs are decorated with matching turned finials. The sizes quoted are for a bed 36 inches wide, but beds of other widths could be made in the same way.

The legs are shown with an allowance for casters. The tops of the legs extend above the top rails by 1 inch. Mark out the rear legs (Fig. 6-7A), including the positions of the rails. Mark out the front legs (Fig. 6-7B) and check that the side heights are the same on all legs.

Mark the four main rails and the lower rear rail together so the distances between shoulders are the same. The top rails will be improved by rounding their tops (Fig. 6-8A). This section looks better if it is part of an ellipse, than if it is part of a circle or just a flat top with rounded edges. Cut down the tenons to miss the curve (Fig. 6-7C). The other rails can have full-depth tenons. Dowels for these joints would not be as strong. Mark and cut the mortise and tenon joints between the rails and legs. Square and smooth the top of each leg, then drill a hole centrally for the finial dowel.

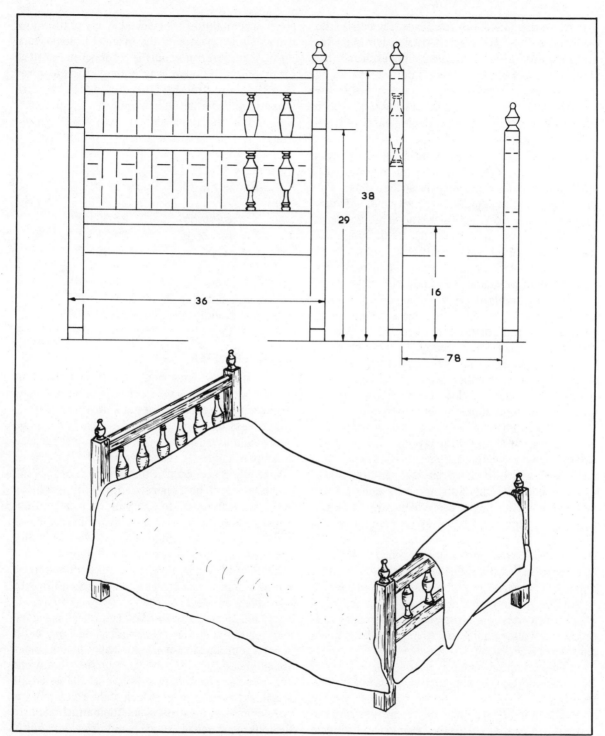

Fig. 6-6. A single bed with spindle-paneled ends.

117

Mark the holes in pairs of rails together so the positions match. To avoid the risk of errors due to turning around later, mark the ends of each pair that should be the same way. Use a drill press or a jig when making the holes, so they are square to the surface. Space the holes evenly (Fig. 6-7D); ¾-inch holes, ¾-inch deep, will give ample clearance to the spindle dowels.

The spindles are longer at the backboard than at the footboard. The designs are related (Fig. 6-8B and C); the main difference is at the center portions. Since the six spindles in each panel are fairly close together, getting them the same shape is important. Particularly important are the heights of the main lines running around the spindles. Check these and their diameters with a rod and calipers. Variations in the beads at the ends are not as noticeable. Overall lengths between the end shoulders must be the same as each other and as the distances between the rail positions marked on the legs, so the whole framework assembles without gaps. Check the dowel diameters with a hole in a piece of scrap wood or with calipers. Aim for an easy fit in the holes and taper the dowel ends slightly. You do not want to stop and adjust any joint while putting together a batch of six spindles and two rails.

The finials (Fig. 6-8D) have matching shapes. Their dowels are longer because they have no other parts with which to share the load, and the strain could be considerable if anyone pulls against a finial. Although the finials are widely spaced on the bed, match their sizes and shapes as near as possible.

Assemble one end at a time, Glue the spindles into the rails and the rail tenons into the legs, then clamp and square the end by measuring diagonals before any of the glue starts to set. Sight across to check for twist before letting the glue harden. Clean up the ends after gluing the other parts. The finials can then be glued in.

The design allows for plain sides, but any of the other methods of supporting a mattress can be used.

The spindles will probably be turned from the same wood as the rest of the bed, so the stain and polish or varnish may be the same all over. You can get an interesting effect by using wood of a different color for the turned parts. Even with the same wood throughout you can stain the framing and not the turnings, or the other way around. Light-colored spindles and finials, surrounded by a dark framework, give an interesting effect, combining Colonial or traditional design with a modern appearance.

## Materials List
## for Spindle-Paneled Single Bed

| | |
|---|---|
| 2 rear legs | 2×38×2 |
| 2 front legs | 2×29×2 |
| 4 rails | 2×36×2 |
| 1 rail | 4×36×1½ |
| 2 sides | 4×79×1½ |
| 6 spindles | 2×12×2 |
| 6 spindles | 2×10×2 |
| 4 finials | 2× 7×2 |

## SEMI-FOURPOSTER

A full fourposter bed has legs extended to support a roof, or tester, from which hung drapes large enough to enclose sleepers, providing privacy and preventing drafts. Although such a bed may be interesting to make and have, the original purpose no longer applies. A change occurred when people realized their bed could be much more open; yet the tradition of high posts persisted, resulting in many beds of a century or so ago with legs carried upwards. There is an attraction about having posts higher than practical requirements would dictate, and these extensions are very suitable places for turned work. Round posts have a lighter and more graceful appearance than square posts, no matter how those are decorated.

This semi-fourposter bed (Fig. 6-9) has some features that follow Early American designs, but it is not a reproduction of any particular model. Sizes are intended to take a 48-inch mattress that drops between the sides. The side, head, and foot rails are all at the same level. Much of the rigidity of the bed depends on these parts and their attachments to the legs. At the head, a wide panel also aids rigidity. It is tenoned into the square parts of the legs and the

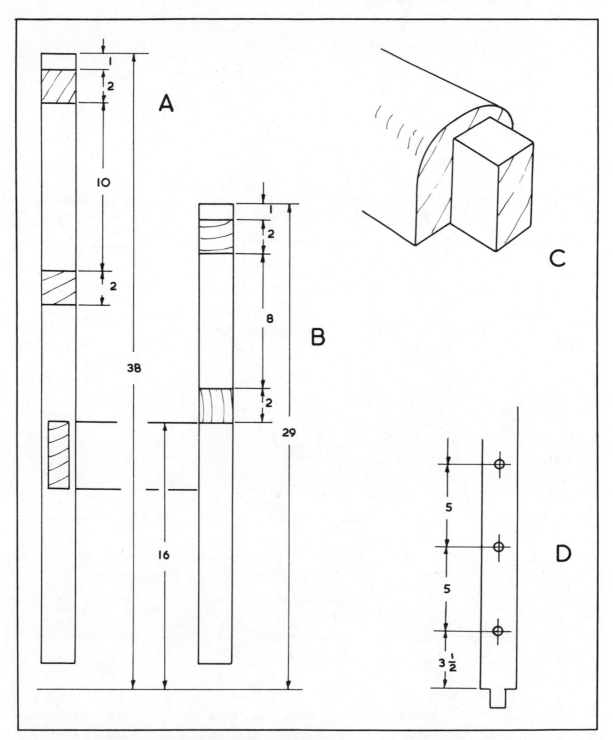

Fig. 6-7. Leg end rail details for the spindle-paneled single bed.

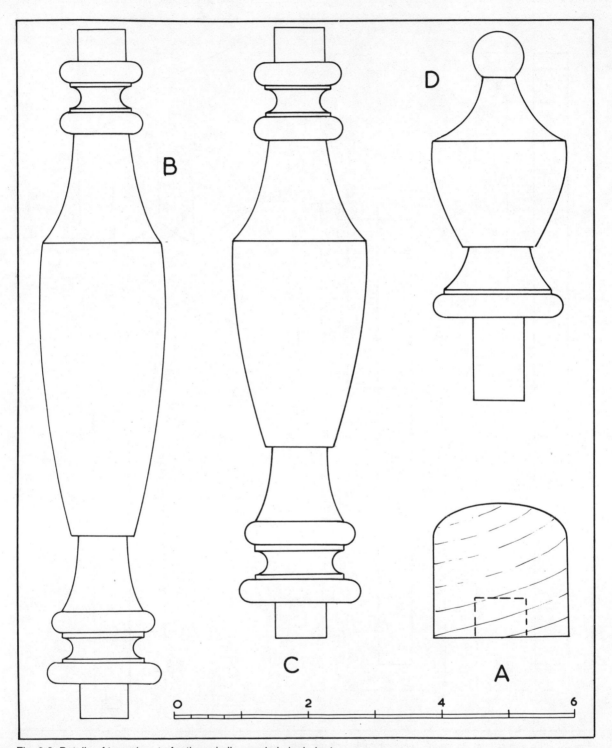

Fig. 6-8. Details of turned parts for the spindle-paneled single bed.

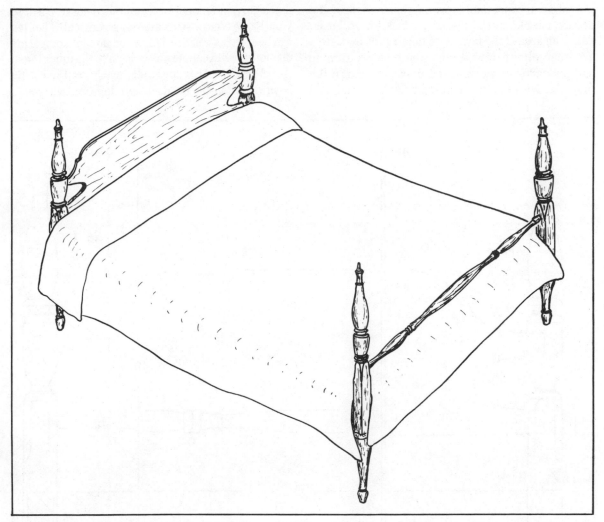

Fig. 6-9. A semi-fourposter bed.

parallel round parts above that. A turned rail is across the foot. Both this rail and the legs may have to be turned in parts to come within the limits of a lathe.

### Bed Ends

From the general drawing (Fig. 6-10) it can be seen that all four legs are the same, except for joint details. The foot rail joins its legs at the same level as the lower tenons of the headboard. If the legs cannot be accommodated full length in your lathe, divide at the top of the square part. A dowel down-

ward would be cut into by joints going the other way; so arrange the dowel upward from the square part (Fig. 6-11A). The top few inches of the square look best if the corners are rounded off (Fig. 6-11B). Careful centering in the lathe is needed, or uneven rounding of the corners will be obvious.

Exact sizes of the various turned parts are not important, but keep the urn shape above the square parallel in the part that will be mortised for the headboard. Whatever the design, there should be a general slimming toward the top, but do not thin the wood so much that it will be weakened. The drawing shows reasonable proportions. Below the square part keep the leg fairly thick for stiffness. Allow an area at the bottom to take a glide or caster. You may either draw a leg fullsize before turning and endeavor to work to the drawing, or turn the first leg, with key measurements as required, and use a certain amount of freedom to curve parts to your liking where sizes are not so critical. That leg can be used as a pattern for a rod and for comparing diameters with calipers as you make the other legs.

Mark the legs together for the rail and side positions. Pair the head and foot legs for their joints

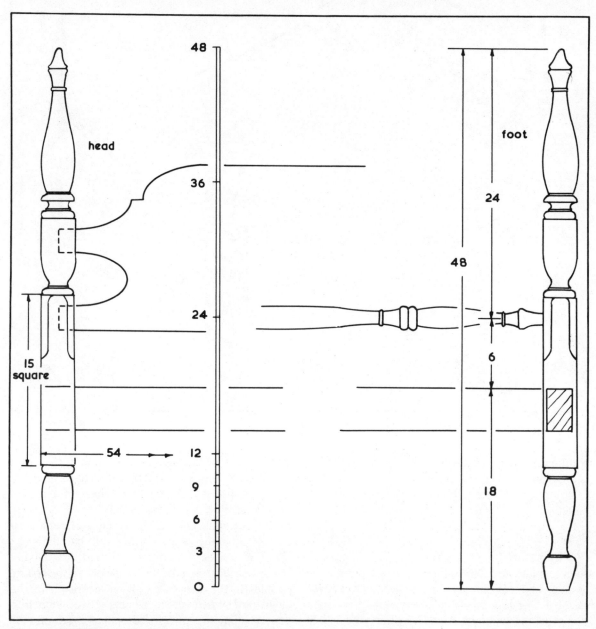

Fig. 6-10. Suggested sizes for the semi-fourposter bed.

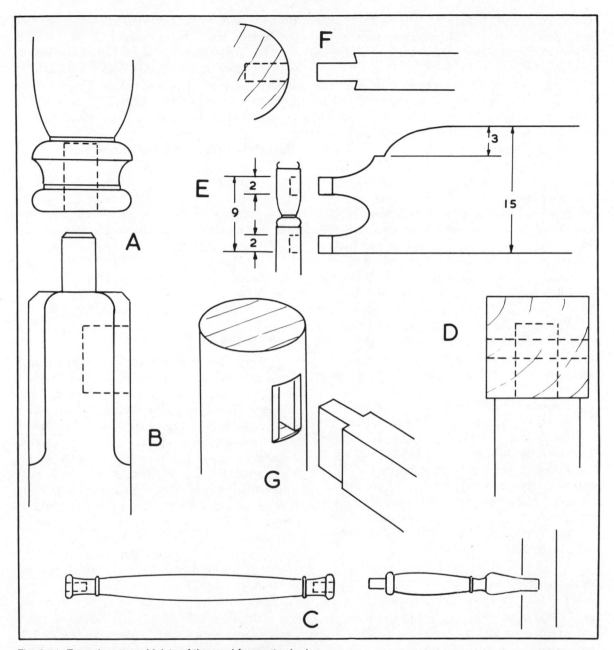

Fig. 6-11. Turned parts and joints of the semi-fourposter bed.

to cross members. If there are slight variations in detail, remember to measure from floor level for joint positions, or the bed may finish with a twist.

The rail across the foot of the bed is fairly slim in relation to its length of 52 inches. Even if a lathe of that capacity is available, the wood would whip while being turned, resulting in a poor finish, with chatter marks due to vibration. It will be easier to make the rail in three parts (Fig. 6-11C), preferably two shorter ends and a longer center section, joined with dowels turned to fit holes. The ends are shown with tapers to allow slight adjustment during assembly, but gaps would show if beads or shoulders were located against the legs.

The sides will be attached to the legs with bolts. Since the rails across the ends come at the same level as the sides, it will be strongest if the tenons on the rails are made long enough for the bolts to pass through them. Take the tenons more than halfway through the legs (Fig. 6-11D), so the bolt hole will come fully in its tenon and not just cut across its end.

Mark out the piece for the bed head, relating its tenoned ends to the mortise positions on the legs (Fig. 6-11E). Taking each tenon less than halfway through its leg should be deep enough. Where the top tenon goes into the round part of the leg, its shoulders may be cut to conform to the curve (Fig. 6-11F), but it would be simpler to flatten each side of the mortise (Fig. 6-11G) so square shoulders will fit closely. Remember to allow for slightly more length between these opposite shoulders than between the lower shoulders which meet the square leg.

Plane and sand the parts for the bed head. Examine the turned parts for scratches from sanding. These scratches will show through any applied finish; so rub them down by sanding lengthwise.

Assemble the bed head, taking care to keep it square and free from twist. When that glue has set, assemble the foot parts over it to keep parts square and true. The lighter-framed foot is more likely to go out of shape during assembly if it is put together without the head as a guide.

### Sides

The bed sides may have their ends cut square, but it helps in stiffening the bed to give them shallow stub tenons into the legs (Fig. 6-12A), since they locate the ends and prevent twist. Drill for each bolt through the parts that are brought together. Cut a mortise for the nut on the inside of the side piece (Fig. 6-12B). The leg may be counterbored for the bolt head and a washer, providing you have a suitable wrench to fit into the hole (Fig. 6-12C). Use a washer under the nut in the mortise.

Both washers ensure tightness since they prevent the head or nut from pulling into the grain.

The simplest way to support a box mattress is with angle brackets inside the sides and end rails at about 24-inch intervals (Fig. 6-12D). You could use wood strips instead (Fig. 6-12E) or fill the area with plywood or slats for the other sorts of mattresses.

### Materials List for Semi-Fourposter

| | |
|---|---|
| 4 legs | 3×50×3 |
| or 2 | 3×28×3 |
| and 2 | 3×24×3 |
| 2 rails | 4×52×2½ |
| 1 headboard | 15×52×1 |
| 1 foot rail | 2×52×2 |
| or 2 | 2×15×2 |
| and 1 | 2×24×2 |
| 2 sides | 2×79×2½ |

### CLUB FOOT DIVAN

There was a fashion for cabriole legs on much classical traditional furniture. Beds, chairs, tables, and other furniture had legs made like stylized animal legs. The paw or claw clutched a ball, which formed the base. Some of these legs were given considerable shaping and were elaborately carved. A feature of the design, no matter what the details were, was the leg which appeared to project diagonally from the corner of the furniture. From this design came a simplified form that could be worked almost entirely on a lathe and may be better described as a club foot. It looks something like a human or animal leg tapering to an ankle above a foot that points diagonally from the framework above it.

This example is a divan or daybed with club feet at the corners (Fig. 6-13). It could be made with the legs set inside a boxed framework (Fig. 5-13), and the top could have slats or crossed webbing. The example, however, is intended to be made with the rails tenoned into the legs. Plywood is arranged inside to support a mattress which fits within the rails. Sizes are arranged to suit a mattress 36 inches wide and 78 inches long.

Prepare the wood for the legs, leaving a little

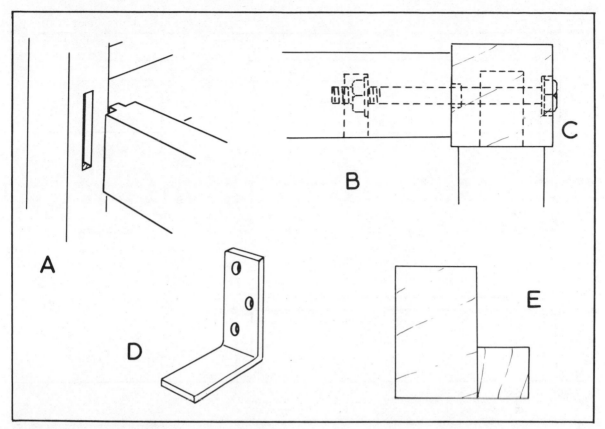

Fig. 6-12. Side to leg joints for the semi-fourposter bed.

excess length at the top to take the driving center in the lathe. Later trim this excess level with the tops of the rails after cutting the joints. Carefully center both ends with pencil lines drawn diagonally across them. Turn the ball that will form the foot (Fig. 6-14A), but leave the wood above that square, except for a narrow part against the ball. There can be a small cylindrical projection below the ball. For the sake of uniformity, it will probably be best to complete all four legs to this stage before doing more work on the first leg.

On one diagonal line at the foot mark another center (Fig. 6-14B). The distance this center is from the main center will control the amount of offset taper the leg will get — ¼ inch may give you a pleasing taper. You may find it worthwhile to turn a piece of scrap wood first, to see how the taper is produced and to judge if it will suit the legs you

want. If you move the center too far, the leg will become very slim above the ball, and the wood may be weakened. If you do not move the center enough the shaping will not be very obvious.

With the tailstock center in the new position, turn the part above the ball (Fig. 6-14C). The wood will be rotating out of true; so work carefully at first with a gouge to rough it to shape, or you may split wood from the angles. Stop and examine the work frequently as cuts progress. You cannot judge the shape easily while the wood is rotating, as you can with a symmetrical shape.

The top of the leg remains symmetrically centered at the headstock end, so you will find the taper blends from the offset shape above the ball to the square top (Figs. 6-14D and 6-15A).

The rails are central both ways in relation to the legs (Fig. 6-15B), but the tenons are cut toward

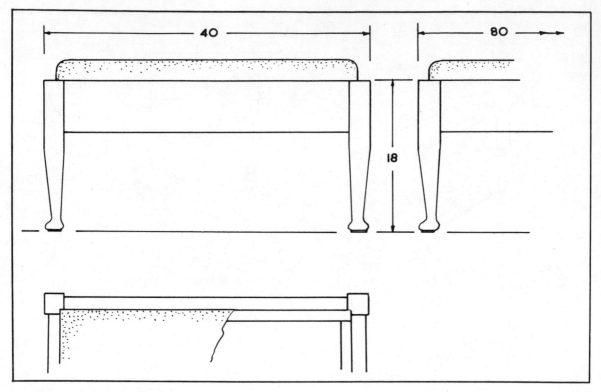

Fig. 6-13. Divan bed with club feet.

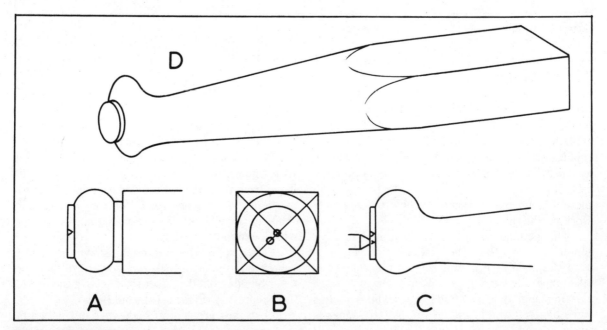

Fig. 6-14. Method of turning a club foot.

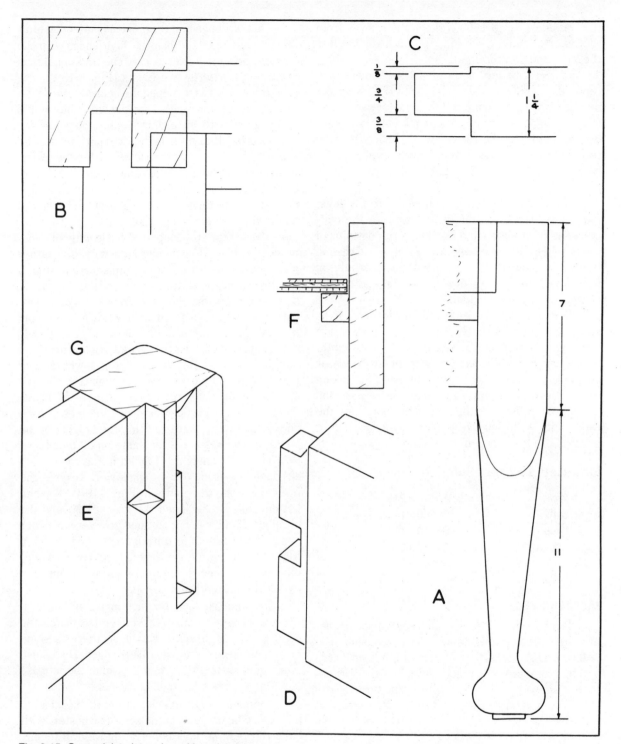

Fig. 6-15. Corner joints into a leg with a club foot.

the outside (Fig. 6-15C) to keep them away from the inner corner, which must be cut away to clear the plywood and the mattress.

Prepare the legs and rails for the mortise and tenon joints (Fig. 6-15D). Cut down the inner corners level with the insides of the rails for two inches (Fig. 6-15E). This will be the depth of the supports on the insides of the rails (Fig. 6-15F). When the tops of the legs have been cut down level with the rails, round the outer angles and corners (Fig. 6-15G).

After the rails have been joined to the legs, glue and screw the supporting strips for the mattress inside the rails and level with the bottoms of the notches cut in the legs. Make a plywood base to fit loosely inside the framework. Drill a few holes in it to allow air to pass through as the mattress is compressed and expanded.

If an attractive wood has been used, the divan can be given a clear finish. An alternative is to leave the legs exposed and cover the rails with cloth, which can match the covering of the mattress or cushion. Use cloth over thin foam padding, taking the cloth over the top edge into the recess, and turning the other edge up behind the bottom of the rail. Nails with decorative heads can be used at intervals to give the effect of buttoning.

## Materials List for Club Foot Divan

| | |
|---|---|
| 4 legs | 2½×20×2½ |
| 2 rails | 6×80×1¼ |
| 2 rails | 6×40×1¼ |
| 2 supports | 1×80×1 |
| 2 supports | 1×40×1 |
| 1 base | 36×78×½ plywood |

## JACOBEAN BED

Jacobean furniture was almost all made of oak, although other available woods were used. The beds were characterized by fairly high headboards and by footboards not much lower, but the particular feature was the use of turnings. The turned parts were often arranged with a twist, but where that extra work was to be avoided a series of bulbous shapes gave a similar effect.

This Jacobean bed (Fig. 6-16) is intended for a 36-inch mattress and has the high ends, with the legs turned simply (Fig. 6-17). The traditional type of turning has screwlike twists (Fig. 6-18A). The direction of the twist is opposite at each side. Twist turning can be done with a special lathe, but, if it is to be done with an ordinary lathe, most of the tooling is hand carving. The turned portion must be shaped to a cylinder, then marked for the twist, which is carved with gouges and sanded. The other form (Fig. 6-18B) can be turned completely by normal lathework techniques. It is assumed you will follow this design.

The legs are too long to be made without joints in most lathes. Dowels can be arranged at either place where the leg changes from square to round. It will probably be better to make the joint above the square portion, but with the dowel on the square part (Fig. 6-19A) to avoid drilling down into a mortise. When turning the legs, cut cleanly at the ends of the square pieces and be careful to avoid breaking out the corners. Round the corners where they meet the round parts. The rear legs (Fig. 6-18C) extend higher, but the front legs (Fig. 6-18D) have the same lower parts. Make sure the legs at each end are matching pairs and that the heights of the joints for the sides are the same on all four legs.

The bed panels are framed in the same way, although the front one is shallower. Groove the framing to take the plywood (Fig. 6-19B). Top and bottom rails do not need the grooves beyond the uprights. If you can cut stopped grooves with your equipment, make them only as far as needed. If you can only plow a groove in the full length of the wood, glue in short pieces where the grooves come between the uprights and the legs.

Use mortise and tenon joints (Fig. 6-19C). Choose plywood with face veneers to match the solid wood, if possible. Cut it so there is some clearance at the bottoms of the grooves. Do not use much glue around the panel, but glue the mortise and tenon joints thoroughly.

The main rails and sides are of the usual sort. Joints may be made as in the semi-fourposter, with bolts through the legs penetrating the rail tenons

Fig. 6-16. A Jacobean bed.

(Fig. 6-12) and bed irons or strips of wood support-ing a box mattress.

The panels are decorated with half-turning glued on. The two pieces (Fig. 6-18E) can be turned as one fully round part and divided. Prepare the wood as two pieces glued together with paper in the joint (Fig. 6-19D). Turn it to the shape you want in the usual way, then split the pieces apart along the paper line with a knife and sand off level the remains of the paper.

Assemble one end and follow with the other over it to match and square the ends.

## Materials List for Jacobean Bed

| | |
|---|---|
| 2 rear legs | 2×44×2 |
| 2 front legs | 2×39×2 |
| 4 rails | 2×38×1 |
| 2 rails | 2×17×1 |
| 2 rails | 2×14×1 |
| 2 rails | 4×79×1½ |
| 2 rails | 4×39×1½ |
| 1 panel | 14×33×¼ plywood |
| 1 panel | 11×33×¼ plywood |

## SOFTWOOD-TURNED BED

If pine or other softwood is to be used for making a bed with turned parts, the sections must be larger than when hardwood is used. The turned parts must be given a fairly bold treatment, so there are no fine details that might break away, either during lathework or in subsequent use.

This softwood-turned bed (Fig 6-20) has sizes that suit a 48-inch mattress. The end panels are fairly open, with a central flat splat and four turned

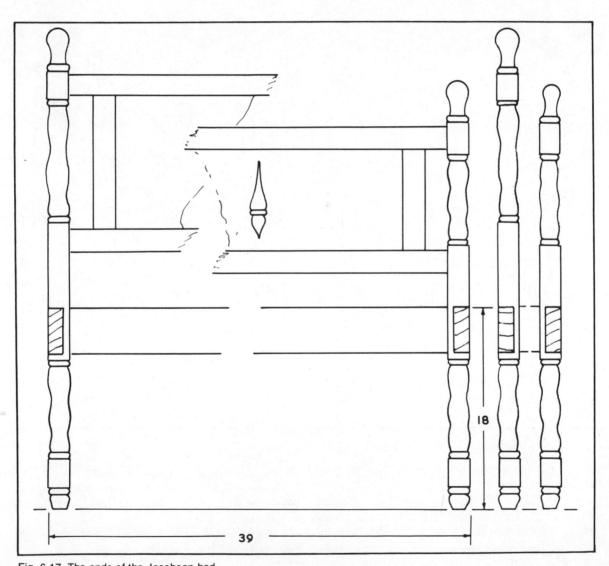

Fig. 6-17. The ends of the Jacobean bed.

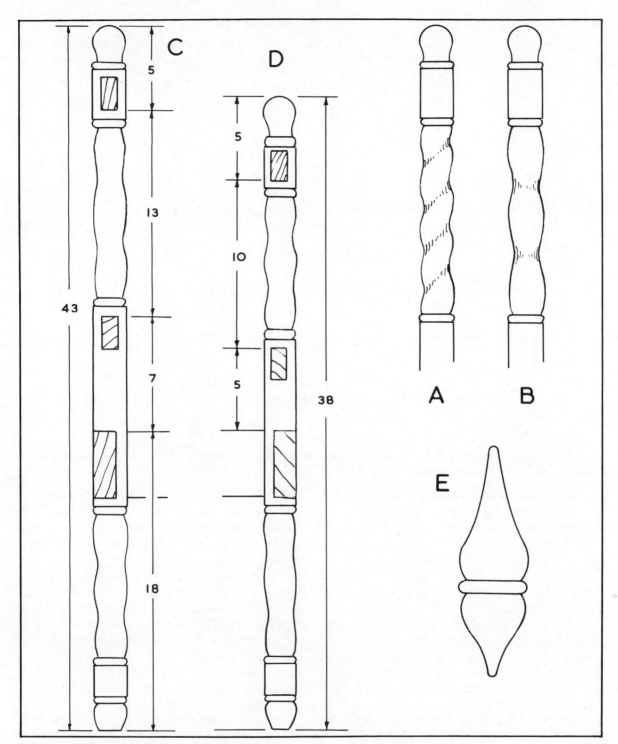

Fig. 6-18. Turning details of the Jacobean bed parts.

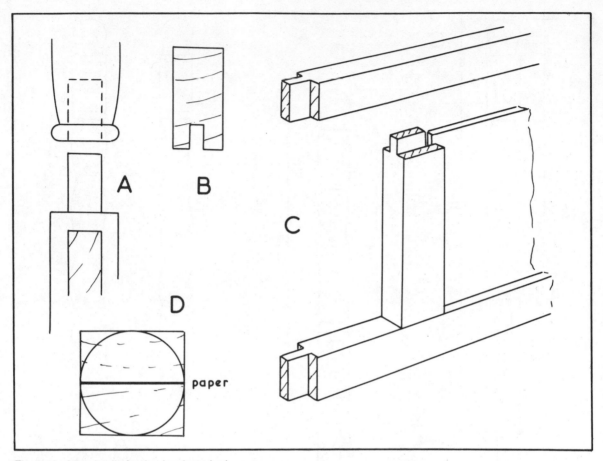

Fig. 6-19. Joint details for the Jacobean bed.

spindles at each end. The head is higher and the foot pattern rises from the main foot rail (Fig. 6-21). It is suggested that you complete the bed with a slat base, but you could use one of the other methods of supporting a mattress if you wish.

Except for the ends of the legs, the turned parts can be all the same size in their shaped sections, so if you mark out carefully, you can use a template (Fig. 6-22A) for the spindles and the legs, although they are different diameters. If you prefer to work freehand, make a rod, to get equal distances. The ½-inch beads in softwood are thicker than would be normal in hardwood, and the other curves are sweeping rather than tight.

The front legs (Fig. 6-22B) may just go between the centers of one of the common lathes. If the rear legs (Fig. 6-22C) are too long, you can

make them in parts, with dowels extending from the square sections into a turned section, as described for some previous beds. Mark the pairs of legs together and get the rail and side heights the same on all four legs.

Turn the matching sections to the template. At the bottom of each leg the shape is like a thick bead. Make the bottom flat and keep it large enough to take a caster. The hollow for the tailstock center can be left since it will provide a location for the caster. At the top of each leg, turn a bead next to the square part, then make a shallow knob above it. A slight pear shape going to a point at the top will loop better than spherical or elliptical curve.

Check the distances between the rails at both ends on the legs, and turn the spindles to match (Fig. 6-22D), allowing for a short parallel piece at

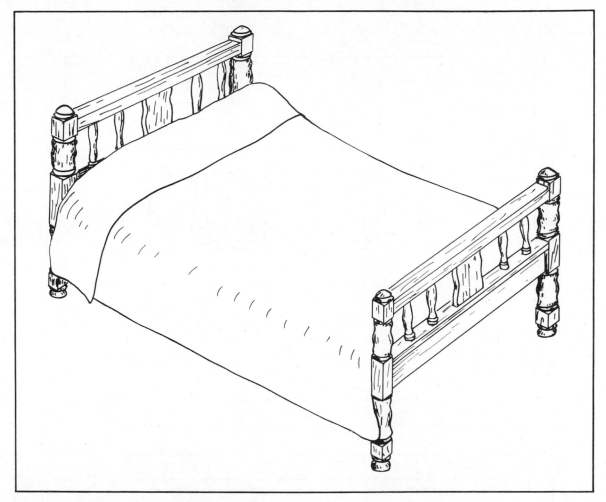

Fig. 6-20. A turned bed made of softwood.

each end and dowels ½ inch long. You can make the splats at the same time (Fig. 6-23A). The distance between shoulders should match the spindles. The outlines of the edges may be cut to similar curves and rounded in sections. The ends are most simply joined to the rails with dowels (Fig. 6-23B), although you can cut short tenons (Fig. 6-23C).

The main rails join to the legs with double tenons (Fig. 6-23D). If the sides will be bolted, take the mortises more than halfway through the legs, so the bolt holes will pass through these tenons. The 3-inch rails may have single (Fig. 6-23E) or twin tenons (Fig. 6-23F). The thin rail that crosses above the main rail at the foot may be doweled into

the legs (Fig. 6-23G) and glued to the main rail. That rail and the 3-inch rails will need to be drilled and mortised for the parts that fit between them (Fig. 6-23H).

Whatever method of attachment is used to join the sides to the legs, it helps to give them shallow stub tenons (Fig. 6-24A) for location and for prevention of twisting. Put strips on the sides to support the slats (Fig. 6-24B), which will be spaced evenly along the bed and may be held with single screws at the ends (Fig. 6-24C).

If you bolt the sides to the legs, use two ⅜- or ½-inch bolts going into nuts let into mortises (Fig. 6-24D). Alternatively, you can use two metal shelf

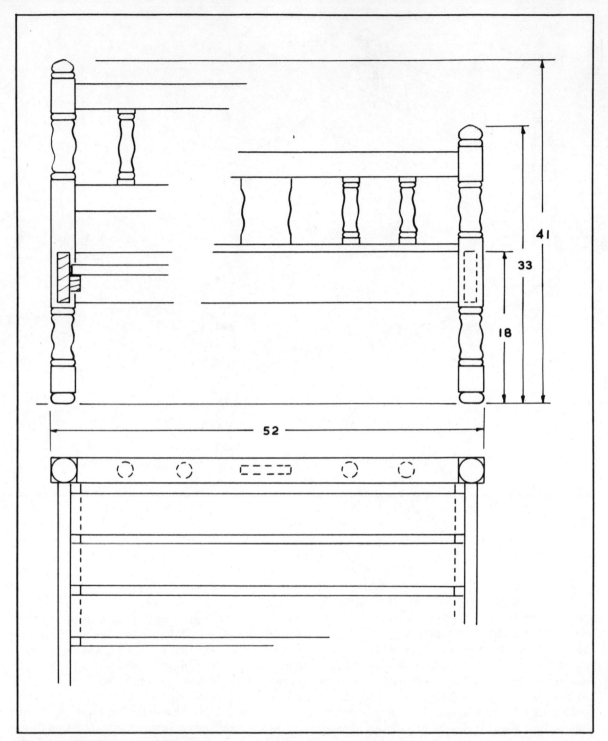

Fig. 6-21. Sizes for the softwood turned bed.

134

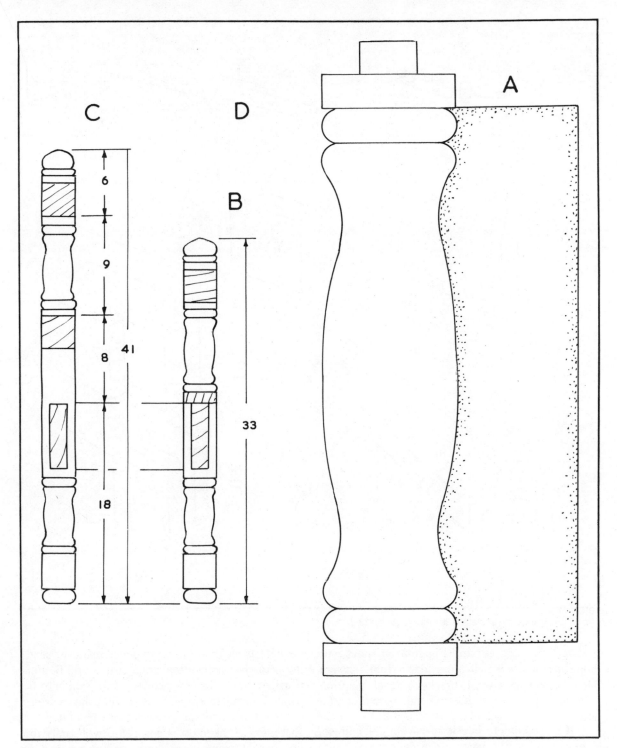

Fig. 6-22. Turned parts of the softwood bed.

135

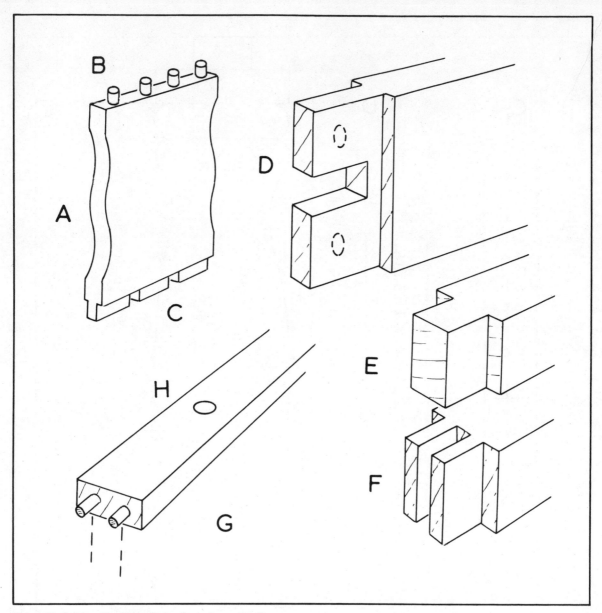

Fig. 6-23. Splat and rail details for the softwood bed.

brackets, at each corner (Fig. 6-24E), held with wood screws or small bolts taken right through. There could be a wood bracket in each position, joined permanently to its side and taken around to screw or bolt to the end rail (Fig. 6-24F).

If the complete bed is to have a clear finish, plane and sand the parts clean before assembly, paying particular attention to pencil marks or sanding scratches across the grain that would be emphasized by varnish or lacquer. If the bed is to be painted, pencil marks and minor blemishes may not matter, but make sure surfaces are level and the sharpness is taken off edges before you apply the first coat of paint.

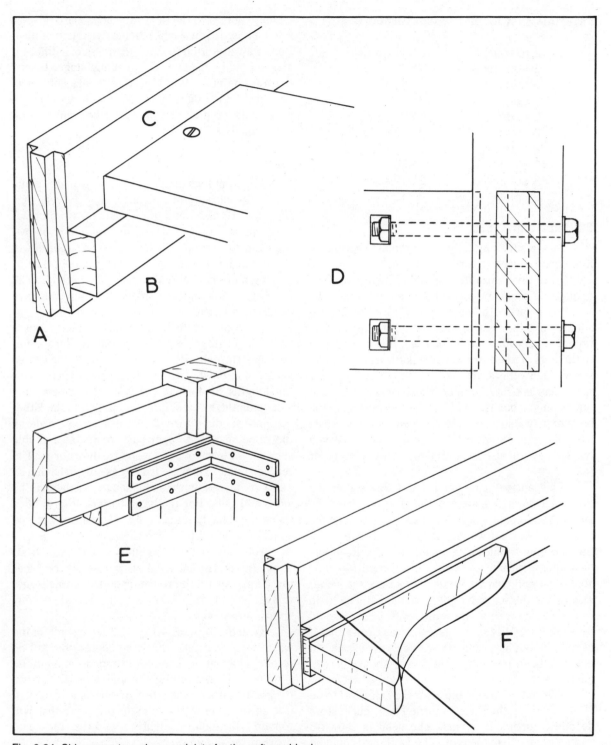

Fig. 6-24. Side supports and corner joints for the softwood bed.

## Materials List for Softwood-Turned Bed

| | |
|---|---|
| 2 rear legs | 3×43×3 |
| 2 front legs | 3×35×3 |
| 3 rails | 3×52×3 |
| 1 rail | 3×52×1 |
| 2 rails | 6×52×1½ |
| 2 sides | 6×79×1½ |
| 2 sides | 2×79×1 |
| 13 slats | 5×50×1¼ |
| 8 spindles | 2×12×2 |
| 2 splats | 6×12×1 |

## SQUARE-TURNED BED

Besides making fully turned round sections, a lathe can be used to form parts which are rounded enough to give a profile, but which have not taken enough off a square piece to be a full circle. The result is a part with four flats left from the original square and the rest of the section rounded. The technique is called *square turning*. It is appropriate to the legs of a bed where some parts are made fully square and others are square-turned so elliptical flat areas appear. Outside these areas there are fully rounded beads. Knobs at the top and feet at the bottom may also have fully rounded sections. Apart from the decorative effect of the flats on curved parts, they can also take mortises conveniently for rails.

This square-turned bed (Fig. 6-25) is intended to suit a 36-inch mattress that fits between the sides. Sections of wood listed are intended for fir, pine, or other softwoods. If hardwoods are used, the sections should be reduced slightly. Each end has square-turned legs and fully turned top rails above flat end boards. Head and foot are the same, except for the extra height at the head. The main rails and sides are at the same level. There should be enough rigidity in the assembly as drawn, but if extra stiffness across the head seems necessary, an extra rail can be fit into the lower square part of each rear leg.

The overall sizes allow for the rail level to be 16 inches from the floor on turned feet, but casters do add a further 2 inches. The head is shown 6 inches higher than the foot. The footboard could be lowered almost to the rail or the headboard raised a few inches, if you wish. Obviously, this modification or an alteration to suit a mattress of a different size should be made at the planning stage. If your mattress is not a box type that would only need support at the edges, you can modify the base to have slats or plywood, as described for several earlier beds.

## Legs

The front legs (Fig. 6-26A) will probably come within the capacity of your lathe, but the rear legs (Fig. 6-26B) may need to be made in two parts. A joint can be arranged above, or preferably, below, the main square part, with a 1-inch or larger dowel about 2 inches long from one part into the other. It may be more convenient to use this method on all four legs, reducing the tendency to whip and leave chatter marks on the wood.

The stock for the legs should be exactly square and straight, then centered accurately. This is important if the exposed square sections on the turned parts are to finish with a uniform appearance. Mark the lengths of the parts that are to remain fully square on the wood before mounting it in the lathe. The intermediate turned sections can be made all the same, with the upper part treated as a double section; so mark out the wood to allow for it. The rear legs differ from the front legs only in having an extra six inches on the main square part above the sides and rails. For the basic pattern (Fig. 6-26C) there is probably no need for a template, but you should use a rod to match the parts.

You should turn the fully round parts first, although you can take the sharpness off the other turned parts with the roughing gouge at this stage, to avoid knocking corners with a tool and possibly splitting the wood.

Turn the top knobs (Fig. 6-26D), except for the waste ends that take the lathe center and will be turned away later. The feet are made in a similar way, but with flat or slightly hollow ends. Turn all the beads, either completely or very nearly to size. Cut squarely in at the ends of the parts that will remain fully square. Slightly round the corners to prevent breaking out.

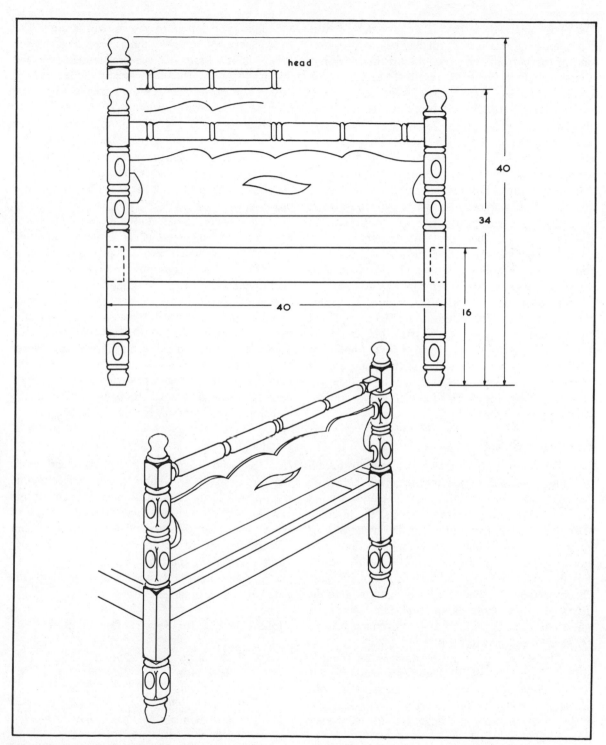

head

40

34

40

16

Fig. 6-25. A square-turned bed.

Turn one section that is to have flats. If you have not done this sort of turning before, work on one of the bottoms of a leg, then if that does not shape exactly as you wish, it will not be very obvious in the finished bed. Round down at the ends to the beads, then turn off the corners between. Stop the lathe and examine the appearance. What you will get is a flat on all four sides that is like an ellipse with flattened long sides. If you turn off more, the ellipse gets narrower. Obviously, if you turn off too much, the ellipse will disappear.

On this first experimental part, you must judge how much to turn off to get a shape that you find pleasing. You can then turn the other sections the same amount. Calipers will help you check how much to take off, but you will need to stop the lathe occasionally to compare different parts.

Sanding while the lathe is rotating tends to blur the edges of the flat elliptical surfaces. You will need to do some sanding in the lathe, but, when you have finished the lathework, use a finely set smoothing plane to take a thin shaving off each flat surface. The sharpness of the outline will be restored, giving the work the distinctive square-turning appearance.

### Bed Head and Foot

The top rails are shown turned fully round, although it would be possible to make them with squared faces to match the legs. The ends are left square and have tenons into the legs (Fig. 6-26E). Although the length might just go into your lathe, it may be simpler to make each rail in sections with dowel joints. You could divide at the center beads, but it may be simpler and stronger to divide into three parts at the other beads. When you glue the parts together, sight along to check straightness and to see that the square ends match and are not twisted in relation to each other.

The main rails could be doweled or tenoned into the legs (Fig. 6-12). The sides could be given stub tenons, for locating, in readiness for bolts through to nuts set into mortises. Alternatively, use special hardware or bracket the sides to the end assemblies.

The two boards are shown with straight bottoms, shaped top edges, and a pierced decoration (Fig. 6-27A). Mark out the end tenons first and match them to mortises marked on the legs. If the turned parts are not exactly as drawn, adjust the mortise and tenon spacing to suit. Tenons are shown fairly thick (Fig. 6-27B) since the legs are much thicker than the boards. Make a template for half the shape of the top or cut the outline halfway on one board and use it to mark the other board, which can then be used to mark the other half of the first piece.

Decoration at the center of the end boards breaks up the plainness of the grain of softwood. You might add some carving or pierce an initial or other design, but the simple motive shown has a traditional basis. Draw its outline (Fig. 6-27C). The halves are the same, so you can use a template for one side and use it the other way, without turning over. The ends of the cutout should go to fine points. Do not try to turn your piercing saw there. Drill for entry of the saw near the center of the pattern, then cut toward the ends, backing to the center after each cut, so the points of the design remain fine.

### Finishing

Take the sharpness off the edges and check that no saw marks are visible, particularly along the top edges. Clean up all the parts by planing and sanding before assembly, especially if the bed is to be given a clear finish. Pull all joints tight, but spread the load of clamps with strips of smooth scrap wood along the legs

Arrange angle bed irons or put strips inside the sides and ends to support the mattress.

### Materials List for Square-Turned Bed

| | |
|---|---|
| 2 rear legs | 2½×42×2½ |
| 2 front legs | 2½×36×2½ |
| 2 main rails | 4×38×2 |
| 2 turned rails | 2×38×2 |
| 2 end boards | 7½×38×1 |
| 2 sides | 4×79×2 |

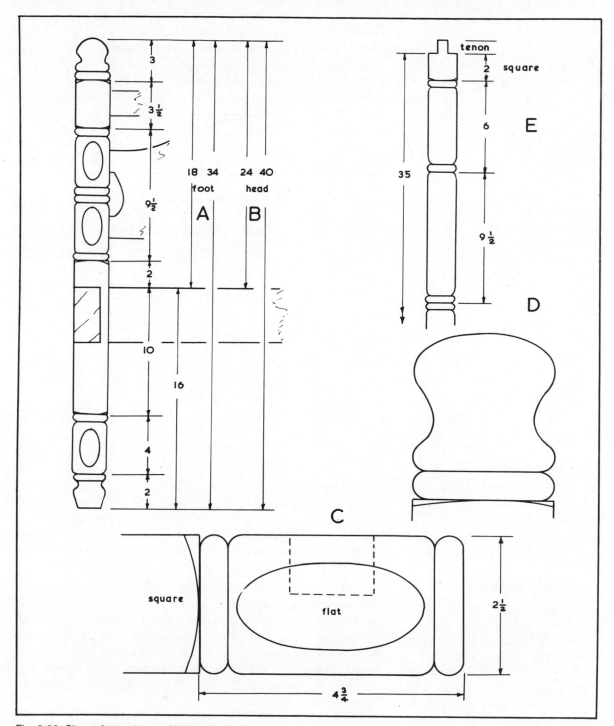

Fig. 6-26. Sizes of turned parts for the square-turned bed.

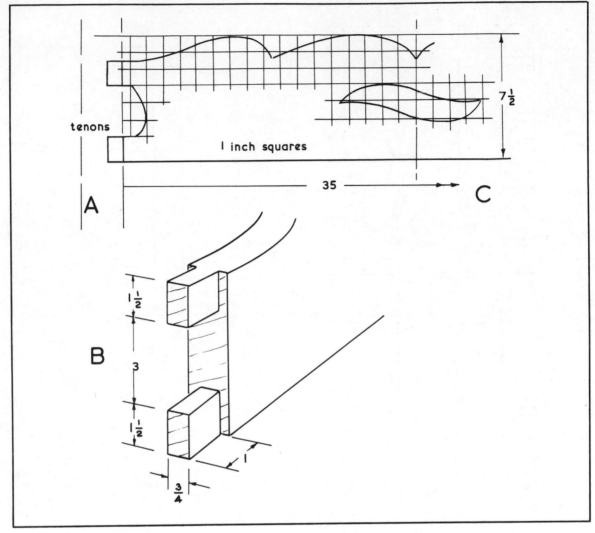

Fig. 6-27. Shape and joints of the end boards for the square-turned bed.

## LOW-FOOT TURNED BED

In most beds with turned parts, the legs extend above the mattress level at the foot. A bed can be made to allow the covering to drape over the foot as well as the sides, so only the head displays the woodturner's skill. This low-foot turned bed (Fig. 6-28) is intended to be made of softwood and will take a 36-inch mattress on slats between the sides. Details can be altered in the ways described for other beds. Sections can be reduced if hardwood is used.

The bed head has spindles which fit into a top rail and the main rail (Fig. 6-29A), instead of into the second rail often used. If you wish to make the bed head higher or arrange the spindles to be more visible above pillows, you can put a gap above the main rail for another, shallower, rail to take the spindles. The rear legs will need to be correspondingly higher.

At the foot, joints are strengthened if the legs go above the rails. They are shown carried up to form knobs 2 inches above the rail level (Fig.

Fig. 6-28. A turned bed with a low foot.

6-29B). The knobs are no higher than the usual mattress, so they will not affect the arrangement of bed coverings. Check the overall sizes of the mattress before cutting wood to size, so it will drop easily into place.

Set out the wood for the rear legs (Fig. 6-29C) and the front legs (Fig. 6-30A). The square parts that enclose joints extend ½ inch above and below other parts. The rail joints are mortise and tenon, cut down slightly to leave more end grain at the mortises (Fig. 6-31A). They could be doweled instead. The sides may have stub tenons for location (Fig. 6-31B) and bolts through to nuts in mortises, as described for earlier beds. Mark out the joints and the limits of the square parts of the legs, before doing any turning. See that the heights of the mattress framing are the same on all legs and the marks on the rear legs are properly paired.

The turned parts should be cut straight in at the ends of the square parts, then these ends rounded. Rough the parts between to cylindrical shapes with a gouge before penciling the positions of beads. Cut wide beads. Do not go in too deeply beside them or very deeply between them as you sweep curves. Most lathes will take the full length of a rear leg, but if not, there can be dowel joints above or below the part with the main rail joints,

preferably with a dowel projecting from the square piece. Turn the bottoms of the legs slightly hollow and leave them a suitable size to take a glide or a caster, if you wish to fit either. The tops of the front legs are like large beads, but at the rear legs they are higher knobs.

The spindles (Fig. 6-30B) are straightforward, but be careful to get the bead at the same position on the whole set, or variations will show in the assembly. One alternative to help prevent you from placing the spindles upside-down is to deliberately make the bead above center, which looks better than below center. Another variation has the beads at different heights, so the bead on the center spindle is higher than those at the sides, with an arc in their locations that carries through the theme of the curve of the top rail.

The top rail is shown with a curved decoration (Fig. 6-30C) and tenons into the legs. Mark and cut the shape symmetrical about the centerline. That edge will be the most prominent part in the complete bed, so finish it smoothly and with slightly rounded edges.

Mark the holes in the head rails together and take care not to turn either end-for-end after marking. Allow for the spindles to go about 1 inch into each piece (Fig. 6-30D). If the holes are slightly too

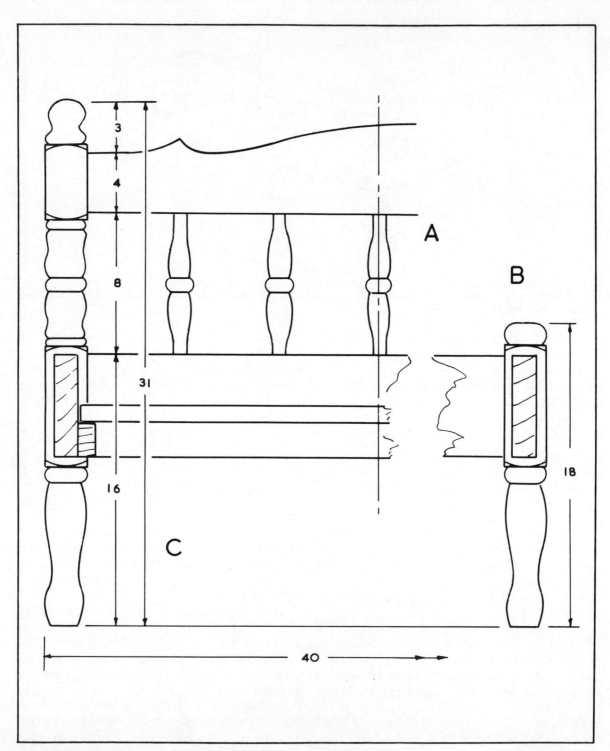

Fig. 6-29. Sizes of the end of the low-foot turned bed.

144

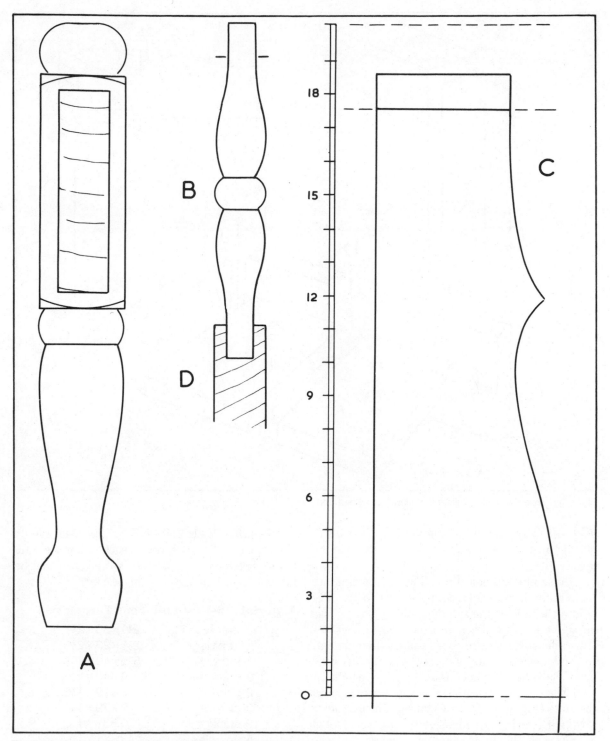

Fig. 6-30. Leg, spindle, and rail sizes for the low-foot turned bed.

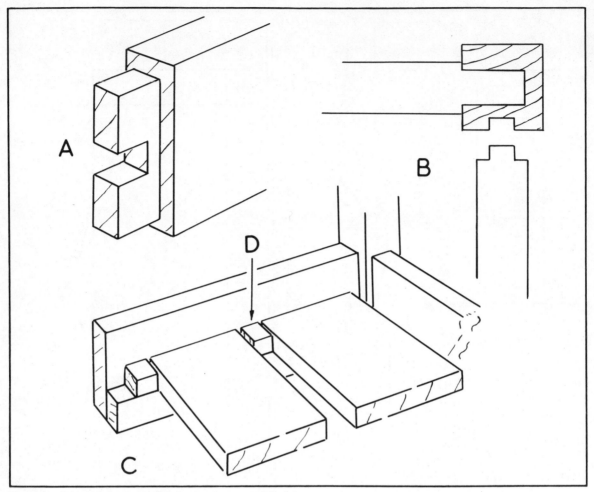

Fig. 6-31. Side and slat details for the low-foot turned bed.

deep you can adjust the spindles during assembly to get the beads in the correct relation to those of the legs.

Assemble the head first. Glue the spindles into their holes in the rails. Join the rails to the legs before the glue on the spindles has set, so they can be moved up or down if necessary. Check for squareness and lack of twist and let the glue set. Assemble the foot in its correct position over the head assembly, to check that the parts match.

Make the sides with strips attached to support the slats (Fig. 6-31C). The strips inside are shown level with the bottom edges of the wide boards, but if you wish the mattress to be higher than the framing, they can be raised. Space the slats evenly along the bed. Place a screw in each end or use little blocks between (Fig. 6-31D), so the slats can be lifted out, making disassembly easier.

## Materials List for Low-Foot Turned Bed

| | |
|---|---|
| 2 rear legs | 2½×33×2½ |
| 2 front legs | 2½×20×2½ |
| 1 top rail | 5½×40×1½ |
| 2 main rails | 6×40×1½ |
| 2 sides | 6×79×1½ |
| 2 sides | 2×79×1 |
| 12 slats | 5×38×1 |
| 5 spindles | 1½×11×1½ |

# Chapter 7

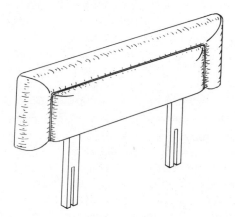

# Special Bed Heads

With the move today from beds with high headboards and only slightly lower footboards, coupled with the change in the methods of providing bed padding, has come a tendency to make the headboard be the design feature of the bed, usually without a footboard projecting above the level of the bedding.

More beds are made with a solid support for a mattress which itself gives all the resilience needed without a flexible support below. This design is seen in many variations of the inverted box form of the bed described in Chapter 5.

Such beds have the covering draped across the foot as well as the sides, so none of the structure of the bed shows. The only opportunity to provide decoration is at the head, where all kinds of finishes and decorations may be tried. An individual can show his own design ideas and personalize the bed head. Although you may not often recline against a bed head without pillows or cushions, an upholstered bed head gives a sense of luxury and comfort.

The bed head does not have to be attached permanently to the bed; so it can be changed if you change the decor or move the bed to a room where a different head would be more appropriate. If the bed is made with legs extending upward to support the headboard, a special head can be attached. Most of these headboards, however, are better temporarily attached with screwed uprights or adjustable posts, or attached to the wall without any connection to the bed.

## SIMPLE UPHOLSTERED HEADBOARDS

A headboard can be made to appear more deeply padded than it actually is. It is this appearance, rather than actual comfort, that is the intention, since it is rare for anyone to want to rest with much weight against the headboard alone.

The simplest form is a plain rectangle of ½-inch plywood, over which is placed a layer of foam not more than 1-inch thick and probably only half that. It is then covered with cloth. On a shape with straightedges you do not need to stretch the cloth to conform, as you do with elaborate outlines; so almost any cloth can be used. It could be a woven fabric. The more open weaves show more tendency to stretch than tightly woven cloth, but in this case, either will do. Some leather-like plastic-coated fabrics are available in bright colors and white, as well as those browns and greys of automobile seats. Any of these fabrics can be used. Some have very little stretch, which might make them difficult to form over a complicated shape, but, for a straight-edged board, stretch does not matter.

### Upholstering

Take the sharpness off the plywood headboard edges and corners. You could give the edges a full rounding, but leaving them square is usually satisfactory. Cut the foam slightly too big. Fitting is easier if the foam is held to the wood with adhesive, which need not be spread all over, but could be applied in strips around the edges. The adhesive prevents the foam from slipping down later. Make sure the adhesive is suitable for the foam. The solvents in some adhesives will attack some plastic foam materials.

If a patterned material is chosen, you will need to arrange the cloth so it will have a symmetrical appearance. A large, prominent pattern may look good, but could result in wasteful cutting to make it look right on the headboard. In any case, arrange the lines of the weave—the *weft* and *warp*—parallel with the edges of the headboard.

Use staples or tacks driven into the back of the board to hold the cloth. With most cloth you should turn the cut edge under to prevent fraying (Fig. 7-1A). Keep the tacks far enough from the edge to leave space for a second row into the rear covering cloth (Fig. 7-1B). Tack along a top or bottom edge at a close enough spacing to stretch the cloth evenly—probably at about 1½-inch intervals. Go to the other long edge and start near the middle of it to stretch and tack similarly, working out towards both corners (Fig. 7-1C). Try to keep an even tension, pulling just enough to round the edges of the padding. On both edges go to about 3 inches of the corners.

Work similarly along the shorter sides. A small amount of cloth will be slack at each corner. Try pulling the cloth at a corner to get an even appearance at the front. Drive in more tacks to keep this neat appearance. Much depends on the cloth. With soft, flexible cloth you can probably pull at the back and fold the surplus to drive tacks through. With stiffer material, such as some plastic-coated fabrics, you may need to cut darts in the edge at the back to get the material to settle smoothly at the front. Remember that it is the front appearance that matters. When you have found a method that succeeds at one corner, treat the other corners in the same way to get an even appearance.

Plastic-coated fabric does not need to be turned under at the back. Instead, you can leave it flat and cut parallel with the edge after covering (Fig. 7-1D). Another piece of similar material can be tacked over it, without turning in (Fig. 7-1E). Woven cloth should be turned under (Fig. 7-1F). Cut across the corners if you are turning cloth under, to reduce the bulk there (Fig. 7-1G).

The simple headboard can be given a buttoned appearance with decorative nails arranged in a pattern (Fig. 7-2A). Measure and drive carefully, since nails out of line will be very obvious.

### Framing

The headboard could also be framed. You could use a narrow strip with a beaded edge nailed on. Miter the corners (Fig. 7-2B). It will be best to cut these strips and check that they will fit, then stain and varnish or polish them before attaching them. It may be best to frame all around, but the bottom edge of the headboard is usually hidden by pillows, so you could omit an edge strip there.

Wider framing might be more effective, and look more like a picture frame than a narrow strip. The frame could be slightly deeper than it is thick (Fig. 7-2C). Counterbored and plugged screws would have a better grip than nails (Fig. 7-2D). If an even wider frame is needed, it is better to attach it to another piece of plywood going behind the main piece (Fig. 7-2E). You can then use molding, even picture-frame molding with the rabbet fitting over the upholstery (Fig. 7-2F).

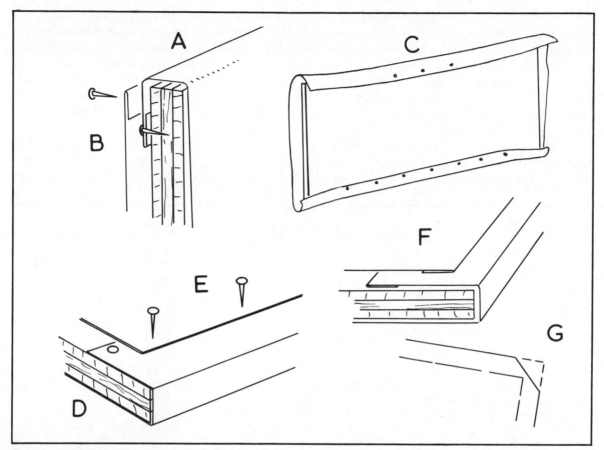

Fig. 7-1. Upholstering over a plywood headboard.

## Hanging

If the headboard is to be attached to the wall instead of the bed, it will not need cloth on the rear surface. It should be hung in some way to hide the rear. You may be able to use screws with screw-in domes (Fig. 7-3A) in two positions, and nails elsewhere. In a small bed head it may be sufficient to just have two of these screws as the only apparent buttoning.

Another method of fitting is with keyhole plates behind the edges of the headboard. One at each side should be sufficient. In a simple form the plate has a large hole to pass over the screw head and a slot to slide over its neck, with holes for small screws to go into the plywood. Drill into the plywood to provide clearance. Fit the plates with the slots upward. The bed head can then be hung on

two screws driven into the wall with their heads projecting slightly (Fig. 7-3B).

If the plywood is too thin to drill, you can use a plate that gives clearance on the surface, by making a piece of sheet metal with a double bend, or *joggle*. The amount of joggle should be just enough to give clearance for the screw head (Fig. 7-3C). If you use brass or aluminum less than 1/16-inch thick, you can hammer the double bend in a vise.

An attraction of the keyhole plate method of hanging is that no fasteners are visible, so no one is likely to lift the headboard off; yet you can remove it easily.

## CURVED UPHOLSTERED HEADBOARD

Thin upholstery on plywood can be made to follow a curved edge without much trouble, since the distortion of the cloth will be slight. A plain rectangular piece of plywood can be improved in appearance by rounding its corners, either to a small radius (Fig. 7-4A) or a much bigger curve (Fig. 7-4B). Cover the board the same as a plain rectangle by first getting an even tension as you tack at the back along the straightedges. Stop a few inches from the beginning of the curves. Manipulate the cloth at a curve by pulling over the back. Even with material which has little stretch you should be able to pull it to a smooth shape over the curve.

At the back you can probably crease and fold a thin, flexible material to tack through the folds (Fig. 7-4C). Do this evenly. Try to avoid gathering more at one part of the curve than another. With stiffer, plastic-coated fabric, you will not be able to fold, but you can cut darts toward the edge at an even spacing around the curve (Fig. 7-4D); then tack into each tab.

A common headboard arrangement has more than one curve. A large central curve meeting a smaller one on each side is often seen. The treat-

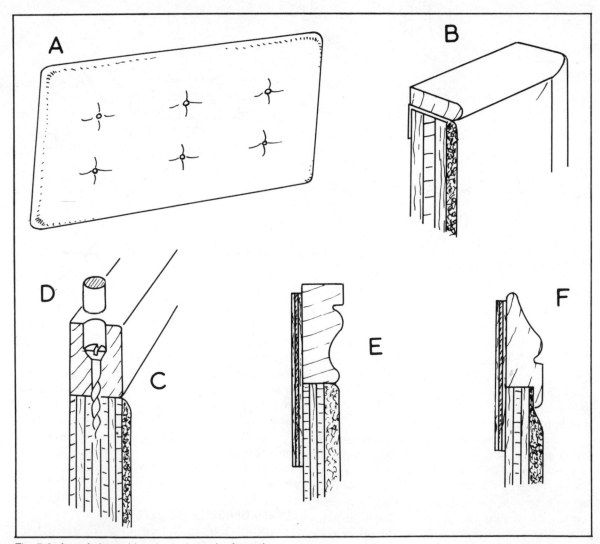

Fig. 7-2. An upholstered head panel may be framed.

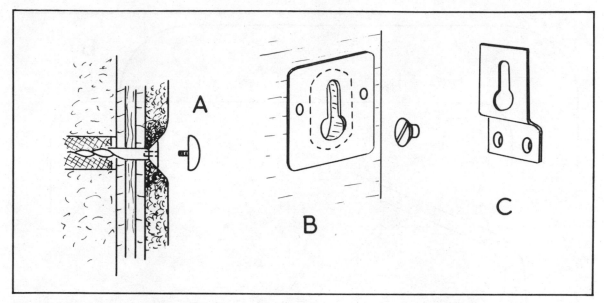

Fig. 7-3. A headboard may be screwed to or hung from a wall.

ment of this arrangement is very similar to that of a curved corner (Fig. 7-4E). Locate the covering cloth and tack on the straightedges. Get it over the curves with temporary tacks at the back, until you are satisfied that the pattern is even and the tension is about right. Usually you will start with a tack behind the center of the top, followed by others at fairly wide spaces out from there (Fig. 7-4F).

To get an even appearance you must give special attention to the places where the curves meet. Pull harder there. At the back, cut toward the meeting (Fig. 7-4G), but not right up to the edge. Tack each side of the cut and the cloth will settle to a good shape on the front. Around the curves you can fold and tack lighter cloth or cut darts at intervals into thicker and stiffer material.

If you put a piece of cloth on the back with edges turned under, the edge of thin cloth may crease underneath without becoming very bulky, but, if there is a tendency to finish too thick, cut darts into the edge before turning under.

There are many possible curved shapes that can be used (Fig. 7-5A). You can draw parts of circles. A semi-circle is often used, but parts of a circle are not considered as attractive as other curves. A semi-ellipse makes a good shape, par-

ticularly for a wide bed, where a semi-circle would go too high.

A simple way of drawing an ellipse uses two nails, a piece of string, and a pencil. Draw a line across to represent the major axis and another square to its center for the minor axis. These lines represent the intended limits of the curve in both directions. From the top of the minor axis measure half the length of the major axis diagonally to it and mark the positions both ways (Fig. 7-5B). Drive in the nails lightly at these points, which are your first centers for a curve. Tie the string in a loop that will go around the nails and stretch to the end of the major axis (Fig. 7-5C). Put your pencil in the end of this loop and start drawing a curve, keeping the string tensioned around the nails (Fig. 7-5D). You should get a semi-ellipse for the top of your bedhead.

If you are not satisfied with the first curve, you can make a higher one by moving the nails closer together and retieing the string in a new loop of the right length. If you want a curve that is not as high, move the nails further apart and adjust the loop size to suit. Of course, the ellipse does not have to go the full width of the plywood. It can blend into other, smaller curves at the sides (Fig. 7-5E).

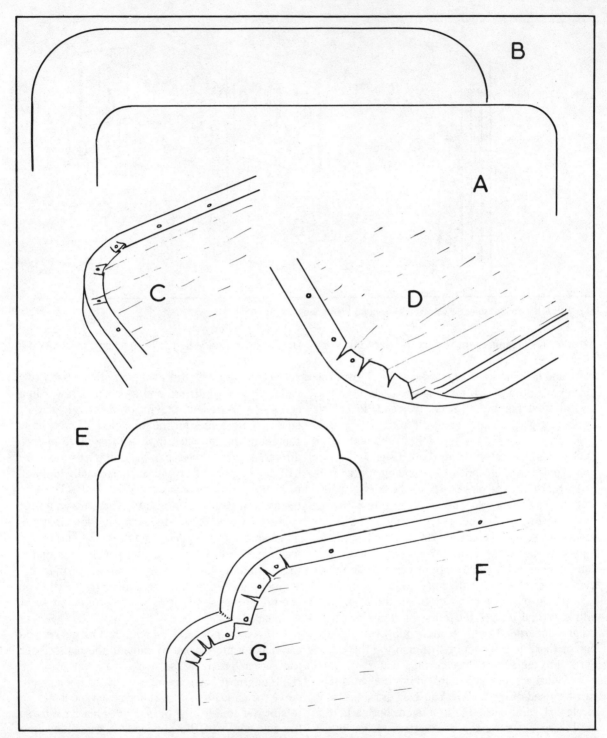

Fig. 7-4. Covering over a plywood headboard may be folded or cut at curves.

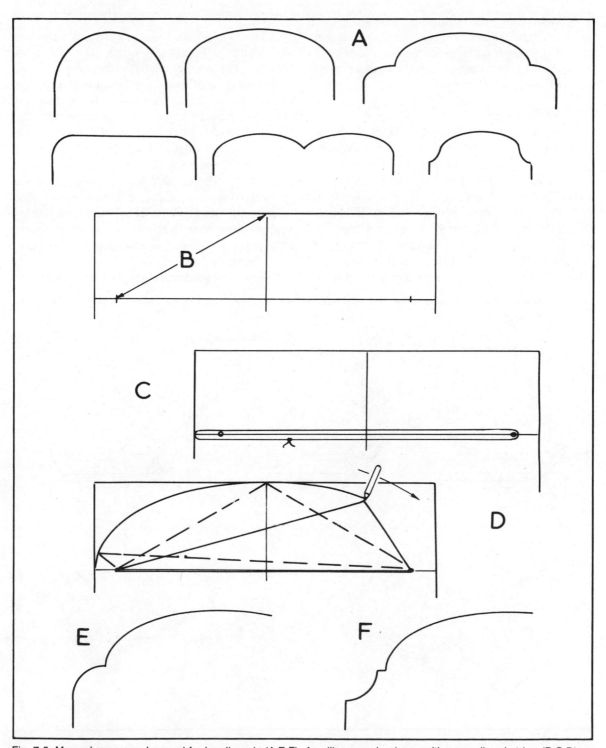

Fig. 7-5. Many shapes may be used for headboards (A,E,F). An ellipse can be drawn with a pencil and string (B,C,D).

Some plain wood outlines have curves divided by short, straight pieces (Fig. 7-5F). Upholstering over that shape is not impossible, but it is easier to join curves to other curves directly, so that dividing straight sections arc avoided.

## DEEP UPHOLSTERY

Foam padding up to 1-inch thick may be regarded as token upholstery. It is certainly softer than plain wood, but it cannot provide much comfort. Its object is mainly to give a luxurious appearance. Thicker padding may look even more luxurious, and it also provides real comfort. Rubber or plastic foam padding 2 or 3 inches thick would be suitable. In general, the method of covering is similar to that for thin foam, but there are some special considerations when using the thicker material.

The finished head looks best if the edges are well-rounded. To allow for this look, the foam should be cut to curve neatly. Merely compressing a square-cut edge would not produce an even and attractive curve. The foam should be cut squarely and slightly oversize. On the standard headboard, ¼ inch all around should do (Fig. 7-6A) for curved as well as straight edges. To make the foam curve properly, the underside of the edge is cut at an angle (Fig. 7-6B). The amount you cut depends on the particular foam—a dense, stiff foam would need more cut off than a softer piece. You may want to try a scrap piece first, but, for the usual upholstery foam, cutting at 45 degrees to about half the thickness should be satisfactory.

You could pull the foam to the curved edge with

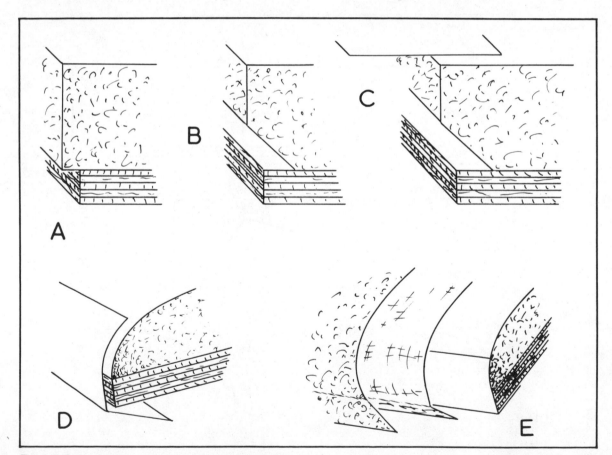

Fig. 7-6. Compress, cut, and pull to get a rounded edge.

the covering cloth, but it is easier to get an even edge if a strip is attached (Fig. 7-6C) and pulled to shape first (Fig. 7-6D). This strip could be cloth held with an adhesive, or you could use self-adhesive plastic strip. Once the covering is on, there should be no load on the strip or its adhesive. Pull the edges to shape and hold the strip behind the wood with more adhesive supplemented with tacks or staples.

If the covering material is to be fairly thick and closely woven, it can be put on directly over the foam. On some beds the head covering material chosen is the same as that used for the bedding, which is rather lighter than the usual upholstery material. In that case, the head should be covered with two layers. First put on a plain, light cloth (Fig. 7-6E) to hold the foam in shape and provide a base for the outer covering, so no unevenness or details of the foam show through. It is this first covering that gives shape to the upholstery; so take care to tension it evenly. You may need to experiment by moving tacks until you get a good appearance on the front.

Put on the outer covering with enough tension to keep it in shape without creases. If there is no inner covering, try to regulate the foam as you go. For curved edges, the method of tacking and cutting darts where necessary is the same as described for thinner upholstery. To a certain extent the greater thickness allows you more scope for stretching over a curve without excessive creasing. Slight creases around a curve may have to be accepted, and they can be treated as design features. However, if there are matching curves at opposite sides of a head, try to get similar patterns of creases in each place.

## BUTTONING

With thicker upholstery on a bed head, some buttoning is almost essential for the sake of appearance. Buttoning also prevents the foam from slipping down. The padding is too thick for nails to be used to simulate buttoning; so you should use buttons and twine as described in Chapter 3. On a plain rectangular headboard the buttons are best in rows—either a single row or two or three rows with

the buttons in vertical lines as well (Fig. 7-7A). You can also stagger the button positions (Fig. 7-7B). If the top of the head is curved, you will need to arrange buttons to suit (Fig. 7-7C). A fairly wide spacing of buttons should be sufficient, but there could be much closer buttoning, like the arrangement on a Chesterfield seat. Close buttoning is more appropriate to leather or a leather-like plastic than to patterned cloth.

Drill the board at the button positions before starting to cover. If the headboard is fairly large, it will be worthwhile to also drill a few larger holes for ventilation as the foam presses in and out. Use a long needle to poke through from the back to get the button position at the front, but be careful that these positions finish in line. You can use a plain button at the back. It would not push out the rear covering cloth much if it is left on the surface, but you could counterbore the plywood slightly to let it in (Fig. 7-7D). Otherwise, use a small dowel, preferably let into a groove (Fig. 7-7E). Knot and adjust the twine as described in Chapter 3, taking care to get a uniform appearance on the front.

The creases that result from the buttons pulling back may be all the decoration needed. You can manipulate them into an even pattern with the point of a needle or awl as you tighten the twine. With light fabric, another way of emphasizing the button pattern is to use a sewn seam between the button positions (Fig. 7-7F). You must prepare the cloth before fitting it, so marking out is important, and it must be located exactly. Pencil the seams on the underside of the cloth and sew through as close to a fold as possible (Fig. 7-7G). Open it out for the stitching to show on the front (Fig. 7-7H), making a crossing pattern between buttons.

## BORDERED UPHOLSTERED BED HEAD

A bed head in which a central panel of padding is bordered by more upholstery has a luxurious appearance as well as the practical advantage of helping to prevent pillows from slipping sideways. The central panel should usually have thinner padding than the border. Covering may be the same all-over, or the pattern of the border may be different from the panel to emphasize the framing effect.

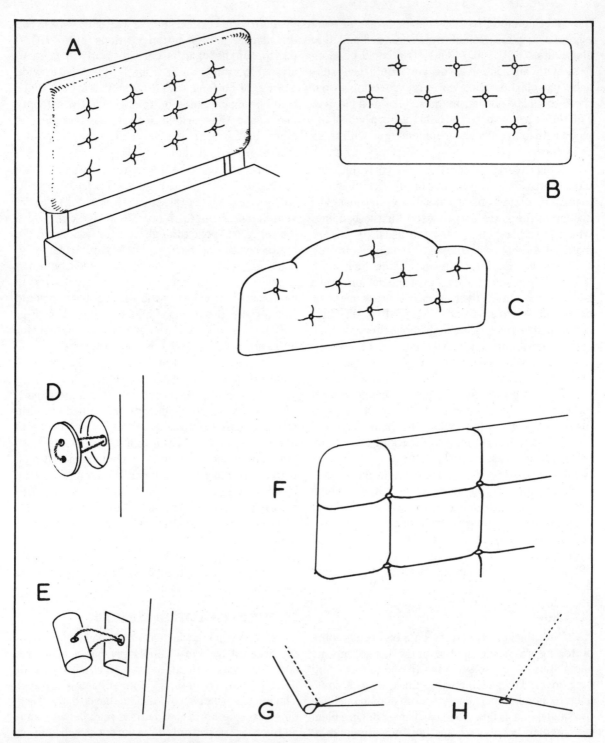

Fig. 7-7. Buttoning improves the appearance of a headboard.

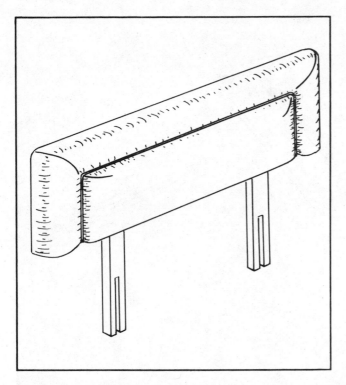

Fig. 7-8. Upholstery can be arranged to give a bordered effect on a bed head.

This bordered upholstered bed head (Fig. 7-8) is for a board with straight sides and rounded top corners, but similar arrangements could be used for a headboard with rounded edges. The border need not be carried across the bottom, since it will be hidden by pillows. For most beds the border can be between 4 and 6 inches wide. The thickness of the foam is not critical, but the central panel could be 1 inch, or up to 2 inches if you want more softening. The border should be about 1 inch thicker than the panel.

Mark the size of the panel on the board and cut the foam to match, with rounded top corners (Fig. 7-9A). If the foam is 1-inch or less thick, it can be left with square edges, but, to get a better curved edge on thicker foam, bevel underneath. Cover the foam with muslin or other thin, plain fabric, tacked fairly closely to hold down the foam edges (Fig. 7-9B). Check that the line of the edge of the padding is kept straight. Cover with the outside fabric. If you are covering with a closely woven, stout fabric or a plastic-coated fabric, you can probably omit the inner muslin. Check for straightness. Make sure

the panel edges are parallel with the outside edges of the board.

Tack piping over the tacked edges (Fig. 7-9C). It could be a matching design or a contrasting color to define the division between the parts of the upholstery. Stretch the piping so the covered cord makes a straight line close to the edge of the panel. Use one length of piping all around, and cut the curved corners with darts in the flat parts.

The border will be back-tacked over the edge of the piping, using strips of stout card about ½-inch wide (Fig. 7-9D), but first the strips of cloth that will make the border must be mitered and sewn together. Cut strips of cloth with ample width to allow for turning under the card and wrapping over the padding and the backboard. Fold under enough cloth to go under the card. Get the length along the fold to mark where the miters go. Also check along the outside edges of the headboard. Allow for turning under at the miters and sew the seams. Excess lengths at the bottoms of the sides can be dealt with after fixing.

The card may be in several pieces. Tack

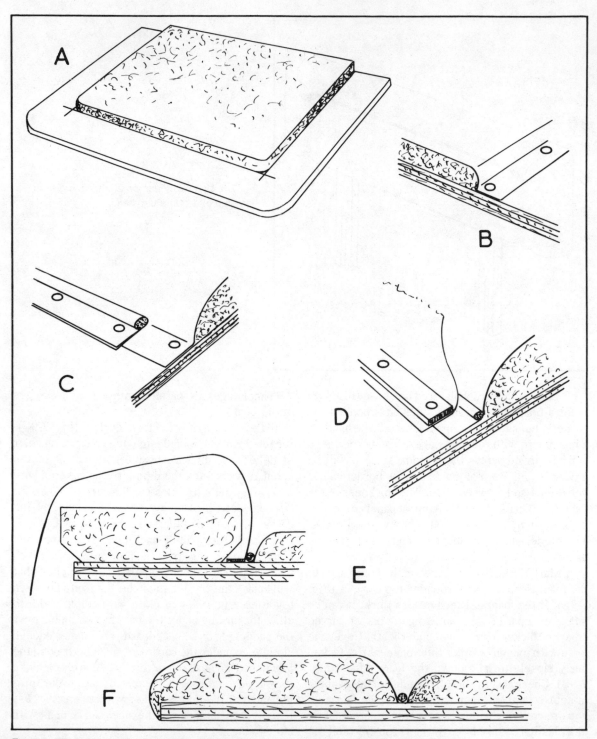

Fig. 7-9. The inner padding is positioned; then the border is defined by piping and back tacking.

through it close to the piping so the folded border covering will be straight and without any appreciable gap. At the corners you can probably manage without card, but if you have allowed much curve, you may want to cut small pieces of card to fit into it.

Foam for the border should be beveled underneath to make a good curve (Fig. 7-9E). Leave it slightly too wide, so it will compress as the cloth is pulled over it. Another way of giving a more rounded and padded edge is to leave the cloth about 1 inch too wide and square. When the cloth is pulled over, some of the foam will go over the edge (Fig. 7-9F).

If an inner layer of muslin must be used, you can manage without sewing miters in it, but the strips overlap at the corners. Back-tack the muslin and the outer covering at the same time; then turn the outer cloth back out of the way while you deal with the padding and the muslin.

The panel, as described, does not feature buttoning. Much depends on how large an area is covered. Even with a small area, you could use two nails with decorative heads to simulate buttons. For a larger area, it would be better to arrange a pattern of buttons and twine (Fig. 7-10A).

With thin foam, buttoning does not give as good a creasing of the cloth, and appearance is not as nice, unless the foam is prepared before covering. You can use the foam untreated and pull the buttons almost to the board. To give a deeper effect on thin foam, slice into the foam between the button positions, going about halfway through (Fig. 7-10B). When the cloth is pulled down by the buttons, creases will extend along these cuts to give a pleasing appearance. Another way of emphasizing the button pattern is to sew between the button positions (Figs. 7-7G and 7-7H). Cutting or seaming in this way is attractive if the button lines come in a diamond pattern (Fig. 7-10C). Put temporary pins in the foam. Hold a straightedge against them (Fig. 7-10D); then use your finger along the straightedge as a depth gauge for the knife. If there

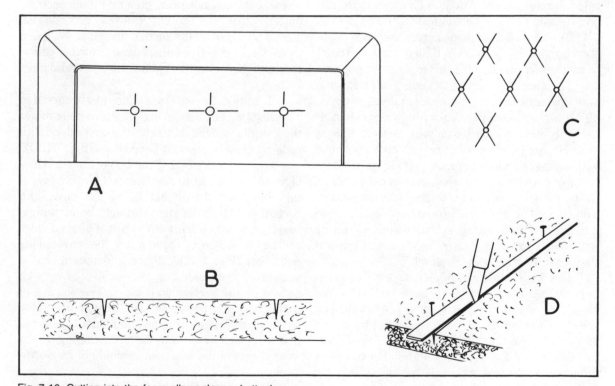

Fig. 7-10. Cutting into the foam allows deeper buttoning.

are a large number of buttons or decorative nails, start fitting near the center of the panel, or you may shape the padding unevenly.

## PIERCED AND CARVED PANELS

There is not much scope for elaborate decoration of wood in modern furniture. In Victorian days people thought it was necessary to carve or embellish almost every surface. A plain piece of wood was regarded as part of a poor design. Although we may not want to return to those days, a headboard or footboard can provide a place for more decoration than would usually be applied to other furniture.

Some earlier beds have shaped top edges to the boards. This shaping can be carried further by cutting through the boards to give a pierced pattern, like fretwork on a larger scale. Some designs intended for cutting in thin wood with a fretsaw might be enlarged for cutting in thicker wood with a piercing saw or jigsaw. A fairly bold treatment is needed (Fig. 7-11A). You must consider the grain in relation to strength. A leaf ending in a fairly fine point would be strong enough along the grain (Fig. 7-11B), but a similar shape across the grain might soon break off (Fig. 7-11C). If there must be a point in that direction, it will need to be more obtuse.

For ease in cleaning the edges after sawing, slim openings should be avoided as much as possible. It is much easier to deal with a wider cutout. It helps to use a piercing saw with teeth as fine as possible, so the edge is left reasonably smooth and without ragged edges to clean. A blade intended for metal or plastic could be tried, but much depends on the particular wood. A coarse grain may not let such a fine blade cut, and resin in other woods may cause it to clog and stop cutting. A blade that is not cutting will soon overheat and char the wood, and you will then have blackness to clean off.

One interesting way of piercing a bed end is to personalize it with initials (Fig. 7-11D). Piercing alone may or may not be satisfactory, depending on the choice of initials. Some letters must be carved as well to make them effective, as described later. In addition to letters, the outline of a badge or emblem can be pierced, or you could cut out the figures of a date.

If your interest is in carving, you can treat a bed end as a panel for relief carving. It will probably be best to keep the carving within a rectangle, then frame the panel (Fig. 7-12A). Obviously, an elaborately carved panel will probably take longer to do than the rest of the bed, but you will finish with a bed which has value in its uniqueness.

You could also include the outline of the board as part of the carving (Fig. 7-12B), but do not allow yourself to be carried away with carving excessive detail along the edge. There may be a few flowing curves, but small points and other fine details are not wanted on a bed.

You may not want, or be able to work, elaborate carving on a bed end, but you can cut in simple lines to make patterns or form letters (Fig. 7-12C). A V tool or deep carving gouge will cut the lines. Another way of cutting these lines is with a router, either used freehand or with a jig. An assembly for cutting house name boards could be used as a router guide for cutting lettering into the end of a bed. These cuts can be given greater prominence by putting stain into the cut grooves. Any surplus should be wiped off the surface immediately. Use a cabinet scraper on the surface later to further define the edge between the lighter surface and darker hollow.

Traditionally, letters and figures are carved in a serif style. You should use a pattern book to get the letter forms, but this technique can be done with ordinary chisels following pencil lines (Fig. 7-12D).

Carving and piercing can be combined. A design may be similar to one intended for relief carving, but, instead of just being cut down the background, it is cut right through. Some things, like leaves, which must stop short if pierced only, can be carried on by carving into the surrounding solid part (Fig. 7-12E). Since a footboard can be seen from both sides, a pierced design may be carved on the surface both sides. The shaping of surfaces, veins in leaves, and similar one-sided work can be repeated on the other side. Unless the bed will stand away from the wall, carving on the second side of the headboard would not be worthwhile.

The decision to carve depends on your inclina-

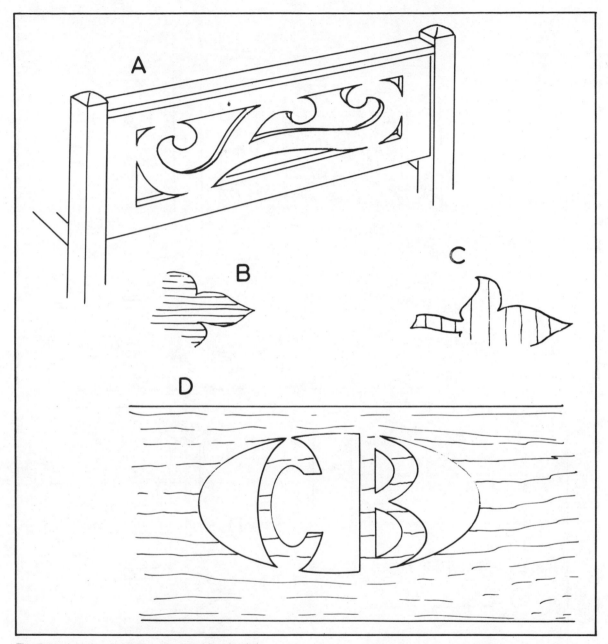

Fig. 7-11. A bed end may be decorated by piercing.

tions and ability. Usually only surface carving is used on the ends of beds and is all that would normally be regarded as appropriate to a modern bedroom, but quite elaborately carved ends have been done in the round and not just on the surface.

The design must be chosen to suit the fairly broad expanse of comparatively thin wood, but such things as intertwined snakes and tangled foliage are possible, if you decide that is what you want to wake up to!

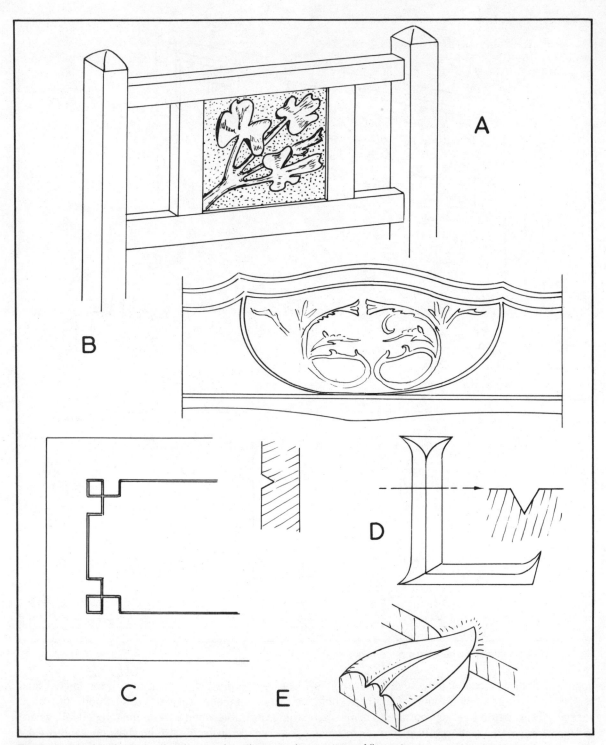

Fig. 7-12. A bed end may be deeply carved, or there can be a pattern of line cuts.

## VENEERED BED ENDS

The possibility of using prepared veneered panels of plywood has been mentioned in the descriptions of simple beds, but you can do your own veneering. Thick plywood might have its edges, as well as the surface, veneered, but glue does not hold well on edge grain. Particleboard takes veneer better on its edges. In most cases it would be better to frame a veneered panel, whether it is a simple geometric pattern or an advanced marquetry picture. Framing allows you to regulate the relationship of the size of the intended panel and the necessary size of the bed. The panel need not be proportional to the bed end. It might just form a central motif (Fig. 7-13A).

If you veneer a thin plywood panel which will be set in a grooved frame, you should veneer both sides, even if the second side is just one piece of plain veneer. Veneering both sides balances the stresses imposed on the plywood and counteracts

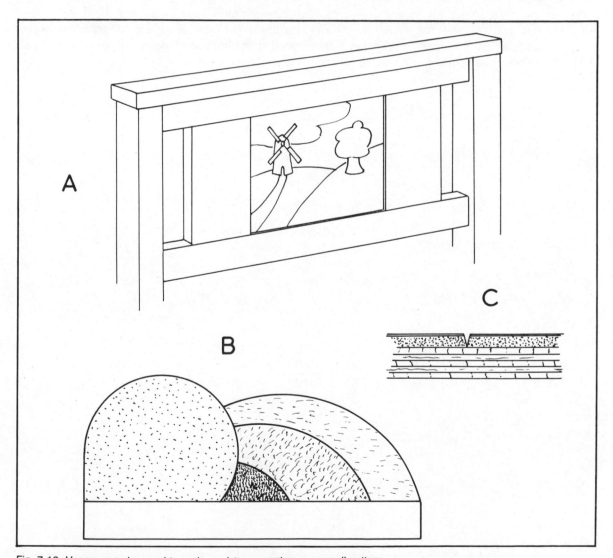

Fig. 7-13. Veneer may be used to make a picture panel or an overall pattern.

any tendency to warp.

A bed end may not be the place for a very finely detailed marquetry picture, nor a picture where the color differences are not very great, since it is unlikely that a viewer will see the pictures to the best advantage. A bold coat-of-arms or a picture made of large contrasting pieces will be more effective than a complicated view of a landscape with subtle differences of shade and grain in the wood.

There are other things besides wood that might be considered as veneers. Laminated plastic materials are made in a great variety of patterns. Some of these have possibilities on bed ends. They could be panels in wood frames, or they may stand alone. With some patterns, a plain expanse may have a rather clinical appearance, but some of the darker materials look more like wood and will match surroundings better.

For a modern effect, pieces of different designs of laminated plastic can be fitted together, rather like marquetry (Fig. 7-13B). It may be difficult to get very closely fitting edge joints, as can be done with thin wood veneer trimmed with a knife, but, if the edges are beveled (Fig. 7-13C), slight discrepancies will be obscured. The best way to fit shaped edges is to cut one and use it as a pattern for marking the adjoining one. Leave some surplus at the edge of a panel and trim that to the wood after you have adjusted the meeting pieces as closely as possible.

# Chapter 8

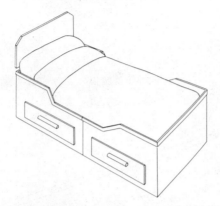

# Children's Beds

A child may sleep in a full-size bed, but in his or her early years may be happier and more comfortable in a bed adapted to his smaller size and particular needs. Usually it is better for the bed to be strongly made, with plainness rather than ornamentation. Plain areas that the child can use to hang pictures will be more appropriate than elaborate decoration that attracts an adult, but means nothing to a child.

There are many possibilities for beds. Quite often compactness is valuable. If more than one child is sleeping in a room, two beds can be arranged in the usual twin bed manner, possibly with one headboard across the two, with built-in table and shelves. If space is more confined, bunk beds are a good solution, and they appeal to the majority of children. Another arrangement features one bed that can fit under the other during the day, to give more play space. It is possible to arrange two beds in a corner, so the foot of a lower one goes under the end of a higher bed. The arrangement allows various sorts of combination furniture, such as a clothes closet or a desk under or against the upper bed. If a child's bedroom is to be kept tidy, there is a strong

case for including drawers under a bed.

The size of a child's bed depends on available mattresses. For a crib or cot the mattress is obviously small and may even be adapted from a cushion or pillow. For larger beds there are mattresses smaller than adult size. A bed can be made to fit around one of these, but there is a good case for making a child's bed full-length and not too narrow. There are mattresses 24 and 30 inches wide, but, if you are considering the long-term use of a bed, it may be better to keep the bed size to suit a mattress 36 inches wide and 78 inches long. The child can be comfortable in this size even when he is small, and there will be enough space for him right up to adult size. You will also be able to accommodate an adult visitor in the bed who will not suffer from the discomfort of pushing his feet out of the end, knocking his elbows against the side, or falling out.

## PLAIN BED

A bed can be made to take a 36-inch mattress, with plain panel ends and a robust construction (Fig. 8-1). It could be built as a permanent assem-

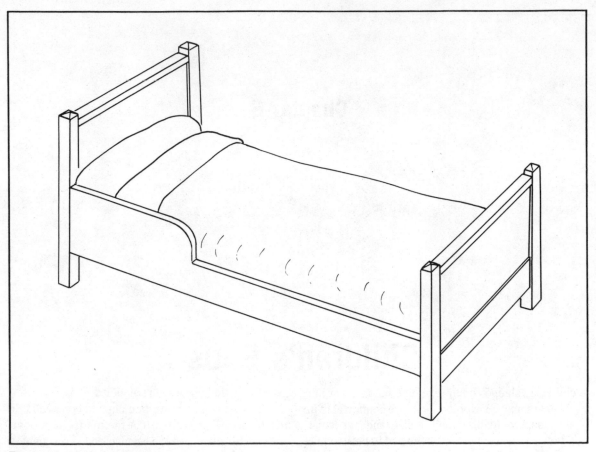

Fig. 8-1. A child's plain bed.

bly, since it is small enough to carry on edge through most doorways, but a method of disassembly is suggested. Softwood could be used and the bed given a painted finish, but it would be stronger made of hardwood. If you are thinking ahead to the time when the bed may have to form part of the furnishing of an adult's room, all of the framework could be stained and varnished or polished, and the panels painted. Once the child has passed the "stick-on picture" stage, the panels could be given another coat of paint and left plain or decorated with decals.

The head and foot have square legs with plywood panels. The head is 7 inches higher than the foot. It would be easy at this stage to alter sizes if you wish. It is assumed that plain ¼-inch plywood is to be used, but you could use hardboard with the

plywood. The hardboard could have laminated plastic on the surface, which would have the advantage of being easy to clean. The panels could be made up of tongued and grooved matched boarding if the lower rails were made thicker to take the wider grooves.

Mark out the pair of rear legs (Fig. 8-2A) and the front legs (Fig. 8-2B) so all four parts match. Mark the positions of the joints to other parts, but don't cut them until the meeting pieces are ready. Leave some excess length at the tops until after the top rail mortises have been cut.

Mark all crosswise rails together, to get the distances between the shoulders the same. Allow for tenons going not more than 1 inch into the legs to keep the rail tenons clear of the tenons from the side pieces.

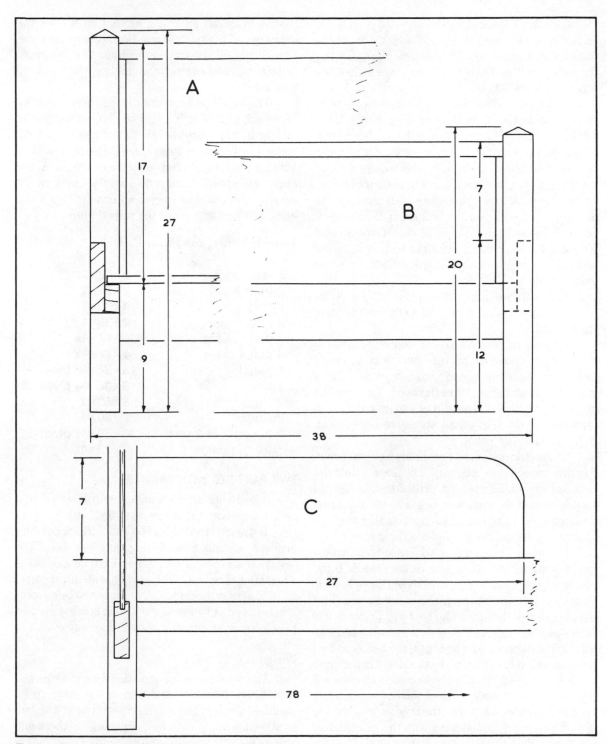

Fig. 8-2. Sizes of the child's plain bed.

Groove the top rail for the plywood (Fig. 8-3A) and arrange twin tenons there. Gauge the widths of the mortises in the legs at the same time. Groove the lower rail and make tenons there below the groove (Fig. 8-3B).

In the other direction the barefaced tenons on the sides may be 1¼ inches long (Fig. 8-3C). If the bed is to be assembled permanently, the tenons will be glued into their mortises. If you expect to disassemble the bed occasionally, the tenons may be made tight enough to be a drive fit in their mortise. Drive screws across—one into each tenon from the outside. This arrangement will stand up to several separations and reassemblies, but, if you expect frequent disassemblies, it might be better to use bolts or special hardware, as described for some earlier beds.

The mattress support is plywood. Fit strips inside the sides (Fig. 8-3D), up to the shoulders of the tenons.

It would be possible to cut stopped grooves in the legs to take the panels, but most grooving planes or other equipment are intended to cut a groove through to the end of the wood. To avoid this problem, the plywood panels fit into grooves in the rails, but at the legs small strips are added (Fig. 8-3E) to hold the panel.

Shape the tops of the legs in any way you fancy. Simple tapers are shown. The tops could be rounded or cut square and drilled to take turned knobs. Round the exposed edges of the top rails. Assemble the head and foot, checking that they are square, free from twists and matching.

For many children it is advisable to provide a guard at the head end, at one or both sides. If the bed is to go against a wall, one should be sufficient, as shown. The guard is a piece of solid wood (Fig. 8-2C) on top of the side. The best way to attach it is with dowels. Arrange three or four downward into the side and three into the leg. If the bed is to be a permanent assembly, glue to the side, then glue to the leg when you drive the side tenons into the leg mortises. If you want to take the bed apart later, glue to the side, but leave the dowels into the leg dry. If you want to dispense with the guard later, the dowels into the side may also be dry, but make

them a drive fit, so young hands cannot coax the joint open. This sort of raised end is seen on some French adult beds; so you can argue that the guard could remain, even when the child says he is too old to need it.

The base that supports the mattress is a piece of ½-inch plywood. It could be divided across the middle if that would be easier for handling. Drill some widely spaced large holes in it—20 should be sufficient to let air in and out of the mattress. At the ends the plywood may be merely cut straight across, or it could be shaped around the legs so its ends rest on the tops of the rails there.

## Materials List for Plain Bed

| 2 rear legs | 2×28×2 |
|---|---|
| 2 front legs | 2×21×2 |
| 2 rails | 4×38×1 |
| 2 rails | 2×38×1 |
| 4 panel sides | ½×17×⅜ |
| 4 panel sides | ½×12×⅜ |
| 1 panel | 18×36×¼ plywood |
| 1 panel | 10×36×¼ plywood |
| 2 sides | 5×82×1 |
| 2 sides | 2×80×1 |
| 1 base (or in 2 pieces) | 36×80×½ plywood |
| 1 (or 2) guards | 7×28×1 |

## TWO-PART BED WITH DRAWERS

A bed with drawers underneath is useful in a child's bedroom. This two-part bed with drawers (Fig. 8-4) has raised sides and ends, which not only prevent a child from falling out, but keep the bedclothes in place, too. An optional headboard is suggested. The bed is in two almost identical parts, divided across the middle; so, if it has to be moved, it is reduced to half-size and should be easy for two people to carry through normal doorways.

### Design

The sizes given are intended for a mattress 36 inches by 78 inches, and they would have to be modified if you prefer a different mattress. The bed is shown with two drawers opening on the same side. You will need to settle on drawer arrange-

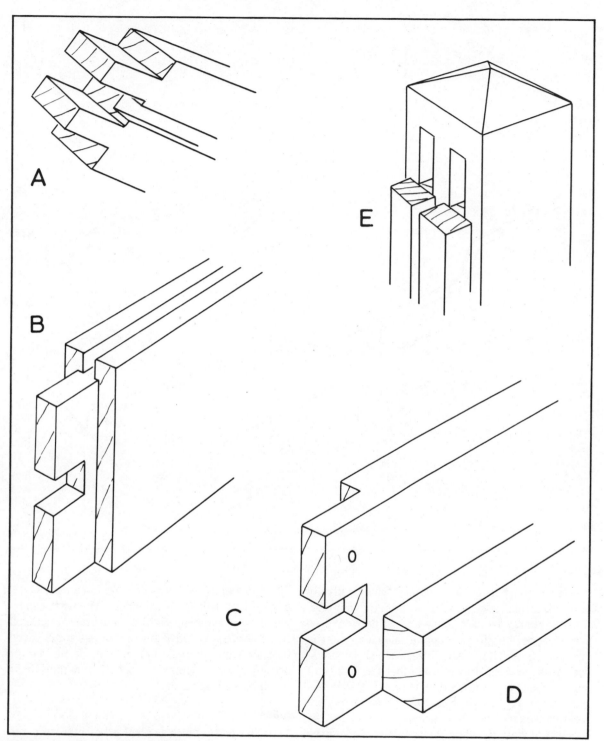

Fig. 8-3. Joints for the plain bed's parts.

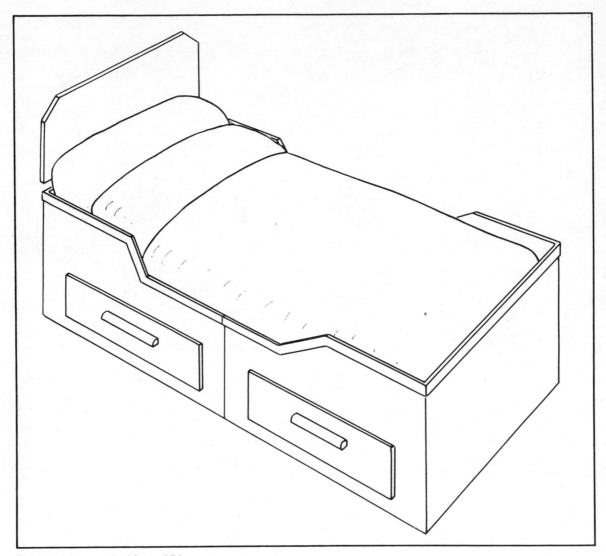

Fig. 8-4. A two-part bed for a child.

ments to suit a particular situation. If there will only be room for a drawer to pull out from the foot end, the other part must be made without a drawer. Two drawers operated from opposite sides may suit the available space. If there is little space at the sides, you could make the drawer in the foot section to pull out endwise, without needing to modify the design very much. As shown (Fig. 8-5) the two parts are identical, except for the pairing necessary for the drawers to work the same way, and the need for the headboard at one end.

Most of the bed is made from ½-inch plywood, framed with 1-inch-square strips. The parts can be glued, with finishing nails driven from outside. If the nails are punched below the surface and covered with stopping, there will be little evidence of their presence on the outside, especially if the bed is finished with paint.

## Sides

The parts which control other sizes are the sides (Fig. 8-6A). Obtain the main sizes from Fig.

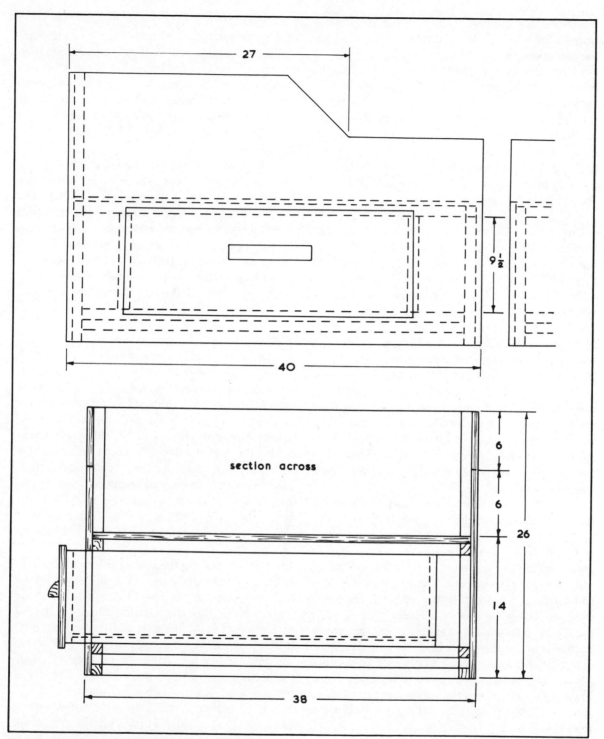

Fig. 8-5. Part sizes for the two-part bed with drawers.

8-5. Note that the corners have these sides overlapping the ends, so leave enough projecting past the framing strips.

Cut drawer openings where you want them, but leave their opposite sides uncut. Give them the same framing, which will be needed to support the drawer guides. At the sides of the drawer openings, set back the vertical strips enough to allow the plywood drawer guides to come level with the opening. It will probably be wiser to leave the final leveling of the plywood on the opening until after the guides have been fitted.

Cut the top edges of the sides straight and square across. They are to be covered with edging. For a simpler construction you could omit the edging and round the plywood edges, but exposed plywood edges do not look right. It is also very difficult to shape and round some plywood without veneers breaking out to spoil appearance.

The ends are plain rectangular pieces, which fit between the sides. Stiffen them at the bottom edge and at the same level as the sides to support the top. The low ends that will meet each other may go to the upper surface of the plywood top, so it will drop inside all four edges. Join the sides to their ends and check that the two assemblies match. You could put in the tops, but it will probably be easier to deal with the drawer guides first. Secure the assemblies squarely. A temporary diagonal batten could be used.

Get the actual sizes of the drawer guides from the assemblies. Each drawer guide (Fig. 8-6B) is a piece of plywood notched to go around the framing strips above and below the drawer opening. It need not be made deep enough to reach the floor, but its top edge will be level with the strips on the sides and will help to support the top plywood. The lower strip on each guide acts as a drawer runner, while the top strip acts as a kicker to prevent the drawer from tilting excessively when it is pulled out.

Fit the drawer guides, but check that they are parallel and square to the sides with the openings. Make sure the kickers and runners are parallel, or you may have difficulty in making the drawer run smoothly.

Fit the tops in two parts with glue and nails.

They should be drilled with a pattern of large holes for ventilation. You will now have two rigid assemblies that meet neatly. If you are satisfied with the fit, you can drill for bolts to hold the low ends together. Two ⅜-inch bolts with nuts and large washers about 6 inches in from the sides and at about half the height of the ends should be sufficient. After a trial assembly, separate the parts for further work.

There are some plastic edging pieces that can be sprung and glued over the plywood edges, but wooden edgings are suggested (Fig. 8-6C). You may find it easier to cut the rabbets if you start with wider pieces, such as two strips back to back, then cut and round the edging after rabbeting. Fit the edging all around on the outside. Miter the bed corners and cut miters to bisect the angles on the sloping parts. Attach the edging with glue and nails driven from inside the plywood.

## Drawers

Drawers could be made from solid wood, with dovetail corners and the bottoms slid into grooves, but a simpler method of assembly with plywood parts is shown. Each drawer has a false front that overlaps the opening in the bed side, so any slight lack of precision there will be hidden. Start by making the drawer sides (Fig. 8-7A) and check that each will slide along its own guide easily. It is unnecessary for drawers to be interchangeable, so mark where each side is intended to go. Cut the front (Fig. 8-7B) and backs (Fig. 8-7C), so their lengths will hold the sides apart at an easy sliding distance.

Put strips along the bottom edges of the front and sides to take the bottom (Fig. 8-7D) and let the back come above the bottom (Fig. 8-7E). Stiffen the corners inside with more strips. Check the slide of each drawer before fixing the bottom permanently. It may have to be adjusted for any slight lack of squareness. Use glue and nails downward through the bottom plywood into the front and side strips, but screw upward through it into the back.

Each drawer should slide in so its front comes level with the bed side. If that is satisfactory, make the false front to overlap all around. Take off the

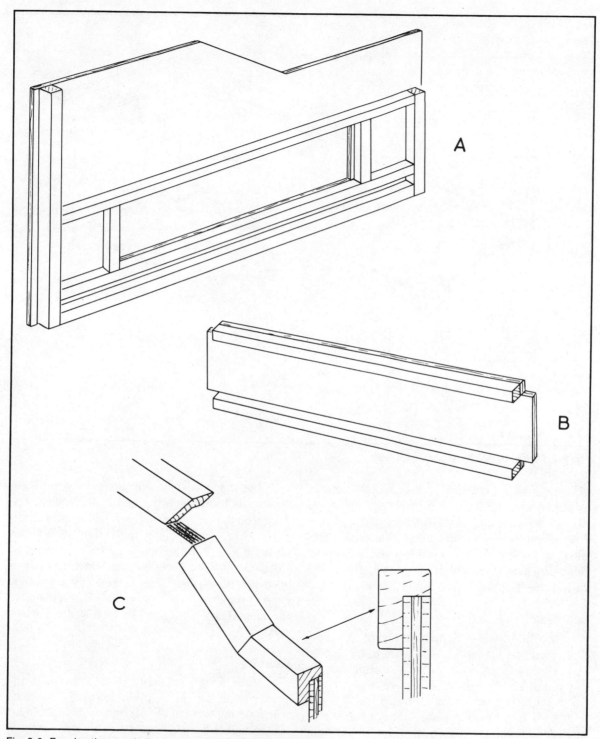

Fig. 8-6. Framing the panels for the two-part bed with drawers.

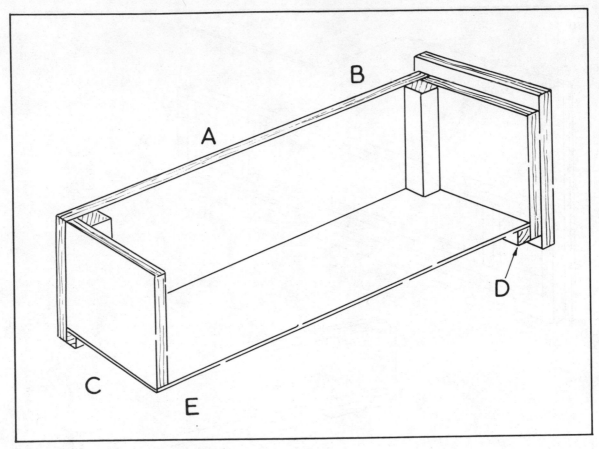

Fig. 8-7. Drawer details for the two-part bed.

sharpness of its corners, and round the exposed edges. Attach it to the main front with glue and screws driven from inside. Handles could be shaped from wood, or you could use metal or plastic handles, preferably of the type which is sunk in almost flush or which has a bail to hang down, so there is little projection for a bare leg to knock against.

## Bed Head

If a bed head is required, any of the types described in Chapter 7 could be used, but a plain type is suggested and used as an example of the method of attachment. A plain piece of plywood is used, with its corners cut to match the bed side angles. It could have all edges except the bottom enclosed by similar edging strips to the bed (Fig. 8-8A).

The supports are slotted strips (Fig. 8-8B) to go over bolts through the bed end. To clear the edging on the top of the bed end, put vertical strips there (Fig. 8-8C). They will also stiffen the plywood. One bolt through at each strip should be sufficient, but you could put one above another in each slot, if you find it necessary. If you will not need to remove the headboard or adjust its height, the supports could be glued and screwed to the bed end.

## Finishing

Make a trial assembly of the two parts together, with the headboard and drawers in place. The meeting parts of the plywood sides should be stiff enough to keep in line. If they are not, a strip of thin plywood can be fitted inside each joint, with screws outward into the side plywood. Of course, the screws will need to be removed if the parts are to be separated. Sand all parts and finish them with paint. If the edging strips have been made of hardwood, you can get an attractive appearance by painting all parts except the edging, treating it with stain and varnish or polish.

## Materials List
## for Two-Part Bed with Drawers

| | |
|---|---|
| 4 sides | 26×42×½ plywood |
| 2 ends | 26×39×½ plywood |
| 2 ends | 14×39×½ plywood |
| 2 tops | 37×41×½ plywood |
| framing from | |
| 36 pieces | 1×42×1 |
| edging from | |

| | |
|---|---|
| 8 pieces | 1½×40×1 |
| 2 drawer fronts | 11×29×½ plywood |
| 2 drawer fronts | 10×28×½ plywood |
| 2 drawer backs | 10×28×½ plywood |
| 4 drawer sides | 10×37×½ plywood |
| 2 drawer bottoms | 28×37×¼ plywood |
| 6 drawer bottom strips | ½×37×½ |
| 4 drawer guides | 12×37×½ plywood |
| 1 bed head | 15×39×½ plywood |
| 2 bed head supports | 2×34×1 |

## STACKING BUNK BEDS

If two identical beds are made with the usual four legs each and ends of the same height, it is possible to put one on the other to make a two-tier bunk bed. You could also put both beds on the floor if there is sufficient space. A double-decker bed allows two to sleep over the space that would

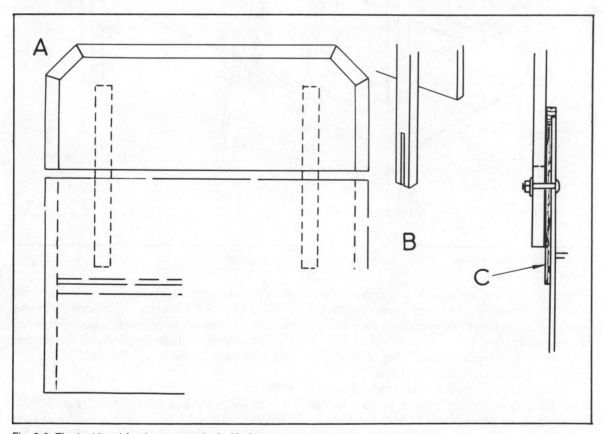

Fig. 8-8. The bed head for the two-part bed with drawers.

Fig. 8-9. Stacking bunk beds.

otherwise be occupied by only one person. Sizes must be a compromise, but sitting headroom can be provided in the lower bed without making the top one too high.

These stacking bunk beds (Fig. 8-9) are intended to take mattresses 36 inches by 78 inches; so the bed could be used by adults as well as children. Close-grained hardwood is advised for the main parts, particularly the legs, because joints are made between the beds with dowels in the leg ends,

and sideways loads might cause soft or brittle wood to split. You could build just one bed now and make the other to match it later, but it is easier to get all the sizes the same if the two beds are marked out and made at one time.

## Legs

The legs are four similar pairs (Fig. 8-10A). Mark the positions of other parts across them all at the same time. The ends have plywood panels be-

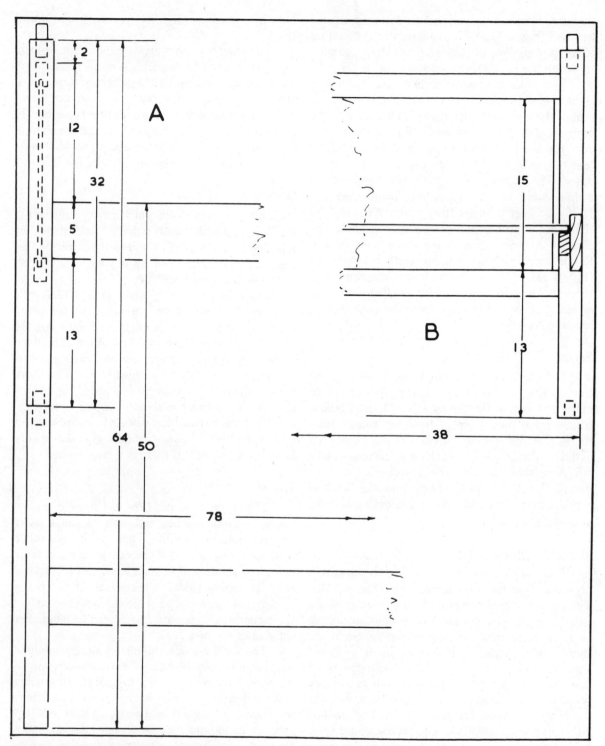

Fig. 8-10. Sizes of the stacking bunk beds.

tween narrower rails, which should be grooved and tenoned (Fig. 8-11A). To avoid the difficult cutting of stopped grooves in the legs, small strips are used to retain the edges of the panels (Fig. 8-11B).

The links between the beds are ¾-inch or ⅞-inch dowels, which must be glued tightly into the tops of the legs, but fit fairly easily into holes on the bottoms of the legs. If one bed will always be the top one, you need only prepare joints on the tops of the legs of one bed and the bottoms of the legs of the other. The drawings show both beds prepared; so either could be the upper one when they are stacked. Carefully mark the centers of the ends of the legs and drill for the dowels (Fig. 8-11C). The dowels should enter each leg at least 1¼ inches. Round and slightly taper the projecting dowel ends (Fig. 8-11D) for easy entry. Round the corners of the legs for appearance and for avoidance of sharp edges against a carpet or where the post may be handled.

### Panels

Cut the plywood panels to fit easily into the framing (Fig. 8-10B), with a little bottom clearance in the grooves, so tightening will not happen before frame joints are tight. Glue the frame joints thoroughly. Be sparing with glue on the edges only of the panels, so you will not have an excess to clean off. Assemble all four ends and check that they match. Try the dowels of one into the holes of another before the glue has set, in case minor adjustments are needed.

### Mattress Support

The sides have strips inside to support a plywood base for a foam mattress (Fig. 8-11E). They could be tenoned into the legs if the beds are to be permanently assembled. The beds are not too large to be carried through a doorway, providing there are no twisting passageways or awkward staircases to pass as well. If the beds are to be disassembled, attach the sides to the legs with dry tenons, as in the previous bed, or by any of the methods described for other beds. The method suggested here uses two bolts at each joint (Fig. 8-11F), with nuts sunk into mortises in the sides.

They give maximum rigidity, yet can still be taken apart.

The mattress support is a piece of ½-inch plywood, in one or two parts. It drops in and need not be screwed down. Drill a pattern of large holes in it for air to pass in and out of the foam mattress. Before going further, try the beds fitted together. If the assembly is easier with a particular bed on top, you could fit that bed with a guard, if you want one. That bed will also be the one to take the ladder.

### Guard

One guard is shown, which may be sufficient if the bed is against a wall, but you could fit two on top. You may wish to fit them to the lower bed as well, if it is to be used by a young child. The materials list allows for one.

Make the frame of the guard (Fig. 8-12A) with open mortise and tenon, or *bridle*, joints (Fig. 8-12B), which can be strengthened with dowels through near the inner corners. After assembly, leave three corners square, but well round the one that projects. Drill for the dowel rods. The short ones need not go very far into the rails, but let two or three go through and into the bed side (Fig. 8-12C). Arrange two short dowels to go into the bed end. If the bed is to disassemble, glue the dowels into the guard, but fit them dry into the bed.

### Ladder

The ladder is shown (Fig. 8-13) hooking over the side of the top bed and with its foot a short distance from the bed line. There are several other ways of fitting a ladder, as can be seen in later designs, including a permanently attached vertical one. A sloping ladder is easier to climb, but a vertical ladder cannot be removed by a child. When the ladder shown is out of use it can be hung over the end of the bed.

The ladder sides should be straight-grained and free from large knots. Most hardwoods will be suitable, but you may have to pick over available softwood pieces to find suitable grain. Five rungs are shown, giving a rise of about 10 inches. If that rise seems too much for your child, you can space six rungs, which would give a rise of about 8 inches.

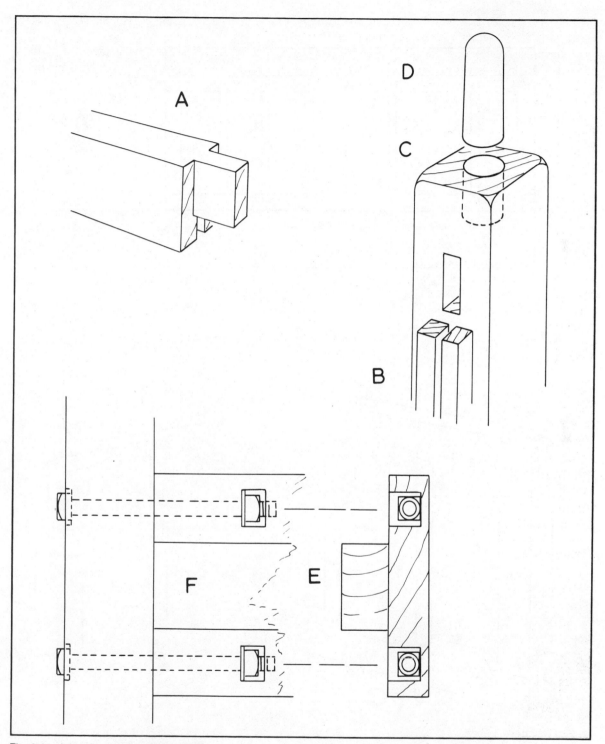

Fig. 8-11. Joints for stacking bunk beds.

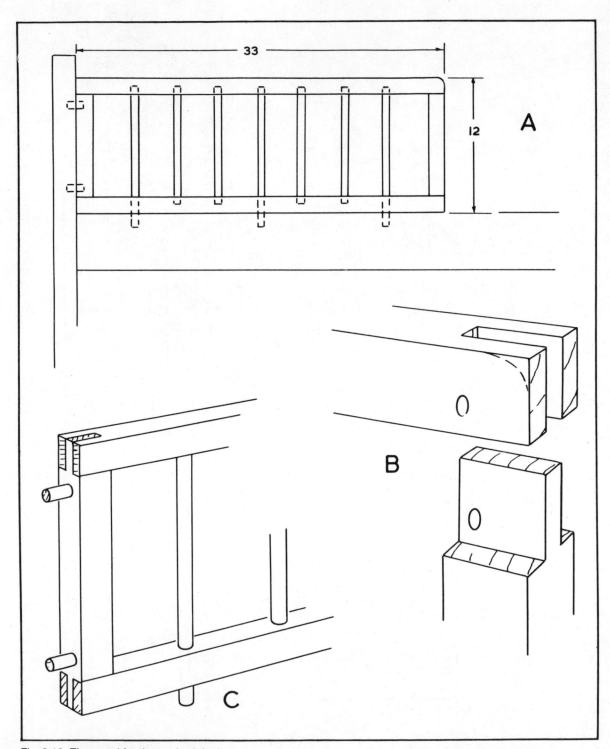

Fig. 8-12. The guard for the top bunk bed.

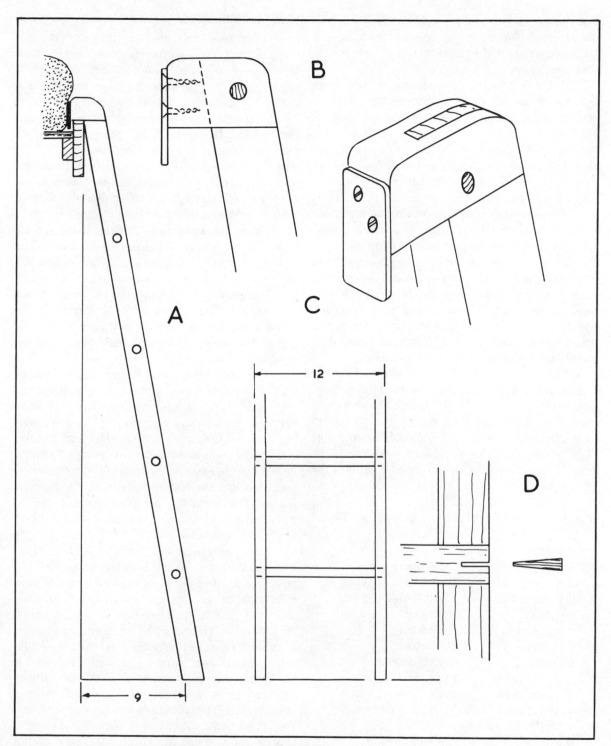

Fig. 8-13. Construction of the ladder for the stacking bunk beds.

You can set the ladder slope and size full-size on the floor (Fig. 8-13A), or it may be sufficient to slope a strip against a bed, then mark and cut the foot bevel, then the height and top angle.

To get the correct rung spacing, the distances that matter are the tops of the rungs and not their centers. Have a centerline on a side and step off equal spacing between the top of the bed side and the floor. Measure ⅜ inch below these points for the centers of the holes for the rungs. Anyone climbing to the top bed then makes exactly the same step all the way from the floor.

At the top there is a strip attached with a bridle joint to each side (Fig. 8-13B). Have the strip too long, trimming it to length after making the joint. Put a dowel through the joint, in the same way as at the corner of the guard, and well-round the exposed corner. At the inside a strip must hang down to hook over the bed side. It could be a piece of hardwood about ¼-inch thick, but it would be better to use sheet metal a little over 1/16-inch thick. Brass or aluminum would do (Fig. 8-13C).

When you drill for the rungs, use a drill press or a template to get the holes square to the surface. Drill right through. It will probably be strong enough to depend on glue, but you can give extra strength by also wedging the top and bottom rungs (Fig. 8-13D). Make a saw cut across and drive in the edge, which can be cut off and planed level after the glue has set.

## Materials List for Stacking Beds (Two Beds)

| | |
|---|---|
| 8 legs | 2×34×2 |
| 8 rails | 2×32×1 |
| 4 panels | 17×38×¼ plywood |
| 16 panel strips | ⅜×16×⅜ |
| 4 sides | 5×80×1 |
| 4 sides | 2×80×1 |
| 2 bases | 37×80×1 |
| 8 joints | ¾×3 dowels |
| 2 guard rails | 1½×35×1 |
| 2 guard rails | 1½×13×1 |
| 7 guard rails | ½×13 dowels |
| 2 ladder sides | 2×60×1 |
| 5 ladder rungs | ¾×13 dowels |

## LOW STACKING BEDS

If two beds are made with minimum heights you can stack them so the combined height is no more than a single bed of normal height. One bed can be used over the other as a bed at night or a divan during the day, possibly without the second bed being apparent. When two beds are wanted, the top bed can be lifted off, to give you a pair of matching beds, rather lower than usual, but otherwise full size. In this way an overnight guest can be accommodated. In a child's room, more floor space is cleared for playing; yet two children will have their own beds at night.

These low stacking beds (Fig. 8-14) are intended for mattresses 30 inches by 78 inches. The mattresses could be 6 inches thick, and sheets and blankets on the lower bed would still clear the top bed. If the lower mattress is thinner, there should be clearance for a pillow as well. However, the pillows or cushions could be scattered on the top bed if the assembly is to be used as a divan or day-bed.

The sizes (Fig. 8-15) give a combined height of about 20 inches on the compressed top mattress, or beds at about 10 inches from the floor when the parts are separated. Except for the means of joining, the two beds are identical. The legs and the ends do not come above the mattress tops. It would be possible to make higher ends on the top bed if you wish, but the bottom bed should be made as shown. For a child's room, the parts could be softwood and painted, but for general use varnished hardwood might look better.

The controlling sizes are at the legs (Fig. 8-16A). Mark out all the legs together, with the positions of other parts. At the bed ends the twin rails could be doweled to the legs, but tenons are shown (Fig. 8-16B). The sides are also tenoned (Fig. 8-16C). There will be no need to make the beds for disassembly since they are shallow enough to be taken through any normal space in a home. If the tenons both ways do not go more than halfway into the legs, they will not interfere with each other (Fig. 8-16D). The sides have barefaced tenons, and the supports for the plywood bottom goes inside (Fig. 8-16E). Round the lower edge, so it cannot

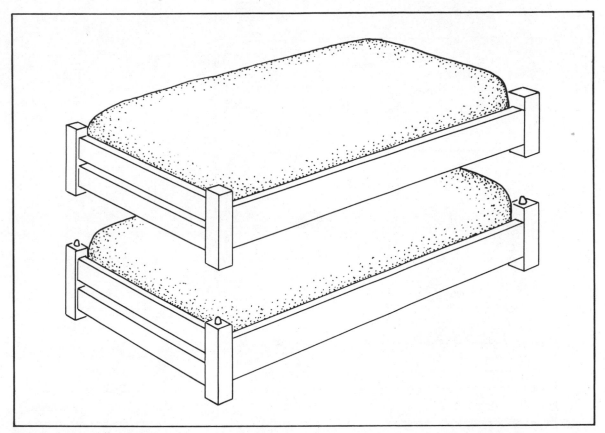

Fig. 8-14. A pair of low stacking beds.

scratch the bedding on the lower bed (Fig. 8-16F).

Round the tops of the legs of the top bed (Fig. 8-16G). At the joints, drill the meeting surfaces centrally for ¾-inch dowels. Arrange the projecting parts of the dowels with a slight taper and rounded tops, so they will enter the holes in the upper parts easily (Fig. 8-16H).

Glue the dowels in the tops of the legs of the lower bed. Assemble the ends and check that the dowels will fit into their holes before the glue has set, in case any adjustment is necessary. Test similarly when you glue in the sides to the legs. Assemble the two beds one over the other while standing on a flat surface, so they go together without twist.

Make the plywood bottoms to fit in. They could be cut around the legs at the corners, but it should be satisfactory to cut the ends straight across. Drill holes in the bottoms for mattress ventilation. The bottoms could be made to lift out, as in most other beds, or you could screw the plywood to its supports to increase stiffness, if there is a tendency to flex when you lift a bed.

## Materials List
## for Low Stacking Beds (Two Beds)

| | |
|---|---|
| 8 legs | 2×11×2 |
| 8 rails | 3×32×1 |
| 4 joints | 3×¾ dowels |
| 2 sides | 6×80×1 |
| 2 sides | 1½×78×1 |
| 2 bottoms | 30×80×½ plywood |

## TRUNDLE BEDS

At one time a fine lady had an elaborate and

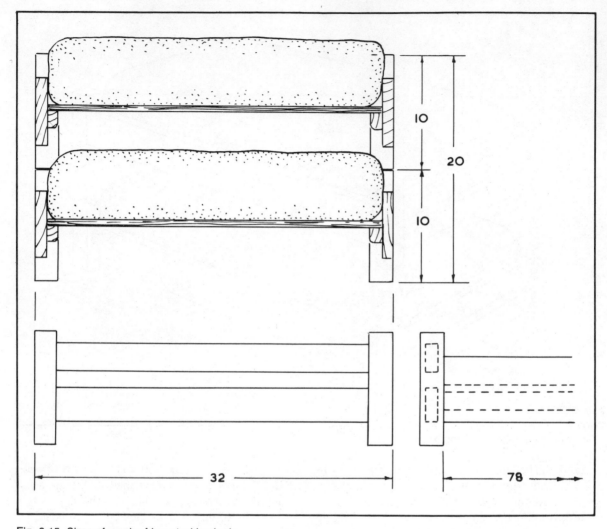

Fig. 8-15. Sizes of a pair of low stacking beds.

luxurious bed, but her maid, who stayed in the same room to be immediately available, slept on a bed that was stowed under the main bed during the day. That was a trundle bed. The idea still has uses in situations where beds are needed, but it is convenient to store them in the same space during the day. In a child's room this compact storage of beds would give extra play space during the day. The low stacking beds just described serve the same purpose. They provide two matching single beds, but the top one has to be lifted off; so two people must work together. If a trundle bed on casters is used, one adult, or one child, can pull out the lower bed, leaving the other bed at the original height, which cannot be altered, but can still be at a reasonable distance above floor level.

In this set of trundle beds (Fig. 8-17), the lower bed is as low as it can be, with the compressed mattress only about 6 inches from the floor. The other bed is about 17 inches high. There is enough space under it for the lower bed to be made up and slid under. The sizes given (Fig. 8-18) allow for both mattresses to be 36 inches by 78 inches. The supports for the top bed are kept far enough out from the ends of the mattress to allow the lower bed to fit between the legs.

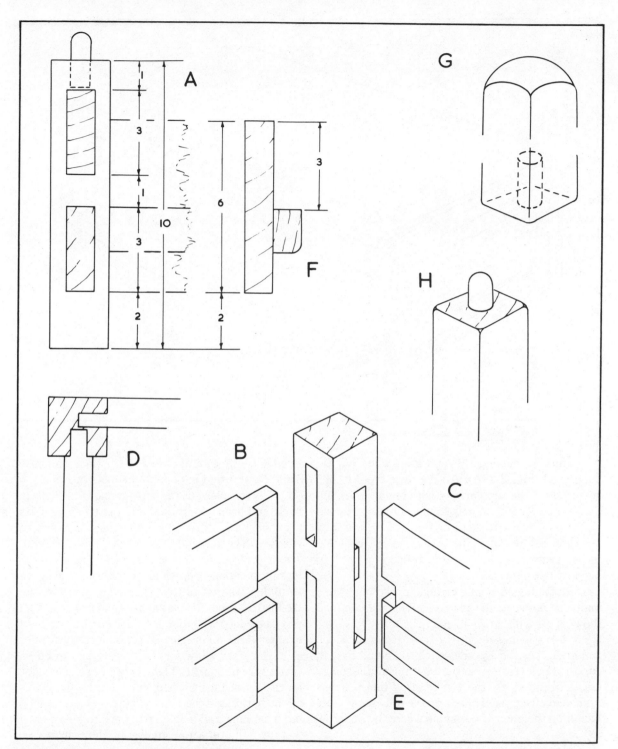

Fig. 8-16. Construction of the low stacking beds.

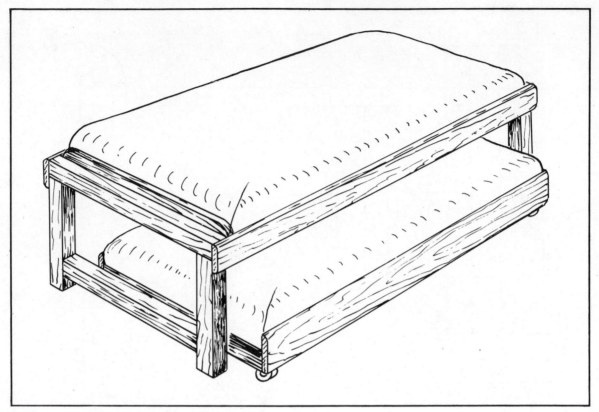

Fig. 8-17. A trundle bed under another bed.

Start by making the end assemblies for the upper bed (Fig. 8-19A). All the parts are 2 inches square. Join the top corners with bridle joints and the lower rails with mortise and tenon joints. Inside the ends come mattress rails (Fig. 8-19B), which go 2 inches below the frame and stand up about 1½ inches, with rounded corners. Inside are strips to support the plywood base.

Make the sides long enough to accommodate a mattress between the mattress rails and continue the support with strips inside (Fig. 8-19C). A mattress 4 to 6 inches deep will stand above the sides and ends, but the woodwork should blend in with curves. Before final assembly, round the outer edges of the sides, the top edges of the mattress rails, and all exposed edges on the end assemblies, including the ends of the sides where they overlap the legs.

Make the plywood base to fit, and drill some

large holes in it for mattress ventilation. The base could be screwed in or left loose as you wish.

The trundle bed is a simple frame with strips in back and front to retain the mattress and its plywood base. Make the frame of 2-inch-square strips with bridle joints at the corners (Fig. 8-19D). The overall length should pass easily between the legs of the other bed, whose lower rails will serve as guides. There will not be space for ends to retain the mattress, but fit sides at back and front, with all exposed edges well rounded. Make a plywood base similar to the other one and screw it to the frame.

The sizes allow for the trundle bed to be on casters about 2 inches high. There is no allowance for casters on the main bed, but you could put glides on the bottoms of the legs. If casters are needed on the main legs, rail heights will have to be adjusted so they will still act as guides for the trundle bed when it is pushed in or out.

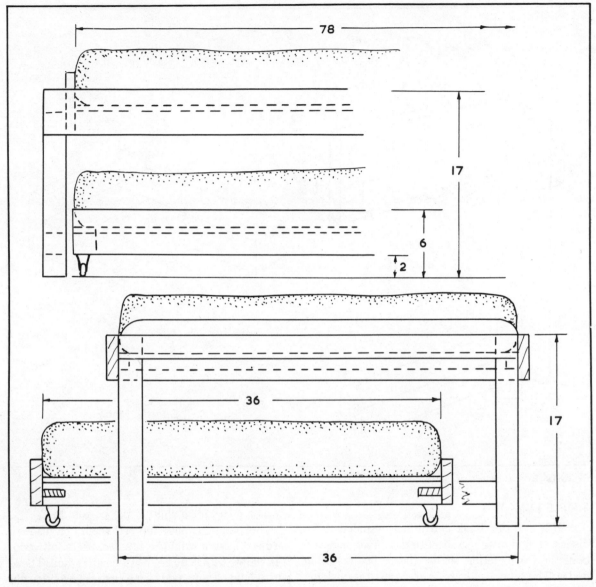

Fig. 8-18. Trundle bed sizes.

## Materials List for Trundle Bed

**Main Bed**

| | |
|---|---|
| 4 end legs | 2×18×2 |
| 4 end rails | 2×38×2 |
| 2 end mattress rails | 5½×38×⅝ |
| 2 end supports | 1×38×1 |
| 2 sides | 4×86×1 |
| 2 sides | 1×82×1 |
| 1 base | 36×78×½ plywood |

**Trundle Bed**

| | |
|---|---|
| 2 sides | 2×80×2 |
| 2 ends | 2×38×2 |
| 2 sides | 4×80×1 |
| 1 base | 36×78×½ plywood |

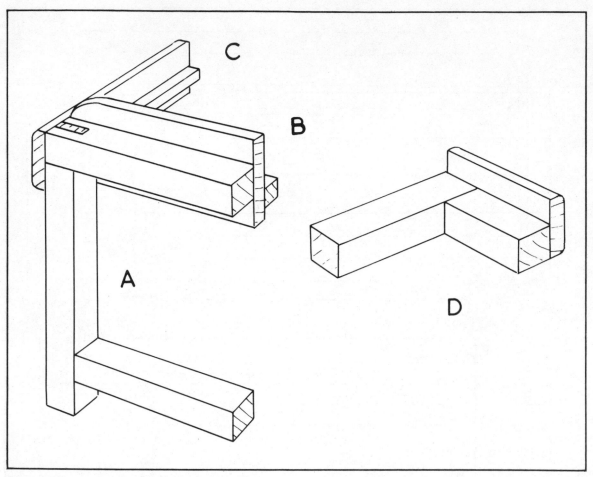

Fig. 8-19. Corner details of the trundle beds.

## SIMPLE BUNK BED

If a two-tier bunk bed is not intended to be disassembled or taken apart to make two separate beds, its construction can be simple. The resulting bed will be robust and able to stand up to a considerable amount of the use handed out by children. This simple bunk bed (Fig. 8-20) is of reasonable proportions to give headroom for the lower user, while not being excessively high. Sizes suit 36-inch full-size mattresses, so the bed could be used by adults without constricting them. The assembly is strong enough for adult use, although the design is intended for children, with permanent ladder and a guard rail for the top bed. The ladder is shown at one end, but if it was put further along it would also

act as a guard for a child in the bottom bed.

For long-term use the bed should be made of hardwood, but it would be satisfactory in softwood. It is shown with slats below the mattresses. These parts could be softwood in any case. Plywood might be used instead of slats, if you wish.

The legs have broad rails across at each bed level and the sides are also tenoned into them (Fig. 8-21A). Mark the positions on the pairs of legs, and leave some waste wood on the ends to cut off after the mortises have been cut. Mark all the rails together, so distances between shoulders will be the same (Fig. 8-22A). Mark the sides in the same way (Fig. 8-22B), but with the shoulder the other way. All of the joints can be made with barefaced tenons,

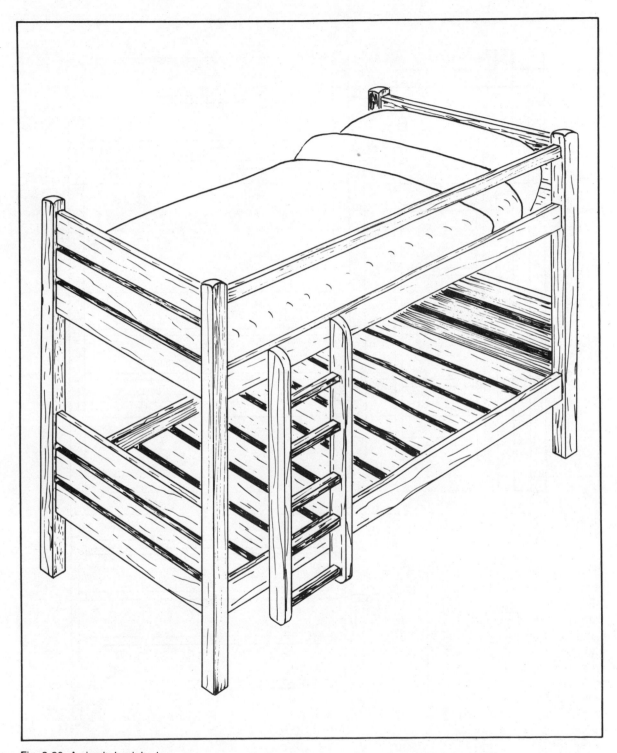

Fig. 8-20. A simple bunk bed.

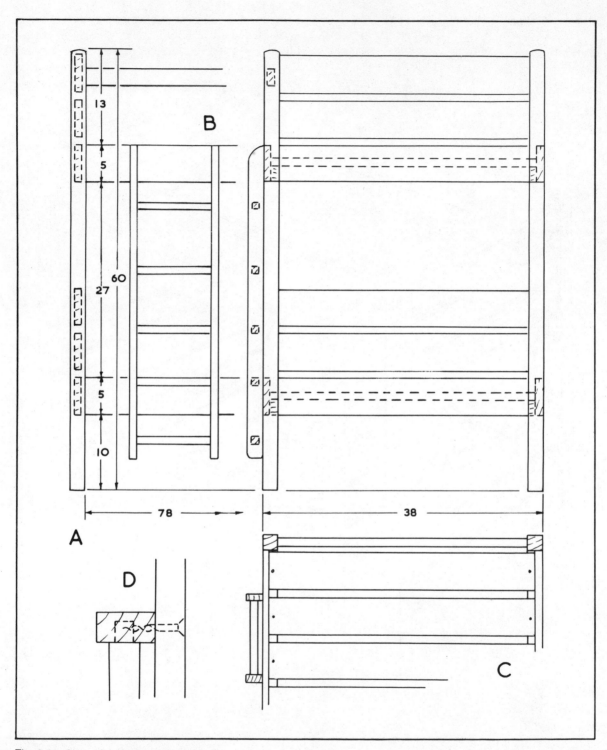

Fig. 8-21. Sizes of a simple bunk bed.

to give better clearance in the leg where the side and end rails must be joined at the same level (Fig. 8-22C). The guard rail over the top bunk can also be tenoned. Only one guard rail is shown and is all that will be necessary if the bed comes against a wall. A rail could be put at the opposite side, if the bed will ever be used away from a wall.

Make up the ends and check that they are square and match. The tops of the legs can be rounded (Fig. 8-22D). If the bottoms will be directly on the floor, take off any sharp angles. Join the ends with the sides and guard rail. Check squareness by measuring diagonals at each end and across a bed level. Pull the joints as tight as possible. They could be reinforced by screws or nails driven from inside. When checking squareness in all directions, see that the assembly stands firm on a level surface.

The ladder shown (Fig. 8-21B) is intended to be screwed to the bed sides. You could use a separate ladder, as described for an earlier bed, if you wish. This ladder need not reach the floor. It is shown ending 2 inches below the bottom rung. Divide the height between the upper side piece and

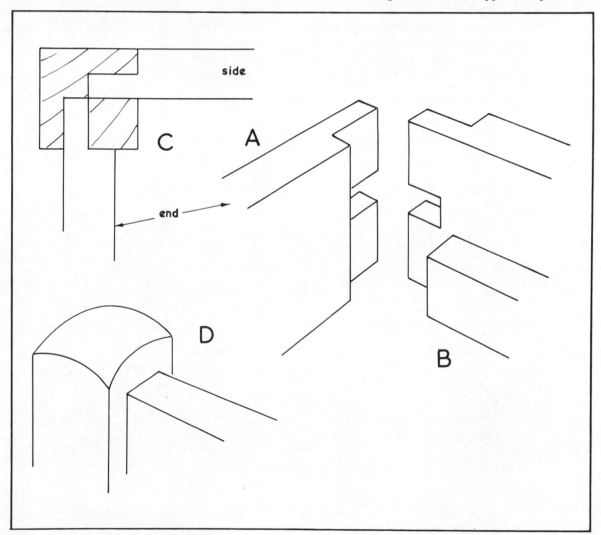

Fig. 8-22. Corners of the simple bunk bed.

the floor into six equal spaces, which will become the upper edges of the rungs (Fig. 8-23A). Mark out the sides to suit.

The rungs could be pieces of ¾-inch dowel rod, but square rungs are shown, with tenons at their ends (Fig. 8-23B). The tenons need not go right through, since there is no need for stiffening, as in a free-standing ladder. Round the tops of the ladder sides to meet the top of the bed side and take off the sharpness of the bottom ends. Leave the rungs basically square, but take off the sharp angles (Fig. 8-23C). Screw the ladder sides from inside the bed sides (Fig. 8-21D).

The bases of the beds are supported on strips inside the sides, whether you use slats or plywood. Take off the sharpness of all exposed angles of the strips and the edges of the upper bed sides where the lower bed occupant may knock against the wood. Space the slats evenly and secure them with a screw at each end (Fig. 8-21C).

The bed should stand steadily anywhere, but if it is going against a wall, movement might be prevented with a few screws into the wall.

## Materials List for Simple Bunk Bed

| | |
|---|---|
| 4 legs | 2×62×2 |
| 12 rails | 5×38×1 |
| 2 sides | 5×82×1 |
| 2 sides | 2×80×1 |
| 1 guard rail | 2×82×1½ |
| 24 slats | 5×38×1 |
| 2 ladder sides | 2×44×1 |
| 5 ladder rungs | 1×13×1 |

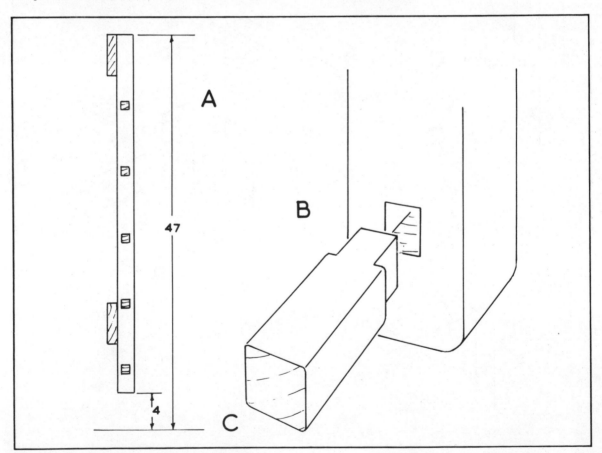

Fig. 8-23. Ladder details for the simple bunk bed.

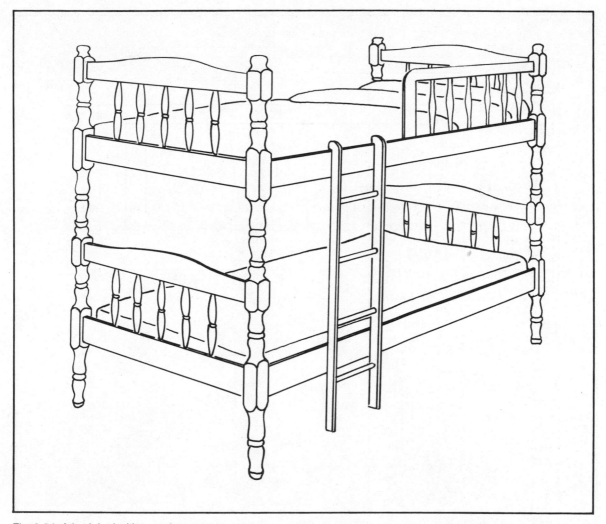

Fig. 8-24. A bunk bed with turned parts.

## TURNED BUNK BED

A two-tier bed with all the main parts turned can look very attractive. It involves the builder in quite a lot of lathework, but the result is worth the effort. Sizes are arranged to come within the limits of a 30-inch capacity lathe. There are two beds which are almost identical, with dowel connections between the legs. This turned bunk bed (Fig. 8-24) is intended for mattresses 30 inches by 78 inches. The mattresses are shown supported on webbing, which provides some springing so the mattresses need not be as thick as they would on solid sup-

ports. However, you could use plywood or slats instead of webbing, if you preferred.

### Design

The beds could be made of hardwood or softwood. The sizes quoted suit softwood. Some parts could be reduced slightly in section if a dense hardwood is used. Hardwoods allow for more detail in turning without producing weak parts; so two designs for the lathework are shown. With hardwood, the ends of the square parts are cut squarely against beads (Fig. 8-25A). With softwood, the

193

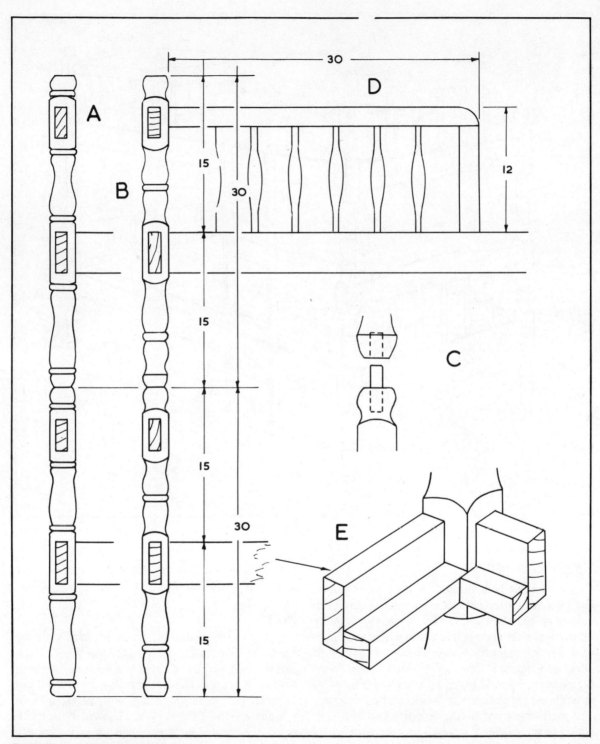

Fig. 8-25. Sizes of the turned bunk bed.

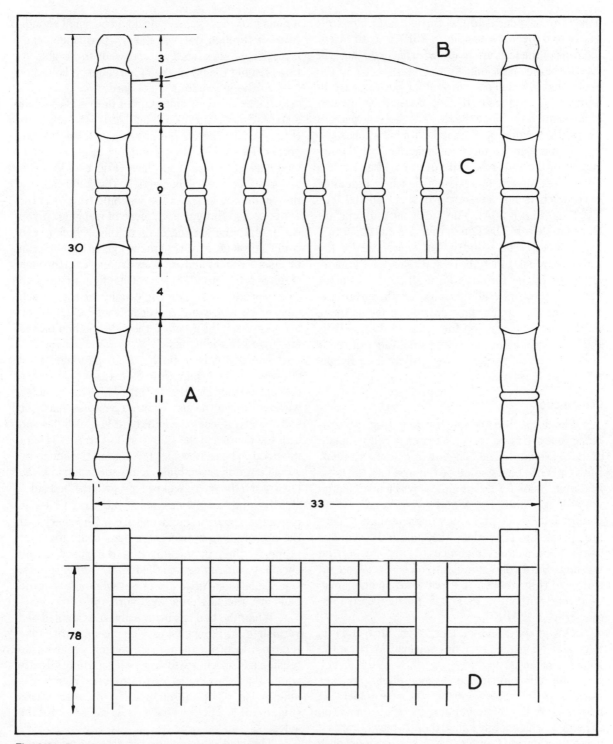

Fig. 8-26. End sizes and webbing arrangements for the turned bunk bed.

beads are avoided and the turned parts blend directly into the squares (Fig. 8-25B). In both cases, the tops of the legs are made with flat ends that will match the flat bottoms; so the joints between the upper and lower legs will match. For the sake of uniformity, the tops of the top bed may be finished in the same way. Since they will not become parts of joints, they could be finished with full knobs.

If you want to increase headroom for the occupant of the lower bed, its ends could be made a few inches higher, but raising the whole assembly very much is not advised. Mark out all the legs together (Fig. 8-26A). The sides and end rails are the same level. The upper rails are cut down to 3 inches deep. The wood is left square where the joints go. Mark 1 inch above and below each joint for the start of the turning. Turn all the legs, taking care that they finish all the same length. The tops of the lower legs might have dowels turned on them, or they could be drilled for separate dowels (Fig. 8-25C). Drill the other legs to suit. Taper or round the ends of the dowels, so they will enter easily, but not finish loosely.

## Construction

Shape the tops of the top rails (Fig. 8-26B). Since four are to be made to match, a half template of the curve is advised. The lower rails are straight. Both rails can be doweled or tenoned into the legs. Mark out holes for the spindles, which need not go very deeply into the wood—½ inch should be enough for ½-inch or ⅝-inch diameter holes. Turn the spindles to suit. Make the ends of the spindles parallel for a short distance before starting the shaping. Hardwood spindles look best with a central bead (Fig. 8-26C), but softwood spindles may be turned without it, as shown for the guard spindles (Fig. 8-25D).

One guard is shown. Decide on which end it is to go and if you need two, or even four. Mark for the guard joint on its leg.

The rails and sides are shown slightly thicker than usual for a plywood or slat base under the mattress. With rubber webbing there is a tension on the sides, which might cause them to bow inwards if made too thin and flexible. Mark out the sides, with

tenons into the legs. A bed should be small enough to pass through doorways, so a permanent construction is suggested. If you want to be able to disassemble the beds, the sides could be bolted or held to the legs with special hardware.

Inside the deep sides comes pieces 1¼-inches square. Similar pieces are put across the end rails (Fig. 8-25E). Before joining the side pieces together decide how the webbing is to be attached. One way is to tack it in place (Fig. 8-27A). Five tacks at each end will be needed. You could nail on a thin strip of wood over the webbing (Fig. 8-27B), with one nail through each piece of webbing. If you use metal clips on the ends of the webbing, you could plow a groove along the wood, so the clips can be inserted and a nail or screw driven down through (Fig. 8-27C). Another way of holding a clip is to plow a groove at a slight angle along the top of each strip for the clip to be pressed in (Fig. 8-27D). If you use a groove, cut it before the side and end pieces are joined to their rails.

The guard is made up of strips joined with dowels or a bridle joint (Fig. 8-28A) and tenons into the leg and the side (Fig. 8-28B). Make the spindles without central beads, whether you use hard- or soft woods. Reduce the ends to fit ½-inch holes and drill the guard and the side to suit. The guard is not intended to be removable. If you want the bed to be suitable for disassembling, leave the tenon into the leg dry, so the guard will remain with the bed side.

Assemble the four ends at the same time and check that they are square and matching. Check that the dowel joints between the beds come together properly. Join in the sides of the guard, again checking squareness and the fit of the dowel joints. Check diagonals in all directions while the stacked beds are standing on a level surface.

When the bed has been painted or stained and varnished, fit the webbing. The pieces across take the most load. Fit them first, getting a reasonable tension and spacing webbing with gaps only slightly wider than the widths of the pieces. Weave the lengthwise pieces through the crosswise strips (Fig. 8-26D). They can have wider gaps toward the sides.

The ladder for this bed is shown upright and

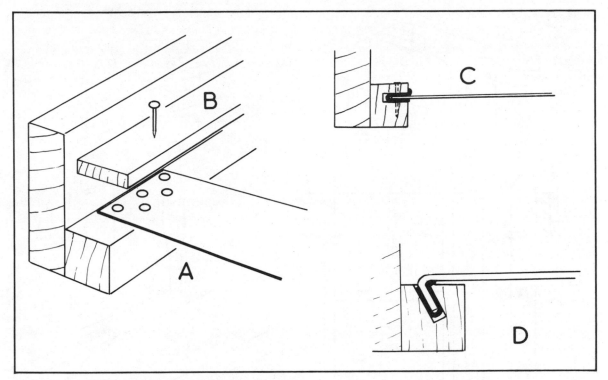

Fig. 8-27. Methods of attaching webbing for the turned bunk bed.

hooked over the side of the top bed, so it can be removed (Fig. 8-28C). It could be made to slope or it could be screwed in place, as described for other beds. The sides should reach from the floor to above the top bed, where there are short pieces with bridle joints and hooks inside the bed (Fig. 8-28D). The hook may be a thin piece of hardwood, or a piece of aluminum or brass may be screwed on. Strengthen the bridle joint with a dowel through. Thoroughly round all exposed edges.

Divide the distance from the top of the bed side to the floor evenly for the rung spacing. If made to the suggested size, 45 inches conveniently divides into five. These positions are the tops of the rungs, so drill below them. Dowels ¾ inch in diameter are suitable. They are stronger taken right through. The top and bottom rungs may also be wedged (Fig. 8-28E). If that is done, the intermediate rungs could be taken only about ¾ inch into each rail. If you prefer square rungs, use tenons, as described for an earlier bed.

## Materials List for Turned Bunk Bed

| | |
|---|---|
| 8 legs | 2½×32×2½ |
| 4 rails | 4×33×1¼ |
| 4 rails | 1¼×32×1¼ |
| 4 rails | 5×33×1¼ |
| 4 sides | 4×82×1¼ |
| 4 sides | 1¼×80×1¼ |
| 20 spindles | 1½×12×1½ |
| 1 guard rail | 2×32×1¼ |
| 1 guard rail | 2×14×1¼ |
| 6 spindles | 1×12×1 |
| 2 ladder sides | 2×50×1 |
| 4 ladder rungs | ¾×13 dowels |

### BUNK BED WITH DRAWERS

Drawers under a bed are always useful, but even more so in a child's room. With children sleeping one above the other, the toys and clothing that must be stowed if the room is to be tidy are increased. Drawers under the lower bed can be

197

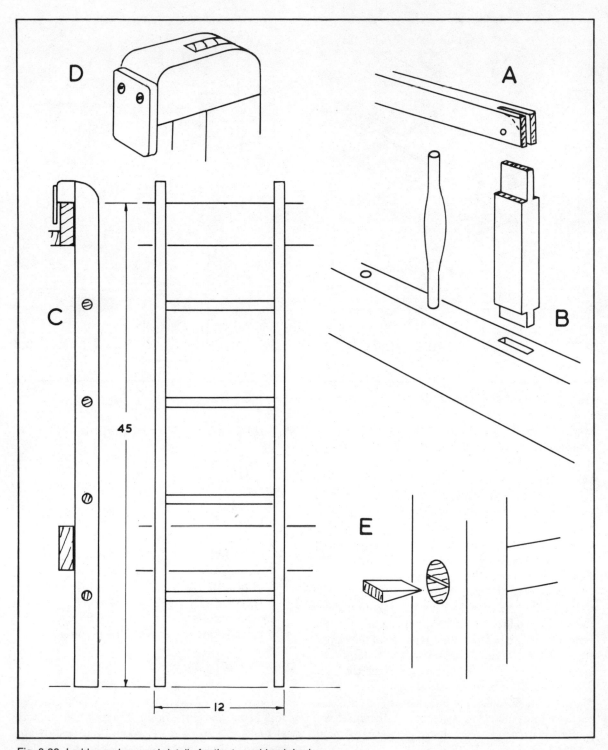

Fig. 8-28. Ladder and general details for the turned bunk bed.

Fig. 8-29. A bunk bed with drawers.

quite spacious. Closing in the space under the bed also prevents dust from getting underneath, or at least removes the need for sweeping in a rather awkward place.

This two-tier bed (Fig. 8-29) takes mattresses 36 inches by 78 inches, supported on plywood bases. The space under the lower bed is enclosed and fitted with two drawers. The top bed is without a raised foot. Its ladder can be hooked on at the foot or at a side. Guards are arranged at both sides.

The combined beds are intended to be treated as a unit, but the top bed can be lifted off for transport. It could be used alone on the floor, but separation is primarily intended to reduce the parts to sizes that will pass through a doorway. The main parts could be made of hardwood or softwood. Available plywood for closing in below the bottom bed may dictate what finish should be chosen. If other woods are mixed, a painted finish may be desired, but plywood with a good face veneer may be used with an attractive hardwood for a stained and varnished or polished finish.

The suggested sizes (Fig. 8-30) may be modified if you have mattresses of other sizes or wish to increase the space between the beds. The lower bed has ends of the same height. The top bed has a head similar to the lower one, but nothing extending up at the foot.

### Legs

Start with the legs. The two pairs for the lower bed are the same (Fig. 8-31A). Mark the positions of the rails and sides and the two strips that come above and below the drawer openings. The sides come level with the outsides of the legs, but the top end rails are central. Below the bottom bed one of the strips laps on to the piece forming the side of the bed. Its upper edge supports the plywood below the mattress and its projecting part below comes behind the side plywood (Fig. 8-31B).

Mark out the legs for the head of the upper bed (Fig. 8-31C). The rail and side joints will be the same as for the lower bed. Mark out the legs for the foot of that bed (Fig. 8-31D). The only joints are for the side and end rails both arranged so the pieces come level with the outsides of the legs. Round the tops of the legs for the top bed after the mortises have been cut (Fig. 8-31E). The joints between the bed legs are made with dowels (Fig. 8-31F), glued in the lower legs and tapered slightly to push easily into holes in the upper legs.

### Rails and Sides

The rails and sides are all joined with dowels or mortise and tenon joints. The two top rails in each bed can have central tenons (Fig. 8-32A), but where the rails and sides must come level with the outsides of the legs, use barefaced tenons (Fig. 8-32B). The 1-inch-by-2-inch strips that come behind the plywood below the bottom bed can also be joined to the legs with dowels or tenons (Fig. 8-32C). The distance between these strips will be the depth of the drawers, and they should be put at the back as well as the front, although the back is not cut away. The rather long, slender pieces will be stiffened when they are attached to the plywood.

The rails and sides are all straight. Mark out all pieces that must match together. Cut the joints. Strips can be put inside the bed sides before assembly. Similar pieces are needed inside the end rails to support the mattress base. For the top bed, the strips should finish level with the undersides of the bed sides. All sharp edges there should be well-rounded off, since they may be knocked by the head of the user of the lower bed. Prepare the parts for the guards before assembly.

When you assemble the lower bed, put strips between the narrow pieces (Fig 8-32D) to provide end support for the plywood, which goes between the legs, up to the bed side piece, and down to the floor. Cut out the openings for the drawers in the front, but leave final leveling of the long edges until after the lengthwise strips are attached. It is easier then to get straight and level edges. Attach the plywood with glue and fine finishing nails. The nails can be punched and covered with stopping, although the panels will come at the level too low for the nail heads to be obvious to a normal viewer.

Plywood panels are fitted similarly all around. Be careful that the lower plywood edges do not come below the level of the legs. The weight of the beds and their occupants must be taken by the legs. If the bed is to stand on a carpet, you may want to keep the plywood about ¼ inch above the leg level, so it does not press into the carpet.

### Drawers

The drawers may go almost the full width of the bed (Fig. 8-33A). They need runners underneath, guides at the sides, and kickers above to

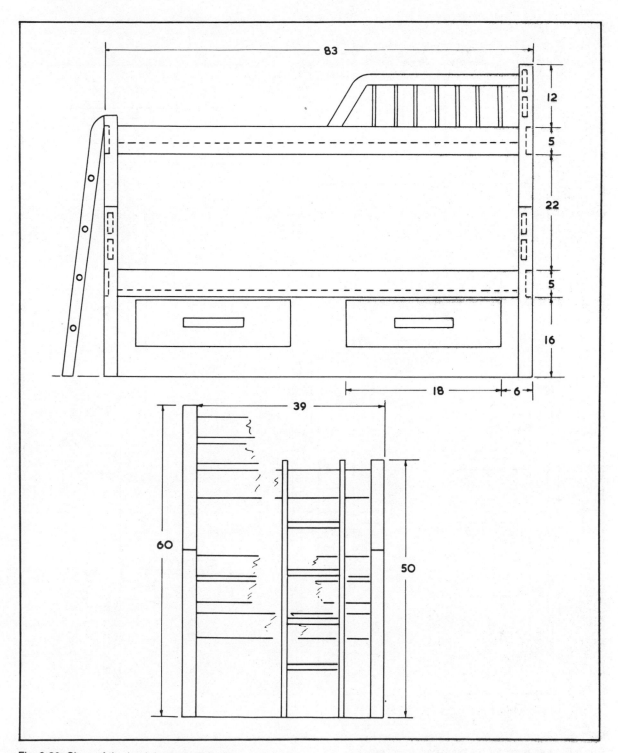

Fig. 8-30. Sizes of the bunk bed with drawers.

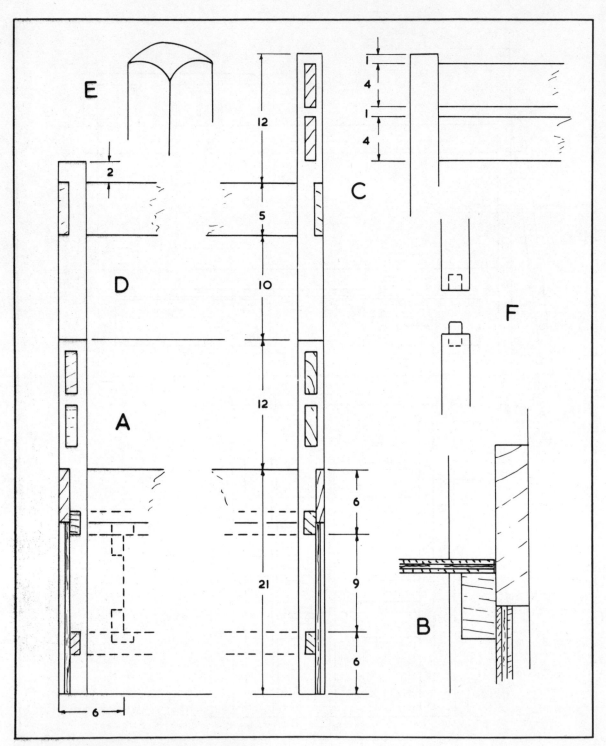

Fig. 8-31. Part sizes for the bunk bed with drawers.

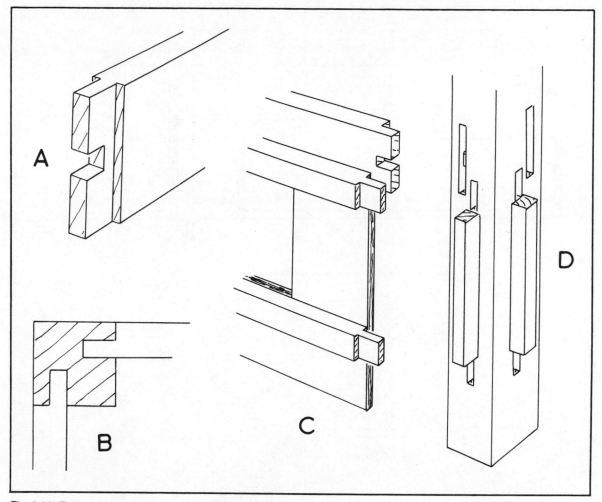

Fig. 8-32. Framing joints for the bunk bed with drawers.

prevent the drawer from tilting. Pieces of plywood could be put across, but assemblies of 1-inch-by-2-inch strips are suggested. Make sure the pieces you use are straight, since any deflection will affect the smooth running of a drawer.

Let the pieces that will form runners and kickers into the long strips at back and front (Fig. 8-33B). Half the width of each piece comes across the opening. On these pieces mount guide pieces (Fig. 8-33C). They need not be let in. Keep ends level with the sides of the openings. Make sure these parts are square to the front and parallel with each other.

The drawers can be made as described earlier

(Fig. 8-7), with plywood sides, a false front to overlap the opening, and handles attached. You may want to put stops on the runners at the back, so stopping a drawer is not done solely by the overlapping front, which may get strained if a heavily loaded drawer is pushed back hard.

Another way of providing a handgrip, without actually using a handle, is to cut away the top edge of the drawer front (Fig. 8-33D). Well-round all the edges that a hand will contact. This grip has the advantage of not leaving anything projecting and is particularly appropriate for drawers in which a child keeps his toys. You could make two cutouts so the child can use two hands.

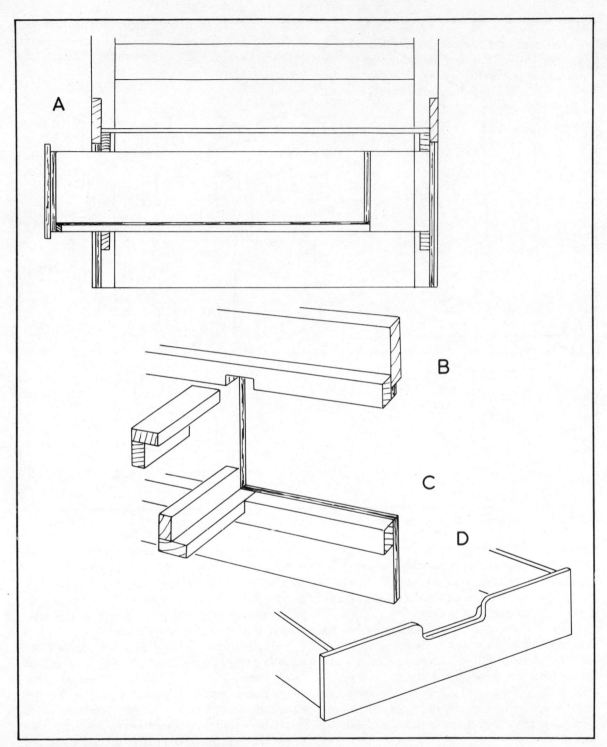

Fig. 8-33. Supports and guides for the drawers.

## Guards

The guards are made of strips with dowel rods to the bed sides. There are simple tenons into the legs, but the fronts are shown with sloping parts (Fig. 8-34A). The exact angle is not important but 60 degrees to the side is suitable. Set this out and cut a bridle joint at the top corner (Fig. 8-34B). For the tenon into the side, the inner edge must slope, but the other edge can be cut square to the surface (Fig. 8-34C). Mark out the dowel holes so one comes fairly close to the bridle joint. The gap lower down will not then be too wide. Well-round over the bridle joint and take sharpness off all exposed edges.

## Ladder

The ladder is made like an earlier one (Fig. 8-13). The end and sides of the top bed are the same, so the ladder can be used at the foot or side of the bed, however at the end it will not interfere with

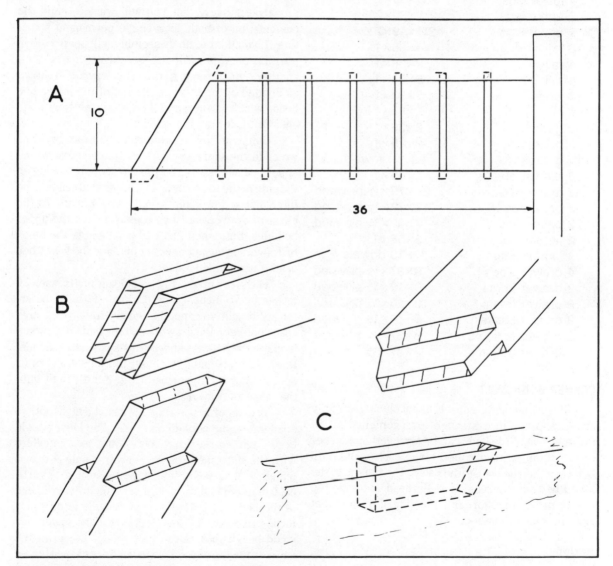

Fig. 8-34. Guard for the top bunk.

205

the use of drawers. Measure the actual height of the top of the upper bed rail and divide it to get the rungs evenly spaced. Five spaces will give a rise of just over 9 inches, but if you think this is too much, six spaces will give 8 inches. Mark these distances to make the top edges of the holes drilled for the rungs.

## Materials List for Bunk Bed with Drawers

| | |
|---|---|
| 4 lower legs | 2½×36×2½ |
| 2 upper legs | 2½×30×2½ |
| 2 upper legs | 2½×19×2½ |
| 6 rails | 4×38×1 |
| 4 rails | 2×38×1 |
| 4 rails | 5×38×1 |
| 4 sides | 5×83×1 |
| 6 sides | 2×83×1 |
| 2 guards | 2×36×1 |
| 2 guards | 2×15×1 |
| 14 guards | ½×11 dowels |
| 16 drawer guides | 2×39×1 |
| 2 mattress bases | 37×79×½ plywood |
| 2 base sides | 17×79×½ plywood |
| 2 base ends | 17×35×½ plywood |
| 2 ladder sides | 2×56×1 |
| 4 ladder rungs | ¾×13 dowels |
| 4 drawer sides | 9×37×½ plywood |
| 2 drawer fronts | 9×19×½ plywood |
| 2 drawer fronts | 10×20×½ plywood |
| 2 drawer backs | 9×19×½ plywood |
| 2 drawer bottoms | 18×37×¼ plywood |
| 3 drawer bottoms | ½×37×½ |

## CORNER BUNK BEDS

It is usual, and compact, to put one bed directly above another in a stacked arrangement, but, if there is space, the beds can be arranged in a corner of the room, with one bed along each wall. Both beds can then be used either way. The person in the lower bed may feel cosy with his head under the top bed or prefer the more open feeling of making that end the foot of his bed.

## Design

This arrangement also opens up another pos-

sibility. The vacant space under one end of the upper bed can be used by another loose piece of furniture, such as a table or desk. There is room for a chair, if someone is to read to a child, or, if the child reads himself, there could be bookshelves. The possibilities are endless and the children may have their own ideas. The furniture could be built-in. In the example (Fig. 8-35) there is a chest of two drawers, with a top at a height of 27 inches that will serve as a working surface for a child.

It is unlikely that you will want to build the combination of beds as a single permanent structure. If you do, the final assembly will need to be in position and you will not be able to move it to another room through normal doorways. It is shown as divided at the level of the top of the lower bed head, which is the same height as the top of the chest of drawers (Fig. 8-36A).

Construction is generally similar to beds which fit the same way over each other, except the upper bed needs an extra post to support one leg on the side of the lower bed. The upper bed can then be lifted off the dowel joints on the lower posts. At the chest of drawers are two legs to match the upper bed legs, but, when that bed is taken off, the block of drawers is an independent unit and the lower bed can be used independently.

The sizes given (Fig. 8-36) suit mattresses 36 inches by 78 inches. The drawer width can be arranged to suit your needs, but try to leave enough space between the drawers and the bed for a person to make the bed. As shown this space is 15 inches. It would be possible to build in more drawers or doors under the upper bed (Fig. 8-36B) to fit onto the chest of drawers.

The upper bed is shown without a high foot, so a ladder can be hooked on there. The ladder could be brought to the front, but would then interfere with the movement of the drawers, unless it was put close against the side of the lower bed. A vertical ladder could be attached permanently to the end of the bed, but it would need to be held off a few inches to allow for toe clearance. The lower bed could be given a raised foot, but it is shown the same as the top bed. The bed heads could be treated in the same way suggested for many previous beds, with slats or turned spindles vertically between rails, or there could be two or more narrow, horizontal rails, but solidly shaped heads are shown (Fig. 8-36C). The extra post at the wall side of the lower bed should be braced to the corner post for rigidity by a panel similar to the bed heads. A single rail would also be sufficient. Extra lower rails are shown across the ends of the fairly long-legged upper bed, to provide stiffness. The rail at the foot also prevents things from falling off the working surface over the drawers. The rail under the head may be used for hanging things beside the lower bed.

## Top Bed

Make the top bed first. The legs at the head (Fig. 8-37A) will be mortised for the other parts. They should extend up 2 inches and be rounded after the mortises have been cut. Mark out the pairs of legs for the foot end at the same time. They have the same details up to the bed side level (Fig. 8-37B), then are cut off and rounded 2 inches above that. Drill the bottoms of all upper bed legs with ¾-inch holes to take the dowels projecting from the tops of the lower legs.

The head panel is shown as a solid board with a straight lower edge and a shaped top (Fig. 8-37C).

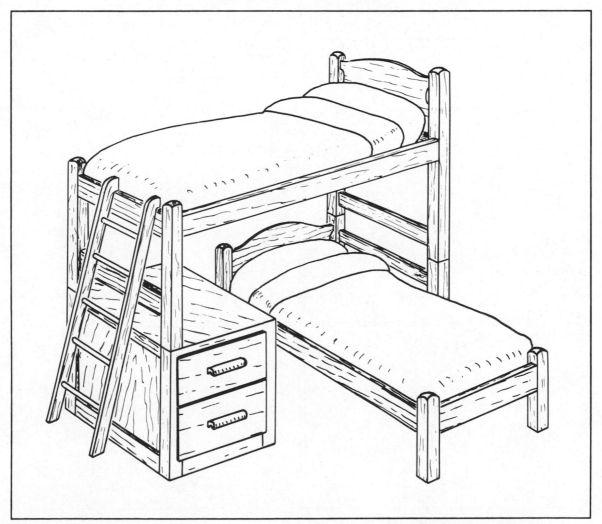

Fig. 8-35. Corner bunk beds.

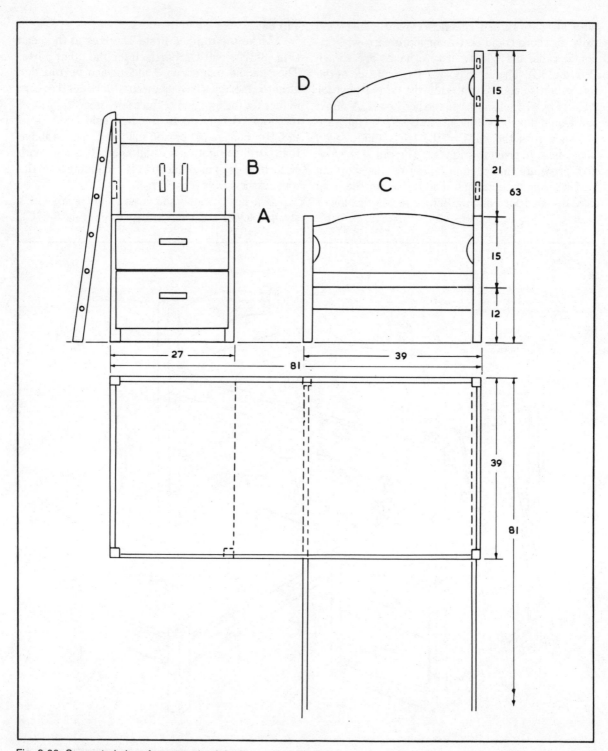

Fig. 8-36. Suggested sizes for corner bunk beds.

208

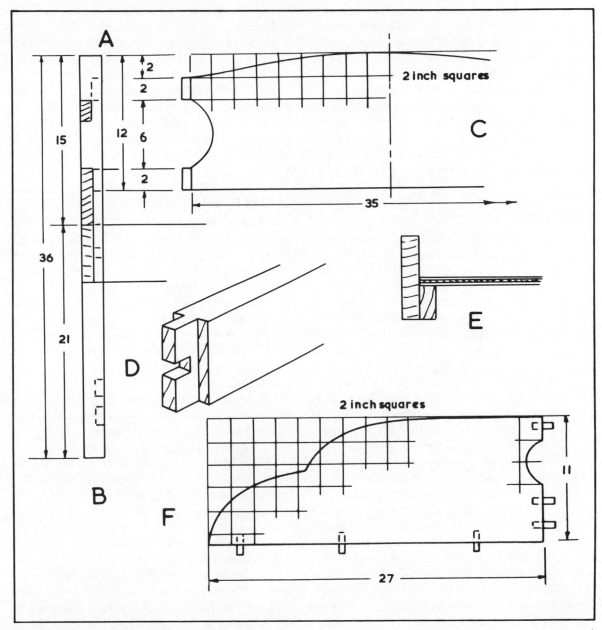

Fig. 8-37. Details of parts of the corner bunk beds.

Its ends are cut down to make two tenons. There will be a similar head for the lower bed, and you may use one at its side instead of a straight rail, so a half template will be worth making. The rail at the side level should be made with a barefaced tenon, so its outer surface comes level with the outside of the leg. The lower, stiffening rail may have central tenons (Fig. 8-37D).

In the other direction are sides with barefaced tenons and the usual supports for slats or a plywood base for the mattress (Fig. 8-37E). Similar slats go across the end rails. Make up the foot of the bed.

If a guard is to be provided, it could be framed with dowel posts or turned spindles as described for earlier beds, but it is shown here as a solid piece to match the bed heads (Fig. 8-36D). Mark and cut the shape (Fig. 8-37F). Its top edge and the shaped parts of the bed heads should be well-rounded before assembly. The guard could be tenoned into the leg, but dowels are better into the bed side; so they are suggested into the leg as well. Glue and dowel the guard to the side first; then assemble and carefully square the other parts to complete the upper bed.

## Bottom Bed

In most details the lower bed is made in the same way as its upper partner. It could be made with head panels at both ends, so it would be suitable for use either way. It could be made with a foot like the other bed at the inner end, but it would still need a high post to take the upper leg in the corner of the room. As drawn, the head will be in the corner and the foot without a raised part will be at the other end, similar to the upper bed.

The head legs (Fig. 8-38A) are shorter than those of the upper bed and are without lower rails. The leg that will not extend to the other bed, and the two legs at the foot, should all have rounded tops. Cut the top of the other leg square.

There must be a post at the side of the lower bed at a suitable distance from the corner to take an upper leg. The bed side away from the wall can have barefaced tenons to bring the wood level with the outside of the legs. This arrangement at the wall side, would extend the extra post out of the bed side into the edge of the mattress; so make the leg level with the inner edge of the bed side at the corner (Fig. 8-38B) instead of at the outer edge, bringing it in 1 inch. Make sure there will still be space for the mattress. If necessary, make the bed a little wider.

At the post position, it will be best to use a halving joint. Cut ½ inch out of the side and make a notch ½ inch in the post (Fig. 8-38C). Get the distance from the corner leg by measuring the distance between the legs of the upper bed. They may not be exactly to size, but that does not matter if you allow for the difference.

You could fit a similar panel to the head between this post and the corner leg, but it is simpler to tenon in a plain rail (Fig. 8-38D) for stiffness. Drill for and fit projecting dowels in the tops of the legs to fit the holes in the legs of the other bed.

For both beds make plywood bases for the mattresses. They could be divided across the middle if that is more convenient. Drill a pattern of holes for mattress ventilation. The plywood could be left loose on its supports, but screwing it down adds stiffness to the assembly.

## Chest of Drawers

The chest of drawers can be made as an independent unit. The key measurements are an overall height the same as the height of the leg and post on the lower bed and a distance back to front to suit the spacing of the foot end legs of the upper bed.

The carcass is made with four 2-inch square posts with ¼-inch plywood in grooves at the side and back. Rails are fit outside the plywood and the top is solid. At the front are top and bottom rails, but there is no rail between the drawers since their false fronts meet.

Mark out the four posts (Fig. 8-39A) allowing for the thickness of the top. Cut grooves to suit the plywood panels both ways in the rear posts (Fig. 8-39B) and to suit the sides only at the front. Make the sides first. Top and bottom rails come outside the plywood grooves and should be doweled or tenoned into the legs (Fig. 8-39C). Make the panels and assemble them into the grooves at the same time as the top and bottom rails are fitted. Glue the plywood to the rails and reinforce with a few fine nails driven from inside.

Make the top and bottom rails for the back and front, with tenons or dowels into the posts. Cut a plywood panel for the back and have this ready to fit. Similarly, have the front rails ready, but do not fit them until you have made and fitted the drawer rails.

At the levels of the bottoms of the two drawers make combined runners and guides (Fig. 8-39D). The surface of the guide must come level with the insides of the legs. The runners must project far enough to support the drawers. Put another strip

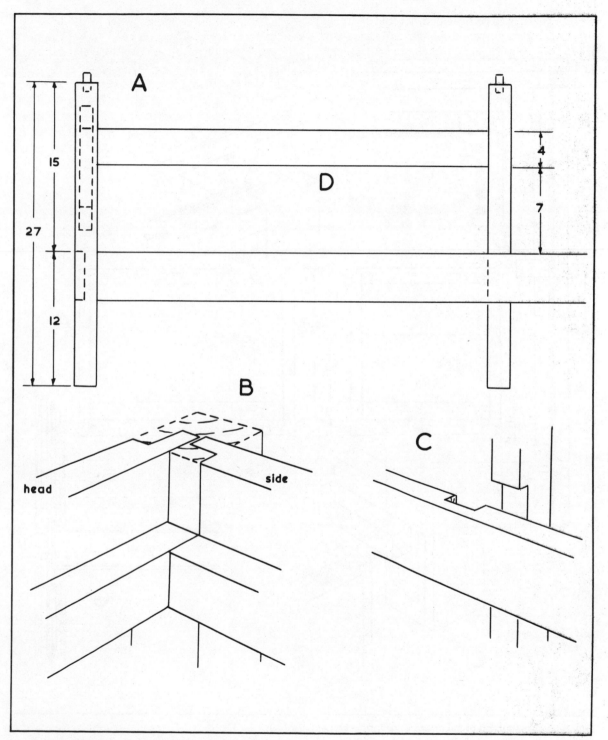

Fig. 8-38. Details at the corner of the lower bed.

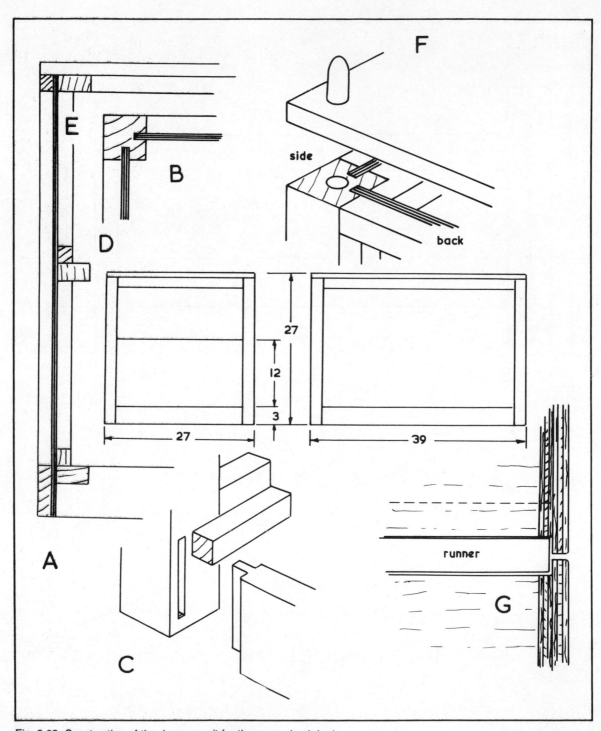

Fig. 8-39. Construction of the drawers unit for the corner bunk bed.

across the top to act as a kicker (Fig. 8-39E). These pieces can be supported with glue and nails through the plywood, although the ends could be doweled or tenoned if you wish. Take care to get them parallel.

The top is shown as a solid piece. It could be thick plywood, with its edge grain hidden by narrow strips fitted around and mitered at the corners. A frame of strips about ¾-inch thick with a panel of thinner plywood could be let into rabbets to form the main surface. This surface might be a place for butcher block construction, using a large number of narrow strips, if you want to match something of that type already in the room.

Make the top to the overall sizes of the carcass (Fig. 8-39F) and fit it. Drill for dowels in the two corners that will fit with the legs of the upper bed.

The drawers could be made with solid wood dovetailed in the traditional way, or they could be made from plywood as described earlier (Fig. 8-7). Let the false fronts overlap the posts and rails, but, where the bottom of the top drawer comes above the lower drawer, arrange for them to come close (Fig. 8-39G) to hide the ends of the runners. There could be stops on the runners to relieve the strain on the fronts when a drawer is pushed in hard. Add handles to the drawers to complete the unit.

### Finishing

You will have no difficulty in fitting the upper legs to the bed below, but be careful not to distort the foot end of the upper bed. Position the chest of drawers so the upper legs can be dropped onto the dowels without forcing them out of true.

The ladder is made in the way previously described (Fig. 8-13). It will hook on the side or end of the upper bed. The height of 48 inches conveniently divides into six spaces of 8 inches, but use these marks as the top of the rungs.

### Materials List for Corner Bunk Beds

**Top Bed**

| | |
|---|---|
| 2 legs | 2×38×2 |
| 2 legs | 2×25×2 |
| 1 panel | 12×38×1 |

| | |
|---|---|
| 1 rail | 4×38×1 |
| 2 rails | 5×38×1 |
| 2 rails | 2×38×1 |
| 2 sides | 5×81×1 |
| 2 sides | 2×81×1 |
| 1 guard | 11×28×1 |
| 1 base | 37×79×½ plywood |

**Bottom Bed**

| | |
|---|---|
| 2 legs | 2×29×2 |
| 1 post | 2×29×2 |
| 2 legs | 2×16×2 |
| 1 panel | 12×38×1 |
| 2 rails | 5×38×1 |
| 2 rails | 2×38×1 |
| 1 rail | 4×38×1 |
| 2 sides | 5×81×1 |
| 2 sides | 2×81×1 |
| 1 base | 37×79×½ plywood |

**Block of Drawers**

| | |
|---|---|
| 4 posts | 2×29×2 |
| 2 panels | 27×39×¼ plywood |
| 1 panel | 27×27×¼ plywood |
| 2 bottom rails | 3×27×⅞ |
| 1 bottom rail | 3×39×⅞ |
| 2 top rails | 1×27×⅞ |
| 1 top rail | 1×39×⅞ |
| 6 drawer runners | 2×39×1 |
| 6 drawer guides | 1×39×⅞ |
| 2 drawer sides | 11×39×½ plywood |
| 2 drawer sides | 12×39×½ plywood |
| 1 drawer front | 11×24×½ plywood |
| 1 drawer front | 12×24×½ plywood |
| 1 drawer front | 12×25×½ plywood |
| 1 drawer front | 13×25×½ plywood |
| 1 drawer back | 11×24×½ plywood |
| 1 drawer back | 12×24×½ plywood |
| 2 drawer bottoms | 24×39×¼ plywood |
| 4 drawer bottoms | ½×39×½ |

**Ladder**

| | |
|---|---|
| 2 sides | 2×52×1 |
| 5 rungs | ¾×13 dowels |

# Chapter 9

# Cots, Cradles, and Cribs

A bed for the smallest and newest member of the family does not need to be very large. It may not be used very long for one child, since he will grow and need a more normal bed. Usually the cot or crib will be used for more than one child, so it is an advantage if it can occupy minimum space or be made to take down or fold until next needed. You may also need to take the bed when you are visiting overnight, which is another reason to be able to reduce it in size.

In the smallest crib sizes, cushions or improvised padding are used, so size is not critical. For larger cribs mattress size will govern the size of the wooden parts. A common size is 24 inches by 48 inches, but you should get your mattress before you start construction.

There are some safety considerations. The assembly must be stable, so the child can not rock it over. He should not be able to get out, if you prefer he does not. A baby will be incapable of making the attempt, but later on the child may regard it as a challenge and do his best to get out. Gaps should be kept narrow. It should never be possible for a child

to get his head through a space and become trapped; so rail spaces must be no more than 3½ inches. In most cribs one side must open, but when it is closed it should be proof against young investigating hands, which can be very persistent.

## FOLDING CRIB

This folding crib is of simple construction (Fig. 9-1) and is made to fold flat. When the mattress support is in place, the crib is rigidly held to shape, but, when it is removed, the crib can be folded flat, still with the same length and height, but only a few inches wide.

Sizes given are for light hardwood. If a softwood is used, the legs should be made slightly thicker. Dowel rods are always hardwood and it is better to make the other parts to match. You could use square strips instead of dowel rods, but their corners would need to be rounded and the ends tenoned. Check the mattress size and work to that, allowing a little clearance all around.

The standard size crib (Fig. 9-1A) will suit a child up to the age when he will need a normal bed.

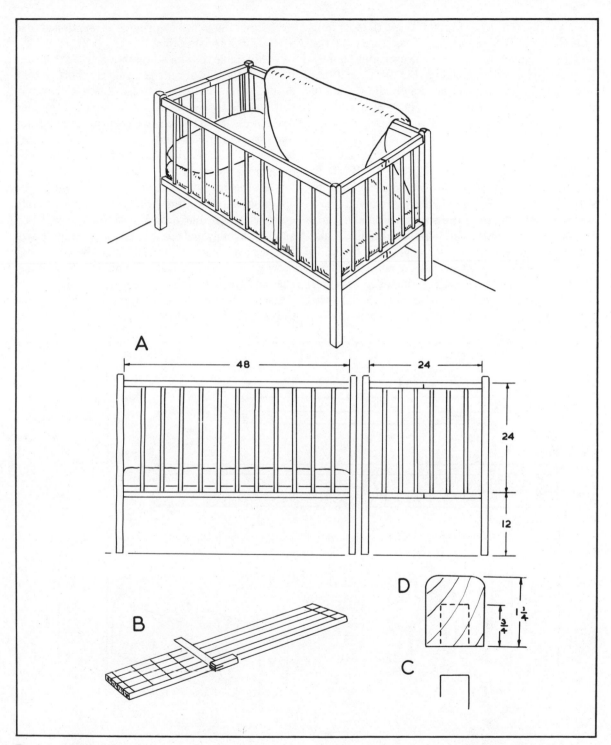

Fig. 9-1. A folding crib.

Mark out the four legs (Fig. 9-2A) and the four long rails (Fig. 9-2B). The sections of wood are not large enough to allow for two dowels in each joint, unless they are arranged diagonally, (Fig. 9-2C) and that spacing is difficult to place accurately. It is better to use mortise and tenon joints (Fig. 9-2D).

### Construction

Mark the dowel hole positions across all rails together, to insure they match (Fig. 9-1B). Drill squarely to the surface and to a regular depth (Fig. 9-1C), preferably using a drill press, so you know the holes are square to the surface. Round the top edges of the top rails (Fig. 9-1D) thoroughly. Take off sharpness from the lower edges of those rails and all edges of the lower rails. Where the joints come in the legs leave the meeting edges square, but elsewhere take off all sharpness. Round the tops of the legs (Fig. 9-2E), allowing them to pro-

ject above the joints to provide strength and also give a place to hang things.

Assemble the sides together and see that they match. If the dowel rods are slightly short so they do not touch the bottoms of the holes, they will settle at the right distance when the rails are joined to the legs. If you try to make them full length, they may prevent the assembly from pulling together properly. Check flatness and squareness by measuring diagonals.

At the ends the rails are divided in the middle and hinged to fold (Fig. 9-3A). To get an accurate end you should make both parts of one end in a single assembly and cut it in two later (Fig. 9-3B). Use an even number of dowels so the cut comes between the center ones. Round and take off any sharp edges of the rails in the same way as those at the sides. It is important that the spacing between the end rails is exactly the same as between the side

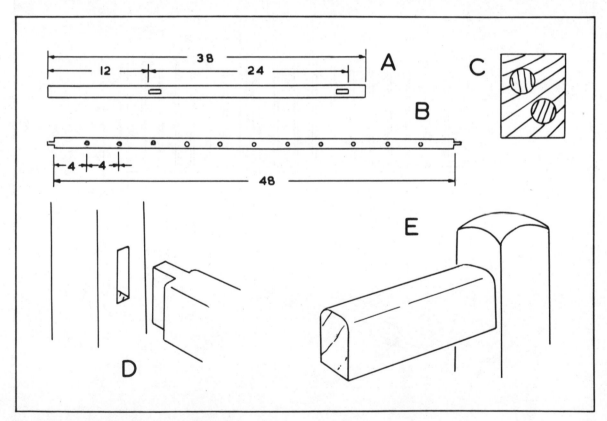

Fig. 9-2. Legs and side rails for the folding crib.

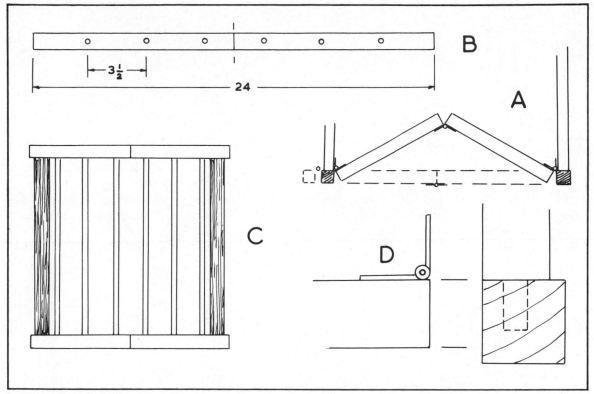

Fig. 9-3. End of the folding crib.

rails. Use temporary pieces as stops during assembly (Fig. 9-3C). Thin nails through the corner dowel joints can be used to prevent movement while the glue is setting. Check squareness and see that opposite ends match.

Separate the parts of each end by sawing across, but be careful that sections do not become turned around or confused with each other. The hinges go on the surfaces (Fig. 9-3D) to give better clearance for folding than when let in. File off any exposed corners. Make sure you drive screws level and do not roughen the heads by letting the screwdriver slip.

## Mattress Support

The mattress support is a frame with its sides extending through the ends and its own ends positioned to come just inside the end dowels and prevent folding (Fig. 9-4A). Fit the support close enough to hold the crib in shape, but give enough clearance for it to be lifted out easily. Get sizes from the assembled crib.

Corners of the support may be doweled or tenoned (Fig. 9-4B). Round the ends of the sides that project through the corner spaces. There are several possible ways of closing the support. A piece of plywood may be nailed on and drilled with a few holes to ventilate the mattress (Fig. 9-4C). Slats could be put across and notched into the side pieces (Fig. 9-4D). Perforated hardboard, or *pegboard* could be used. For hygienic reasons there should be plenty of holes or spaces under the mattress. A different support can be made with wire netting—of the chicken wire or fence type—held to the frame with staples (Fig. 9-4E). Turn under wire ends so none can tear the mattress. Any mattress of this size should be thick enough to provide all the cushioning needed in itself, so there is no need for springing in the base.

217

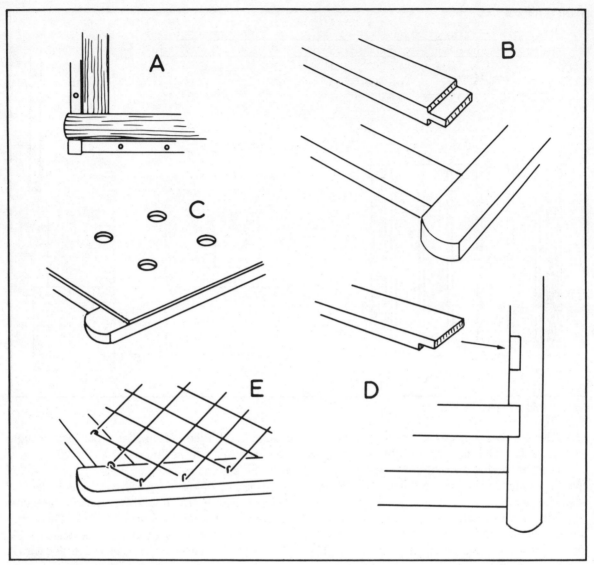

Fig. 9-4. Mattress for the folding crib.

## Finishing

Since the crib is of skeleton construction, there are no broad areas for decoration. A plain varnish finish is usually preferable to paint. It would be easier to keep clean.

### Materials List for Folding Crib

| | |
|---|---|
| 4 legs | 1¼×39×1¼ |
| 4 rails | 1¼×50×1 |
| 4 rails | 1¼×26×1 |
| 2 mattress supports | 2×50×¾ |
| 2 mattress supports | 2×24×¾ |
| 34 spindles | ½×24 dowels |
| 1 bottom | 24×48×¼ plywood |
| or 11 bottom slats or wire netting | 2×24×½ |

## PANELED CRIB

If the sides of a crib are to be deep enough to keep a child in when he is able to pull himself on to his feet, he cannot conveniently be reached by his mother when he is laid flat. One side can be made to be removed, lowered, or folded down. The full depth of a side is more than the height from the floor, so, if the side is to be folded down, only about half of its depth should be hinged. This depth is enough to make access to the mattress easy.

### Design

The crib just described could be divided across one side, so an upper framework could be hinged, but the example shown here is a more substantial piece of furniture and intended to remain full-size. It has paneled ends and the sides are built up with slats instead of dowels (Fig. 9-5A). With broader pieces in the construction there is scope for a painted finish decorated with painted designs or decals. The bed could be made of hardwood or softwood, but the legs would benefit by being thicker if they are made of softwood.

The design is intended for a mattress 24 inches by 48 inches. Obtain the mattress first and adjust other sizes to suit if necessary (Fig. 9-5B). Instructions are given for webbing supports for the mattress. Because of the spring in this support, a thinner mattress could be used. If you fit a solid base, the mattress should be thicker.

Start by making the ends, which are framed with plywood panels. Set out the legs to show the positions of other parts (Fig. 9-6A). The bottom edges of the end framing come level with the bottom edges of the side rails. The mattress support will rest on strips inside these parts (Fig. 9-6B).

A suitable curve for the top rail can be drawn with a center on the floor line (Fig. 9-6C). Use a strip of scrap wood, with an awl through at the correct distance and a pencil against the end, as an improvised compass. Arrange smaller curves to link with this curve at the tops of the legs. The design is shown with a rigid back, since access is usually only required from one side, but both sides could be arranged to drop.

### Joints

Plow grooves to suit the plywood panels in the rails and legs. The leg grooves need not go further than the length of the panel. If you do not have suitable equipment for making such a stopped groove, you can cut the grooves right through, since they are unlikely to be noticed so near the floor. These unwanted groove extensions could also be filled with strips of wood, which would not show when painted over. Round the inner edges of the parts around the panel before assembly (Fig. 9-6D).

Use mortise and tenon joints with short haunches in the top rails (Fig. 9-6E). Since the tenons will be thicker than the width of the grooves, the tops of the grooves will be hidden. The lower joints do not need haunches. Leave the final shaping of the tops of the legs until the ends have been assembled; then you can follow the curves round. Have the mortises or dowel holes for the opposite parts prepared in the legs before you assemble the paneled ends. Assemble the ends squarely and see that they match.

The lengthwise parts are similar overall, except for the extra rails at the joint across the front. A wide central slat allows for decoration, but there could be similar narrow slats all around. Keep spaces less than 3½ inches.

### Drop Side

The drop side must be made as a frame, but its lengthwise parts are similar to the other lengthwise rails. Mark these rails to length, and prepare the ends of the fixed ones for dowel or tenon joints, Mark on the rails the positions of all slats. Key mark one end of each piece so that in the final assembly the risk of incorrect assembly is reduced, since it is unlikely the marking out will be free from slight errors.

Position the wide slat at the center and space the narrow ones equally on each side. Allow for a piece the same width as the end of the frame of the drop side to be put between the top and bottom rails alongside the legs. This piece matches the drop side and provides some stiffening of the legs (Fig. 9-7A).

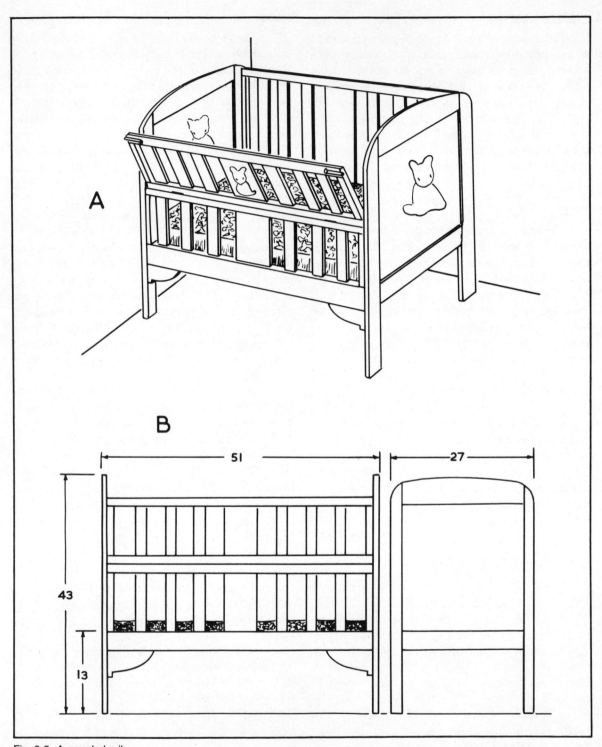

Fig. 9-5. A paneled crib.

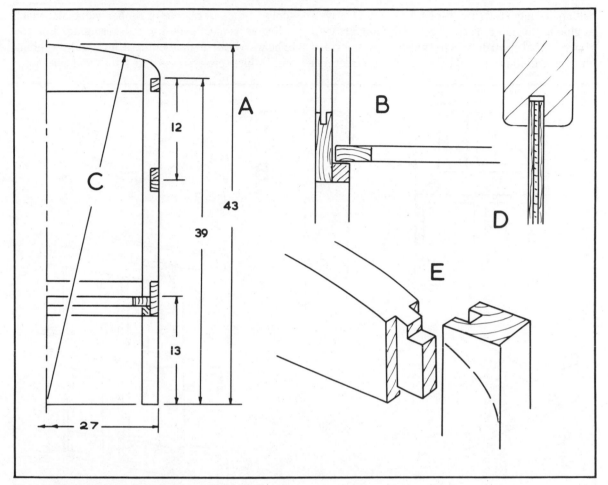

Fig. 9-6. Shape and details of the paneled crib end.

The slats look best, and are safer for a child's hands, if made with a fully semi-circular edge (Fig. 9-7B). They are joined to the rails with barefaced tenons (Fig. 9-7C), which must be cut back to clear the curves (Fig. 9-7D).

The drop side can be made with dowels or mortise and tenon joints at the corners. It joins to the rail below with two or three hinges, so it can be pulled forward and down. The frame may be made the same length as the other rails, then a few shavings taken off so it swings into place without excessive slackness. Assemble the back with slats into rails. Use the back as a guide when assembling the front fixed and hinged parts, which should match the depth and width of the back (Fig. 9-7E).

## Mattress Support

Attach the bearers for the mattress support to the insides of the ends and sides. Assemble the lengthwise parts to the ends. Check the squareness by measuring diagonals at the mattress level, as well as at each side.

Brackets are shown between the legs and the underside of the crib. Glue and screw them in place to improve appearance and to stiffen the legs. Hinge the drop side and arrange bolts to hold the side up. Use the type of bolt that requires a turn before it will slide, so it is very unlikely that a child could operate it.

The mattress support is a flat, rectangular frame. Several corner joints are possible, but a halflap is suggested (Fig. 9-7F). Use screws as well as glue in this joint. You can cover the support with plywood, hardboard, or wire netting, as described for the previous crib. The following instructions apply to the alternative of rubber webbing, which will give some flexibility and springing. For the light weight of a small child, 2-inch wide webbing with 4-inch gaps across the crib should be suffi-

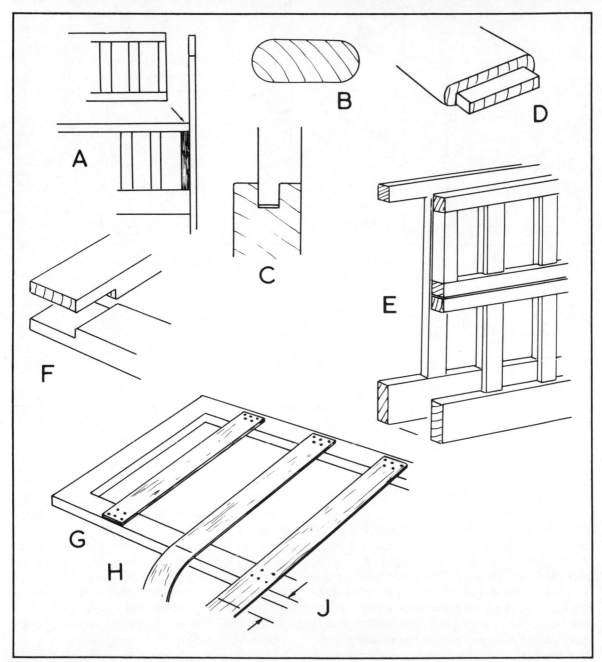

Fig. 9-7. Sides and base of the paneled crib.

cient. If it does not seem to be stiff enough, weave two more pieces lengthwise.

Tack an end of webbing to the frame. Five tacks will do (Fig. 9-7G). Experiment with stretching the first piece to find a suitable tension. Mark the webbing where it comes over the edge of the frame before it is stretched (Fig. 9-7H) and measure how far this mark is beyond the edge when you have the tension required. Mark and pull each of the other strips the same amount before tacking and cutting off (Fig. 9-7J).

Although the crib will not fold, you may wish to keep the mattress support loose, so it can be taken out for cleaning. Finish the crib with stain and varnish, or paint it. Gloss paint is easy to clean, but if you want to apply decals and protect them, it may be better to use paint with little or no gloss, then apply the decals and finish over the paint and decals with clear varnish.

When you have no more use for the crib, you can cut off the legs and use it as a play pen.

## Materials List for Paneled Crib

| | |
|---|---|
| 4 legs | 2×42×1 |
| 2 end rails | 6×25×1 |
| 2 end rails | 4×25×1 |
| 2 end panels | 25×25×¼ plywood |
| 4 rails | 2×52×1 |
| 2 rails | 4×52×1 |
| 1 slat | 6×25×⅝ |
| 12 slats | 1½×12×⅝ |
| 2 slats | 6×12×⅝ |
| 6 slats | 1½×25×⅝ |
| 2 bottom supports | 1×49×1 |
| 2 bottom supports | 1×25×1 |
| 2 mattress supports | 2×49×1 |
| 2 mattress supports | 2×25×1 |
| 4 brackets | 4×8×1 |

## DROP-SIDE CRIB

If one side of a crib can be made to slide down, access is easier than with a swinging section that must be brought forward. In both methods, fasteners at both ends must be released, which may be awkward for a mother with a child in her arms.

However, these fasteners must be accepted as a safety factor. The sliding side has safeguards to prevent a child from releasing it.

This drop-side crib is very similar in its assembled appearance to the crib shown in Fig. 9-1. The sizes (Fig. 9-8A) will suit a mattress 24 inches by 48 inches, but could easily be adapted to another size without affecting construction. It is intended that the crib should be fully take-down, so it can be separated into five flat frames that are easy to store or transport.

### Drop Side

The sliding arrangement depends on some simple hardware, which may be bought, but it is not difficult to make (Fig. 9-9). At each side is a long rod with a head at the top and a screw thread at the bottom (Fig. 9-9A). A ¼-inch rod will do. The head might be made by screwing on a nut and filing it to shape. At the bottom there could be an ordinary nut, but a knurled one allows you to fit it without the need of a wrench (Fig. 9-9B). The rod is held off from the leg about 1 inch with three long screw eyes—one above the top rail, one above the lower side rail, and the other at the limit of lowering (Fig. 9-9C).

At the top of each leg must be a stop which fits under the top side rail and prevents it from lowering. A small amount of clearance is left between the rail and the top screw eye. When the rail is lifted this amount, the stop can be swung clear to allow the side to be lowered. A pair of stops made of sheet metal or plastic can be bought (Fig. 9-9D), but it is possible to make stops from sheet metal and wood (Fig. 9-9E). The metal part is arranged to pivot on a screw into the leg and has holes for screws into the wood part, which is made with a notch to fit under the rail.

It should be possible to make the back to lower as well if you want to be able to use the crib from either side, but the assembly is more rigid if the back is not arranged this way. If you do not want to be able to disassemble the crib, the back rails could be tenoned or doweled into the legs. To allow the crib to be taken down, the rear frame matches the front one, and the rails are cut level at the legs; then

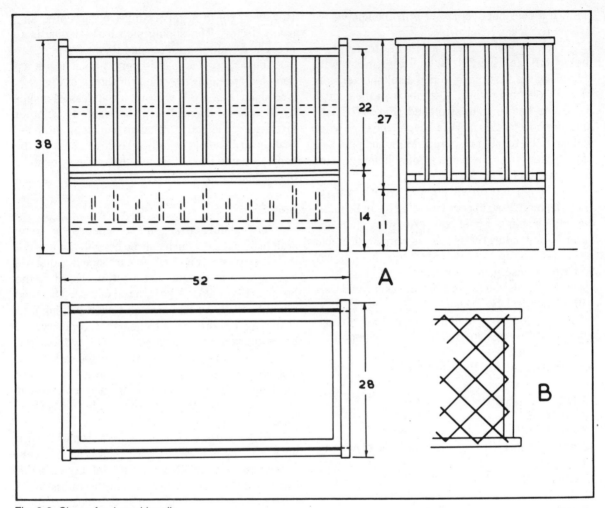

Fig. 9-8. Sizes of a drop-side crib.

a screw through the legs holds the top rail. This screw could be a long wood screw, but its thread does not grip very well into end grain. It would be satisfactory if you only have to disassemble occasionally, but it would be better to use an insert in the wood for a stove bolt or other metal-thread screw (Fig. 9-9F). The metal or plastic insert may be provided with ridges to resist withdrawal, or it may need to be glued in its hole.

At the lower rail there could be similar screws and inserts, but another connection is shown (Fig. 9-9G). There is a strong L screw hook, or *cup hook*, in the leg to fit into holes in the underside of the lower rail. Make the hook end an easy fit; then the

back frame can be dropped onto the two hooks and screws inserted at the top.

### Construction

With the mattress size checked and the hardware available, the actual construction is quite simple. Wood sizes listed suit close-grained hardwood. Softwoods are not advised since they would not be strong enough to take sliding without cracking, and the whole crib might be shaky.

Start with the pair of ends (Fig. 9-10A). The lower rails are tenoned into the legs (Fig. 9-10B), but the tops of the legs can each have a dowel into the top rail, which overlaps slightly (Fig. 9-10C).

The spindle dowels fit into holes drilled slightly too deep so the fit is easy.

The two side assemblies are the same, except for details at the ends (Fig. 9-10E). Drill the ends of the front rails to slide easily on the rods when the ends are fairly close to the legs (Fig. 9-10F). At the back put inserts in the top rail ends, and in the bottom ones if you choose that method of construction. For hooks under the lower rail make the holes an easy fit, but position them so the ends of the rails come close against the legs.

## Trial Assembly

In a trial assembly, position the top screw eyes above where the top rail comes. Locate the stops just far enough below that position for the notch end to clear the rail when it is close up to the eye. This will permit about ¼-inch lift on the side to allow the

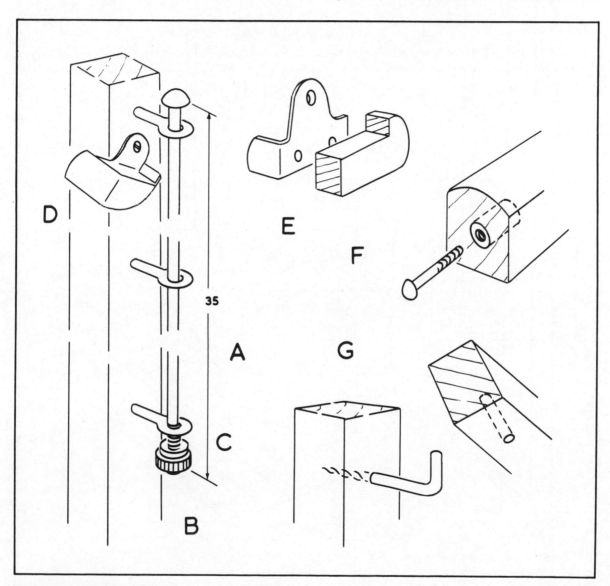

Fig. 9-9. The sliding mechanism for the drop-side crib.

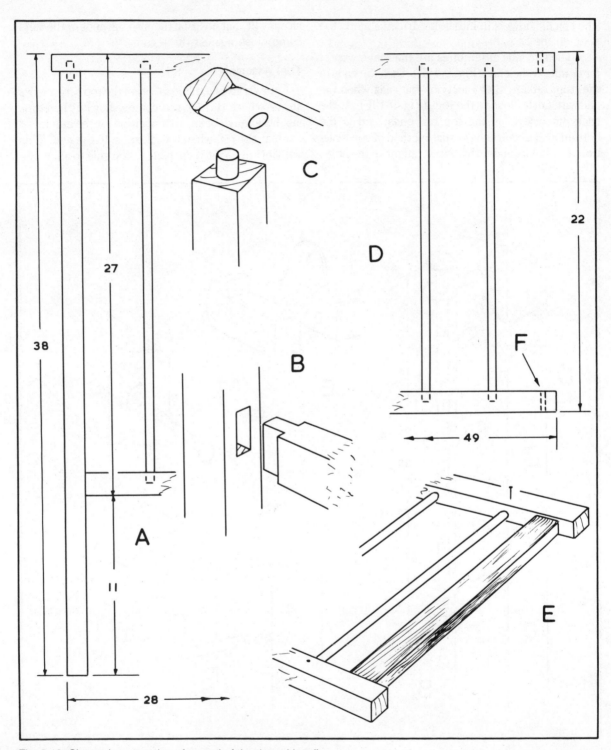

Fig. 9-10. Size and construction of an end of the drop-side crib.

stops to be pulled forward and the side to be lowered. A child would not be able to lift the side and release both stops, since they are too far apart. The second screw eyes are guides to prevent the rod from flexing, and they should come above the lower rail, but not so close that they restrict lifting. Position the third screw eyes at the lower limit for the side—about 4 inches from the floor is suitable, but the length of rod available may control this position.

The trial assembly will give you sizes for the mattress support (Fig. 9-8B). Its sides go through the gaps in the ends beside the legs, and its cross pieces should come fairly close to the end dowels and hold the side pieces near the legs. In that way the mattress supporting frame keeps the crib in shape. The method of mattress support can be your choice. Any of the ways described for earlier cribs could be used, but, if you want to keep the sections light for transport, wire netting is a good choice. Webbing could be used, but slats or plywood would add bulk and weight.

## Finishing

Separate the sections for finishing. Rails should be rounded and sharp angles taken off before assembly. Make sure that the ends of the top rails over the end frames are well-rounded and that the extensions of the mattress frame have sharpness taken off. Like the first crib, this crib is better finished with varnish than paint.

## Materials List for Drop-Side Crib

| 4 legs | 1¼×40×1¼ |
| 4 end rails | 1¼×30×1 |
| 4 side rails | 1¼×51×1 |
| 22 spindles | ½×22 dowels |
| 12 spindles | ½×27 dowels |
| 2 mattress supports | 1¾×53×1 |
| 2 mattress supports | 1¾×25×1 |

## LIFT-SIDE CRIB

An open bed is much better than a crib for getting at the coverings or the occupant, but raised sides and ends are needed to keep a small child in bed. The methods of hinging and sliding one or both sides, as described for the previous cribs, make reaching inside easier, but there is still a low barrier to reach over. This barrier can be removed by arranging for a side to lift out completely. If both sides can be lifted out, you are left with a small bed. A child who feels he is too big for a crib may find this bed acceptable when both sides are removed, since he then feels he is in a proper bed, although it is smaller. Until he gets too tall for the 48-inch mattress he can use what was his crib as a normal bed.

This lift-side crib (Fig. 9-11) is in the usual proportions to take a 24-inch-by-48-inch mattress (Fig. 9-12A). The ends remain at the full height, but both sides can be lifted out. The design is intended to be made in hardwood and given a good finish, so it can remain as a normal piece of furniture much longer than many cribs, which are intended for only a short life.

Prepare the wood for all parts. You should understand how the sides lift out and lock back securely when replaced, since this affects the cutting of legs and rails. The top side rails continue past the legs about 2 inches at each corner and are given tapered notches (Fig. 9-13A). The tops of the legs are notched to match (Fig. 9-13B), and the outer corners are rounded. Only a slight taper is needed (Fig. 9-13C). The notches should be matched so the rails are tight when pushed down fully. The lower rails of the sides carry projecting dowels to fit holes in the main side rails (Fig. 9-13D).

## Bed Frame

Start by marking out the legs (Fig. 9-12B). The rigidity of the crib when the sides are removed depends on the joints of the main side rails into the legs, in the same way it does in a full-size bed. Allow for the usual mortise and tenon joints. The side rails and end rails meet the legs at the same level. Arrange for them to come flush with the outside surfaces of the legs, and cut barefaced tenons. Even then the tenons cannot be taken very far in unless the mortises meet and the tenons are mitered (Fig. 9-13E).

To keep the end top rails clear of the notches in the tops of the legs they are cut down to mortise or

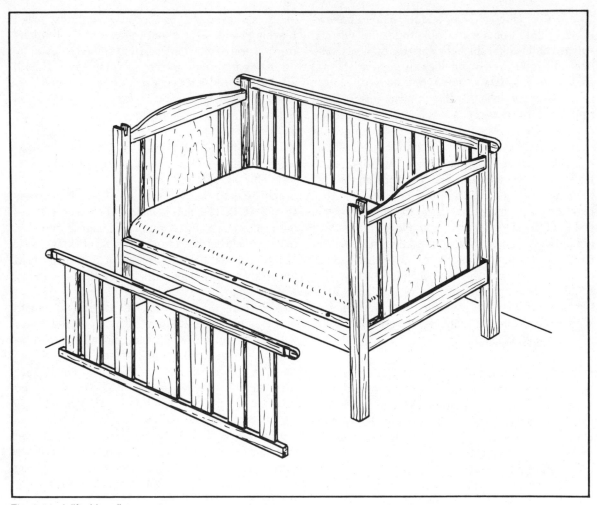

Fig. 9-11. A lift-side crib.

dowel to the legs level with the bottoms of the notches (Fig. 9-12C). Shape both rails to match and well-round the cross-section as well. The plywood panel is enclosed in grooved uprights which are tenoned or doweled into the rails (Fig. 9-12D). Cut the notches in the tops of the legs and the mortises at rail level for the lengthwise parts. Round all exposed edges; then assemble the ends.

Make the two main rails. Inside these rails and across the matching end rails put square bearer strips far enough down to take the mattress supports (Fig. 9-13F). Assemble the side rails to the ends, paying particular attention to squareness. The legs should stand squarely to the side rails so

the side frames can be made correctly.

## Sides

The lift-out side frames are made with a central slat 6 inches wide, 4-inch slats each side of it, and 3-inch slats outside them (Fig. 9-12E). All of these slats are ⅝-inch thick.

At each side make the bottom rail to fit between the legs and the top rail to overlap each leg by about 2 inches. Check if the legs are upright by comparing the length of the bottom rail and the distance between the marked shoulders on the top rail. Notch the top rails to match the leg notches. Round the tops and the outer ends.

228

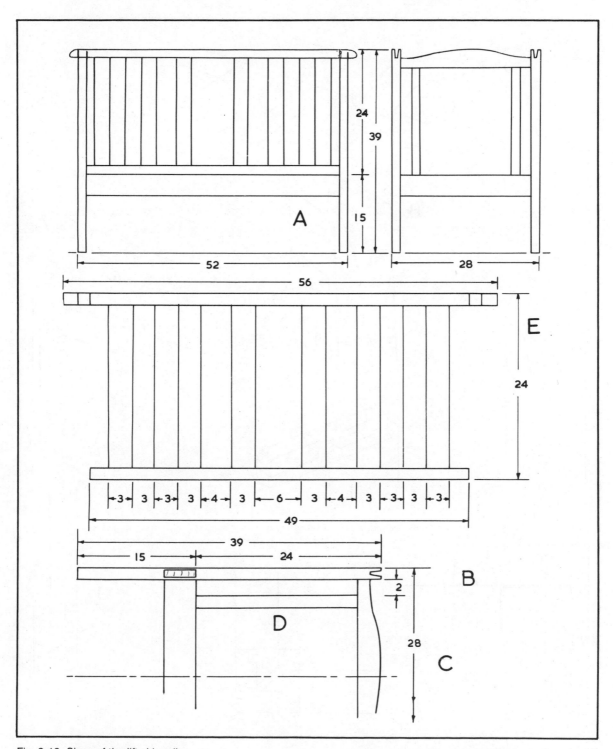

Fig. 9-12. Sizes of the lift-side crib.

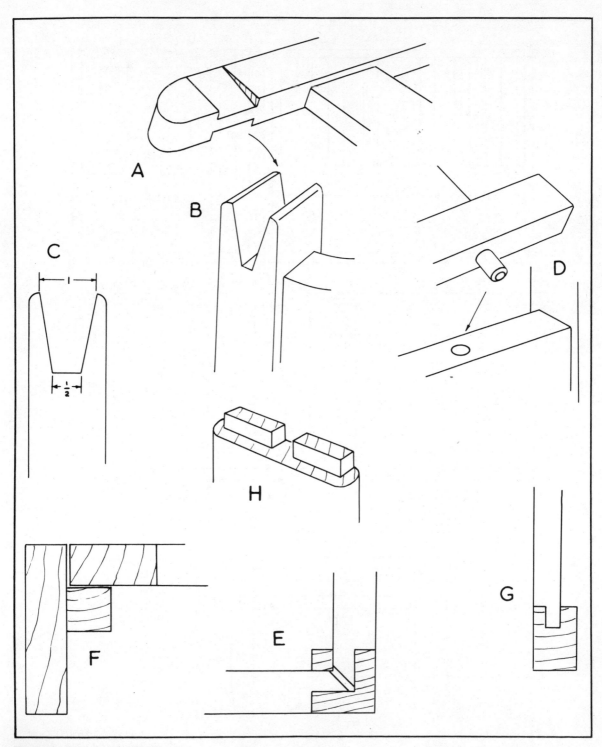

Fig. 9-13. Joints for the lift-side crib.

Drill the bottom rails for central dowels to fit matching holes in the side rails. It should be sufficient to put a dowel a few inches from each end and another centrally along a side, but, if that does not seem enough, you can add more. Taper the projecting dowel ends so they can be located easily in their holes. It is very unlikely that the two sides will be exactly the same, and it is probably wise to assume that will be so. You can then avoid trying to put a side in the opposite space by spacing dowels differently on each side. If the dowel hole near the middle is not exactly central, you will prevent a side from being turned around; so the only way to fit it will be the one decided on during construction.

At one side put the bottom rail in position with its dowels pressed in tightly. Put the top rail in place level with the tops of its legs. Measure the distance between the rails and use it as the distance between the shoulders of the slats.

Make the slats with rounded edges and barefaced tenons so they come level with the inner surfaces of the rails (Fig. 9-13G). Cut back the tenons to clear the curved edges and divide them on the wider slats. (Fig. 9-13H).

## Finishing

Assemble the sides and try them in position. At this stage the notches and dowels should be easy fits, since they will become tighter after paint or varnish has been applied. If a good hardwood has been used and the plywood has suitable surface veneers, the crib will look best with a clear finish over the plain or stained wood. If the plywood does not match the other wood, it could be painted and decorated with decals. As the child gets older, these decals could be scraped off and the panels painted again.

The mattress support is a rectangular frame with the halflap corners glued and screwed. It should drop into place easily, but you should be able to remove it for cleaning. Any of the methods of covering it described for earlier cribs can be used. The top comes level with the side rails, so bedding is easily tucked in when one or both sides are removed.

## Materials List for Lift-Side Crib

| | |
|---|---|
| 4 legs | 1⅜×40×1⅜ |
| 2 rails | 4×52×1 |
| 2 rails | 4×28×1 |
| 2 top rails | 3¾×28×1 |
| 4 uprights | 1⅜×26×1 |
| 2 panels | 20×23×¼ plywood |
| 4 rails | 1⅜×56×1 |
| 2 slats | 6×24×⅝ |
| 4 slats | 4×24×⅝ |
| 8 slats | 3×24×⅝ |
| 2 mattress supports | 2×49×1 |
| 2 mattress supports | 2×25×1 |

## TRADITIONAL ROCKING CRADLE

For the first six months a child does not need much space in which to sleep, and there is no need yet for a crib of the sizes just described. There is the need for the child to be near his mother much of the time. Colonial settlers favored box-like cradles or cots, sometimes with a hood, and usually arranged to be rocked with a foot. Some of these cradles were very basic, while others were made with elaborate decorations. Because families were larger than they are today, a cradle might serve a family for a great many children; so treating the cradle as a fairly permanent piece of furniture was justified. Today you may not want a cradle of this size to last very long, so a simple construction would be justified, possibly arranged so it could be taken apart eventually and the wood used for something else.

This rocking cradle (Fig. 9-14A) is based on a common traditional form without a hood. Original cradles would have been made of boards cut from solid wood. If you want a proper reproduction piece of furniture, the cradle could be made in that way, but it is more convenient to use plywood and finish it by painting. It would be better to use solid wood for the rockers, since plywood might splinter on the edges when used.

Set out the head end first (Figs. 9-14B and 9-15A) since this end settles the shapes and sizes of other parts. The curve of the top can be drawn about 19 inches radius, or you can spring a lath around to

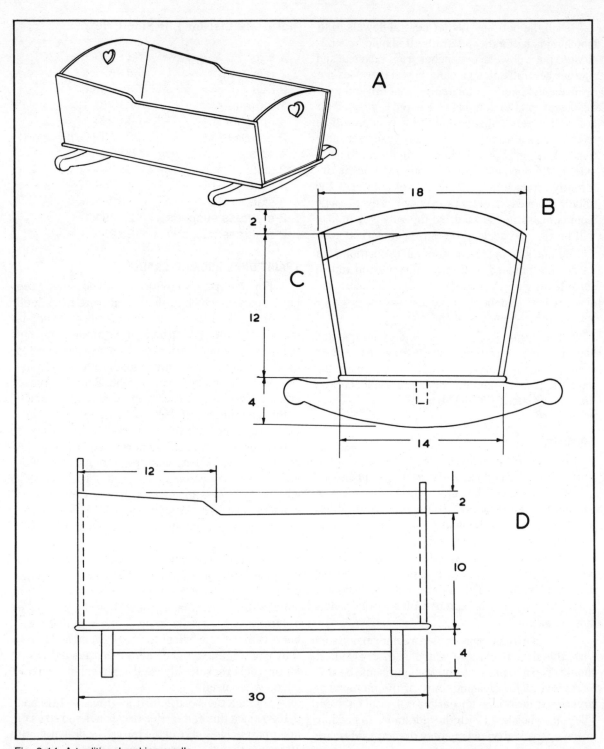

Fig. 9-14. A traditional rocking cradle.

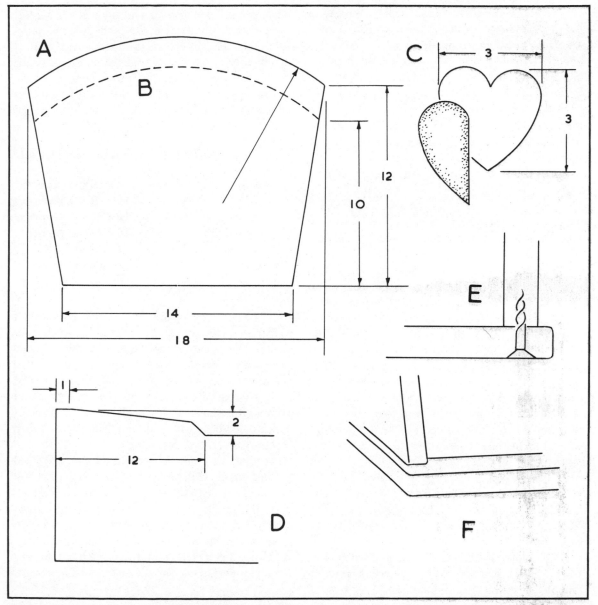

Fig. 9-15. Ends and sides of the rocking cradle.

draw the top curve. The foot end is the same shape, except it is cut off 2 inches lower (Figs. 9-14C and 9-15B). In both cases have the grain of solid wood or the outside veneers of plywood go across the cradle.

The ends are decorated with heart-shaped cutouts (Fig. 9-15C). Besides serving as decorations, these cutouts allow fingers to be put through to lift the cradle. A half template should be made. Cut the openings with a fine jigsaw or fretsaw, so you do not have to do much cleaning of the cuts with a file or sandpaper. Round the edges of the cutouts and the outside top curves thoroughly, but leave other edges square.

233

The sides (Figs. 9-14D and 9-15D) are cut with most of their length parallel; then there is a stepped taper. This edge well-rounded. Traditional cradles made from solid wood have dovetailed corners. Through dovetails show your skill and look well in hardwood, but for plywood construction it is better to let the sides overlap the ends slightly, then screw the parts together (Fig. 9-15E). Bevel the bottom edges of the sides to match the slope. Round the extending end parts of the sides.

The bottom should overlap a little and have its edges rounded (Fig. 9-15F). Screw upward into the other parts, taking care that the assembly finishes squarely. There may be a few holes in the bottom to let air through if you are using a small foam mattress.

The rockers must be symmetrical and match each other. The curve should be part of a circle, so it is unwise to depend on springing a lath around to draw it. The curve finishes with two circles that provide stops when the cradle is rocked (Fig. 9-16A). Use a strip of wood with an awl through it and a pencil against the end as a compass to draw the large curves. One piece could be made and used to mark the other. Turn them over on each other to see if they are symmetrical. You could also use a half template to mark all shapes. Leave the edge that will meet the cradle bottom flat, but take the sharpness off all other edges, particularly so they do not mark carpets.

The rockers could be screwed across the bottom, but a strut between them is advised (Fig. 9-16B). It could join the rockers with dowels or be tenoned (Fig. 9-16C).

Old cradles were left as untreated wood, possibly because suitable finishing materials were unavailable, or because occasional scrubbing was the common practice. Paints of those days were often harmful if sucked by a child. Modern paints are safe, and a plywood cradle would look best if painted in bright colors, possibly with one color inside contrasting with one outside.

The cradle is shown with sloping sides and upright ends, you could alter it to have sloping ends, when it looks more attractive (Fig. 9-16D). The end slopes could be about the same as the

sides, resulting in a compound angle at the corner, slightly more obtuse than the 90 degrees with upright ends. The difference is so slight that there is no difficulty in cutting the edges of the sloping ends to fit against as you try them together. Bevel the bottom edges of the ends in the same way as the sides. Construction is then the same as with upright ends.

## Materials List for Traditional Rocking Cradle

| | |
|---|---|
| 1 head | 14×18×½ plywood |
| 1 foot | 12×18×½ plywood |
| 2 sides | 12×31×½ plywood |
| 1 bottom | 14×32×¼ plywood |
| 2 rockers | 4×25×1 |
| 1 strut | 2×28×1 |

## SWING CRADLE

The next step up for a traditional cradle from a rocker on the floor is one on a stand, in which it can swing. The stand brings the baby and bed higher and easier to attend to and keeps the child further out of the way of pets. The cradle shown (Fig. 9-17A) is based on a Colonial design with Dutch origins. It is shown with a small canopy at the head, which could be omitted and the head made slightly higher than the foot. Swinging is limited, so there is no fear of the cradle being turned over. The extending sides will hit against the supports if an attempt is made to tilt the cradle too far. If you don't want the cradle to swing, the supports could be attached to the cradle ends. Even if you make the cradle to swing and then find that this is not always required, a peg could go through each upright into the lower part of each cradle end to lock it upright.

### Cradle

As shown, the cradle has several wavy or deckle edges. They could be cut by hand, but a fine bandsaw blade or other similar narrow-bladed machine tool would leave an accurate edge that needs little cleaning afterwards. You could alter the design to leave the edges straight, but that would destroy much of the Colonial appearance. The wavy edges should be cut uniformly if the cradle is to look

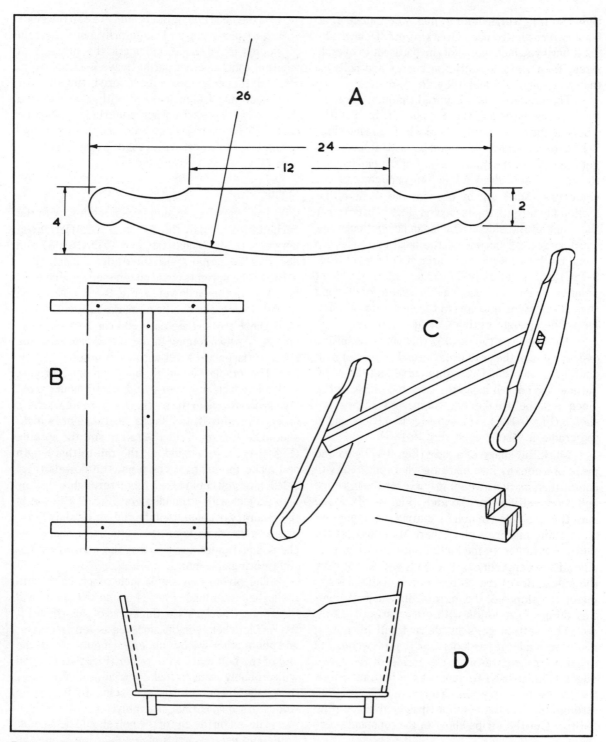

Fig. 9-16. Rocker shapes and construction.

right; so it is worthwhile to make a template of at least two curves to use in marking out. Delay making it until you have some of the parts cut to overall sizes; then you can settle on curves and hollows that will suit the edges they are to mark.

The cradle ends are upright in side view, so they swing between the supports (Fig. 9-17B). There is flair in the sides, and a half drawing (Fig. 9-18A) of the end view should be made full-size, to get the sizes of the many parts. For the end view of the cradle itself, draw a line long enough to be the centerline. Mark out by drawing the shape of the foot end before its top is curved (Fig. 9-18B) to get the slope of the sides, which can be continued upward to get the outline of the head end. The top could be drawn with the center at floor level (Fig. 9-18C) and a radius of 27 inches. Mark the pivot point of the end, and use it as the center for drawing the curves of the bottoms of the ends (Fig. 9-18D). Draw the straight outlines of the supports.

The top over the head is thin plywood sprung over the end of the cradle and an arched piece 1 inch deep (Fig. 9-18E). Draw this curve and the wavy outline. Do not cut away the edge too much, or the piece will be weakened. Suggested shapes are shown (Fig. 9-18F). The top edge of the foot end of the cradle is also shaped (Fig. 9-18G).

Mark the shape of a side (Fig. 9-18H) on one piece of wood, by first marking where the ends will come; then mark a sweeping curve for the top edge and wavy outlines for the ends (Fig. 9-18J). Make sure the two sides match by cutting them together or marking one from the other. Mark and cut the ends, working from the half full-size drawing, each side of the centerlines. The ends will fit between the sides. Bevel the bottom edges of the sides to match the slopes of the ends. Well-round all edges that do not form joints with other parts.

The bottom goes inside and will lift out. It could be made of hardboard or thin plywood. Put supporting strips around the inside of the lower edges (Fig. 9-18K) to support the bottom. Screw the sides to the ends. You may also want to strengthen the joints with strips glued inside (Fig. 9-18L). Cut the strips short of the tops and round them.

At the head end fit the beam between the sides with glue and screws. Temporarily bend the thin plywood top to shape and mark the outlines of where it touches other parts. Leave it a little oversize, but round the front edge before fitting. Bend it into place and fasten it down with glue and fine nails. A screw at each corner would help to hold the curve. Plane the rear edge level and the overhangs parallel to the sides, with rounded edges and corners (Fig. 9-18M).

## Stand

The supports are simple assemblies, with the uprights joined into the feet and a rail arranged between them. Shape the feet (Fig. 9-19A) and decorate the uprights with some edge-shaping (Fig. 9-19B). The uprights could be tenoned into the feet, but they are shown doweled (Fig. 9-19C). Keep the ½-inch dowels clear of the place the rails will come. Glue these parts; then each end can be treated as one piece when joining in the rail. Make sure the inner surfaces are level with each other.

The cradle should fit between the uprights with enough clearance to swing, but without excessive space between the parts. One or more washers on each pivot bolt, to allow a clearance of ⅛ inch, should be enough. Trim the rail to suit the spacing (Fig. 9-17C). You could cut the rail to this length and make the joints to the legs with dowels (Fig. 9-19D), or you could take a tenon through and allow it to project with a rounded end (Fig. 9-19E). It is the accuracy of the ends of the rail, or its shoulders, if tenoned, which keep the support in shape; so check squareness and see that the ends stand upright during assembly.

The pivots may be ⅜-inch coach bolts with their shallow, rounded heads inside the cradle and their square necks in the thickness of the wood. Fit the washers between the surfaces as you assemble, and put another washer under each nut. Cut off the end of the bolt level with its nut (Fig. 9-19F). You will probably want to make a trial assembly first, then take the cradle off the stand to finish the woodwork before final assembly.

The nut on the end of the bolt should be hidden. You could use the brass plates sold for hiding the

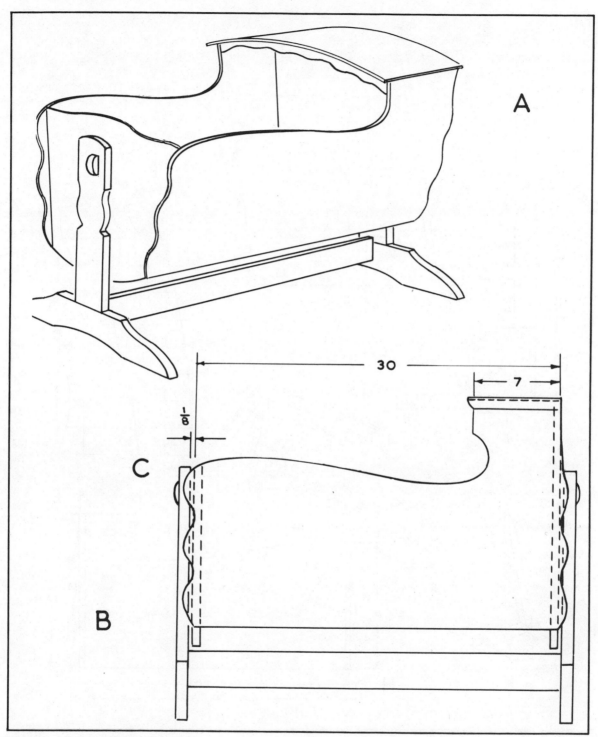

A

C

30

7

1/8

B

Fig. 9-17. A Colonial swing cradle.

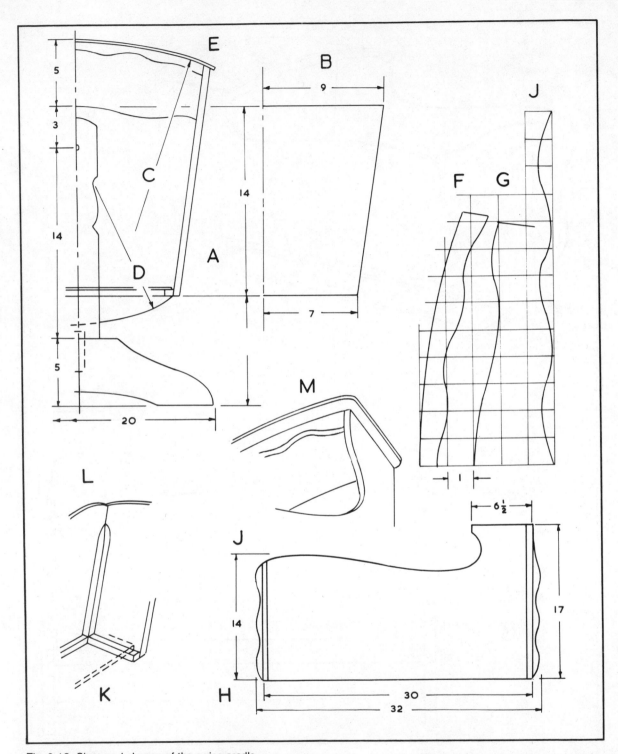

Fig. 9-18. Sizes and shapes of the swing cradle.

ends of bed bolts on larger beds for this purpose. You could turn a piece of wood with a hollow to go over the nut. You could also use a block of wood with enough cut out to clear the nut (Fig. 9-19G).

The cover that is used should be removable so the cradle can be taken apart or the tension of the bolts altered. Screw wood covers on without glue.

The bottom edges of the cradle ends are shown

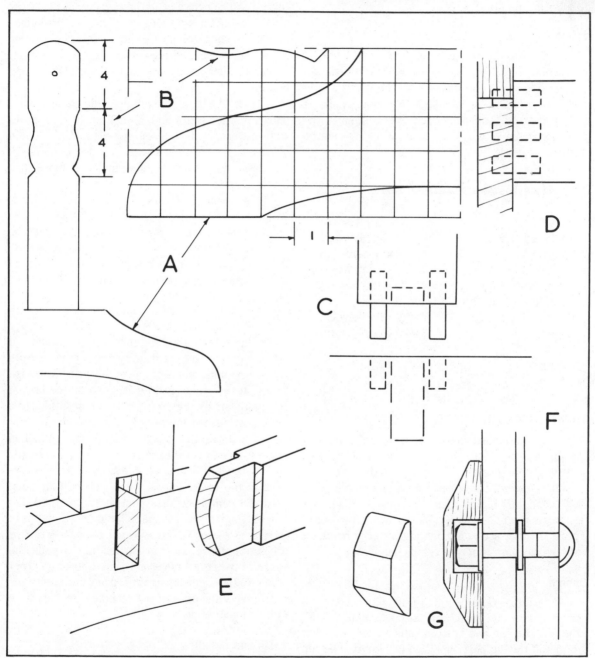

Fig. 9-19. Details of the swing cradle supports.

239

curved. They need not be, although that shape follows the generally curved outlines elsewhere. If you will want to remove the cradle from its stand, the bottom edges are better cut straight across so they will stand on the floor.

## Finishing

The finish depends on the wood. Solid hardwood may look best with a clear finish, although even then the inside could be given a light color so it looks spacious. A plywood cradle is better painted, and a modern effect, despite the traditional lines, would include decals or painted patterns outside.

## Materials List for Swing Cradle

| | |
|---|---|
| 2 sides | 17×33×½ plywood |
| 1 head | 18×19×½ plywood |
| 1 foot | 14×18×½ plywood |
| 1 bottom | 14×30×¼ plywood |
| 2 bottom bearers | ½×30×½ |
| 2 bottom bearers | ½×14×½ |
| 1 top | 7×22×¼ plywood |
| 1 arch | 3×22×½ plywood |
| 2 feet | 5×20×1 |
| 2 uprights | 3×17×1 |
| 1 rail | 3×36×1 |

## TURNED SWINGING CRADLE

Any craftsman can use a lathe to make many of the parts of a cradle, to give it an attractive and lighter appearance than one made with flat boards or square parts. This turned swinging cradle (Fig. 9-20) is slightly bigger than the previous cradle, but its more open construction disguises the size. There is more scope for dealing with the needs of baby without a feeling of restriction.

## Design

As shown (Fig. 9-21), the cradle has turned corner posts and matching, slimmer spindles all around. The top and bottom rails are made of flat wood and the supports are also flat wood. The top rails could be turned, parallel in general form, but

with beads placed between the spindle joints. The support posts could also be turned with a square section at the pivot position and another where the post joins the foot. The two lower rails could also be turned. Much depends on the capacity of the lathe. In the design shown there is no turned part longer than 24 inches, which should fit into almost any lathe, but, if the lengthwise parts are to be turned, you need a lathe with more than 36 inches between centers.

Without a lathe, the cradle could be made with square corner posts and ½-inch or ⅝-inch dowel rods instead of the turned spindles. There could also be square spindles with rounded corners. In any case, do not space the spindles at more than 3-inch centers.

The cradle is intended to be made of hardwood, since this fairly light construction is unsuitable for the weaker softwood, and there would be difficulty in turning the slender parts satisfactorily. A light-colored hardwood with a clear finish gives an airy appearance, but it or a darker wood could be stained to match other furniture.

The cradle is normally hung from the supports and can be rocked. Movement is limited by the knobs on the bottoms of the corner posts, which will hit a lower rail if the cradle is swung very far. Pivots are turned pegs, which can be withdrawn if you wish to lift off the cradle and let it stand on the knobs. Swinging can be prevented with a peg similar to a pivot pin, pushed into a hole at one end.

It will help to set out the main lines of half an end full-size to get the sizes and angles of the rails and posts (Fig. 9-22). First draw the lines representing the lower edges of top and bottom rails, then the centerline of a post at the marked distances, to give you a shape to build on the widths of the pieces of wood. The two ends are parallel strips projecting above the top shaped rail. Divide the space between its edge and the edge of a corner post into three equal parts at top and bottom for the positions of the ends of the spindles, so they flare proportionally in the width.

## Posts and Spindles

Turn the four corner posts (Fig. 9-22A). You

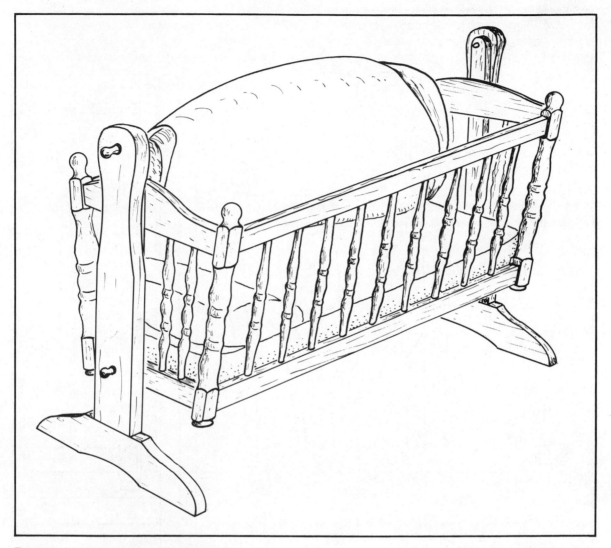

Fig. 9-20. A swinging cradle with turned parts.

can use your own ideas for a pattern, if you wish, but do not cut very deeply and remember that you will need to match the pattern on the thinner spindles. Leave ample square sections for the rail joints. The top knobs will be most prominent, so give them a good, smooth shape and finish. The bottom knobs are not as critical, but should finish smoothly, so they don't scratch or mark anything they are put on when the cradle is taken off its stand.

There is one optical illusion to note. If you divide the piece between the square parts exactly in half for the location of the central turned decoration, it will appear to be below the center in the finished assembly. It is better to arrange that pattern above the actual center, to get a more satisfying appearance.

Turn the spindles to match (Fig. 9-22B). Allow ample parallel parts at the ends. You could make them too long, so you can trim the ends as you fit them. Get the central decoration to finish at the same level as the similar parts of the corner posts. One rod can be marked as a guide for all these

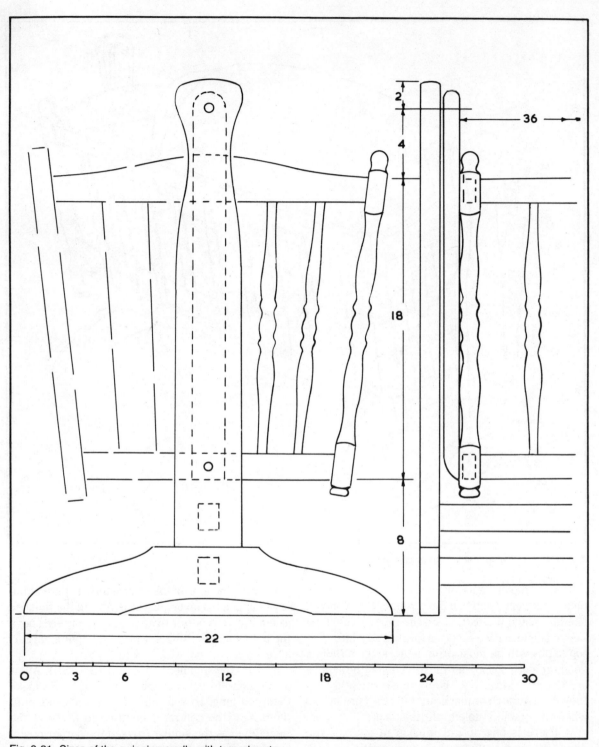

Fig. 9-21. Sizes of the swinging cradle with turned parts.

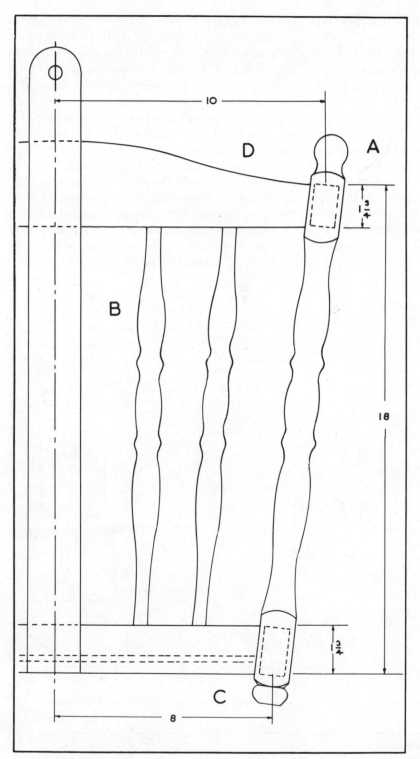

Fig. 9-22. Shape and size of the end of the turned swinging cradle.

243

turned parts. Although the flared posts at the end will be marginally longer than the upright posts at the sides, the difference is so slight that you can ignore it. The parallel ends of the spindles will adjust the size in the rail holes, if there is a little clearance in the depth of the holes.

## Joints

Since not much space is available for joint cutting in places where rails 1-inch thick go into corner posts 1¼-inch square, care is needed to produce strong joints in these places that provide the main strength of the cradle. You can choose between mortise and tenon joints or dowels and screws. For mortise and tenon joints, the mortises should be cut into each other. The tenons may be mitered against each other (Fig. 9-23A). Another, and stronger, way is to make the tenons full depth and notch them over each other (Fig. 9-23B). In this way more tenons fit into the post, with greater glue area.

The end rails could be doweled into the posts. Two ⅜-inch or ½-inch dowels should be used (Fig. 9-23C), with a gap between them wide enough to permit a screw the other way. The side rails then come against the posts and take screws (Fig. 9-23D). Counterbore the holes for the screws, so they can be plugged. The plugs might be regarded as decorative. They would usually be planed level, but you could turn plugs with raised domed heads. If close-grained hardwood is used, a screw should hold well enough in end grain, but, if you are doubtful, put a dowel across from inside to give the

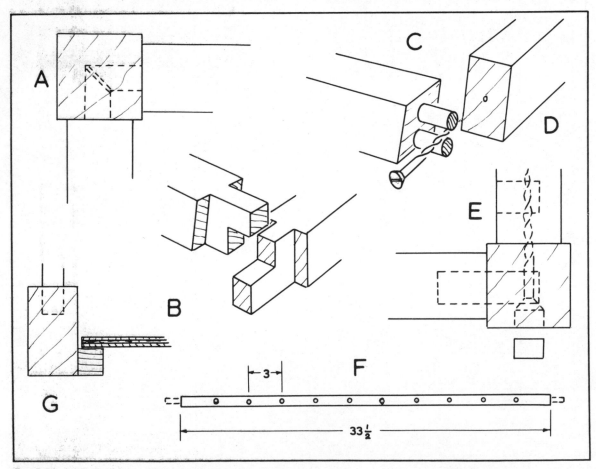

Fig. 9-23. Joints for the turned swinging cradle.

244

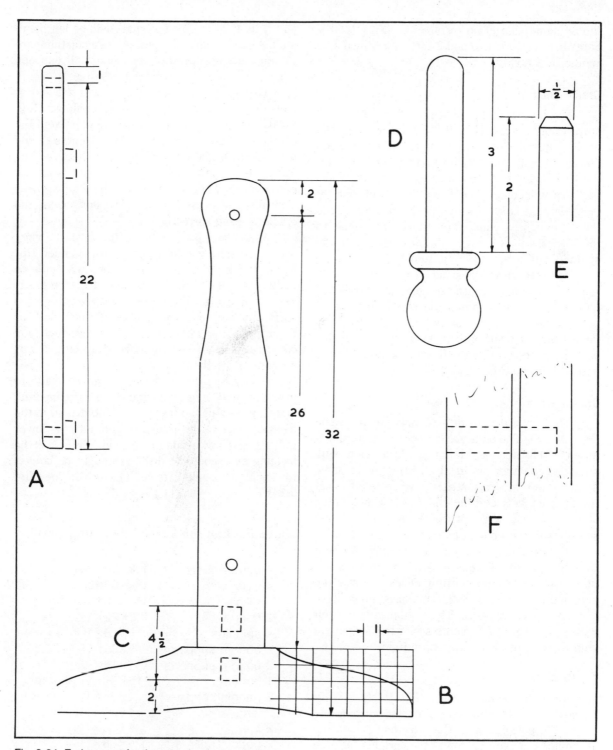

Fig. 9-24. End support for the turned swinging cradle.

thread some side grain to bite into (Fig. 9-23E). Screws 10 or 12 gauge and 2-inch or 2½-inch long should be suitable.

## Cradle Ends

The bottom end rails are parallel and beveled at the ends for joints (Fig. 9-22C). Reduce the ends of the top rails for similar joints and cut the top edges to matching symmetrical curves (Fig. 9-22D). Round the top edges except for the short part that will come against the 2-inch wide upright end. Mark the hole positions for the spindles. Angle the drill slightly, using your drawing as a guide to the slopes. Slight errors will not matter since the spindles will adapt during assembly.

Take off sharp edges and clean off all the parts ready for assembly. Fit the spindles into their holes with a little glue, and join the rails to the corner posts. Check that the parts are symmetrical by measuring diagonals of the first end before the glue has started to set. Use the first end as a pattern for assembling the other end.

## Cradle Sides

The top and bottom side rails are the same (Fig. 9-23F). The ends are cut square, or an allowance is left for tenons. Mark the hole positions with all strips together and drill all holes to the same depth. Use temporary strips of scrap wood to set the distance between the ends while gluing in the spindles if you will not be joining the side assemblies to the ends immediately.

Tenon or screw the sides to the ends and check that the assembly is square. After the glue has set, fit strips inside the bottom edges to take the plywood bottom (Fig. 9-23G), which should have some ventilation holes, The bottom may be left loose, although a few screws into the strips will help to keep the assembly more rigid.

## Cradle Stand

Make the hanging ends (Fig. 9-24A). Well-round the top extensions and curve the bottoms into the cradle bottom rails. Make the end supporting assemblies. Tenon or dowel the uprights into the feet (Fig. 9-24B). The uprights could be left parallel, but some shaping is appropriate when there are turned parts. Shape the feet. Round all exposed edges; then join the uprights to the feet.

The bottom rails are straight and tenoned or doweled into the ends. In the heights shown (Fig. 9-24C), the upper one acts as a stop to prevent the cradle being swung too far. The rail lengths should be enough to allow some clearance between the upright legs and the cradle ends—about ⅛ inch at each end should be satisfactory. Check squareness carefully, since the legs must be upright for the cradle to hang correctly.

Make two pivot pegs (Fig. 9-24D). They should go through and project with rounded tips inside the hanging ends. Turn them carefully to make push fits in the holes. When the cradle is hung, it helps to have washers between the wood surfaces. They could be pieces of thick cloth or flexible plastic, rather than metal, although you could cut discs of ⅛-inch plywood, to be glued as spacers inside the legs.

A peg to prevent swinging can be made to match the pivot pegs, but cut it shorter and taper its end (Fig. 9-24E), so it enters a hole drilled in the hanging piece of the cradle, but not into the lower rail. A peg is only needed at one end. The hole in the hanging end should be drilled through the hole in the leg after assembly, to get it exactly in line (Fig. 9-24F).

## Materials List for Turned Swinging Cradle

| | |
|---|---|
| 4 corner posts | 1¼ × 22 × 1¼ |
| 4 rails | 1¾ × 36 × 1 |
| 2 rails | 1¾ × 16 × 1 |
| 2 rails | 3 × 22 × 1 |
| 28 spindles | 1 × 18 × 1 |
| 2 bottom supports | ½ × 36 × ½ |
| 2 bottom supports | ½ × 16 × ½ |
| 1 bottom | 16 × 36 × ¼ plywood |
| 2 hanging ends | 2 × 24 × 1 |
| 2 legs | 4 × 30 × 1¼ |
| 2 feet | 4 × 23 × 1¼ |
| 2 bottom rails | 1½ × 38 × 1¼ |

# Chapter 10

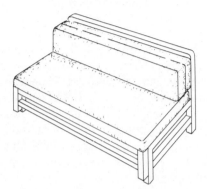

# Folding Beds

Many beds are suitable for taking apart and stowing away in a reduced space. Some standard beds have sides that can be removed from the head and foot, so you have flat ends and separate sides to handle or put into storage. Those methods of disassembly are arranged mainly to allow a large bed to be moved through doorways, passages, and stairs, rather than to allow frequent folding or packing away. In those cases take down and reassembly are only needed on rare occasions, as when furniture is moved to different rooms or to a different home. Besides these standard beds that can be disassembled, others have already been described that will fold flat, with varying degrees of simplicity, such as some of the cribs.

Other beds may be needed for occasional use, such as when camping or when extra guests must be accommodated. The emphasis then must be more on ease of folding and assembly. Some comfort in use is obviously desirable, but a little may need to be sacrificed for the convenience of portability and compactness. Some folding beds include hardware that is made especially for the bed and is not nor-mally available to amateur craftsmen nor of a type easy to make specially. However, there are some ways of making folding beds with no special hardware or with only simple metal items that can be made without elaborate equipment.

Some beds use canvas as the body support, and it is intended to be used without a mattress. The hammock effect can be quite comfortable. It could be supplemented with an inflatable mattress or a piece of soft foam less than 1 inch thick. Other beds are better with a full mattress on top. A point to consider with canvas alone or with thin padding is temperature. If you are camping where conditions may be cold at night, cold rising from below is likely to affect you more than cold air above, so canvas alone may not be sufficient. However, you can adopt simple methods of heat insulation, such as putting sheets of newspaper between the canvas and bedding.

## PIPE STRETCHER BED

The simplest way to provide hammock-type bedding is to use a piece of canvas with pockets sewn on the sides, into which pipes can be slid and be supported by ends which keep them apart. This pipe stretcher bed (Fig. 10-1) can be stored almost anywhere, and assembled to provide a bed close to the floor, for use when camping or in any available space at home in emergency. A person could sleep directly on the canvas or have a mattress or other padding above it. The size suggested is 24 inches between the centers of the pipes, which is about the minimum for an adult directly on the canvas. The pipes should be long enough to suit 72-inch canvas.

Various pipes are suitable. They must be stiff enough not to bow in under a heavy weight. An aluminum alloy about 1¼ inch outside diameter, with walls 1/16 inch thick would be stiff enough. A steel tube of smaller diameter could be used. Stiffness is a combination of outside diameter and wall thickness. If you use a thin-walled tube, the overall diameter must be greater. Select your tubes before making the other parts.

Make the four uprights (Fig. 10-1A) with holes to make a sliding fit on the tubes. Do not draw the top curves with the same centers as the tube holes, but make them a little higher, so the end grain is strengthened. The crosspieces (Fig. 10-1B) should be tenoned into the uprights (Fig. 10-1C) if you want to use the finished bed in your home. If you are only concerned with making a bed for camp use, the parts could be overlapped and nailed or screwed (Fig. 10-1D).

If the tubes make reasonably close fits in their holes they will probably provide ample lengthwise stiffness for the ends, but, to aid them, feet are arranged to pivot under the crosspieces (Fig. 10-1E). For storing they are in line with the crosspieces, but in use they are turned on screws to go across them (Fig. 10-1F). Make the thickness of the feet the same as the projections of the uprights. Use stout screws as pivots—14-gauge-by-3-inches long are suitable.

Use canvas of the type chosen for tents. Simple woven canvas is better than the type impregnated with plastic. It does not matter if it has been waterproofed or not, although waterproofing may be an advantage if you want to store or use the bed in damp conditions. Untreated canvas may ab-

sorb moisture from the air.

Turn in the ends of the canvas (Fig. 10-1G). Besides strengthening the edge and preventing a cut edge from fraying, the "tabled" edge will not stretch as much under load and will prevent pillows or other bedding from falling off the end.

Sew the pockets along the edges so the tubes can be pushed through easily. There is nothing to be gained by making the pockets a close fit on the tubes; in fact it puts a greater strain on the stitching. Turn the edges in and sew through, preferably with two close lines of machine stitches (Fig. 10-1H). The width across the canvas should not be so tight that it is difficult to hold the tubes far enough apart to get them into the supports. There will be some sagging under the weight of a sleeper, but, to give him sufficient comfort, do not allow very much sag in the initial fitting. Almost certainly the canvas will stretch slightly.

## Materials List for Pipe Stretcher Bed

| | |
|---|---|
| 4 uprights | 3 × 10 × 1½ |
| 2 crosspieces | 4 × 28 × 1½ |
| 2 feet | 1½ × 10 × 1½ |
| 2 metal tubes about | 1¼ diameter × 78 |

## CROSS-LEGGED FOLDING BED

If any folding bed may be regarded as traditional, the cross-legged folding bed is it. Metal-framed folding beds may have taken its place in some situations, but the wooden-framed folding bed has been used for camping and in places where large numbers must be accommodated and the beds later reduced to much smaller volumes for transport or storage. Such beds could provide a place for large numbers to sleep, yet could be packed away and transported to another one-night stop without requiring much space for carriage.

### Design

The bed requires some simple sheetmetal-work, as well as woodwork, but that can be done with a few basic tools for cutting, shaping, and drilling metal. The framework should be made from

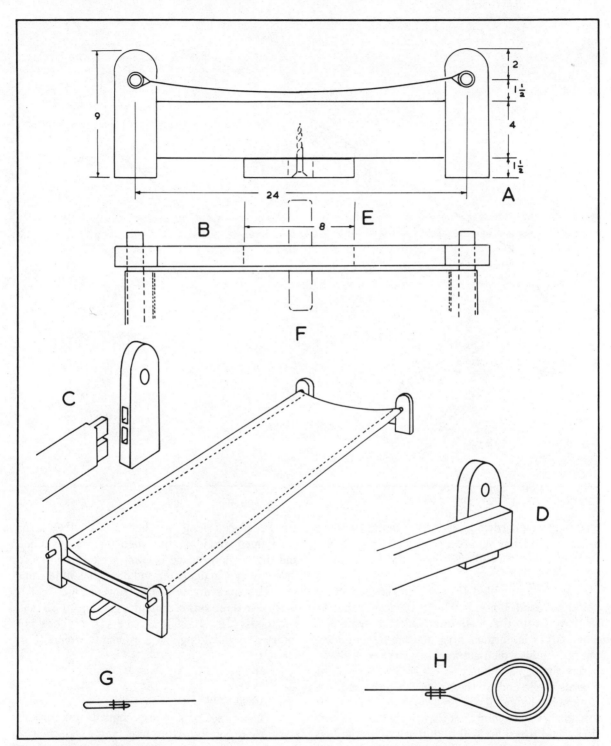

Fig. 10-1. A pipe stretcher bed.

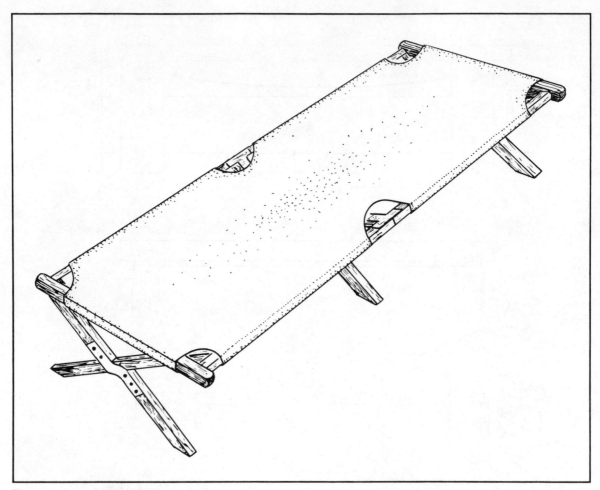

Fig. 10-2. A cross-legged folding bed.

close-grained hardwood, free from knots, since the sections are fairly small for the loads imposed. Soft or open-grained wood might not stand up to use for very long.

When assembled (Fig. 10-2), the bed frame could be used alone, although comfort would be improved with thin foam or an inflatable mattress. The canvas is permanently attached to the sides, but the ends, which act as spreaders and lock the bed in shape, slide into pockets and over projecting dowels in the ends of the sides. When the ends are removed, the sides can be brought together. The folded legs will swing over their sides into line with them, and the sides will fold in half, with the legs there turned back over them. If the two loose ends

are then placed along the other parts and the canvas is wrapped around, all the wooden parts are in line and the whole package is compressed to no more than 6 inches in diameter and 38 inches in length.

The sides divide at the center (Fig. 10-3A). There are three sets of similar legs (Fig. 10-3B) and two ends (Fig. 10-3C). So the canvas does not interfere with folding, cut it around the joints (Fig. 10-3D).

## Leg Arrangement

The arrangement of legs controls other sizes, so set them out first. Draw a rectangle 24 inches by 14 inches (Fig. 10-4A), with a centerline from top to

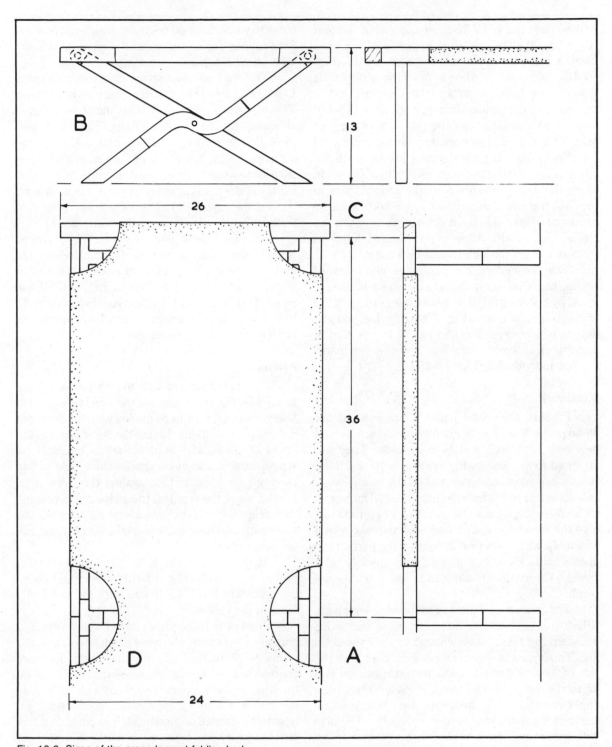

Fig. 10-3. Sizes of the cross-legged folding bed.

bottom, and mark the 22-inches spread of the feet (Fig. 10-4B). The top edge of the solid leg goes from a top corner to one of these points (Fig. 10-4C). Draw another line to mark the width of the wood below this point. Where the center of the strip crosses the centerline draw a circle (Fig. 10-4D) using it as a guide to get the positions of the part legs at the right distance apart to fold along the solid leg. From the top corner draw a line to touch the circle (Fig. 10-4E), and mark the width of the wood along this line. Measure from the 22-inch mark at the foot the same distance along the bottom of the rectangle. From this point draw a line to touch the circle (Fig. 10-4F). A line at the width of the wood from it will go through the 22-inch mark.

That procedure competes the geometry of setting out. Convert to the actual angles and sizes of wood by squaring off the tops of the legs to mark the sections of the sides (Fig. 10-4G) giving you the details of the legs. You can sketch in the central metalwork to avoid confusing the legs when marking out individually (Fig. 10-4H).

## Metalwork

Prepare the metal parts before you cut the wood parts. They can be cut from a mild steel sheet between 1/16 inch and ⅛ inch thick. They are attached to the wood with rivets or bolts and nuts. Rivets are more compact and cannot work loose. Diameters of rivets or bolts may be 3/16 inch or ¼ inch. You should paint the metalwork before fitting it to the wood parts. You may wish to make a trial assembly with bolts first in some of the parts, then disassemble for painting and final assembly with rivets. The rivets should also be painted after assembly.

The four central plates that provide leg pivots (Fig. 10-5A) should be marked out so the space between the two arms is enough to clear the solid leg. This space is shown as 1¼ inch, but check the size of the actual wood, since the part legs must fold on to the sides of the solid leg, preferably with a slight clearance. The arm with two rivets goes on the part leg that extends to join the side. The arm with three rivets goes on the leg that extends to the ground, to give more support to it. The legs cross

close to an angle of 60 degrees, which can be used for marking the central part. Round as shown and take off all sharpness.

The end legs must swing over the sides using L-shaped plates (Fig. 10-5B). Make eight of them. The top arm is narrower than the wood to give clearance for the rounded edges. That rivet goes through a wood side near its end, so round the outline with the rivet hole as center to give clearance as it swings. The internal angle can be rounded a little. Take the sharpness off the outside corner.

At the center of the bed the legs, come centrally under the side joints; so the four metal plates (Fig. 10-5C) extend both ways for pivot rivets. Round them in the same way as the plates for the end legs. Drill all the plates to suit the rivets or bolts. Make the holes a close fit in the metal and wood. It is better to drive a rivet through than to have a loose fit. Closeness helps when riveting and reduces the risk of movement in the joints.

## Assembly

Cut the leg parts to size, using your setting out as a guide. Cut the pieces for the sides (Fig. 10-4J). Use your metal fittings as guides when marking out the end hole positions. Round the outer edges of the sides (Fig. 10-4K) where the canvas will be strained over. The sides should close tightly, and the leg ends should close against the sides (Fig. 10-4L), since they control the shape of the bed and the uprightness of the opened legs. Do not make the ends until you have made a trial assembly and can get sizes from it.

At the ends of the sides fit ½-inch dowels, projecting ¾ inch (Fig. 10-4M). Taper and round the ends which will be linked with the bed ends. Glue in the dowels.

Rivet or bolt the plates to the woodwork. You may get rivets with prepared heads. You can put a round head toward the outside, then hammer another head on the other side (Fig. 10-5D), while the first head is supported on an iron block. It does not matter, except for appearance, if you do not get a perfectly shaped second head. You could countersink the rivet holes in the metal plates. You may get rivets with countersunk heads, then leave enough

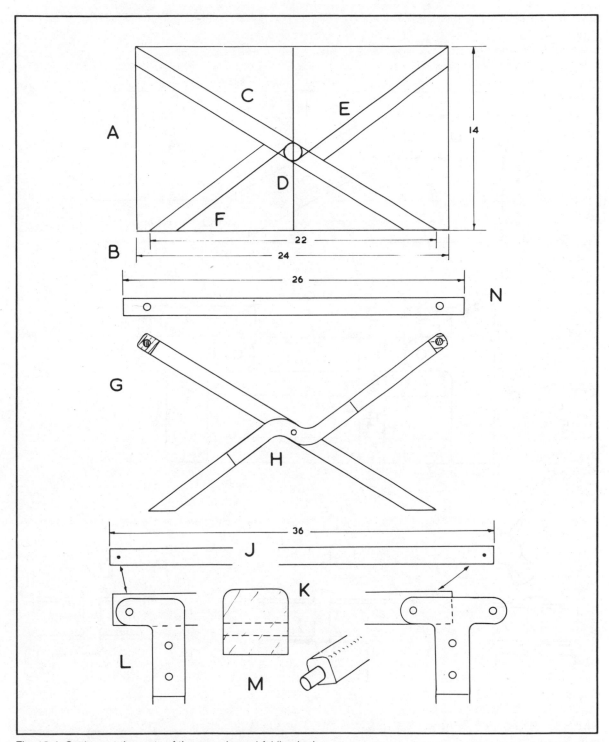

Fig. 10-4. Setting out the parts of the cross-legged folding bed.

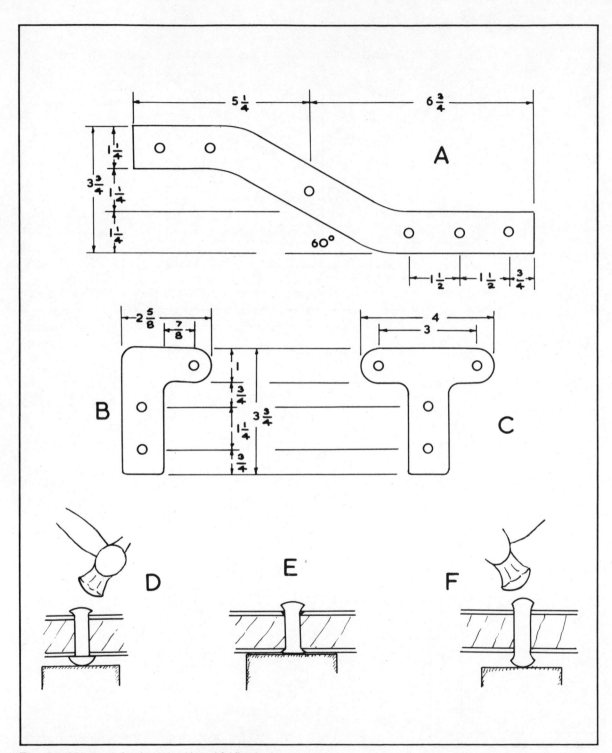

Fig. 10-5. Metalwork for the cross-legged folding bed.

metal at the other end to hammer and fill the second countersunk hole (Fig. 10-5E). You can use a mild steel rod and make your own rivets. Judge how much metal is needed to form heads and cut the rod squarely. Work over an iron block and shape the heads by working a little from each side in turn until you have satisfactory round or countersunk heads (Fig. 10-5F).

## Canvas

The canvas may be fairly stout material, such as is used for heavier tents, and either waterproofed or not. For a cheaper construction you could use burlap. Burlap or untreated canvas would only be suitable for indoor use, since it might absorb moisture from the atmosphere.

Allow enough material for the canvas to wrap over the sides and be turned in for tacking underneath (Fig. 10-6A). The wrap relives the tacks of some strain. How tight you plan to stretch the canvas depends on the material, but even stiff canvas can be expected to stretch in use. For most materials you should start with it fairly tight.

Where the canvas must be cut back around the joints, mark with a template for neatness. A radius of 4 inches is about right. You may find a plate you can mark around. Canvas will fray if nothing is done to protect the curved cut. If it is soft enough, you may be able to turn it under and sew, although this procedure is difficult to do neatly on a curve. It is easier to wrap tape over and sew through it (Fig. 10-6B).

At the ends you need enough canvas to make pockets. They should be easy fits on the wooden ends, and be turned in and sewn (Fig. 10-6C). The corner cutout tape protection should be continued around the openings of the pockets (Fig. 10-6D). Adjust the pocket as you sew it so you can push the wooden end through and spring it on to the end dowels to make the bed top finish with enough

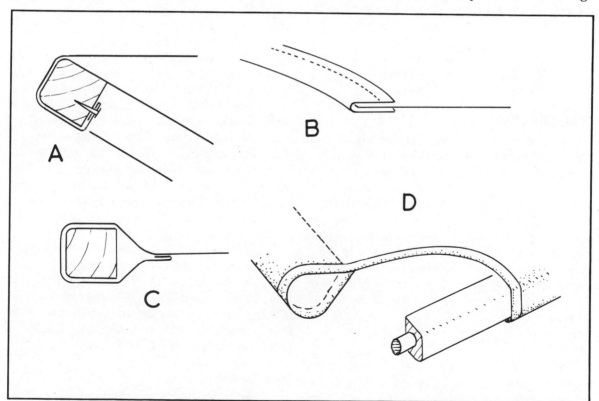

Fig. 10-6. Canvas details for the cross-legged folding bed.

tension lengthwise. Be careful not to have slackness at the ends, or the end pieces may come off their dowels.

## Finishing

With the bed opened and the canvas taut, measure across the centers of the projecting dowels and make the ends (Fig. 10-4N). Round the edges that come against the canvas. Well-round the ends, since they will be exposed in the finished bed.

The finished bed can be left with the metalwork painted and the wood untreated. You could paint the wood to match the metal, but it would look better vanished. It could be treated with linseed oil to prevent it from absorbing moisture, either as the only treatment or under varnish. A final refinement would be to make a canvas bag to hold the folded bed, preferably long enough for the parts to slide in, with a drawstring at the end.

## Materials List for Cross-Legged Folding Bed

| 3 legs | 1¼×26×1¼ |
| 6 legs | 1¼×13×1¼ |
| 2 ends | 1¼×28×1¼ |
| 4 sides | 1¼×38×1¼ |

## SLIDE-AWAY BED

If a bed is to be used in a room that is otherwise occupied during the day, or in a bedroom that becomes a playroom for children, it is useful to be able to convert the bed to something else, preferably a seat. This slide-away bed (Fig. 10-7) is large enough for use by two when opened, but it reduces to half-width, and the parts of the mattress become seat and back cushions. If a loose cover is fitted over the closed bed it looks like a two- or three-seat settee. In both forms it is a satisfactory piece of furniture, without concessions due to the double purpose.

## Design

There is a main assembly (Fig. 10-7A) with a broad, flat seat and a high, upright back. This assembly is made into a bed with an extension that fits to it and brings the bed area up to 48 inches by 78

inches, or whatever size you decide to make the bed. The extension can be lifted over the seat of the main part; then the mattress parts go over it to make the seat and back padding (Fig. 10-7B). The mattress is made up of one slab 24 inches wide and two slabs 12 inches wide, all the same thickness, which could be 3 or 4 inches for reasonable comfort. The two 12-inch slabs may be hinged together with tape sewn to them, or with a zipper, so they can be folded against each other when they form the back of the seat (Fig. 10-7C). The two parts of a zipper could also be sewn to the edges that meet to make up the bed, so they can be drawn together and not slide apart at night.

The framework should be made of furniture-quality hardwood. Sections shown would be too thin for sufficient strength in softwood, but they could be increased if the bed is to be made of softwood to match other softwood furniture in the room. You could use dowels in the joints, but mortise and tenon joints are stronger, and the instructions assume they will be used.

The important sizes are at the ends (Fig. 10-8A). The extension rests on the main part when closed (Fig. 10-8B). The wide mattress slab rests on that to form the seat. The two narrower slabs are folded with their hinge tape to form a comfortable back. They also reduce the seat width, since the full mattress is wider than most people want to sit on. When the extension is pulled out the width is doubled and the mattress parts cover the area (Fig. 10-8C). The plywood tops have the main part cut back and the extension piece extended, so they meet over the center of the thickness of the front rail on the main part (Fig. 10-8D).

There are several possible ways of holding the two parts together, but a simple arrangement features a hook and eye fastener at each end of the bed (Fig. 10-8E). Additional eyes should be screwed into the main part near the rear ends of the side rails, so the hooks can engage with them to hold the extension in place during the day.

## Main Assembly

Start by making the ends of the main part (Fig. 10-9A). Where the lower rails join you can use the

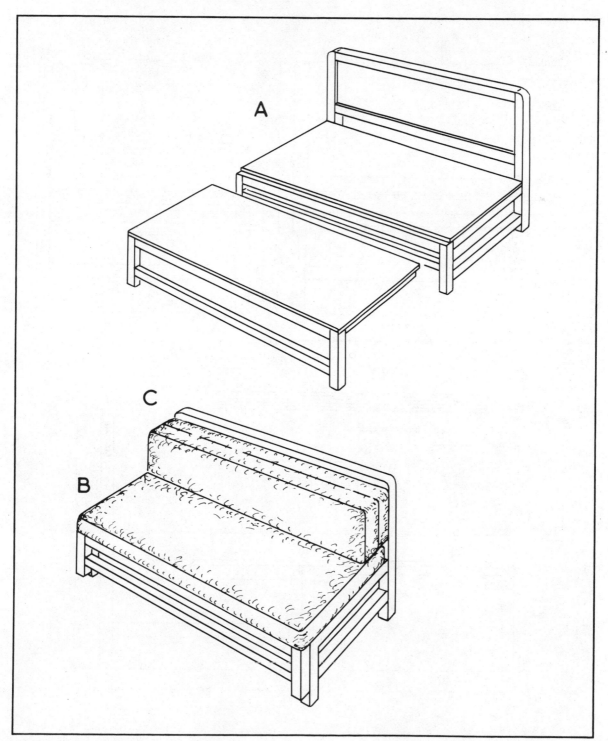

Fig. 10-7. A slide-away bed.

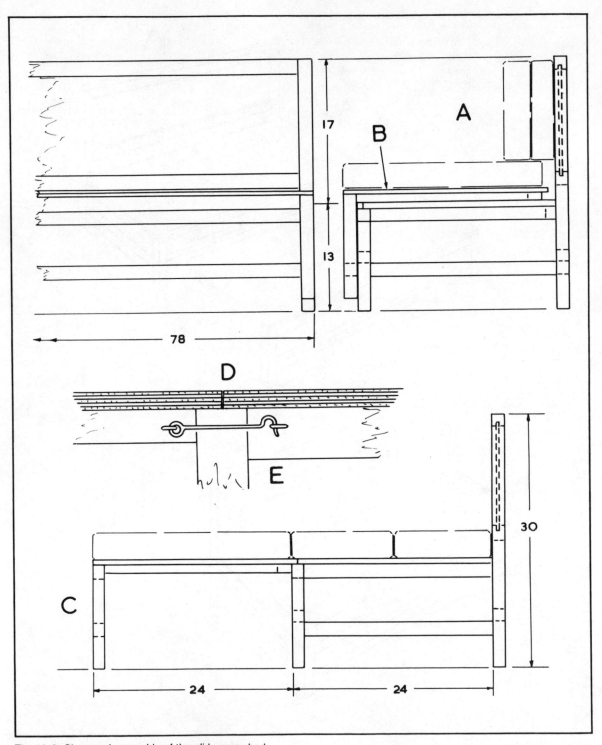

Fig. 10-8. Sizes and assembly of the slide-away bed.

usual central tenons taken into mortises of reasonable depth. At seat level the end and front rails come into the legs at the same level. You can get slightly longer and stronger tenons if you bring them about ⅛ inch toward the outside edges (Fig. 10-9B) and miter them inside the legs. Where tenons come at the tops of the legs, they should be haunched so they do not show (Fig. 10-9C).

Groove the back rails and the rear legs between the mortises to take the plywood panel. Mark all the lengthwise rails together so the distances between shoulders will be the same. Cut the panel to fit easily into its grooves. Round the front outer corners of the front legs. You may leave the edges of other parts square, but remove sharpness. If the furniture will be moved, fit glides to the bottoms of all legs. This piece of furniture is not really suitable for casters.

You can assemble all the components of the main part at this stage or leave them until the extension is ready. Make up the ends first, squaring and matching them. Add the lengthwise rails and the back panel. Thoroughly glue and clamp the joints. The panel may have just a small amount of glue on its edges, which will be strong enough, while preventing an excess of glue from oozing out and needing to be cleaned off.

The seat plywood fits on the frame. Its rear edge and ends come flush with the edges. At the front it is cut back to the center of the front rail (Fig. 10-8D). Make sure this edge is planed straight before fixing. The seat can be held down with glue and a few finishing nails, or it could be screwed in place. Round the corners and exposed edges of the seat back.

## Extension

The extension ends (Fig. 10-9D) are made of legs with rails joined to their tops. The rails are only 1 inch deep, and ordinary tenons would be difficult to make effectively; so a tapered dado joint is suggested (Fig. 10-9E). The front rail can come into a leg with a tenon slightly offset toward the front, in the same way as in the main part to clear the end of the dado piece. The lower rail between the extension legs has ordinary mortise and tenon

joints. The rear rail under the extension top can join the end rails with open mortise and tenon or bridle joints (Fig. 10-9F). Round the outer corners of the front legs (Fig. 10-9G).

Fit the plywood top to the extension in the same way as the top of the main part, but make it flush with the frame at the front and ends, extending it enough to go over the main front rail at its back (Fig. 10-9H).

You should leave a little excess length on the bottoms of the extension legs. When the assembly is used as a double bed, the extension should not slope downward, even slightly. It would be better level or even tilted a little the other way; so trim the bottoms of the extension legs after a first trial assembly.

## Mattress

The three mattress parts can be made from plastic foam. Cover them with cloth, preferably with piping along the seams. The two edges of the narrow pads that must hinge together could be made with one piece of cloth across both edges, but it would be easier to make them as units and sew on a strip of tape as a hinge. In any case, do not use piping along those meeting edges, or where the wide pad meets the other, if you wish to use a zipper there. You will probably find it worthwhile to sew on tapes or cords where the mattress meets rear legs, so it can be tied in to prevent movement at night.

Holes may be drilled in the two top pieces of plywood for ventilation of the mattresses, but, to be effective, they must be in line when the bed is used as a seat. Drill a pattern of holes in the extension top; then locate its position over the main top and mark through for drilling.

## Variations

As described, this is a basic design. It would be possible to give the back some shaping of the top rail. Instead of a plywood panel there could be matched boarding. The back could be taken higher to include shelves for books or other things. The lower part of the rear section could be made as a box, with a top to lift off, so bedding might be stored

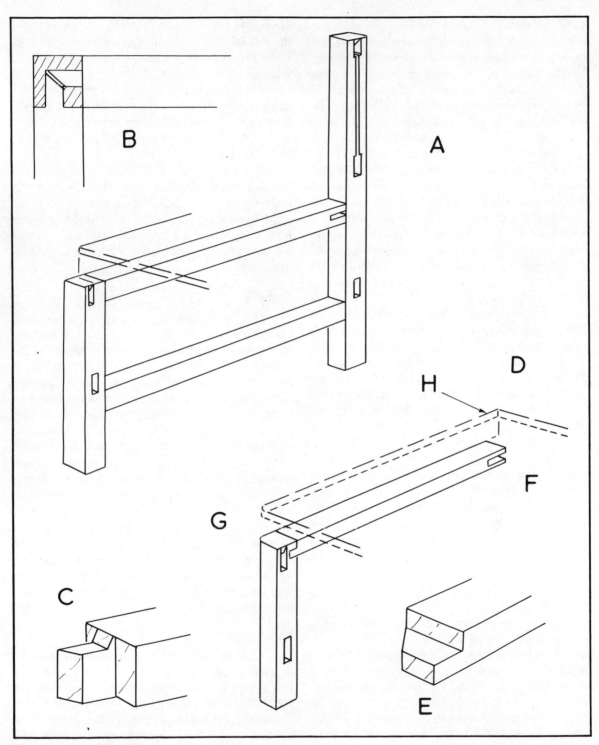

Fig. 10-9. Ends of the slide-away bed.

until it is needed for a double bed. It would be possible to use drawers instead of a lifting top, but you would need to remove the extension to get at them.

## Materials List for Slide-Away Bed
### Main Part

| | |
|---|---|
| 2 rear legs | 1½×32×1½ |
| 2 front legs | 1½×15×1½ |
| 5 rails | 1½×78×1½ |
| 4 rails | 1½×24×1½ |
| 1 panel | 14×76×¼ plywood |
| 1 top | 24×79×½ plywood |
| 1 rail | 1½×78×1 |

### Extension

| | |
|---|---|
| 2 legs | 1½×15×1½ |
| 2 rails | 1½×78×1½ |
| 2 rails | 1½×24×1 |
| 1 rail | 1½×79×1 |
| 1 top | 25×79×½ plywood |

## FOLDING COT

For a very young child it is convenient to have a folding cot or bassinet that can be easily lifted, yet folded flat when out of use. This folding cot (Fig. 10-10) uses a sewn plastic box-shaped bag containing a stiffening base for a mattress and supported on crossed legs that permit folding when the base and mattress are removed. A locking strip prevents unintentional folding when the cot is in use.

### Design

Construction is simple, and the cot could be made as a temporary piece of furniture until the child becomes too big for it, but, if made of good wood and properly finished, it could be long-lasting for many babies. In any case, the wood parts should be of close-grained hardwood, selected for reasonable straightness of grain and freedom from knots, since the sections would not be adequate if the wood had flaws.

The general drawing (Fig. 10-10A) gives suit-able sizes, but they could be altered if you wish. The legs taper toward their ends (Fig. 10-10B), and the diagonal braces are arranged one each way on opposite pairs of legs (Fig. 10-10C). The locking strip (Fig. 10-10D) need only be fitted at one end. The size of an available mattress may determine the size of the fabric bag, but if none is available you can easily cut a piece of plastic foam and cover it with cloth.

### Wood Frame

Set out the end shape. Draw a rectangle and join its opposite corners (Fig. 10-11A). The diagonals will be the centerlines of the legs. To get the sizes for tapering, draw a circle of 2 inches diameter at the center and others of 1½ inches diameter at each corner (Fig. 10-11B). Draw lines to touch these circles (Fig. 10-11C). They represent the tapers to plane the legs. The tops of the legs will follow the curves you have drawn, but at the bottom cut the legs parallel with the floor (Fig. 10-11D).

Make the four legs identical and drill their centers for bolts. You can use ¼-inch bolts, preferably with countersunk heads inside and washers between the legs and under the nuts outside (Fig. 10-11E). If you can obtain domed head nuts, you can cut off the ends of the bolts and seal them out of sight under the domes. Otherwise, cut off any surplus bolt ends and file them level with their nuts.

The stretchers tenon into the tops of the legs (Fig. 10-11F). Keep them far enough down from the rounded ends to avoid any risk of breaking out the short end grain there. Let the tenons go through and finish them with rounded ends (Fig. 10-11G).

Pair the legs when you assemble, so the inner legs slope the same way. The stretchers are of different lengths, since the one across the outer legs must be longer. Assemble the stretchers to the legs and bolt the legs together. If necessary, put temporary struts across the legs lower down until the glue has set.

Mark across the outsides of the legs 4 inches and 14 inches up from their bottoms for the diagonal braces. Prepare the strips of wood with their edges rounded. Put a strip diagonally across the pair of outer legs and mark and drive one screw at each

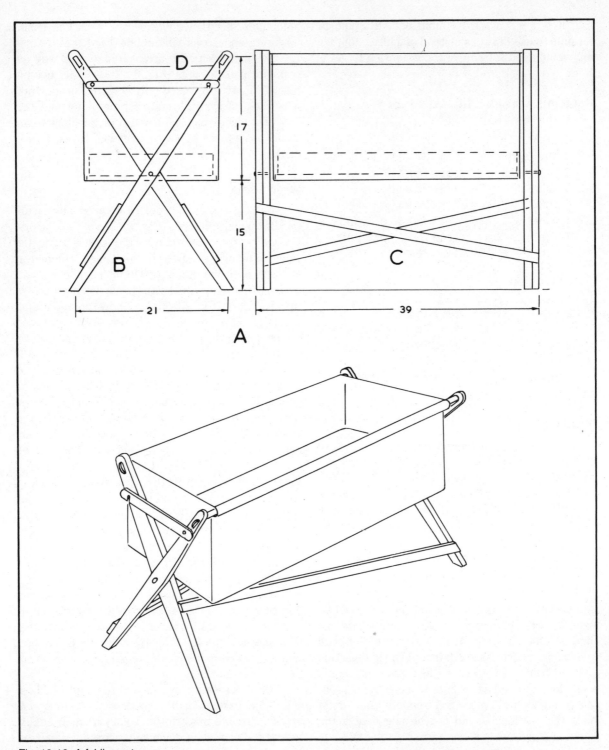

Fig. 10-10. A folding cot.

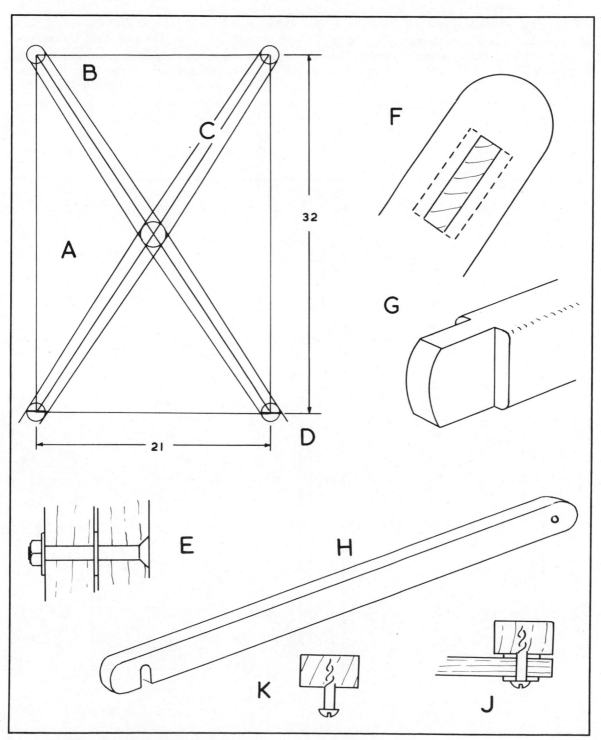

Fig. 10-11. Shape and construction of the folding cot.

end; then cut off the surplus ends of the brace. Do the same the other way on the opposite side on the inner pair of legs. You should now be able to open the framework so it stands steadily when brought to the designed width.

Measure down from the top of the stretcher 5 inches on the legs at one end to get the position for the locking strip. Mark the centers for screw holes on the legs at these positions. Measure between these centers for the size of the locking strip (Fig. 10-11H). It pivots on a round head screw, with washers inside and outside on the outer leg (Fig. 10-11J). At the position on the inner leg drive another round head screw, so it projects more than enough for the strip to hook over it (Fig. 10-11K). Round the edges and ends of the strip, but leave enough projecting to stop the risk of short grain breaking out. Although the screws are at different

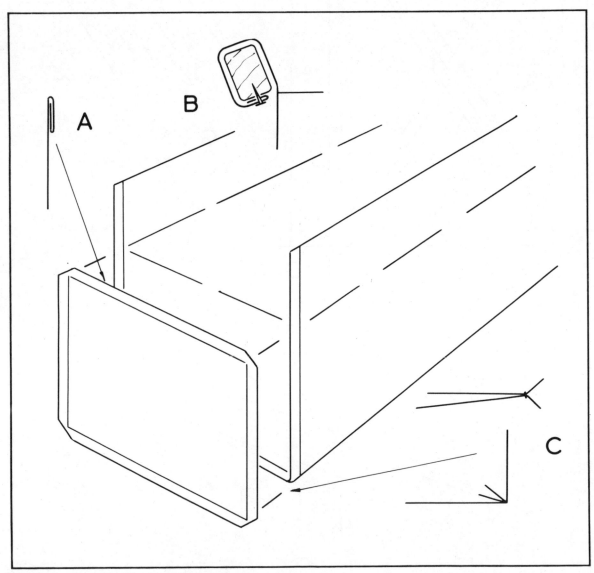

Fig. 10-12. The canvas part of the folding cot.

levels because of the overlapping of the legs, at the distance used, the strip will easily drop into position. When the cot is folded, it will hang along its leg.

## Box-Shaped Bag

The box-shaped bag could be made of any stout cloth, but for easy cleaning it is better made of plastic-impregnated fabric. The weave of the fabric helps the bag keep its shape better than plain plastic sheeting. Choose a flexible material. Although white has a clean appearance, there are some attractively patterned materials that could be used.

Get the sizes from the actual framework. The ends determine the sizes. Cut pieces with about ½ inch extra all around. Turn in and sew the top edge of each piece (Fig. 10-12A). In the other direction cut a strip that will go around, with enough to wrap over the stretchers for tacking underneath (Fig. 10-12B), and enough at the edges for sewing to the ends. Sew the pieces inside out (Fig. 10-12C); then turn the bag the right way. You will probably want to put some extra hand stitches through the seams at their top corners, where most strain can be expected to come.

If the bag is satisfactory, wrap the material over the stretchers and tack underneath so the rows of tacks will not show. Be careful to arrange the amount you turn under at each side so the base of the bag will finish level when the cot is in use. Make the plywood base to fit easily inside the bag. Round its corners and edges. Ventilation holes are not needed, but some ¾-inch or larger holes near each end allow you to get fingers in to lift the base out. Fit the mattress on top of the base to complete the cot. Try to remove the mattress and baseboard, then release the locking strip to test folding. You should be able to fold the framework to only a few inches thick. Much depends on the stiffness of the fabric.

## Materials List for Folding Cot

| 4 legs | 2×42×1 |
|---|---|
| 2 stretchers | 1½×40×¾ |
| 2 braces | 1×42×½ |
| 1 locking strip | 1×20×½ |
| 1 base | 28×35×½ plywood |

# Chapter 11

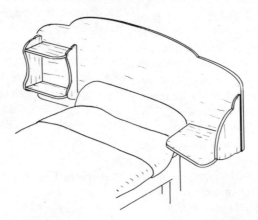

# Combination Bed Heads

A bed must take its place with other furniture. You will need some provision for bedside storage, usually with some form of cabinet or cupboard, or just a table, at each side of the bed. An assortment of separate pieces of furniture may suit the layout and needs of a particular room, particularly if it is spacious. Loose, light tables may be moved or knocked over, however; so the occupants of the bed cannot rely on always being able to reach things, possibly by feel, in the dark.

In many circumstances it is better to have bedside arrangements built into an extended headboard. There are a great many combinations. There may be just shelves or book racks. There could be quite extensive storage places at each side and above the bed. Lights, radio, and many other things could be built in. The ultimate combination is a bed as part of a wall-long block of built in closets for clothes and bedding. There could be a dresser with a stowing stool. There might even be a folding shower unit. The bed is then incidental to a larger range of built-in furniture, the making of which is outside the scope of this book.

Building furniture into the bed head aids in keeping things compact in a small room. If you include bedside tables, cabinets, or book shelves in the bed head you take up less space than if these are independent items, and you free floor space for furniture that must be independent. Once you have built-in furniture, however, it is immovable; so you should be sure that what you make is what you want. If you have separate pieces of furniture, you can move them about.

If you are equipping a child's bed, you can arrange the things he is likely to want within reach, and so discourage him from getting out of bed frequently. Toys and books are less likely to be knocked over.

Whether the bed head is attached to the bed or not depends on its size and how much will project. A board with shelves and a tabletop built lightly and not arranged to project very much might be attached to the bed and move with it when the bed must be moved for cleaning. If the head has more substantial attachments or is very high, as when it carries bookshelves, it is better to attach it to the wall. A full rack of books can be very heavy. Even if a first assembly attached to the bed end seems strong enough, there is a risk that it will sag forward and shed books on to the person sleeping in the bed. It would be better to screw the bed head to the wall and fit the bed into a space between projections from it.

If what you plan to build in will rest on the

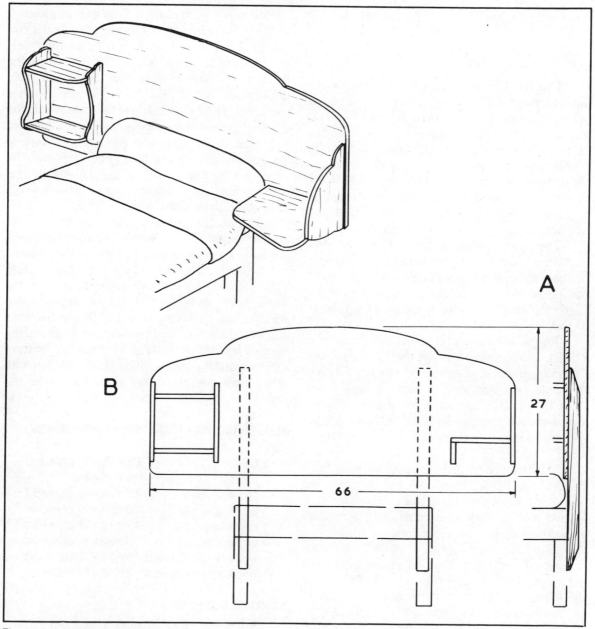

Fig. 11-1. A bed head with racks.

floor, as with tables and storage cabinets with doors, the bed head is better treated as a separate piece of furniture. With its broader base resting on the floor it may stand independently, or you may want to attach it to the wall. If the project is carried the full width and height of the wall, your only concern with the bed is to leave a suitable space for it to push in.

## BED HEAD WITH RACKS

This bed head with racks is an example of a lighter type of combination bed head whose weight can be taken by the bed. You could also attach the bed head to the wall if you wish. As shown (Fig. 11-1) the head is intended for a single bed, with a double rack at one side and a table at the other. The entire head could be made of plywood and finished by painting, although it might be made of veneered or plastic-covered particleboard. Measure the actual bed, but typical sizes are suggested.

The struts to support the bed head are more substantial than for a simple head (Fig. 11-1A). If the bed has legs, rigidity is increased if the struts can follow down them. If it is a boxed bed, stiffen inside the rear panel where the struts will be attached.

The back of the head is a piece of plywood (Fig. 11-1B), which can be shaped at the top. Lay out on it the arrangement of shelves. Try this in position in the room, you may want to increase or decrease sizes to suit available space or arrange different shelves to suit your needs. If the bed is going in the corner of a room, there may be an extension at one side only.

Mark the positions of the struts and make them (Fig. 11-2A). Taper their ends and round the exposed edges, so they will not mark the wall if moved against it. You could glue rubber or plastic foam along them or add rubber buffers.

There are matching curves for the back and the brackets. For the back a half template will help you get a symmetrical shape (Fig. 11-3A). You can cut the lower edge of the back straight across, but a variation has the sides dipping down so the shelves come lower. Much depends on the thickness of the

mattress and the actual height of the person who will use the bed.

The best joints for the projecting parts are dados, but if the material is unsuitable for cutting grooves, you can use small dowels or rest shelves on narrow strips. Pieces that come against the back may be screwed from behind, as well as glued.

The tabletop tapers toward the bed (Fig. 11-2B). The edge nearer the bed has a strut underneath (Figs. 11-2C and 11-3B). At the outer edge the bracket extends above and below the table (Figs. 11-2D and 11-2E). Its outline matches other parts (Fig. 11-3C). By notching the table around the bracket, the end of the dado groove right across can be hidden. Plywood does not give a very strong grip for screws through the back, but strips may be added inside (Fig. 11-2F) to take the screw ends. Screws into particleboard should have enough strength without added strips.

The book rack has parallel shelves, but the supports are different widths. The inner support is narrower to make it easy to remove books when reaching from the bed. The outer support (Fig. 11-2G) should be cut with dados stopped at the front, since shelves and supports are the same width. Shape the outline (Fig. 11-3D). For the inner support, the dados may be cut right through and the shelves notched around (Fig. 11-2H). Give the front edge a matching outline (Fig. 11-3E). Stiffen with strips for the screwed joint at the back, if necessary.

## Materials List for Bed Head with Racks

| | |
|---|---|
| 1 back | 27×66×½ plywood |
| 2 struts | 1½×36×1½ |
| 1 table | 15×15×½ plywood |
| 1 table bracket | 5×12×½ plywood |
| 1 table bracket | 12×13×½ plywood |
| 2 book shelves | 5×15×½ plywood |
| 1 book shelf support | 5×15×½ plywood |
| 1 book shelf support | 3×13×½ plywood |

## STORAGE BED HEAD

A bed head may be made into a storage unit

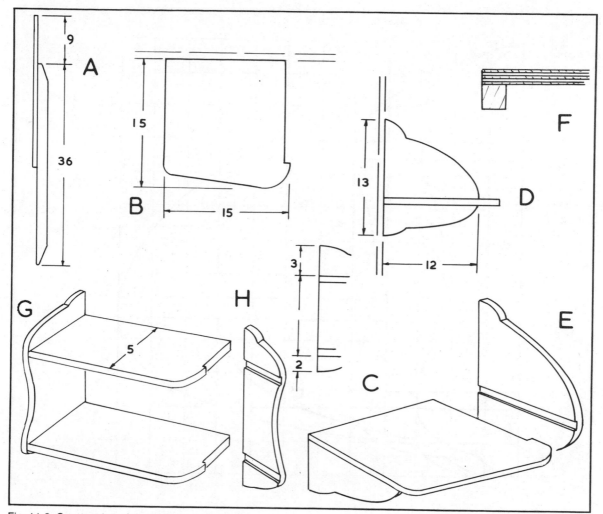

Fig. 11-2. Construction of the bed head with racks.

independent of the bed itself. Its capacity depends on the bed and the layout of the room. It will push the bed forward into the room, so you must allow for an extra 12 inches at least in the bed length if storage space behind the bed is to be worthwhile. The head can then be made as a unit that stands independently on the floor, although it could be attached to the wall as well. The bed fits into it, but can be pulled away.

## Design

You will need to decide what storage you want and arrange the unit accordingly; then adjust its size to suit the bed and the available space beside it. The example (Fig. 11-4) only moves the bed out just over 9 inches, and its side parts only project a little more when the doors and flaps are closed.

The design is shown symmetrical, but it could be made in three parts, if that would suit possible rearrangements or transportation to another home. In that case, the central part makes one unit, with its own sides, and the outer parts are made to come against it. In this bed head the central portion above the bed slopes back and has sliding doors, so it is

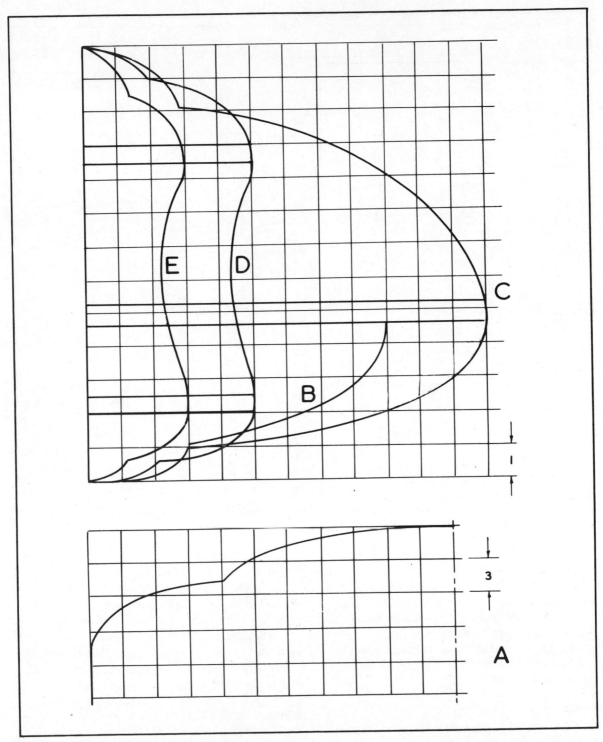

Fig. 11-3. Shapes for bedside rack parts.

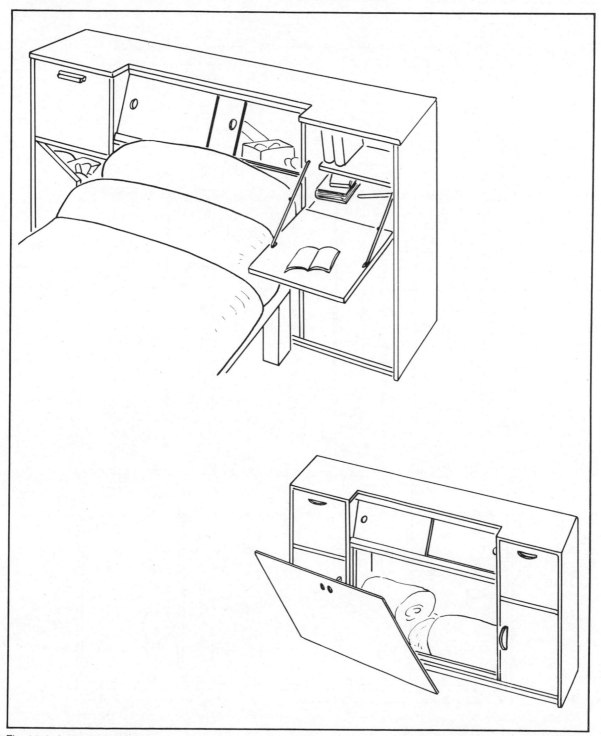

Fig. 11-4. A storage bed head.

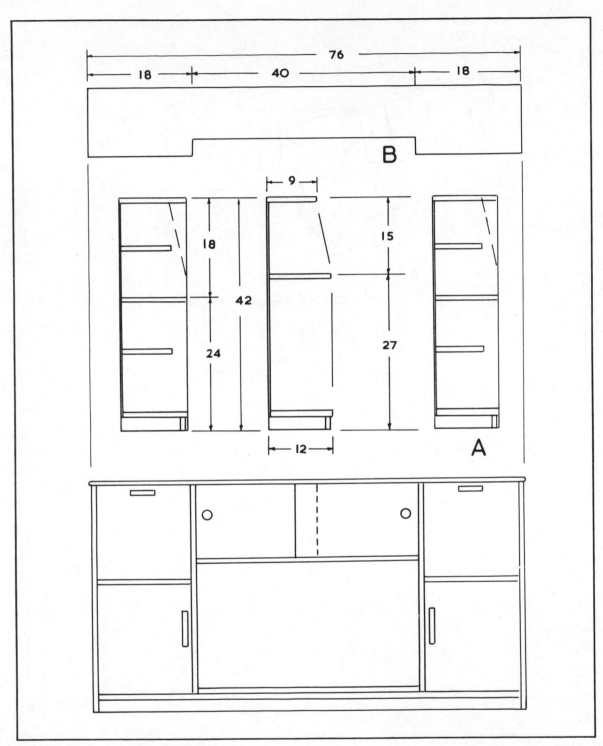

Fig. 11-5. Sizes of the storage bed head.

accessible from the bed. The side parts have doors below and lowering flaps above that can serve as side tables. The portion behind the bed has an opening front. It can be used for storing space blankets and other things only needed occasionally, since it is necessary to pull the bed away to get at them.

Sizes depend on the bed. There should be a few inches of clearance in the recess, which is shown 40 inches for a 36-inch bed. The bottom of

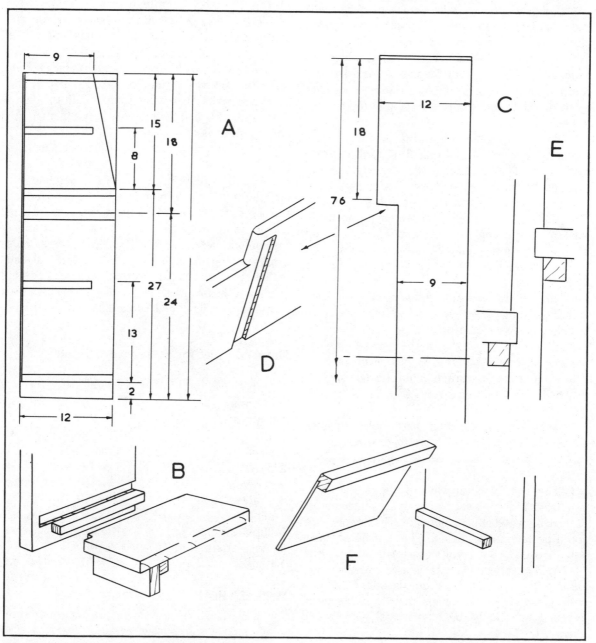

Fig. 11-6. Storage bed head parts and assembly.

273

the top compartment should come well above the mattress level. Other sizes should be adjusted around these widths and heights.

## Construction

Construction may be in solid wood, which will give the best finish, but thick plywood or particleboard with veneered facings could also be used. Start with the four main uprights, which are almost the same (Figs. 11-5A and 11-6A). Mark the positions of other parts on them. The outer uprights go to the floor, but the others stop at the bottom board.

The bottom goes right through and can fit into dados or rest on battens that fit behind the front plinth (Fig. 11-6B). Rabbet the rear edges of the outer uprights to take the plywood back, making the intermediate uprights narrow enough to do so.

Make the top to go right through, but cut it back over the center section (Figs. 11-5B and 11-6C). The joints may be stopped dados (Fig. 11-6D). Dowels would be better for plywood or particleboard.

The central and side dividers may be made with dado joints, but rigidity will be increased with battens below (Fig. 1-6E). Keep them back far enough at the front to clear the flaps and doors. Shelves can rest on battens, so they can be removed if you want to alter storage. Thin plywood shelves may be given solid wood fronts (Fig. 11-6F) to hide the battens.

Assemble all the main parts before making doors. Close the back with plywood, which should be one piece or small pieces with joints over solid parts.

There are several ways of making the doors and flaps. The simplest way is to use single pieces of thick plywood or particleboard. Thinner plywood could be let into frames to give a paneled effect when closed and a level surface when open (Fig. 11-7A). Thin plywood could be used on each side of a frame (Fig. 11-7B). This could be edged with thin solid wood strips. The flaps could be arranged to swing down and be held horizontal with hinged stays (Fig. 11-4).

Another way to arrange support is to use the

doors below. The flap swings down (Fig. 11-7C). The door has to swing out to engage with it behind the handle (Fig. 11-7D). Put a block on top of the door, to fit into a recess when closed (Fig. 11-7E). Make a wedged piece behind the flap handle (Fig. 11-7F) so the block on the door will run on to it.

The sliding doors on the central section are pieces of plywood with finger holes instead of handles. Stout glass could be used in the same way. Cut guide strips with plowed grooves (Fig. 11-7G). Make the grooves at the top twice as deep as the bottom grooves; then it is possible to lift the doors in and out, although their weight keeps them in the bottom grooves in normal use.

The front of the bottom compartment behind the bed is best made to lift out. It is a piece of plywood that rests against stops all around the opening. Put strips of wood inside the panel edges and across the bottom, with the upright pieces long enough to fit inside the strip across the bottom of the compartment (Fig. 11-7H). Another strip goes across the top inside the stop (Fig. 11-7J). Make all of these parts an easy fit. Arrange magnetic or other catches at the top. Make finger holes in the plywood so the top can be pulled forward and up to remove the panel.

## Materials List for Storage Bed Head

| | |
|---|---|
| 2 ends | 12×42×¾ |
| 2 uprights | 12×40×¾ |
| 1 bottom | 12×76×¾ |
| 1 top | 12×78×¾ |
| 1 divider | 12×42×¾ |
| 2 dividers | 12×18×¾ |
| 4 shelves | 9×18×¼ plywood |
| 4 shelves | 1×18×1 |
| 1 plinth | 2×76×¾ |
| 6 flaps and doors | 18×22×¾ plywood |
| Panel frames from 4 | 1½×48×½ |
| 1 back | 42×76×¼ plywood |

## TWIN BED HEAD

If two single beds in a room project from a wall, a combined bed head makes a neat arrangement and usually looks better than two individual heads. It

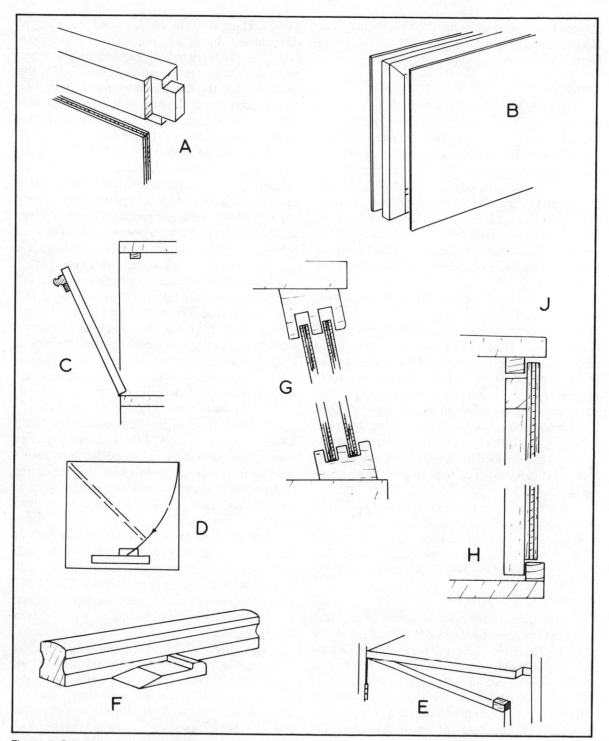

Fig. 11-7. Storage bed head door details.

provides an opportunity for arranging a matching layout, although there is scope for individual treatment if you wish.

## Design

The suggested twin bed head (Fig. 11-8) has cabinets of uniform design. The outer cabinets are similar, and the one between the beds is wider. Over these cabinets goes a board of plain outline, but with a pattern of moldings on the surface.

The cabinets are made as units. The headboard is made in two parts and has legs extending down to fit behind the cabinets. If the assembly must be moved, it can be reduced to these units by removing screws. There should be sufficient stability in the assembly, but there could be screws into the wall as well.

The whole bed head will look best in matching woods for all visible surfaces. An attractively grained veneer on the back plywood will be the main feature. Other wood should be arranged to match it, although the edging of the board could be in wood of a different color, and the doors could contrast with the other wood. The framing behind the board could be softwood since it does not show. Solid wood will make the best combined head and cabinets. Cabinet parts could be made from plywood and finished by painting, or you could use faced particleboard. The following instructions are for solid wood.

Sizes given are intended for a pair of 36-inch beds, allowing 3 inches of clearance. Check your beds and relate cabinet heights to the actual height of users when sleeping on the mattresses, rather than the height of the bed when out of use.

## Assembly

The cabinets are made the same (Fig. 11-9). Mark out the three pairs of sides to the sizes shown (Fig. 11-9A). Rabbet the rear edges to take the back plywood. Dowels will make simple, satisfactory joints. Use ¼-inch or 5/16-inch dowels at about 2½-inch spacing. Across the tops of the sides put stiffeners to come between the rails (Fig. 11-9B). Mark where the other pieces are to come. The bottom and the shelf fit in the same way (Fig.

11-9C). There could be another shelf inside any of the cabinets, but it will probably be best to put battens on the sides and let the shelf rest on them, so it can be taken out. In any case, do not bring the inside shelf to the front, as it would obstruct your view of anything in the bottom part. A width of 8 inches should be enough. At the bottom, set back a plinth underneath (Fig. 11-9D).

Assemble the parts you have made, and fit the back plywood to hold the cabinets square. Make the cabinet tops with the grain across. Carefully square the wood so the rear edge covers the plywood back and the other edges are parallel ⅛ inch in (Fig. 11-9E). Glue the tops on and secure them with screws driven up through the rails and stiffeners.

Doors can be solid wood, or plywood or particleboard edged around. They could be framed and paneled as described for the previous project. The outer doors should be hinged on the side further from the bed. Put small blocks as stops under the shelves and arrange magnetic or ball catches to keep the doors closed. In these positions it is better not to have catches which need turning or other action to release. A sleepy operator may not cope. Fit handles fairly high.

The two parts of the headboard go within 3 inches of the outer edge of the side cabinets. The framing goes behind the cabinets, but the plywood rests on their tops. There is a joint over the center of the middle cabinet. A strut overlaps this joint at the back, and there is a piece of molding over most of it at the front.

Cut the two panels to size. Mark the front lightly for the molding (Fig. 11-10A). At the back the framing could merely butt together, but it would be stronger with dowels or stub tenons (Fig. 11-9F) where the upright struts meet the top horizontal pieces. The fillers across the bottom edge need not have joints cut.

The upright struts are spaced to suit the edges of the cabinets. Check that you match the actual cabinet widths. The struts go 12 inches below the panel (Fig. 11-10B) and will be screwed into the backs of the cabinets. Attach the framing with glue and small finishing nails, punched and covered with stopping. Arrange the place where the molding will

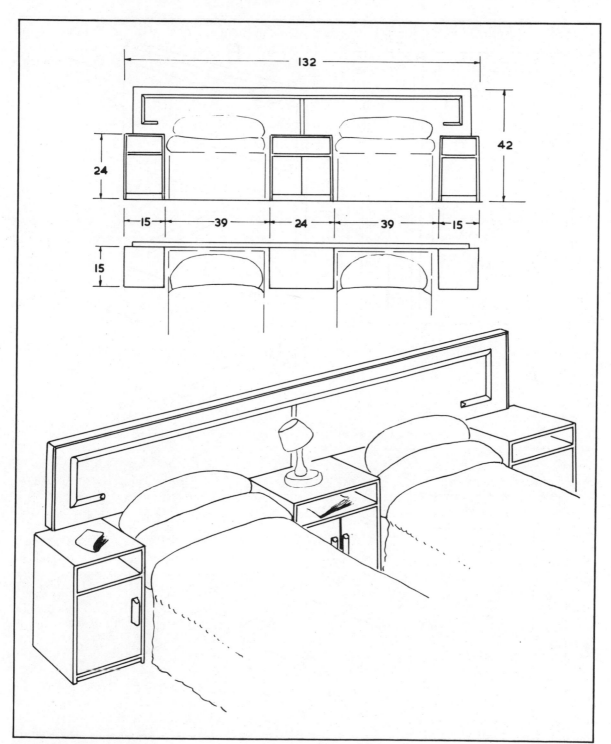

Fig. 11-8. A twin bed head.

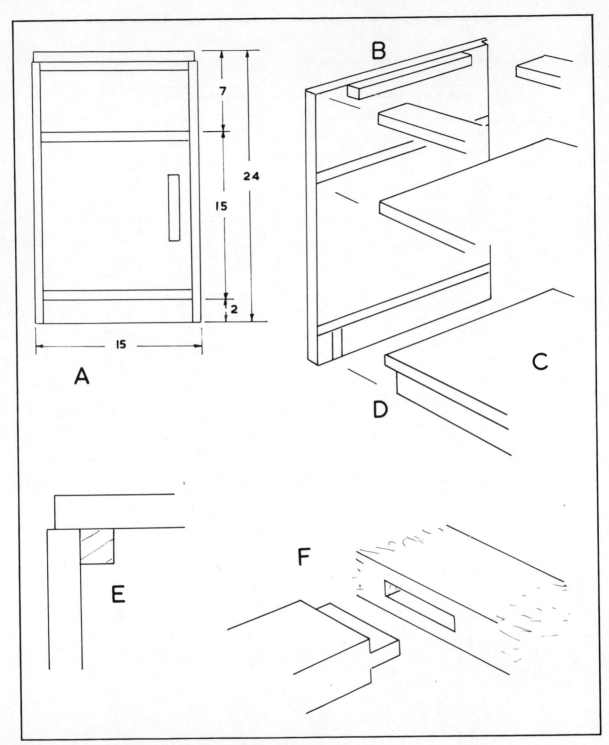

Fig. 11-9. Cabinet sizes and construction for the twin bed head.

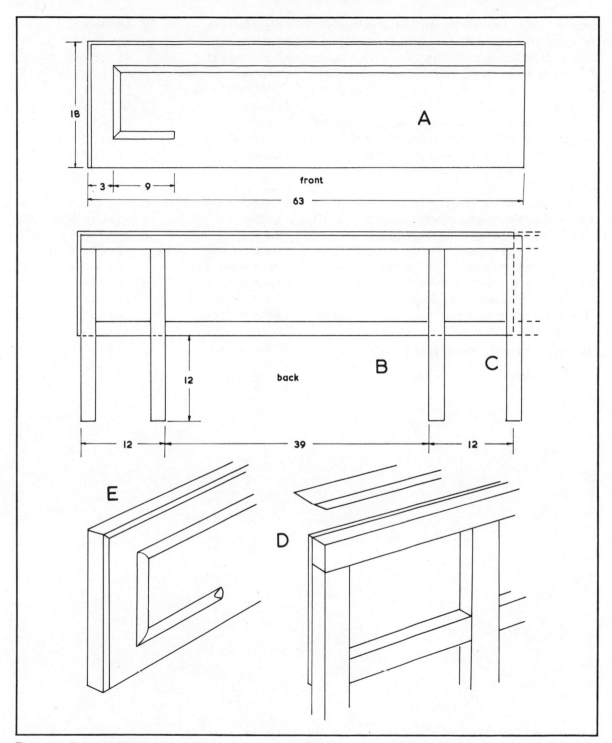

Fig. 11-10. Twin headboard construction.

come to hide some nails. Where the two parts meet, one strut will overlap the joint (Fig. 11-10C). It can be permanently attached to one panel. Use screws through the other panel, without glue, close enough to the edge for the screw heads to be hidden by molding on the front.

When all of the framing has been attached and the edges trued, fit edge strips (Fig. 11-10D). There is no need to cover the bottom edges, nor the place the panels will meet, but miter the top outer corners.

On the front put molding in the marked positions with closely fitting mitered corners (Fig. 11-10E). Use a little glue as well as punched and stopped finishing nails. Bevel or round the inner ends of the bottom pieces. Cut the meeting ends at the center to fit closely. Make a piece of molding to cover the central joint when the head is assembled. Attach the molding with a few nails, so it can be levered off to disassemble the bed head.

## Materials List for Twin Bed Head

| | |
|---|---|
| 6 cabinet sides | 15×25×¾ |
| 2 cabinet tops | 15×16×¾ |
| 1 cabinet top | 15×25×¾ |
| 4 bottoms and shelves | 15×16×¾ |
| 1 bottom and shelf | 15×24×¾ |
| 2 plinths | 2×15×¾ |
| 1 plinth | 2×24×¾ |
| 2 doors | 15×16×¾ |
| 2 doors | 12×16×¾ |
| 4 top rails | 2×15×¾ |
| 2 top rails | 2×24×¾ |
| 6 top stiffeners | ¾×12×¾ |
| 2 backs | 15×24×¼ plywood |
| 1 back | 24×24×¼ plywood |
| 2 back panels | 18×64×⅜ plywood |
| 7 back frame struts | 2×30×1 |
| 2 back frames | 2×64×1 |
| 4 back frames | 2×12×1 |
| 2 back frames | 2×40×1 |
| 2 panel edges | 1¼×64×½ |
| 2 panel edges | 1¼×19×½ |
| 2 moldings | 1×62 halfround |
| 5 moldings | 1×15 halfround |

# Chapter 12

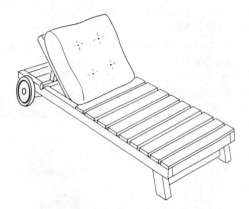

# Special Beds

Any bed has a head and a foot, and sides that support a base that, in turn, supports a mattress. Within these requirements there are a great many forms of beds. Most of these beds have been described already, but there are a few that do not fall into any regular category or are sufficiently different to need special treatment. Some of these beds may be regarded as freaks and therefore are only of limited interest and use.

Most people expect their bed to give them space to spread and move while asleep. They also want to be able to sit up without knocking their head and not be restricted in the bed width or length. Some unusual beds fall short on some of these requirements, so are not described.

Sometimes a bed needs special firmness or local padding to suit an infirmity, but that is usually taken care of by the choice of mattress. If two people wish to sleep together and only one needs special support, two different mattresses can be joined at the center on a double bed, or two single beds can be brought together and joined; so the mattress on one may be very different from the other. No special construction of the beds is required, except for some means of linking them, probably with strips across the ends. If two different mattresses are used on a double bed, they can be linked with a zipper.

## FRENCH BED

There is a form of bed of French origin in which the mattress is more boxed in than is usual in other beds. In addition, there are higher parts at the sides, at head, and foot (Fig. 12-1). The effect is like a bunk in a ship, where there are raised sides to prevent the sleeper from rolling out with the ship's movement. In this bed the sides help prevent a child from rolling out or a restless sleeper from pushing the bed covering on the floor.

As shown, the bed is intended to be made in softwood; so the sections are bigger than they need to be for hardwood. For the main parts the softwood should have reasonably straight grain and be free of large knots. Smaller knots may be regarded as decorative features, if the wood is smoothed properly and given a clear finish. The sizes are intended for a double bed with a 54-inch mattress, but they could be adapted to other widths. In any case, obtain the mattress before starting work. Use sizes that will allow it to drop in with a good clearance, since much of the bedding will need to be tucked away between the mattress and the wood sides.

The sizes (Fig. 12-2) show both head and foot going below the mattress line. Both ends are made in the same way, but the head is 12 inches higher than the foot. The sides could be joined to the ends in any of the ways described earlier, but the type of hardware that links with a hooking action is preferable. Because of the extra depth from the pieces

built up on the sides at their ends, there is space for two of the hooked parts, allowing the bed to be assembled with greater rigidity than usual. If you prefer, you could use tenons from the sides into the legs, or you could use screwed brackets inside.

Start with the ends. The legs at both ends are generally similar, except for different lengths (Fig. 12-2A). Mark the legs in pairs for the positions of the rails and sides. The tops will be rounded (Fig. 12-3A), but it will probably be best to mark the shapes and wait to cut and shape the ends until after you cut the joints.

Mark all the rail lengths together. They are

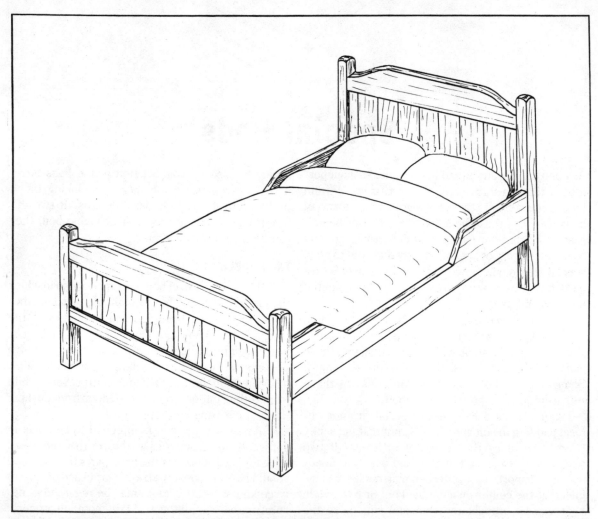

Fig. 12-1. A French bed with raised sides and matched board ends.

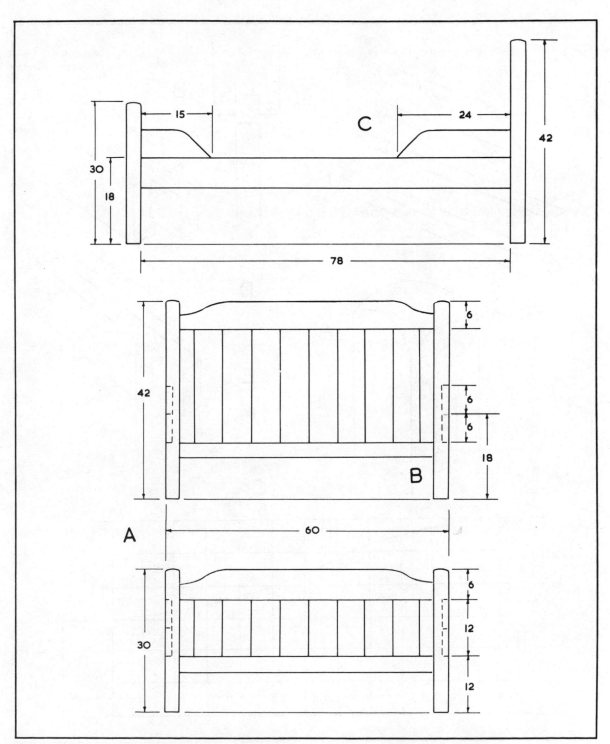

Fig. 12-2. Sizes of the French bed.

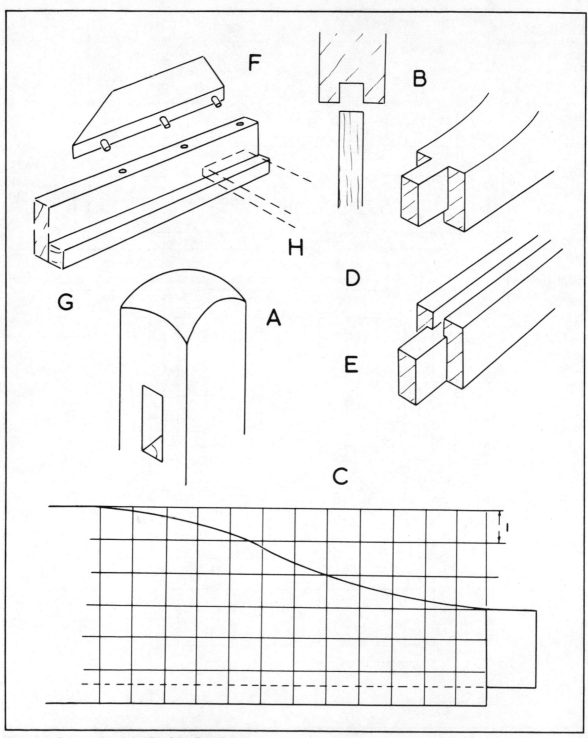

F

B

H

G

A

D

E

C

Fig. 12-3. Constructional details of the French bed.

shown tenoned to the legs, but dowels could be used. Allow for the tenons going almost halfway into the legs. Groove the edges to take tongued and grooved matched boarding (Fig. 12-3B), which should be a fairly close fit since it will not be glued.

Shape the top rail ends (Fig. 12-3C). Be careful to get all four shapings the same, since discrepancies will be obvious in their prominent positions. The shaping brings the rail ends down to the same size as the lower rails. Cut tenons on the ends (Fig. 12-3D), cutting back the tenon depth to the bottoms of the grooves (Fig. 12-3E). Make mortises to match in the legs.

Make up the matched boarding panels. Cut the boards to a length that will not quite reach the bottoms of the grooves. Take off any sharpness or raggedness on the ends. Arrange the boards so they will be symmetrical in each panel by making up the width with pieces of the same breadth at each side,

even if you must cut pieces down the middle (Fig. 12-2B). You then have square edges to come against the legs. When you assemble, glue those side strips, but leave the other boards unglued; then they can expand or contract slightly without splitting. Assemble one end over the other to see that they match.

Make the sides with square ends. The wing pieces at head and foot are cut at 45 degrees, and their top angles are rounded (Fig. 12-2C). Well-round all edges that will be exposed. Join the wings to the sides using glue and dowels (Fig. 12-3F). Make sure the assembled ends are square both ways.

There are several ways of supporting the mattress. You could follow the instructions for one of the earlier beds, but, for a modern mattress, it is satisfactory to use slats across. Put supporting strips for the slats inside the sides (Fig. 12-3G).

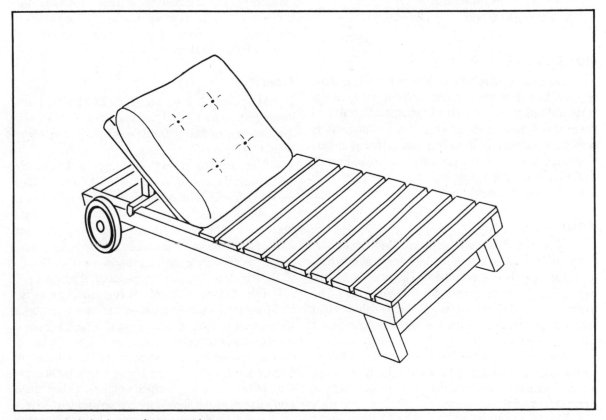

Fig. 12-4. A chaise longue for use outdoors.

Arrange the slats across (Fig. 12-3H). You could place them in position when you put the mattress in, or you could drive a screw through each end. Check squareness of the bed by measuring diagonals before screwing in the slats.

## Materials List for French Bed

| | |
|---|---|
| 2 legs | 3×44×3 |
| 2 legs | 3×32×3 |
| 2 top rails | 6×60×3 |
| 2 bottom rails | 3×60×3 |
| 2 sides | 6×80×1½ |
| 2 sides | 6×26×1½ |
| 2 sides | 6×17×1½ |
| 2 sides | 1½×80×1½ |
| 13 slats | 5×55×1¼ |
| 1 set ¾-inch matched boarding to cover | 14×56 |
| 1 set ¾-inch matched boarding to cover | 26×56 |

## CHAISE LONGUE

*Chaise longue* is a French term for a long chair or a day bed. It is usually adaptable for use near flat at its full length or with a back support adjustable to several different angles. To call it a *chaise*, as is sometimes done, is incorrect since that is a carriage. Chaise longue is a peculiar mixture of French and English, which may be expressive, although something of a hybrid.

### Design

This sort of daybed can be used indoors or out. Some indoor ones are more like adjustable sofas, with the upholstery attached. The one described here (Fig. 12-4) is intended for outdoor use. The mattress is in the form of two or three cushions that can be taken indoors when the chaise longue is left outside overnight.

For outdoor use the bed is shown with wheels, so the other end can be lifted and the bed moved about. For indoor use you may want to have legs at that end as well.

The sizes suggested (Fig. 12-5A) allow ample length for an almost flat bed, with a width of 27 inches. There are three possible reclining positions. It would be possible to adapt the design to other sizes and sitting angles. For occasional outdoor use, the wood could be softwood and painted, but for an indoor bed, sections might be reduced slightly for hardwood, to be finished by staining and polishing. If it will stay outside year-round, it should be made of a durable hardwood.

The main frame is rectangular. It is shown with square ends, but you could provide handles, extending about 10 inches. Mark out the sides (Fig. 12-6A) and the crosspieces. Corners should be joined with bridle joints (Fig. 12-7A). If there are handles, use plain mortise and tenon joints (Fig. 12-7B). Stronger square corners could be made with single dovetail joints (Fig. 12-7C), which would be almost as simple to cut as bridle joints. If there are handles, shape them after cutting the joints (Fig. 12-7D). Saw the outline; then thin the ends since 2 inches is more than a hand can comfortably grip. 1½ inches will be better. Reduce the end to octagonal and then to round.

### Assembly

Make the back pieces (Fig. 12-6B), with the lower ends semi-circular around the bolt holes and the tops rounded away from the slats. Bolts may be ⅜ inch or ½ inch.

The parts that form the struts (Fig. 12-6C) are made with the crosspiece long enough to go over the main frame. The other parts are tenoned to it (Fig. 12-6D). Get the spacing between the joints from the other parts of the bed, but allow for washers on the bolts between the moving parts. Shape the undersides of the crosspiece (Fig. 12-6E) so they fit into the notches without slipping.

The drawing shows three notches (Fig. 12-5B). At the highest position the back is at about 45 degrees and the strut is upright. The other positions give lower reclining positions. The notches in the frame must be cut at slightly different angles in each position. An average shape might be acceptable, but, for the best shaped notches, either make a full-size drawing showing each position, or have a trial assembly, so you can mark each notch to match

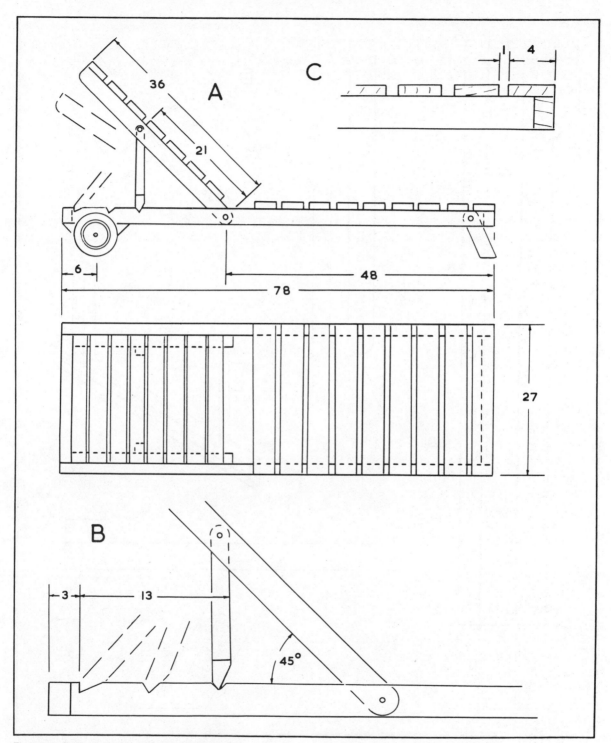

Fig. 12-5. Sizes and action of the chaise longue.

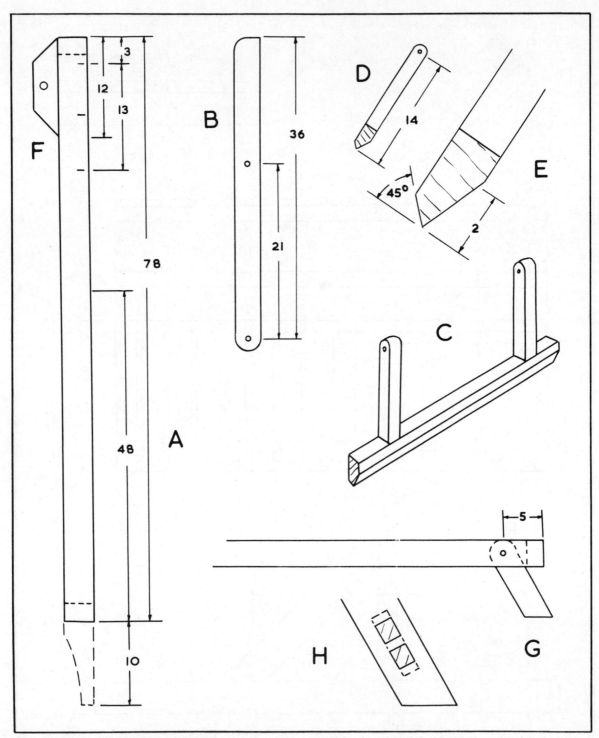

Fig. 12-6. Main parts of the chaise longue.

the strut in that position. There is no need to cut the notches more than 1-inch deep.

The arrangement of the axle block depends on the choice of wheel and axle. The drawings assume wheels about 8 inches in diameter. The axle diameter will need to suit the wheels, but will probably be about ½ inch in diameter. It goes through the blocks (Fig. 12-6F) which are glued and screwed to the frame sides.

The front legs come inside the main frame and are pivoted so they will swing up to fold the bed. When down, they rest against the front part of the frame. Make the legs so they support the bed level (Fig. 12-6G). Their length depends on the height of the wheels at the other end. Put a rail between the legs, preferably joined with double tenons (Fig. 12-6H).

The strips that form the slats across are all the same width. Cut them to come level with the outsides of the frame and around the edges that will be upward. Space them evenly (Fig. 12-5C), using glue and two nails or screws at each end. Check squareness of the main frame during assembly. The slats will hold it and the back to shape.

Make a trial assembly with bolts loose in their holes. See that the legs fold fully and the back is secure at all positions. Remove the bolts and paint or otherwise finish the woodwork. For final assembly, put washers on the bolts between wood parts and lock the nuts.

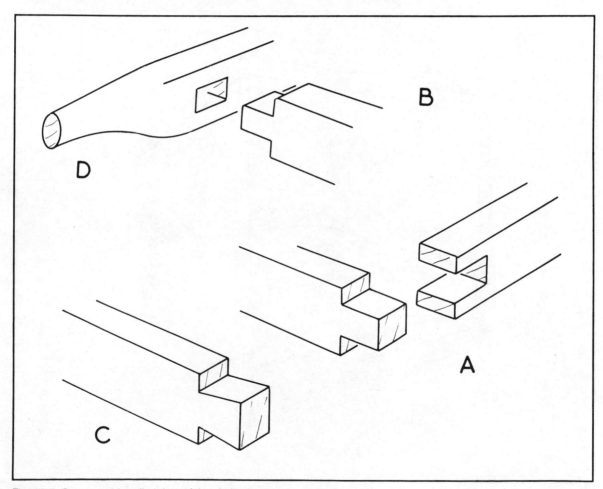

Fig. 12-7. Corner and handle joints of the chaise longue.

Cushions can be made 3 or 4 inches thick. One should match the size of the back. For the flat part you could use one cushion or make up the length with two, linking them with a canvas strip, so they will fold compactly and not come apart in use.

## Materials List for Chaise Longue

| | |
|---|---|
| 2 sides | 3×79×2 |
|   or with handles | 3×89×2 |
| 2 ends | 3×28×2 |
| 2 axle blocks | 3×13×2 |
| 2 backs | 3×39×2 |
| 2 legs | 3×14×2 |

| | |
|---|---|
| 1 leg rail | 4×27×1 |
| 9 seat slats | 4×28×1 |
| 7 back slats | 4×24×1 |
| 2 struts | 1¼×18×1½ |
| 1 strut | 3×28×1½ |

## FOURPOSTER BED

The fourposter bed with a roof, or *tester*, and curtains or drapes all around was developed to provide privacy and exclude drafts. As these needs were reduced, some of the curtains were removed until only those at the head remained; then they went, and with them the tester, leaving beds with high posts that served no purpose. The posts were

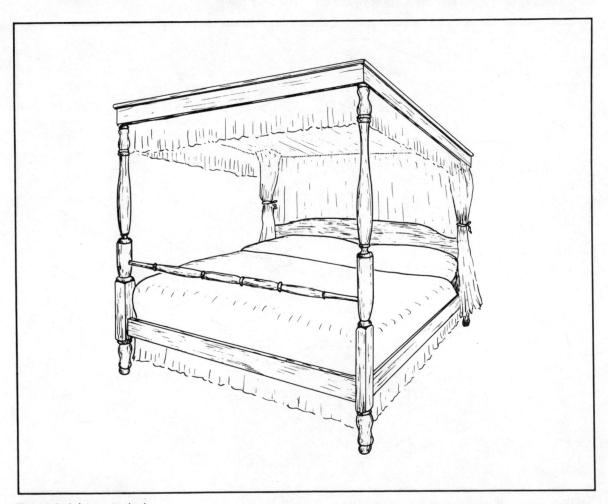

Fig. 12-8. A fourposter bed.

shortened, leaving a bed form with which we are all familiar. However, there is an attraction and an old-world charm about a fourposter with its tester and a few curtains that are decorative rather than functional.

The basic fourposter has a flat tester. In some examples it may have had a solid wood top, but cloth is adequate and lighter. Another version that developed was given a curved top to make a canopy. The canopy led to some reduction in size, particularly at the posts, which may have been a turning problem in their greater length. The effect was decorative when the need for the original privacy and draft exclusion had gone. An example of that form follows a design for a full fourposter with a flat tester.

Most fourposters were double beds, and some were even larger; so this design is intended to take a modern double mattress (Fig. 12-8). Get the sizes of your mattress and make the bed to suit. As described, it is assumed that the sides will have bolts through the legs or be fitted to them in one of the ways described earlier. Slats across will support a mattress.

The sizes shown (Fig. 12-9) allow for the tester to fit onto dowel ends on the posts, so it can be lifted off. With the sides removed the two ends may be sufficiently portable as they are, although you could make dry dowel joints in the posts, so upper turned sections can be removed. A feature of earlier beds worth retaining is the arrangement of ends. At the head is a decorative board (Fig. 12-9A), but at the foot is a rail across at mattress level and a turned rail above the covering (Fig. 12-9B). In some beds the turned rail was allowed to rotate as a roller. It provides a place for a spare blanket that you may need in the night. It can also be used for the covers when making the bed.

## Bed Frame

The posts are shown turned. Shaping with a lathe is always advisable since this type of bed looks very heavy and plain if the posts are left square. It is unlikely that you will have a lathe capable of taking the full length of a post, but you can divide the post into sections that can be turned in the normal lathe

with about 30-inch capacity. One joint may come at the top of the square part 24 inches from the floor (Fig. 12-9C), another joint comes above the backboard level (Fig. 12-9D), and another 27 inches above that (Fig. 12-9E), leaving only a short piece to the tester.

Although the foot rail might be in two parts, it is probably stronger to make it in three parts, with a 20-inch center section and two 17-inch outer sections (Fig. 12-9F). For the joints in this rail and the posts, have dowels and holes as large as can reasonably be used. It should be strong enough to have dowels 1 inch in diameter taken 1½ inches into the other parts (Fig. 12-9G).

Make the four posts. Up to the joints 37 inches from the floor, the complete bed is made in a very similar way to many of the beds described earlier. Join the parts of the posts up to this level, but don't add the upper pieces until after you have cut the joints for the rails and head.

An outline for the headboard is suggested (Fig. 12-10A). The lower tenons go into the square part of the post, but the upper part meets a turned section. The shoulders of the tenon there could be shaped around the curve (Fig. 12-10B), or you may prefer to cut flats each side of the mortise (Fig. 12-10C). If you cut flats, the shoulders of the upper tenons must be cut longer than the lower ones by the amount you have cut into the curve.

If you turn the ends of the foot rail down to 1¼ inch it can go into holes of that size in the posts. If you want to use smaller holes, turn shouldered dowel ends to suit, but do not make the shaped diameter smaller.

Make the sides in the usual way, with strips inside to support the slats under the mattress (Fig. 12-10D). Cut and drill the sides for bolts through the posts. The end rails are plain pieces tenoned into the posts. Assemble the bed ends as prepared to this stage. If the upper parts of the posts are to be removable, glue the top joints, but leave the dowel joints into the assembled bed ends dry; otherwise glue them in. Check post straightness.

## Tester

The tester is kept light, but, to give stiffness,

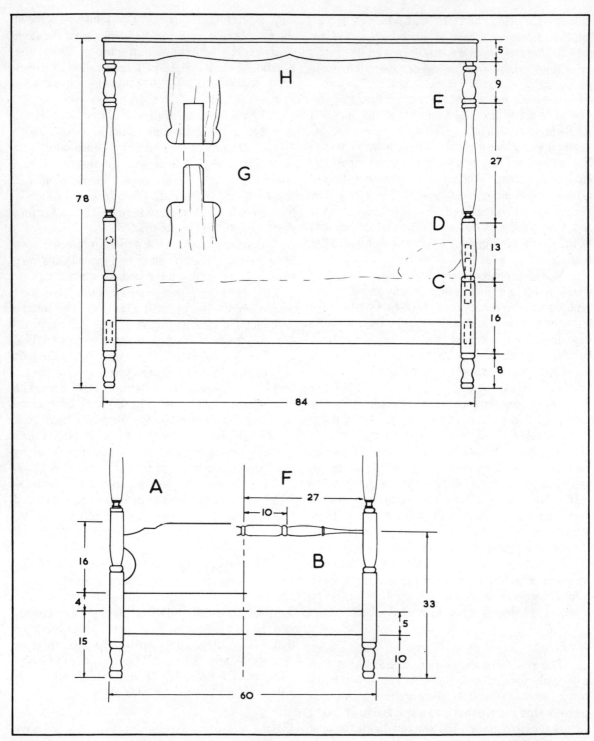

Fig. 12-9. Sizes of the fourposter bed.

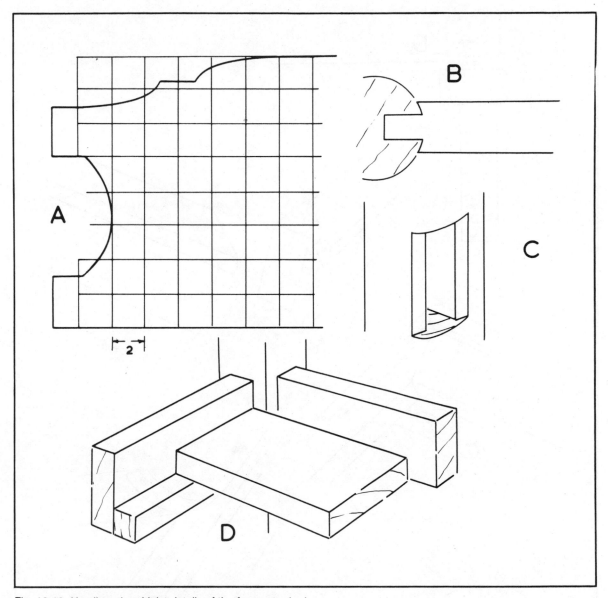

Fig. 12-10. Headboard and joint details of the fourposter bed.

the tops form a T section with the sides (Fig. 12-11A). Round the outer edges of the top. The sides could be left straight, but some shaping improves appearance (Fig. 12-9H). Do not cut too far into the width since that would weaken the section. Shaping it 1 inch at its deepest point will be enough. Use a template to insure symmetry and take the decoration around ends, as well as sides.

At the corners the tester must fit onto dowel ends on the posts. Be careful to get overall sizes to match. Check measurements at bed level, so the posts will finish vertical, even if in a preliminary assembly they tend to move a little out of true. The visible parts of the tester corner should be mitered and fitted around the block inside (Fig. 12-11B). Drill each block to fit on a dowel projecting from the

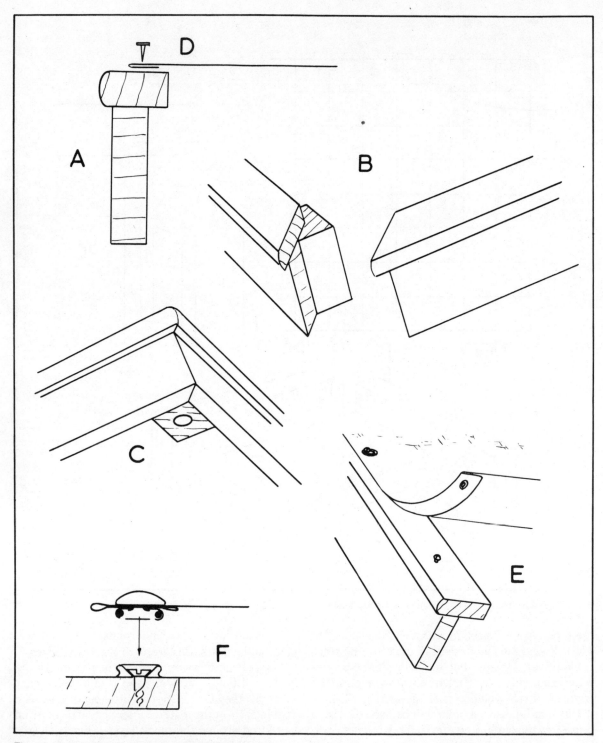

Fig. 12-11. Details of the tester on the fourposter bed.

post (Fig. 12-11C). This should be a push fit, not glued. The assembled tester is quite large, but it would pass through a normal doorway. If you prefer to be able to disassemble it, the sides may be glued to the corner posts and the ends held with screws only.

The simplest way to fit a cloth top is to stretch it over, turn in its edges, and use tacks (Fig. 12-11D). When the cloth must be removed for washing, you would then need to lever out the tacks and drive them again later. This may be the only satisfactory way if you use very thin, light cloth. With slightly stouter cloth eyelets could be fitted at intervals of about 12 inches, so they can be put over screw heads (Fig. 12-11E). You could use press studs (Fig. 12-11F). The top cloth will probably be white, but you could match it with any curtains that go around the sides.

In a modern setting curtains could be light and airy, but traditionally they were often dark and heavy. You could arrange narrow curtains to hang 12 inches or so from the tester all around. There could be a curtain hanging to below the headboard behind, and others from the tester gathered around the posts at the head end. A tester bed is not fully effective visually without curtains somewhere on it, even if they are not required for any practical purpose.

## Materials List for Fourposter Bed

| | | |
|---|---|---|
| 4 posts | 3×78×3 in parts |
| 2 sides | 5×80×1½ |
| 2 sides | 1½×80×1½ |
| 2 ends | 5×60×1½ |
| 1 headboard | 16×60×1½ |
| 1 foot rail | 2½×60×2½ in parts |
| 16 slats | 5×60×1½ |
| 2 tester sides | 4×86×1 |
| 2 tester tops | 2×86×1 |
| 2 tester ends | 4×62×1 |
| 2 tester tops | 2×62×1 |
| 4 tester blocks | 2× 6×2 |

## CANOPY BED

A popular version of the fourposter bed in Co-lonial days used a curved cloth-covered top instead of the wood-framed tester. This canopy achieves a more graceful look with only the draperies showing. If these draperies are made of a light material with plenty of frills and lace or other decoration, the result is a charming, feminine appearance, if that is desired. There may be matching hangings around the posts, but it is unlikely that fully encircling curtains would be desired.

The instructions that follow are based on the bed part of the fourposter just described. Instead of the tester, the posts are cut off at joint E (Fig. 12-9), making the overall height at the corners 14 inches less. Everything below those joints is made in the same way as described. The materials list is the same, except for the parts of the tester.

The canopy is given a curve that brings its center to about the same height as the tester would be (Fig. 12-12), with a light wooden framework over which the draperies are fitted.

The framework (Fig. 12-13A) has curved sides supported on two pieces across the ends. These pieces have holes to fit on dowel ends on the posts. Three intermediate crosspieces are shown. If stiff, straight-grained wood is chosen, this assembly should be adequate. For a wide bed there could be an intermediate arched piece, and you may fit more crosspieces.

The important parts are the arches. They finish 1¼-inch deep, but they must be cut from wide boards, unless wood bending facilities are available to spring them to shape from single strips. It would be possible to join short pieces end-to-end, but a strong, simple way uses vertical lamination. The finished section of 1¼-inch deep by 1-inch thick is made up in two overlapping layers of ½-inch wood (Fig. 12-13B).

Make a compass from a strip of wood, with an awl through one end and the other end 79½ inches from it. Put a notch at 78 inches for the pencil to mark the inner curve (Fig. 12-13C). With this compass draw a curve, at least half as long as the finish arch, on the floor or piece of plywood, to use as a guide when assembling arch parts.

Using the compass, draw curves on the blanks for the arch parts (Fig. 12-13D). With the length

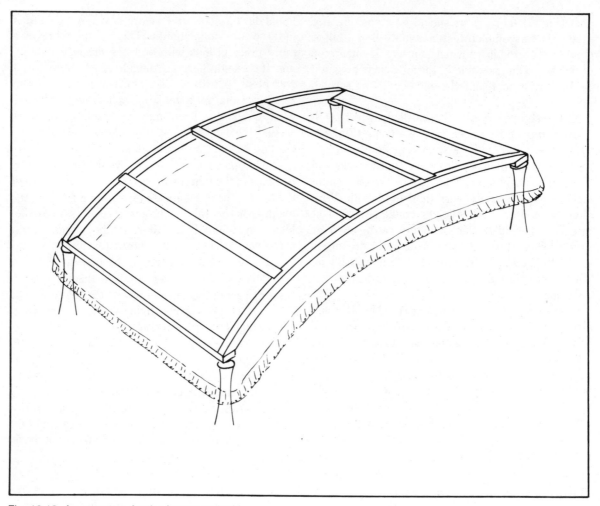

Fig. 12-12. A canopy top for the fourposter bed.

shown you will need eight for each arch. Cut the curves, but leave final shaping until the parts have been joined together. Cut one piece in half to make up at the ends, so the sections overlap to their centers (Fig. 12-13E). Cut the ends to meet closely. The cuts need not be radial. Assemble each arch slightly longer than it will be finally, using the template as a guide. Glue the parts together and drive in finishing nails as well. The number of nails depends on the wood, but ¾-inch nails at about 3-inch intervals should be enough. Make sure the two arches match.

When the glue has set, smooth the edges and mark out the length and the positions of notches for the crosspieces (Fig. 12-13F). So they don't weaken the arches unnecessarily, the notches only come in one thickness of the wood.

Mark the end pieces (Fig. 12-13G) and drill them to match the dowels on the posts. Make a trial assembly with these pieces in position. Check the sizes of the arches before cutting their ends. Glue and screw the arches to the end pieces and the intermediate crosspieces to their arch notches.

Round all edges that will come against cloth. Finish the wood with paint or varnish, although if the drapery material is an open weave or translucent, it will be better to color the wood to match the cloth.

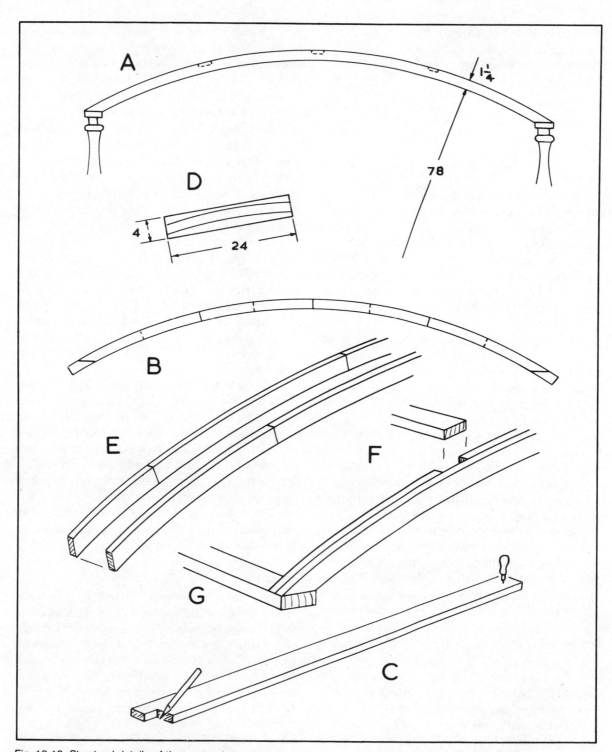

Fig. 12-13. Structural details of the canopy top.

## Materials List for Canopy Bed
(to be used in the place of the tester material int he Fourposter Bed list)

| | |
|---|---|
| 2 ends | 3×62×1 |
| 3 crosspieces | 2×62×⅞ |
| 16 arch sections | 4×24×½ |

## WATER BED

Comfort in bed comes from the spread of support given by the mattress. The greater the area of body and mattress that are in contact, the more comfortable you will be. Modern spring and foam mattresses go a long way toward achieving large and even contact areas, but the most even spread of support over the largest area of your body, no matter how you move in your sleep, comes from a water bed.

The major problem is one of weight. The water in a double bed will weigh close to 1 ton. Will your floor take this load? It is a particular problem if the bed is to be upstairs. According to most building codes, a floor, as built normally, should take the weight, but there may not be much of a safety margin if the floor only just complies with the regulations.

Water in the bed will settle at room temperature, which is some way below body temperature. If you slept on an unheated bed, the water would take away your body heat; so electric heating must be provided. The bed must be filled in position, and you must be able to empty it, but that can be done with a garden hose. It is unlikely that a water bed of modern construction will leak, but there is always this risk; so the mattress full of water must be kept within a liner that could hold any water that leaked.

### Design

A water bed must be treated as a very different constructional problem from a normal bed. The mattress full of water must be enclosed in a strong box. That box must be supported in a way that spreads the load on the floor as much as possible. If the bed was made on four legs in the usual way, one fourth of the total weight would come on the few square inches of floor under each leg. To avoid this localized loading, it is better to have a box-like support and a broad contact with the floor all around.

Water bed manufacturers work to very close tolerances and the wooden frame built to take the bed must match. The makers will supply details of the surrounding sizes they recommend. The wood frame must support and enclose the mattress and a plastic liner, which must be fitted and attached to the wood. It is important that the box-like assembly is without twist and is square, or the filled mattress will not settle to its correct shape.

The design described here is offered mainly to suggest constructional methods. It will be necessary to adapt some details to suit the water bed that is used. Here it is assumed that the mattress is 54 inches by 84 inches and that 7-inch sides will be high enough (Fig. 12-14). The bed is shown with a head containing shelves, but any other sort of head could be used, either attached to the bed or to the wall behind it.

Because of strength factors, you should not make a water bed structure to disassemble to the extent that other beds do, but this bed (Fig. 12-15) can be made as a box to hold the mattress with a supporting frame about the same size and base pieces that could be left attached or unscrewed for transport. The head unit is separate. The separated parts should pass through a doorway, but if you need to reduce the size more, you will need to assemble it without glue, so you can unscrew down to individual pieces of wood, if necessary.

### Assembly

The mattress box (Fig. 12-16A) must be made to suit the size of the mattress. It is given a base of solid boards, below which is the supporting frame, set in with a few screws driven down to maintain location (Fig. 12-16B). There are two pieces across (Fig. 12-15A) to give support under the main area of mattress. Under this support are base pieces (Fig. 12-16C) that project to the size of the bed and spread the load on the floor.

Corners of the box could be held with any of the usual corner joints, but through dovetails are best.

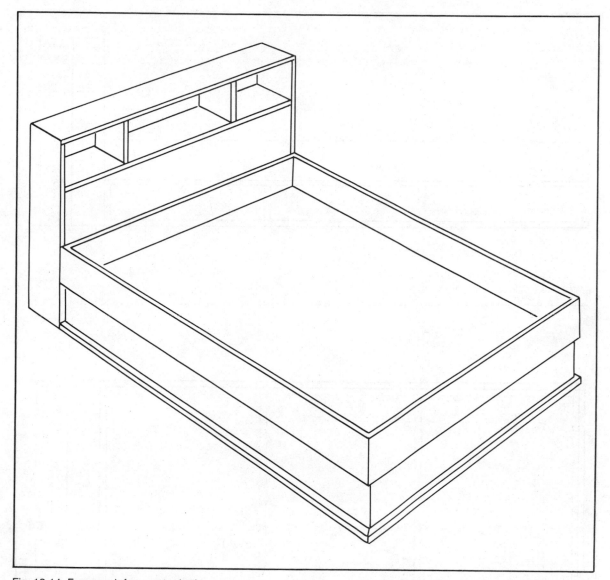

Fig. 12-14. Framework for a water bed.

If you use other joints, reinforcing angle plates could be screwed inside, but make sure nothing sharp is exposed. Square the assembly as you attach the bottom boards, which may be nailed or screwed from below. Keep edges close. The top edges of the sides and ends must be rounded, but follow the instructions of the mattress maker. In some cases upholstery on the edge is required.

Make the supporting frame in the same way, with similar corner joints. Keep the overall sizes about the same as the inside of the box, so the support is set in and you can screw down through the box bottom. Arrange the two supports across, spacing them evenly and checking that the top surfaces are level. They could be fitted into dados at the sides, but screwing should be sufficient.

Make the base pieces to the same overall size

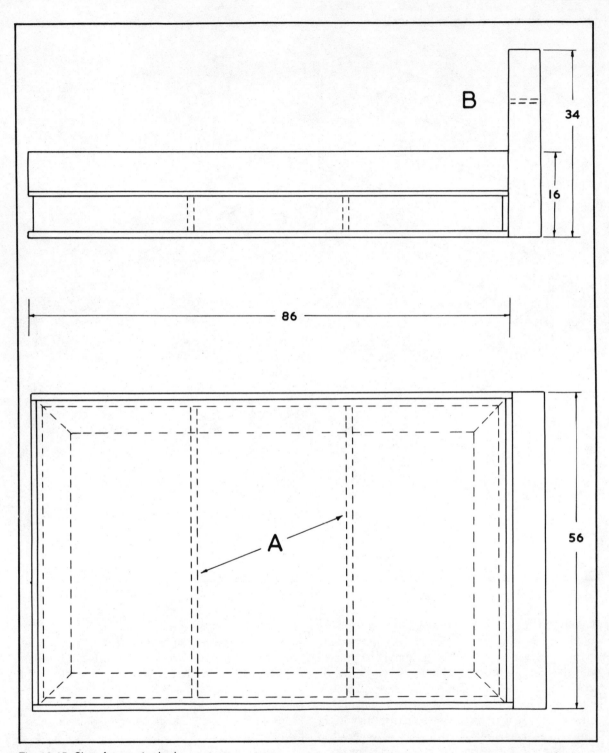

Fig. 12-15. Sizes for a water bed.

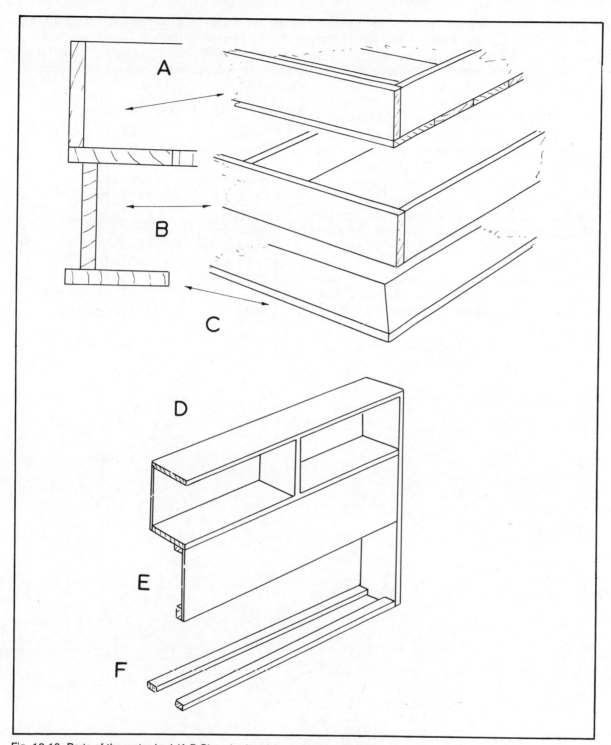

Fig. 12-16. Parts of the water bed (A,B,C) and a head for use with it (D,E,F).

as the box and miter the corners. Screw the base strips to the underside of the supporting framework. If the miters are cut accurately so they meet neatly, there should be no need for glue or any additional stiffening of the joints. When the bed is in use, the miters will be held close.

The suggested head (Fig. 12-15B) must be made high enough for the shelves to come above the bed pillows. Two uprights are joined to two shelves with spacers between (Fig. 12-16D). A plywood panel fits in and is carried to below the level of the bed box. This panel can be held against strips (Fig. 12-16E). Two more strips at floor level (Fig. 12-16F) hold the sides at the correct width. The head can stand between the bed and the wall, without attachment to either.

When you assemble and position your bed, locate it exactly where it is to stay. Once it is filled, you cannot move it. The heater supplied with the mattress will have a thermostat that must be screwed to the side of the bed. You will need to take a plug to a suitable outlet, preferably a short distance away and where the cord cannot be tripped over.

## Materials List for Water Bed

| | |
|---|---|
| 4 sides | 7×87×1 |
| 4 ends | 7×57×1 |
| 2 supports | 7×57×1 |
| 8 bed bottoms | 7×87×1 |
| 2 bases | 7×57×1 |
| 2 bases | 7×87×1 |
| 2 head shelves | 5×57×¾ |
| 2 head sides | 5×36×¾ |
| 4 head stiffeners | 2×57×1 |
| 2 head dividers | 5× 9×¾ |
| 1 head back | 12×57×¼ plywood |
| 1 head front | 15×57×¼ plywood |

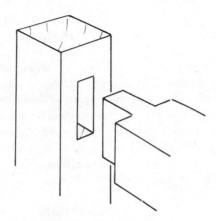

# Glossary

**arris**—The line or sharp edge between two flat or plane surfaces.

**back tacking**—In upholstery, tacks positioned through a card strip so the fabric may be turned back to hide them. Also called blind tacking.

**barbed ring nail**—Nail with teeth cut around it to resist withdrawal.

**barefaced tenon**—Tenon cut with a shoulder at one side only.

**bassinet**—Basketlike bed for an infant. May be on wheels.

**bed head**—The vertical board behind the head end of a bed.

**bed irons**—Hardware used to join bed parts or support a mattress.

**blind**—In woodworking, a hole or recess that does not go right through.

**bolster**—Constructionally, a pad to take a thrust. A lower pillow.

**boxing**—In upholstery, using a separate covering strip around the edge of a mattress or cushion to produce a square edge.

**bunk bed**—One bed above another.

**buttoning**—In upholstery, putting buttons on the surface with twine through the padding.

**case hardening**—The effect on the surface of wood of power planing with blunt cutters. A method of putting a thin steel surface on iron.

**caster**—Arrangement with an offset wheel for moving furniture.

**chaise longue**—French, literally meaning a long chair, but used for a day bed with adjustable head end.

**chipboard**—Alternative name for particleboard.

**counterbore**—Sink a screw head below the surface so a plug can be inserted over it.

**cradle**—Bed for a baby, usually smaller than a crib.

**crib**—Bed for a baby, fitted with high sides.

**divan**—Upholstered couch or bed without raised ends.

**dome of silence**—Smooth metal domed piece to fit to the bottom of a leg for sliding furniture.

**dowel**—Cylindrical piece of wood, particularly used as a peg when making joints.

**dressed and matched boards**—Boards cut to fit edge-to-edge with tongue and groove joints.

**finial**—Turned decorative piece projecting upwards from a post.

**footboard**—A board arranged vertically at the foot end of a bed.

**fourposter**—Bed with the legs at each corner continued upwards, originally to support a tester, but the name may be used when the posts do not go high enough for that.

**foxtail wedging**—Using wedges at the bottom of a blind mortise to spread the end of a tenon driven in.

**French bed**—Bed with head and foot boards and the sides deepened at both ends.

**gimp**—In upholstery, prepared decorative strip of tape used to cover a tacked edge of cloth.

**glide**—Alternative name for a dome of silence.

**haunch**—A short part on the side of a tenon where it goes into another part at its end.

**headboard**—A vertical board at the head end of a bed.

**joggle**—A double bend in a strip of metal.

**knot**—A flaw in wood where a branch left the trunk. The method of joining twine.

**laminate**—Construct in layers with several pieces of wood glued together. Used to build up curved parts.

**matched boarding**—Alternative name for dressed and matched boards.

**mortise and tenon joint**—Common method of joining wood parts, where the projecting tenon on one part fits into the hollow mortise in the other.

**particleboard**—Manufactured board made of chips of wood embedded in synthetic plastic resin.

**piping**—In upholstery, cord enclosed in cloth and sewn into a seam.

**seasoning**—Drying excess moisture from newly felled wood.

**shake**—Natural crack along the grain of wood.

**slat**—Strip of wood. In beds, one of many pieces across to support a mattress.

**splat**—The central strip of wood, sometimes decorated, in a chair back or a bed head.

**stacking beds**—Beds arranged to be put one over the other when out of use.

**stuffing**—The padding, of any sort, used in upholstery.

**template, templet**—Shaped pattern to draw around when marking out parts.

**tester**—The roof or covering of a fourposter bed.

**triangulation**—Using the properties of a triangle to test an assembly for symmetry or squareness, when it is too large to test with normal tools.

**truckle or trundle bed**—A bed which will stow under another one when it is not needed.

**tufting**—In upholstery, similar to buttoning, but using tufts of wool instead of buttons.

**tusk tenon**—A tenon that goes through the mortised part and projects, where it may be wedged.

**water bed**—A bed in which the mattress is filled with water.

**webbing**—In upholstery, a straplike strip made from flax, cotton, or hemp. Also made with rubberized fabric for elasticity.

**winding**—Twisting, particularly a board or an assembled frame.

**veneer**—Very thin slice of wood, to be glued to a backing piece to give it a more attractive appearance or to match other woods.

# Index

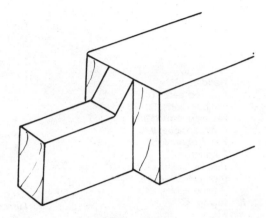

# Index

Edited by Suzanne L. Cheatle